MW00824902

Korean Studies of the Henry M. Jackson
School of International Studies

James B. Palais, Editor

Korean Studies of the Henry M. Jackson
School of International Studies

OFFSPRING OF EMPIRE

The Koch'ang Kims and the Colonial
Origins of Korean Capitalism, 1876–1945

Carter J. Eckert

University of Washington Press
Seattle and London

Library of Congress Cataloging-in-Publication Data
Eckert, Carter J.
    Offspring of empire : The Koch'ang Kims and the colonial origins
of Korean capitalism, 1876–1945 / Carter J. Eckert
        p. cm.—(Korean studies of the Henry M. Jackson School of
International Studies)
    Includes bibliographical references and index.
    ISBN 0–295–97533–4 (alk. paper)
    1. Businessmen—Korea—History. 2. Kim family. 3. Industry and
state—Korea—History. 4. Korea—Dependency on Japan—History.
5. Capitalism—Korea—History. I. Title II. Series.
HC466.5.A2E25   1991   90–47159
338.9519—dc20   CIP

For Emeline J. Eckert

Contents

Illustrations

ix

Maps

Preface

South Korea's rise to global economic prominence in the last three decades is one of the great stories of our time and has captured the interest and imagination of scholars throughout the world. There is no need here to recite familiar statistics. Suffice it to say that we are confronted with an economic achievement so dramatic that it has become popularly known as the "Miracle on the Han" and even forced some of the less doctrinaire minds of the New Left to question their most basic ideas about capitalism and economic growth in the Third World.[*] If Western observers once shrank from describing the "meanness" of Seoul, like the late nineteenth-century traveler and geographer Isabella Bird Bishop, they are now more likely to vie with one another in searching for new superlatives to depict the economic vitality and wealth of the old capital city and the country as a whole.[†]

---

[*]See, for example, Bill Warren, "Imperialism and Capitalist Industrialization," *New Left Review* 81 (Sept.–Oct. 1973): 1-92.

[†]Mrs. (Bird) Bishop was a colorful writer, and never one to mince words: "I shrink," she wrote,

> from describing intra-mural Seoul. I thought it the foulest city on earth till I saw Peking, and its smells the most odious, till I encountered those of Shao-shing! For a great city and a capital its meanness is indescribable. Etiquette forbids the erection of two-storied houses, consequently an estimated quarter of a million people are living on 'the ground,' chiefly in labyrinthine alleys, many of them not wide enough for two loaded bulls to pass, indeed barely wide enough for one man to pass a loaded bull, and further narrowed by a series of vile holes or green, slimy ditches, which receive the solid and liquid refuse of the houses, their foul and fetid margins being the favorite resort of half-naked children, begrimed with dirt, and of big, mangy, blear-eyed dogs, which wallow in the slime or blink in the sun. There too the itinerant vendor of 'small wares,' and candies dyed flaring colors with aniline dyes, establishes himself, puts a few planks across the ditch, and his goods, worth perhaps a dollar, thereon.

Isabella Bird, *Korea and Her Neighbors* (London: KPI, 1985), p. 40. In contrast, Alice H. Amsden, who has written one of the most recent and interesting studies of the

There is, of course, no simple, single explanation for South Korea's stunning transformation; the very complexity of the phenomenon has in fact been an essential part of its fascination and perhaps the main reason it has attracted so many scholars in a variety of disciplines. A major problem exists, however, in that interest in South Korean development per se has grown so much more rapidly in the last twenty years than the broader field of Korean studies itself; as a result, many of the development analyses to date, and especially those undertaken by scholars with little or no formal training in Korean language, history, and culture, have been constructed on a very limited, and often questionable, empirical base of English-language works about Korea. It is one of my hopes that this book will improve that empirical base and contribute to further cross-fertilization between the social sciences and the more humanistically oriented Korean studies field, an interaction from which, I believe, everyone interested in Korea will benefit.

I must also confess to another, even more cherished, agendum. In nearly all of the existing studies of South Korean development the explanations put forward have focused primarily on the period of rapid export-led growth in the 1960s and 1970s and relegated the country's earlier history more or less to the status of background material. In this book I attempt to place Korean history itself at the center of the debate by asking the reader to consider in what ways and to what extent Korea's pre-1960s history, its colonial experience in particular, helped mold the South Korean political economy of today. I hasten to add that in so doing I have no wish to celebrate either the past or the present. To neglect or deny the role of colonialism in Korea's modern transformation would be to omit a fundamental piece of the puzzle. On the other hand, the colonial legacy is also filled with deep shadows and Faustian ironies. If one finds in it enlightenment and progress, one also finds national subjugation, shame, and betrayal, political authoritarianism and violence, and profound human suffering. These darker aspects of the legacy must also be addressed, for they are as yin to yang in the composition of the whole, and they serve as a salutary reminder of the staggering price exacted by history for the South Korean "miracle."

---

contemporary South Korean economy, calls the country "Asia's next giant," and sees it as a model "from which others may learn." Alice H. Amsden, *Asia's Next Giant: South Korea and Late Industrialization* (New York: Oxford University Press, 1989), p. 3.

Interest in the colonial legacy leads naturally to the Koch'ang Kims and the Kyŏngsŏng Spinning and Weaving Company (Kyŏngbang) as a focus of study. Not only was Kyŏngbang the first Korean-owned (and managed) large-scale industrial enterprise in the country's history; its growth and expansion during the colonial period was nothing short of remarkable. The Kyŏngbang story, however, is much more than a tale of corporate success. The company and its people provide a window through which one can explore at a concrete and human level the origins and early development of Korean capitalism itself, a subject that embraces some of the most intriguing and controversial issues of modern Korean history and political economy: the Korean response to imperialism, modern class formation and conflict, class-state interaction, war-related colonial industrialization and social mobilization, nationalism, and, not least of all, the very sensitive subject of Korean-Japanese social, economic, and cultural interaction. All of these areas cry out for further study, and I hope that this book, if it does nothing else, will convey to younger scholars in the field some sense of the human complexity, archival richness, and intellectual challenge of a period whose historical significance has too long lain hidden under a blanket of comfortable clichés and distortions.

No scholar is an island, and I would like to take this opportunity to express my appreciation to some of the many people who have contributed to the making of this book. I alone, of course, am responsible for any errors or omissions.

My thanks, first of all, to Bill Chaney and Elisabeth Koffka, whose lectures and conversation at Lawrence College over two decades ago first ignited a passion for history that has only grown stronger over time. To Jim Palais of the University of Washington, friend, colleague, and mentor, I owe an irredeemable debt of gratitude for nine years of unstinting encouragement and support on every front, and for providing in his own person and work an inspiring model of scholarly thoroughness and integrity. I have also benefited immeasurably from the scholarship, advice, and support of Bruce Cumings, formerly of Washington, now of the University of Chicago, whose pathbreaking work on the Korean War has so richly expanded the intellectual contours of modern Korean studies. Mike Robinson of the University of Southern California, an old friend and fellow explorer of the colonial past, was a splendid sounding board, critic, and cheerleader through the whole process of research, writing, and revision. Ed Wagner of Harvard was the perfect senior colleague, generous to a fault with his own time, and always willing to stretch the rules to give me as much latitude as I needed to get the book done. Ed Baker of the Harvard-Yenching Institute was also there in the final crunch to share his knowledge, lawyerly logic, and friendship, even when he had far more urgent things to do. Others, including Peter Bol, Al Craig, Kent Guy, the late Gregory Henderson, Ken Pyle, and Ezra Vogel, read all or part of the original dissertation or book manuscript and offered valuable comments and suggestions.

Research for this book required the help of many individuals and organizations in three countries. With respect to South Korea, I would particularly like to thank the Koch'ang (Ulsan) Kim and Kwangsan Kim families, and especially Dr. Kak-Choong Kim (Kim Kakchung), the executive chairman of Kyŏngbang, who gave me unrestricted access to all Kyŏngbang's extant colonial records and papers and provided me with a personal introduction to his father and company predecessor, Kim Yongwan, as well as to Kim Sanghong, the chairman of Samyang. This book could never have been written without the very generous cooperation of Dr. Kim and other members of the two Kim families. I am also grateful to the many company employees of Kyŏngbang and Samyang who took precious time out from their own work to be congenial hosts, answer questions, give guided tours, and photocopy documents for a meddlesome outsider. My research in South Korea was expedited, as always, by the collegiality of Young Ick Lew; among many other things, Professor Lew first called my attention to Kim Yongsŏp's brilliant and courageous article on the Koch'ang Kims, a work that caused me to reevaluate completely my thinking about Kyŏngbang and colonial capitalist development. An Pyŏngjik, Kim Chunyŏp, Kim T'aejin, Kim Yongsŏp, and Hong Sŭngjik also all had a hand in making my visits to South Korea pleasant and productive, as did the staff of the Asiatic Research Center and the main libraries of Koryŏ and Seoul National University.

With respect to Japan, I am indebted above all to Hanabusa Yukio of the Institute of Developing Economies, who took a total stranger under his wing and put him in contact with all the right people and institutions. My thanks also to Kimura Sunako and others at the Economics Department Library of the University of Tokyo, to the staff of the Constitutional Documents Room of the National Diet Library, and to Kobayashi Hideo and the late Kajimura Hideki. Sekiya Masahiko, the son of Sekiya Teizaburō, kindly allowed me to microfilm his father's papers and provided the picture of his father that appears in this book.

In the United States my research was greatly facilitated by the splendid resources, librarians, and staff of the East Asia Library at the University of Washington and the Harvard-Yenching Library at Harvard. I am especially grateful to Yoon-whan Choe of Washington, and to Toshiyuki Aoki and the late Sungha Kim of Harvard-Yenching. Numerous friends and colleagues in all three countries, including Peter Bartholomew, Roger Chan, Nancy Deptula, Milan Hejtmanek, Betty Hoyt, Dawn Lawson, Joe Nowakowski, Pak Myŏnggyu, Soon Won Park, Edwin O. Reischauer, Barry Rosenstock, Bill Schoen, Jim West, Kozo Yamamura, and Yu Yŏngsu helped move the process along by providing information or assistance whenever asked. Namhi Kim Wagner and Haruko Iwasaki were reservoirs of patience and good humor in explaining the mysteries of *sōrōbun* and checking my Japanese translations. Kyu Hyun Kim was a hard-working and long-suffering assistant in the preparation of the glossary and maps. Margery Lang was the kind of intelligent, dedicated, and sensitive editor every author hopes to have.

At various stages on the road to publication I was the fortunate recipient of a number of fellowships and grants, including several National Resource Fellowships, a Fulbright-Hays Fellowship for Doctoral Dissertation Research Abroad, doctoral research and write-up grants from the Social Science Research Council, a graduate dissertation fellowship from the University of Washington, and generous allocations from the Committee on the Professorship in Modern Korean Economy and Society at Harvard.

Finally, I would indeed be remiss if I did not include a special note of thanks to David Grose and Joseph Dauben for providing consistently sage advice on the Real World, to Jim and Chris Nicolson for keeping me well fed and reasonably sane during the final throes of writing, and, not least of all, to Kyunghoon and Bernadette Lee for making even the rainy days in Seattle shine.

C.J.E.
Cambridge, Mass.

Man is what has happened to him, what he has done. Other things might have happened to him or have been done by him, but what did in fact happen to him and was done by him, this constitutes a relentless trajectory of experiences that he carries on his back as the vagabond his bundle of all he possesses. . . . *Man, in a word, has no nature; what he has is . . . history.*

José Ortega y Gasset

OFFSPRING OF EMPIRE

The Koch'ang Kims and the Colonial
Origins of Korean Capitalism, 1876–1945

PART I

THE RISE OF KOREAN CAPITALISM

In 1876, on the eve of the Kanghwa Treaty that would open Korea's ports to international commerce, Min Tuho and Pak Munhoe were roughly the same age and were both residents of Kyŏnggi Province. Their relative positions in Yi (Chosŏn) dynasty (1392–1910) society, however, were starkly different. Min was a member of one of the wealthiest and most powerful families in the country. His uncle, Min Ch'igu, was the maternal grandfather of the king, and before his assassination in 1874, Tuho's first cousin Sŭngho (Chi'gu's son) had been both the reputed leader of the clan and the adoptive brother of the queen.[1] Pak, on the other hand, was a poor peasant eking out a meager existence on land that was not even his own but belonged in fact to the Min family.[2] There was little opportunity for two such men to meet on a social basis in Yi Korea's highly status-conscious, aristocratic society, but even if by some quirk of fate they had found themselves in the same room, there would hardly have been much common ground for discourse.

By 1945 — and indeed, long before — things had changed. By then, the sons and grandsons of these same two men were members of the same exclusive social club in Seoul.[3] Unlike their fathers, who had been separated by a chasm of land and lineage, the younger Mins and Paks had been brought together in a burgeoning new class where possession of capital, or "shares," had become a common bond. The Mins had become bankers, the Paks, merchants, and both were investors in industrial enterprise.[4] In the seventy years between the opening of Korea's ports and Liberation, Korea had witnessed the birth and growth of a bourgeoisie.[5]

For many South Koreans, the genesis of the country's capitalist class during this period is difficult to accept because for much of the period between 1876 and 1945 Korea was under the direct or indirect influ-

1

ence of Japan. Indeed, for half of those nearly seventy years (1910–45) the country was a Japanese colony. To acknowledge that capitalism had its origins in this period is thus to suggest that the roots of the vibrant and internationally recognized capitalism of South Korea today might in some way be traceable to Japan. In a country where national pride is not only a very sensitive issue but one closely connected with anti-Japanese sentiment, the idea of Japan as an agency of *kŭndaehwa,* or "modernization," is psychologically wrenching. Many South Koreans would naturally much rather believe that the original impetus for capitalist growth came from within Korea itself.

Anti-Japanese feelings are by no means limited to the southern half of the peninsula. In North Korea as well there is still a deep residue of bitterness toward Japan that continues to defy the passage of time. In both North and South Korea, moreover, there is a common heritage of historical thought that indirectly tends to encourage a nationalistic view of history often quite impervious to facts. The terms and categories used by Koreans bespeak a linear and universalistic conception of history as a whole that is essentially Marxist in inspiration, and both sides share a desire to glorify Korea's position vis-à-vis other nations within the universal historical framework by placing the origins of capitalist development as far back as possible in Korean history, and certainly before the impact of Western or Japanese imperialism. This desire has, in turn, been intensified by anger at earlier Japanese historians working within the same mode of discourse who had emphasized the stagnation of the Korean economy before the advent of Japanese rule.[6]

The result of all these largely unarticulated attitudes has been a rather remarkable convergence of scholarly opinion in both Koreas in spite of all the barriers to a free exchange of information across the thirty-eighth parallel. Both North and South have seen the rise of similar schools of nationalistic scholarship that attempt to demonstrate the existence of the "sprouts" *(maenga)* of capitalist growth in the Yi dynasty. Korean scholars of this propensity have focused their attention on the increasing commercialization of seventeenth- and eighteenth-century Yi society in the wake of the disruptive Japanese and Manchu invasions that weakened the control of the state. They call attention, for example, to such factors as a growing monetization of exchange relations; the rupture of the established system of privileged government merchants and a corresponding rise of a new group of merchants oriented toward the market, some of whom were beginning to invest their profits in the production process itself; the supersession of government artisans by private artisan-entrepreneurs; and the beginning of a free wage labor force whose appearance is related to the commercialization and rationalization of agriculture in the countryside. In short, such scholars suggest that many of the key elements in the process of development toward Western industrial capitalism first delineated by Marx can be found simultaneously in traditional Korea in embryonic form.[7]

It is not my purpose here to attempt a detailed critique of such research. Much of it is meticulous and stimulating. It is also a useful and long overdue corrective to the earlier depiction of the Yi dynasty as economically stagnant. There can no longer be any doubt that Yi society was experiencing internal economic change long before 1876, even though the extent of such change needs to be more fully explored. In spite of the enthusiasm of Korean scholars for the topic, the actual evidence presented thus far does not suggest a scale of commercialization in Yi Korea comparable, for example, to that seen in Tokugawa Japan — let alone in preindustrial Europe.

Even if we grant economic growth and ignore the problem of scale, however, the question of the ultimate significance of such development still remains. There is no clear evidence that the indigenous economic changes described by Korean scholars altered the basic social structure of Yi society. Indeed, the best evidence we have points to exactly the opposite conclusion: that the society was controlled to the very end by a small aristocratic group of landed families like the Mins, who were able to perpetuate an oligopoly of wealth and power by strategic marriage alliances and domination of the state examination system, through which important political posts were granted.[8]

In addition — and more to the point — is the question of whether the economic changes depicted by Korean scholars may properly be considered incipient Korean capitalism. Here we must be very clear in our understanding of what constitutes the basis of capitalist society. It is not enough, I believe, to point out that there was a furtive market economy at work and that there were private merchants and artisans accumulating capital. Private ownership of property had been recognized in Korean society at least two hundred years before the alleged "sprouts" made their appearance in the seventeenth century, and, as Weber noted long ago, the adventurous acquisition of capital is a phenomenon that can be found in all types of societies where money and opportunity are available.[9] It is similarly incorrect to see in the mere existence of private artisans and hired labor a symptom of capitalist growth. Manufacture in its original sense, that is, handicraft production, however developed and widespread, did not in itself have the technical capacity to provide the basis for industrial capitalism.

And here we come to the crux of the matter. Capitalism as an economic system cannot be separated from industrialism. It is inconceivable apart from the technology that alone makes possible large-scale industrial production and concomitant transformation of the peasantry into an industrial work force. It is an economic system characterized not simply by market relations and private ownership of the means of production, but also by the predominance of machine industry. As Thorstein Veblen has written: "The material framework of modern civilization is the industrial system. . . . This modern economic organization is the 'Capitalistic System' or 'Modern Industrial System,' so called. Its characteristic features, and at the same time the forces by virtue of which it dominates modern culture, are the machine process and investment for a profit."[10]

Veblen, of course, was not saying anything here that had not been said earlier by Marx himself. But even though the Korean historians enamored of the "sprouts" argument produce works replete with Marxist assumptions and terminology, they seem to ignore Marx's own perception of the crucial relationship between capitalism and technology: "This workshop, the product of the division of labor in manufacture, produced in its turn—machines. It is they that sweep away the handicraftsman's work as the regulating principle of social production. Thus, on the one hand, the technical reason for the life-long annexation of the workman to a detail function is removed. On the other hand, the fetters that this same principle laid on the dominion of capital, fall away."[11]

"Ignore" is perhaps too strong a word. It is doubtful that any of the Korean scholars of the sprouts school would actually deny the importance of the link between capitalism and industrialism. This awareness, however, poses no problem for their argument because they are working on the assumption of the universality of the capitalist development first described by Marx. To make their point it is sufficient for them merely to locate those aspects of economic growth in Yi society that are similar to various features of the preindustrial European economy emphasized by Marx as part of the historical development of capitalism. Their belief in universality allows them to assume that the unimpeded development of these signs of economic change would inevitably have blossomed into industrial capitalism quite independently of the West.

In the end one is forced to conclude that such scholars seem bent on a futile quest for apples in an orange grove. There is, of course, no way to prove decisively one way or the other whether Korea would have eventually produced an industrial revolution of its own. But why bother? From an historical perspective, the question of capitalist sprouts in the Yi dynasty is important only in so far as it affirms a particular Korean nationalist bias of limited interest to outsiders and ultimately of little relevance to Korean history. We will never know what might have happened, but history in this case tells us unequivocally what did happen: modern industrial technology in Korea was imported, not invented. It is thus only after 1876 that we can begin to speak seriously of the growth of Korean capitalism.[12]

It is precisely this crucial period of imperialism and colonialism, however, that many Korean historians are most inclined to discount in their discussions of Korea's socioeconomic development. According to the conventional academic view, the early sprouts of indigenous capitalism that first began to appear in the seventeenth century had not sufficiently matured by the time the country was thrown open to foreign influence and were therefore unable to withstand Japan's economic penetration. With the annexation in 1910 and Korea's descent into colonial status, native capitalist development was largely stifled until 1945. In its most extreme form, this view amounts to a total denial of any colonial contribution to Korean socioeconomic development whatsoever. Consider, for example, the following statement by Cho Kijun: "It is impossible to talk of the modernization of the economy of a colonized people through an analytical measurement of the economic growth within the colony. Such growth was no more than an economic extension of the invading country; it was not a reflection of the level of income or the economic capacity of the colonized people. . . . Without liberation from imperialist domination, 'modernization' is no more than an empty word."[13]

Cho is correct in describing the colonial economy as "an economic extension of the invading country"—a pattern of economic development whose aspects and political implications I will discuss in detail in parts 2 and 3. But he is wrong in suggesting that Korean "modernization" under colonial rule was no more than an "empty word." In retrospect, what is striking about the colonial period to the student of Korean socioeconomic history is, first of all, the extent of industrial growth that did take place in spite of Korea's colonial status. Second, and even more interesting, is that colonialism did not preclude considerable numbers of Koreans from taking an active part in such industrial growth. Cho's own extensive studies of Korean entrepreneurship during the colonial period clearly, if inadvertently, show this to have been the case, and Cho only very narrowly manages to escape being caught in a massive contradiction by asserting that such entrepreneurship was "national capital" (*minjok chabon*) that developed outside and, indeed, in opposition to the imperial system. Such a formulation raises more questions than it answers, and, represents, as we shall see later, the very reverse of what actually happened.

For the truth, as always, is complex. And it is only by acknowledging the true origins of Korean capitalism that we can begin to grasp its character and significance. The Japanese in Korea were actually both agents of socioeconomic change and oppressors at one and the same time, and it is therefore quite reasonable to talk of economic modernization within the context of imperialism. Imperialism and colonialism were, in fact, only selectively oppressive and affected different classes of Koreans in different ways. Among the least oppressed was the nascent Korean bourgeoisie. Indeed, it is questionable whether the Korean bourgeoisie may be justly considered a victim of Japanese aggression at all—at least in an economic sense. As we shall see, imperialism provided the original impetus for the development of Korean capitalism. And if imperialism was the catalyst of change, colonialism was the crucible in which Korean capitalism first took shape. For their own reasons, the Japanese quite deliberately and purposefully fostered the growth of a Korean bourgeoisie. Korean capitalism thus came to enjoy its first real flowering under Japanese rule and with official Japanese blessing.

CHAPTER 1

Merchants and Landlords

The Accumulation of Capital, 1876–1919

Imperialism came to Korea in the 1870s, but the old civilization did not immediately shrivel up and die. While the forms and patterns of capitalist society, as well as the technology, were now available for Korean adaptation, the actual growth of a Korean industrial bourgeoisie was nevertheless an evolutionary process. Ultimately it would require the appearance of a new generation of Koreans schooled in the language and skills necessary for capitalist success and an economic and political framework conducive to industrial entrepreneurship. Such prerequisites were not much in evidence before 1919.

On the other hand, the impact of imperialism had the effect of drawing Korea for the first time into a vigorous new international market economy dominated by the great capitalist powers — though, as far as Korea was concerned, increasingly centered on Japan. The new market provided a basis and impetus for the accumulation of substantial amounts of capital by certain social elements in Korea's traditional polity, especially merchants and landlords. The more enterprising members of these groups went on to become the core of a nascent industrial bourgeoisie in the 1920s and later. While the process of bourgeois development was thus gradual and complex, it all began in 1876 with the impact of the international market and the hitherto inconceivable opportunities for capital accumulation.

The New Market Economy

While one can point to certain notable trends toward commercialization in the Yi dynasty, the traditional society nevertheless lacked a basic prerequisite for sustained and substantial accumulation of capital: a large-scale and expansive market. This was true even in comparison with Tokugawa Japan. In Japan the political settlement of the late sixteenth century created a captive samurai market (between 7 and

10 percent of the total population) in the towns and stimulated extensive urbanization. Eighteenth-century Edo was a huge metropolis of one million people.[1] Its great trading houses and exuberant merchant culture, which produced so much of what we today consider an essential part of the Japanese aesthetic tradition, were the envy of the samurai themselves, to whom commerce and its accompanying extracurricular activities were strictly (though not always successfully) forbidden.[2]

In Yi Korea, on the other hand, the aristocracy never lost its close link to the land, and urbanization was accordingly limited. What we know of pre-1876 Seoul, then as now Korea's major city, makes it seem small, poor, and dull by comparison with either contemporary Edo or Osaka.[3] Korean scholars of the sprouts school have had to comb deep and laboriously through an assortment of long-forgotten documents to demonstrate the mere *existence* of a market-oriented commercial class, while the still familiar works of Saikaku, for example, with their colorful descriptions of Tokugawa merchants, provide immediate and eloquent testimony to the great scale and depth of Tokugawa commercial life.[4] The evidence produced so far has given no indication of any traditional Korean merchants in Seoul or elsewhere on a scale that even begins to approximate such Tokugawa merchant houses as Kōnoike or Mitsui.[5]

Scholars of the sprouts school have made much of the foreign trade with China and Japan, especially in ginseng, carried on by the independent merchants of Kaesŏng. Kang Man'gil, for example, has even called Kaesŏng of this period "the most important commercial city in the country."[6] Much more work needs to be done before it is possible to say anything conclusive about the scale of such trade, but it was undoubtedly hampered and limited by its illegality. Like Tokugawa Japan, Yi Korea followed a strict policy of forbidding private foreign trade. International commerce, to the extent that it can be said to have existed at all, was officially restricted to tributary trade primarily with China and, to a lesser degree, with Japan.[7] At best the Kaesŏng trade appears to have been only a well-organized form of smuggling, with little in common with the sophisticated international commercial transactions of today or even of the late nineteenth-century capitalist world economy.

This interpretation is supported, moreover, by Kaesŏng suffering a gradual decline as a national commercial center after 1876.[8] For all their alleged skills and experience in international commerce, most of the old Kaesŏng merchant families were unable to adjust to the demands of the new international economy. Those few who did manage to survive and prosper were able to do so not so much because of their traditional business expertise but largely because they were able to send their children to Japan, where they received both a modern education and invaluable practical experience in one of the new centers of Asian commerce. Kim Chŏngho, the founder of the Kaesŏng Electric Company — and Cho Kijun's prime example of a successful Kaesŏng entrepreneur in the period after 1876 — is a case in point. Kim's background is somewhat obscure, and he may, in fact, not have been the progeny of a Kaesŏng merchant family at all, but the son of a wealthy Kaesŏng landlord. What is clear is that he was born ten years after the Kanghwa Treaty, thus eliminating the possibility that he himself might have been a Kaesŏng merchant in the period before 1876, and that he graduated from Meiji University in Tokyo with a degree in law.[9]

In spite of all the enthusiasm in recent years about economic growth in Korea before 1876, in the end one is still left with the impression that both the internal and external market opportunities in Yi Korea were quite limited, especially in comparison with Japan or even China. The comments of nineteenth-century Western observers are by no means always the best sources of information on traditional Korean commerce, but the following statement by Ernst Oppert, a German adventurer of the 1860s intensely interested in the Korea trade, may not have been too far off the mark in its rather bleak comparative assessment of pre-1876 commerce on the peninsula: "Nowhere is there a trace of the life and bustle met with even in second and third-rate Chinese towns, and it almost looks as if the commercial spirit of the people were fast asleep, and would only be roused when the country is opened to foreign intercourse and trade."[10]

With the Kanghwa Treaty of 1876 Korea's commercial isolation from both its neighbors and the rest of the world was effectively ended. Korea not only became an export market for foreign machine-manufactured goods (especially cotton textiles) but became an exporter itself of grains — especially rice — to Japan. It must be noted, however, that change was gradual. Korea's economy was not transformed overnight. The country's main ports were wedged open and developed by Japan and the other powers only slowly and in piecemeal fashion — Pusan in 1876, Wŏnsan in 1880, Inch'ŏn in 1883. Mokp'o and Kunsan, two of the most important ports in the rice trade, were not opened until 1897 and 1899, respectively. It was also not until the 1890s that manufacturing in Japan began to replace agriculture in relative importance and increased the need both for export markets and for rice to feed a growing industrial work force. It also took time for manufacturers to break into the Korean handicraft market. For example, foreign goods supplied only about one-fourth of the total Korean demand for cotton textiles in the period before 1894. The foreign cloth that was being imported at that time had not yet been adapted to popular Korean needs and tastes, and most Koreans continued to buy the more expensive native cloth because it was three times more durable than the foreign fabric.[11]

In the end, however, foreign economic penetration of the Korean economy proved to be irresistible, and it was the Japanese who eventually emerged as the dominant economic force on the peninsula. This is not to suggest that economic gain was the primary motivation behind the Japanese imperialist thrust into Korea. Indeed, it seems quite clear that initially at least Japanese interest in Korea was essentially political and strategic rather than economic.[12] As Peter Duus has pointed out, however, the Meiji oligarchs, while publicly scorning the pursuit of private profit, nevertheless had a keen appreciation of the close relationship between national wealth and national power, and this was reflected in their increasingly frequent and aggressive demands for economic concessions in Korea after 1894.[13]

Even before 1894, indeed, from the very onset of Korea's opening of its ports in 1876, the Meiji government was making some attempt to promote Japanese trade with Korea. In 1876, for example, Ōkubo Toshimichi, the home minister, personally encouraged the well-known businessman Ōkura Kihachirō to go to Pusan and help launch the Korea trade. Later that same year the government guaranteed Mitsubishi an annual five-thousand-yen subsidy for the company to open a steamship line to Pusan. Such examples of official Japanese interest and intervention in the Korea trade are to be found throughout the period between 1876 and 1894.[14]

With the official blessing and often financial support of the Meiji government, private Japanese business interests began to take note of the new Korean market. The site of the Japanese settlement near Pusan, the first Korean port to be opened, was little more than a "miserable colliery" at the time of the Restoration, and even in 1875 — the year before the Kanghwa Treaty — only about 100 Japanese were in residence there. By 1882, however, the Japanese town had some 1,800 people, along with a bank, a shipping company, a hospital, and even its own newspaper published in Japanese (and Chinese).[15] As more and more of Korea was officially opened to foreign trade and Japan consolidated its political position on the peninsula, Japanese commercial establishments spread throughout the country. Even Kaesŏng, the jewel in the capitalist sprouts school mentioned above, acquired its share of Japanese merchants. In a visit there in 1895, the redoubtable world traveler Isabella Bird Bishop noted that "the native traders now have to compete with fourteen Japanese shops, and to suffer the presence of forty Japanese residents."[16] Ultimately such public and private efforts were to give Japan a dominant role in the Korean economy that the annexation only confirmed and enhanced.

The new market economy did not work solely to the benefit of the Japanese, however. During the period between 1876 and 1910 or, more accurately, between 1876 and 1919, Korea's economic position as a Japanese granary and export market for manufactured goods provided the basis for the accumulation of capital by a significant number of enterprising Koreans, who gradually became the core of a native bourgeoisie. Because of their particular role in the new market economy after 1876, merchants and, even more important, landlords were to be the pivotal transitional figures in the emergence of this native bourgeois class.

Merchants

In general, Yi Korea's merchant class does not seem to have adjusted well to the country's gradual incorporation into the world economy. We have already noted the decreasing importance of Kaesŏng in international commerce after 1876. This was due in part, of course, to Kaesŏng's eclipse by the new international treaty ports, but even more, perhaps, to so much of the Kaesŏng trade having been linked to ginseng, which after 1898 became a strictly controlled government monopoly.[17]

Seoul's leading merchants, including the *yugŭijŏn*[18] and the tribute merchants (*kongin*), fared even worse than Kaesŏng's. Both clung as long as possible to their respective official and quasi-official roles as purveyors to the court and central government. In 1895, however, all such official privileges were abolished.[19] With some notable exceptions like Paek Yunsu,[20] Seoul's traditional merchants failed thereafter to adapt themselves to the new conditions. In spite of the increasing influx of foreign items and the growing importance of Japanese yen as a medium of exchange,[21] they continued to deal in native goods and to accumulate Korean copper and nickel coins. For many of them the currency reform of 1905, which virtually destroyed the value of the old Korean cash, was a coup de grâce from which they never recovered. In 1907 the *Hwangsŏng sinmun* observed that "an ugly result of the nickel cash readjustment measures two years ago last July has been a great depression in the business world. Businessmen are in disorder. Some have closed shop and run away; others have taken poison and committed suicide."[22]

Not surprisingly, those merchants who did manage to prosper during this period were the ones most closely connected with the expanding international trade in rice and manufactured goods, the *kaekchu* or *yŏgak*.

The origins of the *kaekchu* are obscure and may possibly be traced to the Koryŏ period (918–1392). During the Yi dynasty, however, the *kaekchu* were important as intermediaries in the commerce between town and countryside. Like other wholesale merchants, they were engaged in buying cheap and selling dear, but because of their special position as middlemen in the national commercial network, they gradually became involved in a host of diverse and complex business activities, including warehousing, consignment selling, and transport. In connection with these pursuits, they also branched out into innkeeping and banking to provide inexpensive lodging and financial services for their merchant customers en route to or from business transactions.[23]

The skills the *kaekchu* developed in such activities were to prove extremely useful after 1876. In the early years of the treaty ports, foreign merchants were forbidden to travel to the interior of the country, and even as more and more of the country was opened up to them, they were still severely restricted by their ignorance of the language and customs of the local areas. It was the *kaekchu* who came to the foreigners' rescue. With their intimate knowledge of the country and extensive commercial connections, they were in a perfect position to act as middlemen in the international trade — buying, selling, storing, and transporting the rice and manufactures that flowed in and out of the treaty ports. Their traditional role as de facto bankers in the network of domestic trade, moreover, had given them invaluable experience that could be readily applied to a successful career in international commerce. Such basic commercial and financial expertise was, of course, improved and developed after 1876 through constant interaction with foreign customers.[24]

As yet no statistics have been uncovered that would allow us to gauge in any really accurate fashion the scope of *kaekchu* capital accumulation during this period, but we can get some idea of the considerable sums that must have been involved by examining the sudden change of fortune of some of the most notable participants. Some of the most successful *kaekchu* were originally poor young peasants or townsmen, for whom the *kaekchu* enterprise offered the promise of quick and often spectacular wealth. One such figure was Pak Sŭngjik, about whom there will be more to say in later chapters, when our analysis leads into a detailed study of the operation of the Kyŏngsŏng Spinning and Weaving Company (Kyŏngsŏng Pangjik Chusik Hoesa). For now it is enough to note that Pak rose from rural poverty to become one of the leading Korean businessmen of the colonial era and that he began his career as a *kaekchu* dealing in foreign cloth imported through Inch'ŏn.[25]

Another such rags to riches figure was Pak Kisun, whose son, Pak Yŏngch'ŏl, later became president of the Chōsen Commercial Bank (Chōsen Shōgyō Ginkō) and another well-known and well-connected colonial business figure. Pak had been born into a poor family in Iri in 1857. When he was only twelve years old, his father became ill and unable to support the family, and Kisun was sent out to work as an errand boy for a merchant family. At eighteen, he established his own rice-trading business and took advantage of his strategic location near the rice-rich plain of North Chŏlla Province to accumulate a fortune. He invested his profits in land and in time became a major landlord in the area.[26]

Pak also invested some of his money in modern business ventures. He was by no means atypical. From around the turn of the century many of the *kaekchu* who had battened on the international market economy began to transfer some of their profits to other forms of enterprise, especially modern banking. Of the two principal founders of the Kup'o Savings Company Limited (later the Kup'o Bank) established in 1908, for example, one had been a North Kyŏngsang landlord and the other—Chang Usŏk—a *kaekchu* who, like Pak, had become wealthy through the export rice trade.[27] Like these other *kaekchu*, Pak too developed an interest in banking. In cooperation with a number of other prominent Korean landlords and *kaekchu*, he founded the Samnam Bank in Chŏnju in 1919. Around this same time he also became a shareholder and board member in some Japanese ventures in the region, including the North Chŏlla Railway Company and the North Chŏlla Livestock Company.[28] For Pak and others, the lucrative *kaekchu* trade had made possible a leap out of poverty that would have been inconceivable before 1876.

While the *kaekchu* life had been good while it lasted, it gradually became more and more difficult. By the late 1890s the country was wide open to foreign—and especially Japanese—influence, and more and more Japanese firms were spreading throughout the country. By then many Japanese traders themselves had acquired years of experience and practical wisdom in the Korea trade, and the importance of the old intermediary role of the independent *kaekchu* was accordingly diminished.

To counteract this threat, many of the *kaekchu* formed cooperative associations in the treaty ports.[29] Others, as we have seen, and especially those who had already made their fortunes, became landlords or moved into other businesses, often in cooperation with Japanese businessmen. In 1907, for example, Pak Sŭngjik, who by that time was running his own drygoods store in Seoul, managed to turn the increasing threat of Japanese competition to his own benefit by forming a separate new international trading company with a Japanese partner.[30] Pak was not unique. By 1911 over 50 percent of the total paid-up corporate capital of the country was held by joint Japanese-Korean firms.[31]

Around the turn of the century one of the two major social components of the nascent Korean bourgeois class—the traditional merchant element—had thus already more or less reached the limits of its ability to accumulate capital without altering its traditional commercial form. It therefore began to imitate the successful capitalist models that imperialism had introduced into Korea and take on the form of a modern Korean bourgeoisie through the establishment of modern banking and trading corporations, more often than not in cooperation with Japanese businessmen.

Eventually such *kaekchu* capital also found its way into industry. While the Kyŏngsŏng Spinning and Weaving Company founded in 1919, for example, was essentially a landlord effort, among its original promoters was at least one member of a former *kaekchu* family.[32]

Landlords

A recent joint study of South Korean entrepreneurship by the Harvard Institute for International Development and the Korea Development Bank discovered from a sampling of some three hundred South Korean businessmen that no less than 47 percent were the sons of "large-to-medium landowners" and that it was primarily the larger landowners who had produced entrepreneurs. The study concluded that "very few entrepreneurs have risen from the poor masses represented by tenant

farmers and rural and urban laborers. The industrial elite were recruited from the pre-industrial elite rather than from society as a
whole."[33]

The figure of 47 percent of course, can only be approximate. It
is based on the necessary assumption that the respondents in the sampling were telling the truth, and Koreans, with their intense regard
for social status, have a long historical legacy of lively exaggeration
when it comes to social background.[34] Still the figure of nearly 50
percent is highly suggestive and may even be too low. The study found,
for example, that 16 percent of the respondents' fathers were "factory
owners," 6 percent, "civil servants," 4 percent, "teachers," and 7 percent, "professionals."[35] Any one or, indeed, all of these groups might
well contain many people whose families were substantial landowners
during the colonial period and before.

When we consider the social origins of the nascent Korean bourgeoisie of the colonial period, it is clear that the predominance of the
landlord element in the class is a phenomenon that has deep historical
roots. Much more research needs to be done before any definitive
statements can be made, but the work that has been done so far on
this question by Cho Kijun and Kim Yŏngmo, for example, clearly
suggests that the formation of a Korean bourgeois class during the
late Yi and colonial periods represented to a significant extent the
transformation of landed wealth into capitalist enterprise.[36] Cho and
Kim are wont to distinguish between "bureaucrats" and "landlords,"
both of which are seen as crucial groups in the transition to capitalism,
but, in class terms, the two groups tended to overlap, and for us the
distinction is more confusing than illuminating.[37] Moreover, those
yangban-bureaucrats who established banks and other businesses with
their own funds like Kim Chonghan,[38] one of the principal founders
both of the Hansŏng Bank and the original Bank of Korea (Chosŏn
Ŭnhaeng), were clearly able to do so because of their income from
extensive landholdings. Observations by Koreans at the time also tend
to confirm the view that the capitalists were emerging largely from
the old landed elite. In a statement on the "Characteristics of the Present Stage of the Korean Revolution" drawn up in 1929 by the Korean
Communist party, it was noted that "most of the bourgeoisie are in
the landlord class."[39]

The preponderance of the landlord element in the Korean colonial
bourgeoisie is really not surprising. Even more than the *kaekchu*, it
was the landlords who reaped the fruits of the new international market economy after 1876 and accumulated the excess capital that could

be used to establish and finance modern business enterprises. As the export rice trade to Japan expanded, so did the profits of those who owned the land on which the rice was grown. Little wonder that the *kaekchu* themselves often invested their first profits in paddy and strove to become big landowners.

Even the landlords, of course, had problems during this period. From around the turn of the century and especially in the aftermath of the Russo-Japanese War, a number of Japanese began to descend upon Korea and buy up land to settle down in the peninsula as landlords themselves.[40] In 1908 the quasi-official Oriental Development Company was also created by the Japanese Diet, and it began a rapacious acquisition of land that would eventually make the company not only colonial Korea's single biggest landlord but the infamous symbol and epitome of Japanese oppression to many Koreans.[41] To protect its own landlords in Japan, moreover, in 1905 the Japanese government placed a 15 percent tariff on foreign rice imports, thus throwing a wrench into the buoyant free trade in rice that had prevailed since 1876.[42]

While such things inevitably put a damper on the capital accumulation process, they nevertheless did not seriously diminish the general prosperity of Korean landlords between 1876 and 1919. The attraction Korea held for Japanese landlords during this period was limited. Even later, at its peak, Japanese ownership of Korean agricultural land probably never exceeded 25 percent of the total.[43] Japanese acquisition of land, moreover, did not necessarily entail a corresponding diminution of Korean landlord property. When private Korean land passed into Japanese hands, it was more often than not a poor peasant owner or owner-tenant and not a rich landlord who had been the loser.[44] And often the land acquired by Japanese landlords had originally been part of the public (or royal) as opposed to the private domain. Much of the land controlled by the Oriental Development Company, for example, consisted of former palace and government properties acquired from the Korean court and central government and of unreclaimed forests and fields obtained from the Government-General after 1910.[45] The company's grandiose plans to colonize Korea with Japanese settlers also turned out to be a dismal failure.[46] In the end, a decision by the colonial authorities to work through rather than against the existing landlord system was clearly reflected in the results of the cadastral survey completed by the Government-General in 1918. One of the survey's main results was official colonial reaffirmation of the existing Korean landowning structure—at the expense of many of the traditional customary rights of the tenant farmers.[47]

The Japanese tariff on foreign rice imports was a more important threat to Korean landlords than competition from Japanese colonists because the tariff struck a blow to the market itself. The Japanese grain merchants in Korea were also naturally concerned, and the Federation of Japanese Chambers of Commerce and Industry in Korea sent a petition to the homeland protesting the tariff and calling for its abolition. In the end, the original tariff rate of 15 percent proved to be highly flexible. Between 1905 and 1913 it was frequently both raised and lowered according to Japanese needs and from time to time even temporarily set aside altogether, and in 1913 it was finally abolished.[48] Eventually the economic boom of the First World War created a bullish market for rice that Korean exports could hardly keep up with, and between 1914 and 1920 the price of rice in Japan nearly tripled.[49] The boom, while it lasted, was a time of unprecedented prosperity for Korean landlords and wiped out the memory of the drier years of the previous decade.

The period between 1876 and 1919 was thus in general a halcyon era for the Korean landlord class. The larger landlords, including many of the late Yi bureaucratic elite, were content for the most part to leave practical matters in the hands of their stewards while they and their children enjoyed the more exciting life of the cities, and especially of Seoul. For those who were less affluent when the market began to open up in 1876, the period through 1919 was a time for more direct involvement in the commercialization that was taking place in the countryside, and many of the more enterprising of these smaller landlords were also able to accumulate considerable amounts of capital. One such landlord family was the Koch'ang Kims, whose rise to eminence as industrial entrepreneurs during the colonial period is the main focus of this book and a yardstick for measuring and analyzing the development of Korean capitalism before 1945. It is time now to introduce this remarkable family, whose own history has been so closely intertwined with some of the deepest currents of modern Korean history itself.

The Koch'ang Kims

In 1876 the Kims were small landowners in Kobu (now Koch'ang) County in the northern part of North Chŏlla Province. The head of the household at the time was Kim Yohyŏp, whose grandsons Sŏngsu and Yŏnsu would eventually found and manage the Kyŏngsŏng Spinning and Weaving Company. As a boy, Yohyŏp's economic prospects had been dim. He had been born into a poor scholarly family in Changsŏng County in South Chŏlla Province, and he was also the youngest of three sons, giving him no hope of a substantial inheritance.[50]

His family lineage seems to have saved him, however. As a branch of the Ulsan Kim clan that had produced Kim Inhu, a noted Neo-Confucian scholar of the sixteenth century and a contemporary and disciple of the illustrious Yi Hwang (T'oegye), the family had clung tenaciously to an increasingly marginal yangban status, and Kim's father was able to arrange a good marriage for his third son with the daughter of a very wealthy landlord in Koch'ang County. Kim's father-in-law subsequently arranged for the new couple to receive some land in the area, and Kim moved north to Koch'ang County.[51] It was a modest beginning for a family that in time became so fabulously land-rich that Koreans were wont to say that the Kims "could wander all over the Chŏllas without ever stepping off their own property."[52]

Ultimately, of course, it was the opening of the export rice market that made such acquisition possible, but the Kims enjoyed a special geographical advantage that gave them an edge even over many other Korean landlords competing in the market. From the beginning, more-over, the family also seems to have had a good nose for business — an instinct brought to bear on all its undertakings, including the management of its landholdings.

Geography

To take a trip to Koch'ang County even today is to take a step backward in time. The South Korean economic "miracle" that stretches out on both sides of the highway between Seoul and Pusan has still scarcely begun to penetrate the Chŏllas. There, in a landscape of thatched-roof villages connected by narrow, unpaved roads, it is easy to imagine oneself in another century or, easier still, perhaps, back in colonial times.

In the coastal township of Haeri, for example, at the Samyang Salt Company owned by Kim Yohyŏp's great-grandson, one finds an old rice mill built by the family in the pre-Liberation period to service what was then Haeri Estate, one of the Kims' many colonial tenant farms (nongjang).[53] The mill is still being used. Since 1945 South

Korea has, of course, experienced land reform and not a few changes of government, but around the Samyang Salt Company much of the land is still owned by the Kims, who had originally reclaimed a good deal of it from the sea with the help of Government-General subsidies.[54] The villages that lie at the edges of the salt works are all composed of Samyang's tenants, who still deliver their rent to the old rice mill in kind.[55]

The most striking feature of the landscape, however, is the land itself, and it is here that we find one of the important geographical keys to the Kims' economic ascension. Generally speaking, Korea is a rocky and mountainous country. Writing in the late nineteenth century, for example, the missionary and amateur Korean historian James S. Gale described the configuration of the land as a "succession of mountain ranges" and quoted a Korean expression he had heard frequently: "Over the hills, hills again, hills without number."[56]

But the Chŏllas—and particularly the great Honam Plain in the northern of the two provinces—are unusual in Korean geography. There the unsuspecting midwestern American traveler is startled to find himself for the first time feeling at home in the Korean terrain. Instead of the usual view of jagged hills and mountains, he suddenly finds himself confronting a sweeping agricultural vista of regular geometric patterns stretching on and on to the horizon—Illinois or Iowa by another name.

The main crop, however, is not corn, but rice. The Chŏllas are, in fact, Korea's "rice basket." In North Chŏlla alone, 67 percent of the cultivated area is paddy, compared with a national average of 56 percent, and the province today provides about 17 percent of South Korea's total annual rice production. Within North Chŏlla, the Honam Plain is the most productive area of all, accounting for nearly 75 percent of the rice harvested in the province.[57]

The land that Kim Yohyŏp received from his wife's family was located in the southern part of the Honam Plain, where Koch'ang County pushes northward into the sea. It was (and still is) easily some of the best rice land in the country. It was also surrounded by land that was equally good or even better, and when the Kim family was in a position to expand its holdings, it would find no more fertile or convenient place than its own front and back yards. The champaign character of the land also proved to be a great advantage much later (in the 1920s) when Kim Yohyŏp's grandson Yŏnsu began to consolidate the family's landholdings into large-scale, contiguous estates.

Another blessing of geography was the land's proximity to the ocean. This meant, first of all, that any holdings bordering on the coast might be extended through drainage into the sea itself. Such a location also offered an additional advantage—easy access to a key port. In this case the Kims were particularly lucky. Just across the inlet to the northeast lay the coastal town of Chulp'o. As international trade developed, Chulp'o gradually became an important entrepôt in the distribution of North Chŏlla rice—and especially of rice from Koch'ang County, which lay at Chulp'o's back door. The Koch'ang rice passed from the interior of the county through Chulp'o and then on by ship to Kunsan, which was only about seventeen nautical miles away. From Kunsan the rice was transferred to larger vessels and shipped to Japan.[58] Chulp'o's proximity both to the Kims' land-holdings and to the international port of Kunsan would in time make it a natural and convenient maritime base for the family's expanding agrobusiness in Koch'ang and other counties. In a word, the Kims in 1876 occupied a position in the North Chŏlla countryside that placed them near the very heart of what would later become one of the main arteries of the most profitable rice trade in the country.

Enterprising Landlords

Favorable geography notwithstanding, the new international market was a boon only to those who took advantage of it. To do so on a scale achieved by the Kims required a keen business sense and not a little ruthlessness. Family tradition has it that the Kims' commercial acumen stemmed originally from Yohyŏp's wife, whose frugality and strict household management were mainly responsible for the family's endurance and increasing prosperity in the early, leaner years of the marriage.[59] In any case, Yohyŏp's two sons, Kijung and Kyŏngjung, and later his grandchildren—and even today his great-grandchildren—have all exhibited a consistent ability to gauge the winds of change and head in the most profitable direction. During the First World War, for example, when many landlords were using their proceeds from high-priced rice sales to buy up more land, Yohyŏp's son Kyŏngjung left his profits in the bank to collect interest and bided his time. After the war, when both rice and land prices plunged, he was able to purchase three to four times the amount of land he could have bought earlier.[60] Later, his sons, Sŏngsu and Yŏnsu, always seemed to acquire new properties just as their previous owners were tottering on the verge of bankruptcy and desperate to sell; in most cases they were able to use their knowledge of the market and their personal contacts to revive or transform the dying companies into profitable enterprises. Even political change, as we shall come to see in this study, has never presented an insurmountable obstacle to the Kims. They have invariably—if not always with the same degree of enthusiasm —made their peace with the ruling authorities, from the late Yi dynasty down to contemporary military regimes in South Korea. In the early 1980s, for example, Kim Yŏnsu's son Sanghyŏp served as prime minister of the country under Chun Doo Hwan.[61]

Such adept economic and political opportunism was much in evidence between 1876 and 1919. The family's move to Chulp'o in 1907 was impeccably timed. First, Chulp'o represented a local bastion of political security in what was becoming an increasingly unstable area. The coercive transformation of Korea into a Japanese protectorate in 1905 had given birth to a rebel movement known collectively as the "righteous army" (*ŭibyŏng*), which was receiving strong support among the Korean populace, especially the poorer peasants, in the countryside. In its frustration with such popular backing for the rebels, the Japanese gendarmerie in turn had resorted to wholesale atrocities against entire villages. By 1907 much of the countryside, especially the densely populated and highly tenanted agricultural regions of the southwest like North Chŏlla from which the rebels drew much of their strength, had seen the development of dangerous zones of guerrilla warfare, and those Koreans suspected of collusion with the ruling authorities (more often than not the wealthy landlords) frequently became the object of *ŭibyŏng* hatred and vengeance.[62] The Kims, who had initially accepted official protectorate posts, including that of county magistrate, may have been one such family singled out for *ŭibyŏng* reprisals.[63] Family tradition has it, for example, that one of the reasons for the move to Chulp'o in 1907 was the constant threat at the time of "robber bands" who had been attacking the homes of the more prosperous families, including that of the Kims themselves. Chulp'o, with its garrison of Japanese forces, was a haven from such peril.[64]

There were also economic reasons for moving to Chulp'o at this time. About 5 percent of the Kunsan export trade in rice was passing through Chulp'o,[65] and most of this rice was coming from Koch'ang County, where the Kims had their original holdings. Chulp'o was, in effect, Koch'ang's door on the international rice market, and it was quite natural that the Kims should eventually come to view the town as a suitable base for their expanding operations. In time Kim Yŏnsu would build a rice mill and a dock and even purchase two eighty-ton ships to transport the rice to Kunsan, thus indeed making Chulp'o the center of the family's rice business in the North Chŏlla region.[66] In 1907, however, the move to Chulp'o and subsequent purchase of property both in the town and surrounding area seems to have been a shrewd investment in the future. Certainly the economic signs were already very encouraging in 1907. The export business was booming as never before. Total exports out of Kunsan—most of which were rice—had jumped from about 650,000 yen in 1906 to nearly 2,000,000 yen in 1907, and thereafter they continued in general to climb higher and higher, reaching a peak of about 26,500,000 yen in 1919.[67] A good part of the change in figures was of course due to inflation, especially during World War I, but such inflation did not hurt those who owned the rice land. On the contrary, it provided an incentive to landlords to try to increase the profits from their estates.

Estate management was the main key to the Kims' capital accumulation between 1876 and 1919. It was an occupation that called forth their more severe economic instincts, for land or estate management during this period meant largely the collection of the highest possible rents through the most efficient handling of tenants. Later, when the Government-General adopted a policy of keeping rice prices low while simultaneously increasing the volume of production through large-scale subsidized irrigation and reclamation, the Kims would begin to take a much greater interest in agricultural improvement and production as well as rents. Before the mid-1920s, however, the family seems to have pursued a management policy based almost solely on maximization of rents through pressure on tenants.

Such pressure took a variety of forms. First, the Kims frequently changed tenants each year, with such changes often accompanied by a corresponding rise in rent for the particular plot of land. Where the prospective tenants were strangers to the family—and especially after a rise in the rent—the Kims also required the peasants to name guarantors (pojŭngin) who would accept responsibility for the rents should the new tenant fail to meet his obligation. Second, the Kims attempted whenever possible to shift the burden of the land tax onto the tenants themselves. Third, the family strove to implement a fixed-rent system (as opposed to sharecropping) on its lands. Not only was the fixed-rent system generally more profitable in terms of rent; it was also customary for the tenant to assume the responsibility for the land tax in a fixed-rent system.[68]

As the Kims continued to acquire more and more land, often in scattered strips located far from Chulp'o, stewards (kwalliin) became increasingly important in management. In 1918 Kijung's side of the family—which included Kim Sŏngsu—employed thirty-eight stewards in all. Kyŏngjung, whose holdings were said to be between two and two and one-half times larger,[69] undoubtedly had a correspondingly greater number under his authority. Stewards were generally, though not always, selected from among the tenants themselves. Their primary duty was to collect the Kims' rents and other fees, such as the interest on rice loans and charges for the use of livestock. Often the family also had its stewards store the rice in their own homes until the price rose sufficiently or the family needed more funds. In return for such services the steward received a fixed percentage (from 7 to 10 percent) of the total rents collected.[70]

Under such an arrangement the stewards obviously had a vested interest in extracting high rents from the tenants. The Kims, however, believed in the stick as well as the carrot when it came to controlling their stewards. Like common tenants, the stewards were changed frequently, and the Kims often tried to lower their percentage of the rent. In addition, they held their stewards accountable for any losses incurred. Harassed stewards in turn sought to reduce their insecurity and make up their losses through pressure on the tenants. The strict manipulation of stewards thus worked to the Kims' benefit in two crucial ways: it tended to keep rents as high as possible and it served in some measure to deflect tenant anger at such high rents away from the Kims themselves and onto the hired local agents who actually carried out the family's exactions.[71]

The Fruits of Enterprise

Lucky geography and hard-headed land management in the context of a flourishing international market in rice ultimately proved to be a profitable combination for the Kims between 1876 and 1919. It is difficult, however, to trace the family's accumulation of capital in any great detail. We know approximately how much land the family owned in 1909 and 1919, but there is almost no indication in any of the available sources of how much land Yohyŏp began with in 1876 or how much land he originally received from his father-in-law at the time of his marriage.

The father-in-law appears to have been a major landowner in the area. Kim family tradition has it that he was a *"mansŏkkun,"*[72] a vague term used by Koreans in much the same way we tend to use the term "multimillionaire." To the extent that wealth and membership in a bureaucratically prominent clan tended to overlap in the Yi dynasty, we may assume that Yohyŏp's father-in-law, as a Yŏnil Chŏng, was indeed reasonably well-off.[73] However, we simply do not know how generously Chŏng treated his new son-in-law. According to stories passed down within the family, the early years of Yohyŏp's marriage were far from comfortable economically, and the accumulation of capital was gradual.[74]

While the details thus elude us, there are a couple of indicators to help us measure the Kims' economic ascent after 1876. One such series of markers is provided by the expansion of the family compound in Inch'on, the hamlet in Koch'ang County where Kijung and Kyŏngjung and later Sŏngsu and Yŏnsu were all born. The gradual erection of this great house, which even today dominates the countryside around it, was material testament to the family's growing prosperity during the late nineteenth and early twentieth centuries.

The first building was completed as early as 1861. Unfortunately, the significance of this initial construction is not clear. On the one hand, it seems to imply that Yohyŏp and his parsimonious wife were applying the techniques of land management discussed earlier long before the opening of the country to international commerce in 1876. This would hardly be surprising, as landlord pressure on tenants had always been a common aspect of Korean rural life. It is also possible, however, that the money for the new house came all or in part from Father-in-Law Chŏng—perhaps to help his daughter and her husband establish a suitable home for their growing family. (Kijung had been born only two years before; Kyŏngjung would be born in 1863.) In any case there was no further construction until after 1876. It was only then that the house began to acquire the form it exhibits today —a compound of numerous buildings with separate but connected domiciles for two families (Kijung's and Kyŏngjung's), each with its own detached reception (*sarang*) and family (*an*) quarters, storage buildings, servants' quarters, and private entrance. Such additions to the house were made by Yohyŏp and his sons in 1879 (main reception quarters), 1881 (minor living quarters), 1893 (gatehouse of main reception quarters), and 1903 (minor reception quarters). By 1907, when the family moved to Chulp'o, all the major buildings of the compound were in place.[75]

The Kims' increasing economic prosperity may also have been reflected in the family's mounting acquisition of bureaucratic posts during this period. Until its abolition in 1894, the traditional civil service examination, although dominated to a large extent by a few aristocratic families, was nevertheless a necessary rite of passage for anyone, regardless of family background, who had serious bureaucratic aspirations. The more important offices, in particular, were generally awarded only to those who had successfully passed the higher civil examination or *munkwa*.[76] Even after 1894, there was no radical change in this basic pattern until the Japanese established a protectorate in 1905. As before, success in the traditional examinations continued to be an important prerequisite for high office.[77]

Nevertheless, while it is undoubtedly correct that the very highest offices — where the real power lay — remained largely in the hands of the *munkwa* passers right down to the end, the case of the Kims suggests that even before the official abolition of the traditional examinations, the old system of recruitment may have been starting to show a few cracks at some of the lower and middle levels of the bureaucracy. Of the three adult males in the Kim family in the period before 1894, only Kijung passed the lower-level examination and received the *chinsa* degree, an achievement that would ordinarily have made him eligible only for admission to the National Academy, not for a regular official post. We do not know whether his father and younger brother even tried to pass the lower-level exam, but, in any case, neither obtained even a *chinsa* degree.[78]

All three men, however, managed to acquire a number of posts in the late Yi period, some of them of fairly high rank.[79] All three, for example, were at one time or another appointed to the office of county magistrate (*kunsu*), a post that carried with it a rank of 4B. Yohyŏp also made it to the lower echelons of the State Tribunal (Ŭigŭmbu), the Council of Ministers without Portfolio (Chungch'uwŏn), and the Royal Secretariat (Pisŏwŏn).

There is no way to be certain, but such positions may well have been purchased with the growing wealth of the family. Certainly the sale even of high office was a practice that was being decried at the time.[80] Many of the Kims' posts, moreover, were acquired even before the official abolition of the examination system in 1894, including, in Yohyŏp's case, the positions in the State Tribunal (1885) and a county magistracy (1888). That the appointments may have been pecuniary is also suggested by their failure to follow a regular pattern of bureaucratic advancement. Yohyŏp, for example, began his bureaucratic career in 1872 as a *kamyŏk* in the Royal Repair and Construction Office (Sŏn'gonggam) with a relatively high rank of 2B. In 1885 he then received minor appointments (*tosa; pongsa*) to the State Tribunal that carried rankings of somewhere between 6B and 8B. The following year (1886) he dropped to the very bottom of the bureaucratic ladder (9B) as a royal tomb official (ch'ambong). Two years later, in 1888, he was elevated to magistrate of Hwasun County in South Chŏlla. Such a bizarre career pattern may perhaps be explained by the Kims purchasing whatever official posts happened to be on the market as profits from the rice trade flowed into the family coffers. And indeed, it was certainly the period after 1876 that was the golden age for the Kims as far as bureaucratic appointments were concerned. In 1876 Yohyŏp was already forty-three years old but he had obtained his first appointment only four years before. All his other appointments came only after 1876, and especially in the years after 1885.

Such architectural and political signposts give us some idea of the family's economic advance during the late nineteenth century. By the time of his death in 1909, Yohyŏp was able to leave his two sons a considerable inheritance. Kijung, the older son, received land producing approximately 1,000 sŏk of rice per year; Kyŏngjung received only about one-fifth that amount.[81] By 1919, however, the original inheritance in each case had multiplied many times over, and the two brothers' relative economic positions stood reversed, with Kyŏngjung in possession of more land than his older brother.

They were both extremely rich. By Korean standards, the amount of land owned by the two brothers in 1919 was nothing short of Croesian. About 80 percent of Korea's rural population at the time consisted of tenants or owner-tenants.[82] The vast majority of Korean owners, moreover, possessed holdings ranging from a mere 1 tan (0.25 acres) to 2.5 chŏngbo (6.1 acres).[83] The estate records (tojobu) of Kijung and his sons, however, show that the older brother's branch of the family alone possessed about 750 chŏngbo (about 1,800 acres) in 1918, over 90 percent of which was paddy. The rent for that year in rice amounted to about 7,200 sŏk[84] collected from well over a thousand tenants, a few of whom may well have been Japanese.[85] We do not have the actual land records for Kyŏngjung's estate, but it was reputedly in the neighborhood of 1,300 chŏngbo (3,185 acres), 900 chŏngbo (2,205 acres) of which were paddy.[86] By 1919 the Kims had thus become one of the wealthiest families in the country. For them, as for many other Korean landlords, the four decades of Japanese imperialism after 1876 had indeed been a time of untold opportunity.

CHAPTER 2

An Industrial Bourgeoisie

Transition and Emergence, 1919–45

The year 1919 was in many ways a watershed in modern Korean history. It is best remembered today for its politics, for the idealism and unity of March First independence movement, when Koreans from all walks of life joined together in a massive nationwide protest against Japanese domination—before the reality of Japanese power and the bitter class divisions of the colony's subsequent industrialization turned such naïve faith and simple harmony to ashes. But in retrospect 1919 was also an important turning point in Korea's socioeconomic development, as the merchants and landlords who had accumulated substantial amounts of capital before 1919 began to take a serious interest in modern industry. In the period that followed, Korea experienced its first great surge of industrialization, and although it was Japanese capital that was given the starring role, Korean capital was also assigned a minor part in the development process. The result was the emergence between 1919 and 1945 of the country's first industrial bourgeoisie—of which the Koch'ang Kims were one of the most prominent examples.

Earlier Industrial Efforts

There were, of course, previous Korean efforts, both public and private, to develop modern industry in the country. Like the early Meiji authorities, the nineteenth-century Korean monarchy, under the prodding of progressive officials, established various industrial offices in the bureaucracy and even set up a few model factories in the Meiji manner. Thus an official textile department (Chikchoguk) and a model textile factory with European equipment and Chinese technicians could be seen in Korea as early as the mid-1880s.[1]

Such programs, however, do not seem to have been part of a determined and comprehensive goal of national industrial development as in Meiji Japan, but only half-hearted and poorly conceived attempts to mollify domestic and international pressure for reform. And lack of will was only one of the problems. The government could set such factories up, but even a more enthusiastic attitude than the government exhibited would not in itself have sufficed to keep the factories going indefinitely. The absence of a stable national financial system that could supply regular and sufficient working capital and a general dearth of Korean managers or private entrepreneurs willing and able to participate in industrial development ultimately rendered such facilities official white elephants.

With the Kabo Reforms in 1894, the government finally began to take a more positive attitude toward industrial development. An official department of industry (combined with agriculture and commerce) was established, and for the first time retired officials (including those of the highest rank) were allowed and encouraged to engage in commercial pursuits.[2] Such official exhortation, along with the gradual proliferation of study societies, newspapers, and magazines devoted to ideas of national "self-strengthening" through economic activity also seems to have helped to stimulate some private interest in industrial development. Thus from around the turn of the century some merchants and landlords, including politically well-placed yangban like Min Pyŏngsŏk, became involved in setting up small-scale private or semiprivate textile factories. Such landlord investment in nonagricultural sectors, however, was relatively limited before the 1920s. And more often than not landlord investments went into banking rather than manufacturing.[3]

Korean investments in the textile industry during this period fell far short of creating modern spinning and weaving operations. The zenith of the Korean textile industry's development before the 1920s, for example, was probably represented by the Kyŏngsŏng Cord Company (Kyŏngsŏng Chingnyu CH). This company had been founded in 1910 as an unlimited partnership but was converted to a joint-stock company in 1911 with an authorized capital of 100,000 yen.[4] It is not known for sure who the actual founders of the company were, but the well-established landlord-yangban family that produced Yun Ch'iho and later Yun Posŏn seems very early on to have played a major role in the company's affairs.[5]

The company appears to have been one of the largest industrial enterprises established by Koreans before the Kim family founded the Kyŏngsŏng Spinning and Weaving Company (Kyŏngbang) in 1919 and also the first textile company in joint-stock form of which we have actual primary evidence. Although the capital was never fully paid up, it did reach 75,000 yen by 1917 and the company seems to have had a substantial labor force. A Government-General statistical survey for that year noted that the company's workers had increased between 1910 and 1917 from 32 to 75. Earlier, however, the *Maeil sinbo*, in reporting a strike at the factory in 1915, had said that the factory employed as many as 150 workers.[6]

In spite of its size, it is difficult to characterize the company as a modern factory. While it does seem to have made some use of power machinery from the beginning, most of the company's assets were in goods produced rather than plant and equipment. The company appears to have relied as much or more on old-fashioned manual labor as on machinery, and the use of machinery was actually decreasing.[7]

The company remained very much geared toward a limited, if not moribund, traditional market that did not really demand standardized machine products. It made little attempt to reproduce the Western broadcloth that was becoming increasingly popular in Korea; instead, as its name implies, it concentrated on the production of *chingnyu*. This is a rather amorphous term in Korean and difficult to capture with a single English word, but "cord" or "belt" comes close, so long as we understand that such items were woven from cotton yarn. Such cords or belts were used by Koreans primarily as traditional clothing accessories, for example, the *taenim* used by Korean men to tie down their billowy trousers at the ankles. The company also produced socks, gloves, and even some cloth, but cloth production never amounted to even as much as 10 percent of the cord production.[8]

The Kyŏngsŏng Cord Company thus represented a kind of halfway mark between the old and new in Korean industrial production. While in form it seemed to belong to the new industrial capitalist civilization that had been penetrating Korea since 1876, in substance it was still largely traditional. As such, it had little future in a society where the demand for traditional clothes was on the decline and a growing new market required more large-scale machine production.[9] In retrospect, it seems almost inevitable that the company would eventually fall into the hands of a family like the Kims, who had more modern and decidedly more ambitious ideas than the factory's original owners.

The Transition to Industrial Capitalism

Around 1919 Korea saw the coalescence of three factors that together worked to stimulate the transfer of Korean landlord capital into industry. One was the coming of age of a new generation of Koreans who were imbued with nationalistic and progressive ideas of economic development and had both the means (inherited from their parents) and the skills (acquired largely in Japan) to put them into practice. A second factor was a change in economic conditions around this time that made investment in land somewhat less attractive while increasing the appeal of industry to a landowning class that had more excess capital than ever before. Finally, and most important, the crucial hinge on which the whole transition turned was the change in colonial development policy—with its dual economic and political character—that occurred around this time. Let us consider each of these factors in turn, beginning with a look at the new generation of wealthy Koreans. The Koch'ang Kims were in the vanguard of this new generation.

The New Generation: The Koch'ang Kims

Within the Kim family itself the new generation of Koreans was best typified by Kim Sŏngsu (1891–1955) and his younger brother Yŏnsu (1896–1979). Both were Kyŏngjung's natural sons, but Kijung, who lacked a son of his own, made Sŏngsu his adoptive heir when the boy was very young. Since both families lived in the same compound in Inch'on as well as Chulp'o, the two boys grew up together and developed a close personal relationship that carried over into adulthood, when they began to lend each other support and assistance in a wide assortment of business ventures.[10] Such cooperation strengthened the already potent financial power of each as individuals, since Sŏngsu's adoption had made each the main heir to a major Korean fortune.

Of the two brothers, it was Yŏnsu who in time emerged as the more active industrial entrepreneur and who thus merits most of our attention in this study. Until his death in 1955, Sŏngsu's interests ran more to journalism and publishing, education, and politics, where in each case he also left a legacy that is still very much alive in South Korea today.[11] Nevertheless, it was the elder brother Sŏngsu who first came to grips with the great socioeconomic changes that were occurring in Korea in the early twentieth century and who first led the family into industrial investment. And, as we shall come to see in the course of this study, the various interests of the two brothers often and conveniently overlapped during their golden era under the Japanese.

What gave the new generation of Koreans, including the two Kim brothers, its particular character was that such young men had been born and raised after the opening of the ports in 1876 and at a time when Japanese influence was reaching its preannexation peak. Both Sŏngsu and Yŏnsu were born in the 1890s and both entered their twenties shortly after the annexation in 1910. Unlike their parents and grandparents, who had been born into a remarkably stable[12] early nineteenth-century society that looked back nearly five hundred years into the past for its roots and identity, the younger Kims grew up as the old world of their parents was collapsing from external pressure and a new twentieth-century Korean world was struggling to be born.

For Koreans of this period Japanese imperialism had become a matter of intense and passionate concern. After 1905 Japan had no rival imperialist powers to contend with for control of the peninsula. A protectorate regime was established that year under Japanese tutelage, and with the forced abdication of the Korean emperor in favor of his feeble-minded son in 1907, Korea lay completely open to Japanese political domination. Japan's economic penetration of Korea had been steadily growing since 1876, and from the 1890s on Japanese merchants and Japanese goods began to move toward a dominant position in the Korean economy. Japan's assumption of de facto political control over Korean affairs in 1905 hastened this process considerably.

Japanese imperialism intensified the nationalism that had been developing in Korean society since 1876 as Koreans were forced to come to terms with the possibility of losing their country. In response to this threat, not a few Koreans, like the "righteous army" guerrillas, chose the route of armed resistance. In general, however, the upper class adopted a more cautious attitude of protest through the promotion of a "patriotic enlightenment movement" that stressed national "self-strengthening" through education and economic growth, including the development of Korean commerce and industry, a theme that had first been sounded in the 1880s by members of the Enlightenment party (Kaehwadang).[13] From the 1890s on, especially after the establishment of the protectorate in 1905, the country saw a proliferation of "study societies" (*hakhoe*) and magazines that sought to "enlighten" Koreans about various aspects of modern (i.e., Western) culture, for example, family management, nation-building, government, law, and agronomy.[14] Such educational efforts, it was argued, would enhance the wealth and strength of the country and somehow (never carefully explained) ultimately help Korea regain control of its own affairs. Commercial and industrial development was also promoted through study societies and magazines like *The World of Commerce* and *The World of Industry*, which emphasized particular aspects of what was generally referred to as the "new learning" or "new thought."[15] During this period many private schools devoted to the new learning were also founded by progressive and nationalistic landlord-bureaucrats to supplement their children's education in the traditional, Confucian-oriented private schools (sŏdang).[16]

Such then was the atmosphere of nationalism and economic reform, inseparably linked, in which Kim Sŏngsu and Kim Yŏnsu grew up. It was an atmosphere that was part and parcel of their home environment. The new civilization had come early to the Chŏllas in the form of international trade and Japanese merchants, and the family's move to Chulp'o in 1907 gave sixteen-year-old Sŏngsu and his eleven-year-old brother a chance to experience it—if only peripherally—from an early age.[17] Even more important was the milieu of upper-class nationalism and progressive ideas in which the boys grew up. Both Kijung and Kyŏngjung, for example, seem to have been generally sympathetic to the goals of the Enlightenment party, which in many ways looked to Meiji Japan as a model for Korean national development. Such affinity was reflected in the family's active participation in the reformist government that came to power with Japanese support in 1894.

While the upper-class reformist tradition of the family basically accepted Japan as a successful modernizer and symbol of enlightenment, it did not necessarily condone Korea's economic or political subjugation by the Japanese, at least at first. One of the tragedies of Korean history is that later, when the Japanese forced the Korean elite to choose between their class interests and their sense of nation, many chose the former, a subject that we shall consider at some length in chapter 8. Before the late 1930s, however, it was still possible for a Korean to claim with some conviction to be both a member of the emerging bourgeoisie *and* a nationalist at the same time. Both Kijung and Kyŏngjung thus served the protectorate government until Japanese interference and arrogance became intolerable and they resigned (Kyŏngjung in 1905; Kijung in 1907). After leaving the government they joined other Honam landlords in assuming positions of leadership in the "patriotic enlightenment movement" that had been sweeping the country in the wake of the establishment of the protectorate. In 1908 Kijung founded Yŏngsin School in Chulp'o to propagate the new learning in the family's new hometown.[18] Kyŏngjung became a trustee and important financial backer of the Honam Study Society, which published a monthly journal, the *Honam hakpo*.[19]

As a result of his father's attitude, Sŏngsu was allowed to receive what at the time was a rather progressive education. His wife's family undoubtedly also played an important role here. Following the Korean traditional custom of early marriage (and early grandsons), Sŏngsu had been married in 1903 at the age of twelve[20] to the daughter of another nationalistic and progressive landlord-bureaucrat, Ko Chŏngju, a wealthy South Chŏlla landlord (Tamyang County) who had received the *munkwa* degree in 1891 and become an official in the prestigious Royal Library (Kyujanggak) in Seoul. Like Kijung and Kyŏngjung, however, he had resigned his position and returned to Ch'angp'yŏng, his hometown, where he established a private school (today Ch'angp'yŏng Elementary School) dedicated to the new learning. He was also one of the original promoters of the Honam Study Society in 1907 and became chairman of the society soon after its formation that same year. In 1906, after a number of years of *sŏdang* study, Sŏngsu was sent to Ch'angp'yŏng to study such subjects as English, Japanese, and mathematics in his father-in-law's school. Later Kijung also permitted him to study at the Kŭmho School in Kunsan, which had regular courses in Korean, mathematics, history, geography, English, chemistry, physical education, and vocal music, as well as night classes in Japanese and weaving.[21]

The progressive attitude of the older generations, however, had its limits. Education and scholarship had long been the pursuits of a gentleman in Korean society, and to make a shift in emphasis from study of the Chinese classics to the new learning of the West was far less radical than actively participating in the new capitalist civilization itself. As we have already noted, some Korean yangban — including members of the royal family — were, of course, already beginning to do just that, and in time others would be persuaded by their children to involve themselves in business pursuits. In general, however, the older generations, especially during this period, seem to have preferred to emphasize study rather than action. Sŏngsu's grandfather, Yohyŏp, for example, is said to have considered commercial activities a violation of Confucian principles.[22] While such moralism had not constrained him from taking advantage of the international rice trade to make a fortune, he probably would have been loath to establish a formal company or call himself a businessman.

As longtime practicing landlords, Yohyŏp and his sons were basically more concerned with agriculture than commerce or industry. One looks almost in vain, for example, through the pages of the *Honam hakpo* to find even passing references to nonagricultural economic development, whereas lengthy articles on agriculture appear regularly in every issue. The essentially agrarian interests of the two older generations appear all the more striking when one considers that during this same period, a younger generation of Koreans was already forming its own study societies and publishing journals that emphasized instead the crucial importance of commerce and industry in national development. In Tokyo, for example, a group of Korean students centered around Yun Chŏngha and Mun Sangu, both of whom would later assist Sŏngsu and Yŏnsu in setting up and running the Kyŏngsŏng Spinning and Weaving Company, organized a group called the Great Korea Study Society (Taehan Hŭnghakhoe). The society published a monthly journal in Korean called *The World of Commerce,* which featured informative articles on banking and other commercial matters, including the proper use and meaning of various common commercial terms in Korean, Japanese, and English. The magazine deplored the traditional upper-class Korean contempt for business activities and made Korea's commercial development a precondition for economic independence of the country.[23]

Japan was the natural training ground for the new generation of wealthy landlords who in the 1920s would start transferring some of their families' assets into modern industry. Much of what the Koreans came to consider "modern" between 1876 and 1919 was actually to a large extent Japanese in origin—Western civilization filtered through a Meiji or Taishō prism. It had been Japanese rather than Western gunboats that had originally forced open Korea's ports in 1876. And in 1881, when King Kojong formed an official party to study and report to the court on the nature and conditions of the new civilization, he had dispatched the group not to Europe or America, but to Japan.[24] By the first decade of the twentieth century the study-trip abroad, especially to Japan, had already become a kind of extended Korean version of the nineteenth-century British Grand Tour for the children of the wealthy.[25]

Kijung originally opposed such a trip for Sŏngsu not on principle, but because he preferred to keep his precious adopted son close to home. But Sŏngsu was determined. Together with Song Chinu, his best friend from Ch'angp'yŏng School and the person who would later become his confidant and alter ego in business and politics, he left Korea for Tokyo in 1908.[26] Eventually the family accepted Sŏngsu's fait accompli and saw to it that he was well supplied with funds, enough for him to cover the expenses of friends and his own not inexpensive hobby of horseback riding.[27] Later, when Yŏnsu started showing similar signs of an impatient desire to go to Japan, the family put up little protest, requiring only that he first get married in Korea.[28]

The importance of the time spent in Japan by the two boys can hardly be overestimated. In each case, the period of study was not only long but critical in its timing, involving the formative years of late adolescence and early maturity. Sŏngsu arrived in Tokyo at the age of seventeen and returned to Korea six years later as a young man of twenty-three. For Yŏnsu, the study abroad must have had an even greater impact. He left Korea in 1911 at fifteen and did not return home until 1921, a full decade later.[29]

There were also other factors that made the years in Japan significant. First of all, they provided each boy with his first direct encounter with the new capitalist civilization and ensured that his concept of "modernization" would thereafter tend to have a distinctly Japanese tint. The boys' entire higher education, from middle school through university (Sŏngsu majored in political economy at Waseda; Yŏnsu in economics at Kyoto Imperial)[30] took place in Japan and in the Japanese language. Such training gave them a linguistic and cultural background that would later allow them to move comfortably and with assurance in the very highest circles of colonial business and politics. Finally, and perhaps most important, was that Japan became for both of them an inspiring symbol of modernity, a model from which to construct a vision of Korea's own development.

Like their parents, Sŏngsu and Yŏnsu probably considered themselves Korean nationalists and regarded the knowledge they were gaining in Japan at least in part as a valuable tool for a future Korean version of national development in which they, as members of the country's educated elite, would have a major role. While their sense of nationalism was essentially an unconscious identification of class with country that would eventually be put to the test and shattered, during this period neither they nor their family falls easily into the category of "pro-Japanese" in the sense one might apply the term to, say, Song Pyŏngjun or other members of the Ilchinhoe who openly campaigned for the annexation.[31]

On the other hand, to recognize such nationalism as a factor in the Kims' psychology should not blind us to the importance Japan held for them as a successful model of development. Like their ideological seniors in the Enlightenment party, the Kims were intoxicated with Japanese ideas of the new civilization. The atmosphere in which they had grown up had convinced them that Japan had somehow mastered the secrets of the West, and, indeed, proof of Japan's growing prosperity and strength seemed to be everywhere, not least so in the country's startling victories over China and Russia. The Kims' extensive Japanese education and experience worked to reinforce such impressions and to provide them with concrete images of the shape of modern society. Even their personal role models seem to have been Japanese rather than Korean. Kim Sŏngsu, for example, consciously modeled himself not on past or contemporary Korean heroes but on the famous Meiji "patriot and statesman" (Sŏngsu's words) Ōkuma Shigenobu, who — whether Kim realized it or not — had initially joined Saigō Takamori and Itagaki Taisuke in demanding a military expedition against Korea during the celebrated *seikan ron* of 1873.[32]

What, then, was the national model of development that the Kims so much admired? During the period in which one or the other (or both) of the boys was in Japan, that is, 1908 to 1921, the country was undergoing an important transition. Since the Restoration, Japan had gradually been developing into an industrialized nation, and the agricultural share in the net domestic product had been correspondingly decreasing. In 1885, agriculture had accounted for about 45 percent of the total net domestic product and industry for only about 15 percent. By 1910 the figures were 32.5 percent and 26 percent, respectively. World War I subsequently brought a new wave of industrialization to Japan. The industrial growth rate reached 9.3 percent per year during the war — much higher than either before or after the conflict — and the farm population declined by about two million people, most of whom were absorbed into the urban industrial sector. By the end of the war any thought of a return to an economic policy centered on agriculture was out of the question. Thereafter, with a slight decline in the 1920s, Japan's industrial output would continue to grow, accounting for about 50 percent of net domestic production in 1940 as compared with only about 19 percent for agriculture. The capitalist model that the Kims were able to observe firsthand was thus one in which industry was gradually dominating the development process.[33]

Of all industries at the time, the textile industry was the most important. Japanese industrialization had begun after the Restoration with the development of financial institutions and had gradually come to encompass sea transport, railroads, infrastructure (postal service, telegraph, roads, etc.), mining, and finally manufacturing. While there had been a significant expansion of the heavy and chemical industries during the First World War, the principal industry within the manufacturing sector before the 1930s was export textiles. Here silk led the way, but cotton also became increasingly important.[34] By the 1890s Japan was already exporting its own cotton goods to Korea. Later (after the Russo-Japanese War), the cotton cloth market was extended to Manchuria and China proper. The industry had begun to stagnate in the years immediately before the outbreak of the World War, but the war turned the situation around. War mobilization, the uncertainty of marine transport, and the shortage of ship bottoms all drastically curtailed European cotton exports to areas east of the Suez Canal, and Japan was able to move into Asian markets in China and elsewhere —including India, Iran, and remote parts of Africa—that had hitherto belonged to the West.[35]

When Kim Sŏngsu returned to Korea in 1914, the great war boom had not yet begun, but the importance of the textile industry in Japan's pattern of development was already clear. Korea itself had been steadily inundated with foreign textiles from 1876 on, and after the 1890s more and more of them were being produced in Japan.[36] Kim did not immediately turn his attention to industry, but like his adoptive father, and in imitation of his hero, Ōkuma Shigenobu, the founder of Waseda University, he established a school—Chungang Hakkyo—where Yi Kanghyŏn, an old acquaintance from the Tokyo years, was given a teaching job.

If Kim needed any persuading about investing in the textile industry, Yi was the man to do it. Like Kim, he was of the new generation (born 1888) and had been educated in Japan. His education, however, had been at the Tokyo Higher Industrial School, where he had majored in cotton textiles, and he seems to have been a tireless promoter of Korean industrialization after his return to Seoul in 1911. He wrote numerous articles on the subject for the *Sanggong wŏlbo,* the monthly journal of the Seoul Chamber of Commerce and Industry, in which he noted the trend toward industrialization in Japan and stressed that industry was the "keystone for the foundation of a nation." A modern textile factory for Korea was Yi's dream, but he seems to have had little money of his own to invest in such a venture. In Kim Sŏngsu, however, he found a sympathetic patron. The relationship between the two men, based at least in part on a similar vision of the country's future, was an important element that led to the establishment of Kyŏngbang in 1919.[37]

The Economic Transition

Whole decades of Korean scholarship have stressed the aspect of nationalism in the Kims' various business and educational pursuits, and there is no reason to deny that the nationalism described above was one element in what was surely a complex of motives behind the family's founding of Kyŏngbang in 1919. Whether it was the decisive element, however, is an arguable point. Certainly the family's history of sound and hardheaded economic sense both before and after 1919 does not lead one to believe that any of the principals would have been likely to expend his assets simply in an outpouring of enthusiasm for a noble cause. And, indeed, there were very sound and hardheaded economic reasons for at least a partial shift to industrial investment in 1919.[39]

In 1919 Korea's wealthy merchants and landlords could look back on over four decades of relative prosperity. The First World War, in particular, had been a boom period of unprecedented profits. Japanese rice prices nearly tripled during the war, and such inflation had spilled over into Korea as well (see chap. 1, n. 49, above). After the war, however, the situation changed dramatically, and once again the economic link with Japan was responsible.

Skyrocketing prices during the World War had benefited Japanese landlords, merchants, and industrialists, but wages had not kept pace with inflation, and the high prices had also been a terrible burden on the small farmers and tenants. The result in 1918 was a nationwide explosion of discontent among the Japanese urban and rural poor that became collectively known as the "Rice Riots." The frightened Japanese government immediately halved the price of rice and set about working to stimulate rice production at home and in the colonies. The purpose of such agricultural promotion was essentially to keep rice prices as low as possible and thereby pacify the country's growing industrial labor force, but such policies also helped contribute to a severe postwar agricultural depression both in Japan and Korea.[38] In Korea, rice prices suffered a precipitous drop after the war, revived slightly in the 1920s, and then proceeded to slide downward in the 1930s.[39] According to family estate records, for example, Kim Kijung received as much as 26 yen for one sŏk of rice in 1919. In 1920, however, the best price the family could obtain was only 13.6 yen — a drop of almost 48 percent. By 1924, the family was receiving between 15.7 and 20.0 yen per sŏk, but prices were again starting to decline. By 1931 the best price obtainable was no more than 7 yen per sŏk, and colonial agricultural experts like Nishimura Kenkichi were calling the fall in the price of rice the "cancer of Korea's rural economy."[40]

To compensate for the lower rice prices, landlords had basically four options during this period, any or all of which were used in combination. One obvious option, of course, was to shift the burden to tenants by transferring leases and raising rents, and most landlords, including the Kims, did so.[41] There were limits, however, to which such pressure could be applied without endangering the efficiency of the operation. While fear and desperation led many tenants to give in to landlords' demands until exhaustion and hunger finally forced them to forsake their tiny plots altogether and to seek alternatives to starvation as temporary laborers or emigrants, this same fear and desperation led not a few others to challenge their oppressors in the courts, or more directly, through "noncropping strikes" and violence.[42]

A second option for landlords was to work to increase the productivity of their holdings through land improvement programs (such as reclamation and irrigation) and increased capital investments (e.g., farm buildings, machinery and tools, manures and fertilizers). Here the colonial government led the way. In response to the Rice Riots in Japan, the Government-General adopted an extensive plan for increasing rice productivity in Korea to ensure a steady supply of cheap rice for Japanese workers. The plan called for such land improvements and capital investments as listed above, and the Government-General undertook to provide landlords with substantial subsidies and long-term, low interest financing.[43] With rice prices so depressed, however, such official inducements appealed only to the larger landlords like the Kims, and, even then, considerable time and effort had to be expended by the landlords themselves to transform their traditionally scattered holdings into the kind of large-scale, contiguous estates in which such improvements and investments would be most effective.

A third option open to landlords to counteract the effect of falling rice prices was to increase the extent of their holdings by buying more land. Land values tended to be directly proportional to the price of the agricultural products grown on them, so the abrupt drop in the price of rice after 1919 also lowered the price of paddy,[44] and landlords like Kim Kyŏngjung, who had been wise enough to bank their earnings and wait until prices went down before buying more land, were able to increase their holdings substantially after the war. We know from the family's estate records, moreover, that Sŏngsu's adoptive father Kijung also purchased more land (about 121 *chŏngbo* [296 acres]) for himself and his sons between 1918 and 1924.

Profits of the war boom had been so great that investment in land, especially at bargain-basement prices, covered only a portion of the total surplus accumulated. Even before the war some of the biggest landlords had found it possible to use some of their earnings to found banks and other enterprises, including private schools designed to instruct young Koreans in the new civilization. As we have already seen, even the older generation of Kims had taken some steps in that direction with the founding of Yŏngsin School in Chulp'o (today Chulp'o Elementary School) in 1907. By 1919, of course, the Kims, like other landlords, were even richer as a result of the wartime rice exports.

For landlords with such excess capital there was a fourth option to help offset the loss in rice revenue — investment in the nonagricultural sector, including industry, which was beckoning those with money as never before. The First World War had transformed Japan into an industrial nation once and for all, and the profitable advantages of industrial investment, especially in the cotton textile industry, were obvious to all who cared to look at the Japanese model. In the war years immediately preceding the founding of Kyŏngbang, the Japanese cotton textile industry had experienced an unparalleled boom because of the European withdrawal from Asian markets. The export demand had been so great that even the rapid expansion of new facilities simply had not been able to keep pace. Paid-in capital in the industry had increased about 200 percent between 1913 and 1919. Spindleage had gone up about 50 percent, and the number of looms in operation had nearly doubled. Company dividends had climbed to the 50 percent level during the war, in spite of a concurrent tripling of corporate reserves between 1914 and 1920.[45] To anyone with a bit of extra capital during this period, the textile industry must have looked very attractive indeed.

There was a basic problem, however. The colonial government established in Korea in 1910 had adopted a policy of maintaining Korea as a simple agricultural colony and market for Japanese manufactured products, including Japanese cotton textiles. In general, only those industries that served the needs of agriculture — railroads and rice mills, for example — were allowed to develop, and even then, Korean entrepreneurs tended to suffer from official favoritism toward Japanese businessmen. Attractive economic conditions notwithstanding, landlord investment in industry was simply out of the question unless there was a significant modification of colonial policy. Such a change occurred in 1919.

The Change in Colonial Policy

The change in colonial policy in 1919 was both economic and political. The economic aspect paved the way for the beginning of a more diversified and industrialized economy on the peninsula. The political aspect insured that Koreans as well as Japanese would be permitted to participate in the proposed economic program.

The colonial government that assumed control of the peninsula in 1910 had not originally contemplated developing Korea's economy beyond the rudimentary level required to maintain the country as a source of cheap agricultural raw materials, especially rice, for Japan. Such industrialization as did take place between 1910 and 1919 was more or less confined to the establishment of a minimal infrastructure of roads, port facilities, railroads, and communications, and to those industries related in one way or another to agriculture, such as rice mills. The other side of this policy of deliberate underdevelopment was to preserve Korea as a secure market for Japanese manufactured goods.

Neither Korean nor Japanese private investment was extensively sought or encouraged during this period; indeed, such investment was rigorously restricted through the promulgation of the so-called Company Law in 1910, which stipulated that all new companies had to be officially licensed by the Government-General. The law also compelled foreign (including Japanese) companies wishing to open subsidiaries or branch offices in Korea to obtain formal permission from the government and warned that any company that made false reports or violated the Company Law would be subject to closure or even dissolution.[46]

Such official curtailment and strict control of private enterprise by Korea's colonial rulers immediately provoked the same kind of strong reaction from many of Japan's capitalists that would later be directed against the Kwantung army's initial attempt to undertake an anticapitalist development of Manchuria in the 1930s. In an interview with the *Tōkyō asahi shimbun* in 1911, Japan's foremost entrepreneur, Shibusawa Eiichi, denounced the Company Law as reflective of a "militarism" (*sāberushugi*) in the Government-General that was inconsistent with Japan's status as a "constitutional nation." Such a law, Shibusawa predicted, would result in the official protection of specially privileged merchants and lead ultimately to the "extinction" of commerce and industry in Korea.[47]

Public discussion on the matter gradually widened to the point where the Japanese press began to question the actual authority of the Government-General to make such a law at all, and the matter even became the subject of debate in the Imperial Diet. In the end, the Diet confirmed the Government-General in its role as the ultimate lawmaker in Korea, but the problem remained of what to do in the event of a conflict between Japanese and Korean law—as, for example, in the case of a Japanese company with branch offices in Korea. To resolve such contradictions, the Company Law was revised twice in the period between 1911 and 1920, but its core provision that all new companies be subject to a system of government licensing remained in effect until the law's abolition in 1920.[48]

By that time the World War had significantly altered Japan's economic situation and made continuation of the Company Law untenable. First of all, the withdrawal of the European powers from the world market east of Suez enormously increased the demand for Japanese manufactured goods, not only in those areas that had been largely the commercial preserves of the West, but in Japan's own colonies as well. As noted earlier, Japanese manufacturers—in spite of a considerable expansion of facilities and production—were not able to meet the sudden and overwhelming new demand, and the Government-General was consequently forced for the first time to consider the necessity of promoting a certain amount of development of the manufacturing sector in Korea itself. The cotton textile industry was a natural candidate because of the steadily growing demand in the colony for machine-made cloth and because of Korea's ability to produce substantial quantities of its own raw cotton. The result was the announcement in 1917 of the establishment of the Japanese-owned Chōsen Spinning and Weaving Company (Chōsen Bōshoku KK) in Pusan—an event much heralded at the time as the advent of large-scale factory production in Korea and a symbol of the colony's bright industrial future.[49]

Second, the World War transformed Japan overnight from a debtor to a creditor nation and created a wealth of surplus industrial capital that needed an outlet. Both during the war and afterward, when recession and curtailment of production in Japan itself severely hampered large-scale domestic reinvestment of the surplus capital, Japanese manufacturers sought capital markets overseas, including the colonies. Thus, in spite of their concern about potential conflict with home export industries, the colonial authorities allowed themselves to be persuaded by capital investors into relaxing their restrictions on the development of colonial industries, and from about 1917 private Japanese industrial investments expanded in both Korea and Taiwan. As Nakamura Takafusa has put it, "The wave of industrialization and incorporation brought by World War I was also the beginning of industrialization in the hitherto suppressed colonies."[50]

In Korea such changes in the Japanese economy resulted in the complete abolition of the Company Law in 1920 and in the adoption of a system of routine legal registration of companies identical to that in effect in Japan itself. The existing tariff barriers between Korea and Japan were also largely eliminated after the war, permitting the free flow into Korea of the Japanese capital goods so essential to the establishment of modern machine factories.[51] In a word, Korea was more or less fully incorporated economically into the Japanese capitalist system. As the factory laws were gradually implemented in Japan, moreover, Korea's special position within the Japanese economic system but outside the jurisdiction of such social legislation made the peninsula an even more attractive haven for Japanese surplus capital investment.[52]

There was also a third reason the Government-General began to encourage limited industrialization on the peninsula at this time: Korea was coming to be regarded more and more as an economic stepping-stone for Japan's growing and increasingly aggressive imperialist ambitions on the Asian continent.

Formal territorial acquisition had begun in the 1890s after Japan's victory in the Sino-Japanese War, when China had been forced to cede Formosa, the Pescadores, and the Liaotung Peninsula in the Treaty of Shimonoseki (1895). Russia, France, and Germany had intervened a week after the treaty was signed to force Japan to return the Liaotung Peninsula, but the other territories acquired were internationally accepted as part of a new Japanese empire. In the Portsmouth Treaty (1905) following the Russo-Japanese War, moreover, Japan was awarded the southern half of Sakhalin Island and finally given a firm foothold on the continent with the acquisition of Russia's leaseholds in Manchuria (including Liaotung and the South Manchuria Railway), preparing the way for formal political control and later annexation of Korea. With the outbreak of World War I, Japan moved quickly to seize Germany's concessions in Shantung and sought to extend its privileges on the continent even further through the infamous Twenty-One Demands (1915). Later, in 1918, after the Russian Revolution, Japan joined European and American forces in their support of counterrevolutionary elements in Siberia. In all, over seventy thousand Japanese troops were dispatched to occupy major Siberian ports, and the Japanese eventually extended their occupation of eastern Russia to the northern part of Sakhalin as well. By 1925 Japan had been persuaded by international objections to withdraw from most of these areas, but between 1919 and 1921, when the Korean Government-General was in the midst of formulating its new economic policies, the exploitation of these newly acquired territories, as well as of earlier continental acquisitions, was very much on the minds of the officials concerned.[53]

The Government-General, in fact, had long since begun to develop economic ties with the north. The Bank of Chōsen, for example, was already effectively serving as a key instrument for Japanese economic penetration of the continent. An imperial ordinance in 1917 had made the bank's notes the sole legal tender in the Kwantung Leased Territory, and by the early 1920s the bank was actually doing more business in Manchuria than in Korea itself.[54] With the Japanese seizure of Shantung in 1914, the Government-General began to take a keen interest in northern and central China as well, and in 1917 a quasi-official economic fact-finding mission under the auspices of the Hansŏng Bank was sent there (and to Manchuria) to explore the possibility of economic connections between Korea and China. The report issued by the mission on its return emphasized the importance of Korea's unique geographical position as the basis for economic links between Japan and the Asian mainland.

This same theme was taken up by the Government-General's industrial commission of 1921, which set forth the general long-term development goals of the colonial authorities in the wake of economic changes wrought by the First World War. It is clear from the proceedings of this commission that Korean industrialization was viewed by the Government-General as an integral part of Japan's ongoing economic penetration of the Asian continent. Korea's new textile industry, for example, was to be as much (or more) an industry for export to new continental markets as an industry to meet domestic Korean needs.

The emphasis on development for export was to some extent an inevitable consequence of the Government-General's desire to avoid friction with Japanese textile manufacturers, who looked upon Korea as their own special preserve, but it was also part and parcel of the imperialist perspective of Korea's colonial officials—and of the particular businessmen who were given the Government-General's blessing. One of the main promoters of the Chōsen Spinning and Weaving Company (Chōbō) in Pusan, for example, was none other than Yamamoto Jōtarō, who was also one of Japan's most enthusiastic and active commercial empire builders—the former head of Mitsui Bussan and future president of the South Manchuria Railway.[55] At the industrial commission in 1921, Vice-Governor-General Mizuno, the commission chairman, after echoing the increasingly popular Government-General

theme that the importance of Korea (and Korean economic development) lay in the colony's central geographic position between Japan
and the Asian continent, went on to stress the importance of exploring
new markets in China and the Russian Far East. In the final report
of the commission, the section dealing with industrial development
also gave particular attention to the export trade.[56] Korean industrialization was thus from the onset inextricably linked to an imperialistic
vision of Japanese economic expansion on the Asian continent.

The political aspect of the change in colonial policy had its roots
in the Korean March First independence movement of 1919, which
destroyed a number of budding colonial careers and shook the
Government-General to its very foundations. As the Japanese would
learn years later in China, nationalism could not be controlled with
brute force. Force, in fact, only tended to intensify nationalistic feeling
against the imperialist aggressor.

Between 1905 and 1918 such nationalism was steadily on the rise
in Korea. By 1919, two harsh, militaristic colonial regimes had succeeded in alienating virtually all segments of the Korean population
with their oppressive and discriminatory rule. Even Korea's emerging
bourgeoisie — at least one element of which had been willing to cooperate with the Japanese from the beginning — had grown disaffected
with colonial policy, and especially with the Company Law, which
not only prevented industrial development in general, but was being
used by the colonial authorities to block native entrepreneurship on
behalf of Japanese businessmen.[57] Japan's ready resort to military
force and brutality during the thirteen years since the establishment
of the protectorate, however, had stunned Koreans into relative quiescence, and the Japanese, perhaps falling victim to their own propaganda on the beneficence of colonial rule, had mistakenly taken such
silence for submission.

The outburst of demonstrations for Korean independence on March
1, 1919, therefore, came as a complete shock. When the Japanese
finally realized the scope of the phenomenon they were confronting,
they overreacted, responding with violence to what was initially a
peaceful expression of nationalist sentiment. The harsh response naturally fanned the flames of Korean nationalism still higher and provoked
suicidal resistance on the part of many Koreans throughout the country. By the time it was all over, a total of no less than one million
Koreans (in a population of about sixteen million) had taken part
in various demonstrations around the country. Of these, possibly as

many as fifty thousand had been injured or killed and about twenty thousand arrested. The governor-general had resigned in disgrace, and Japan had been forced to reexamine its colonial policies.[58]

Under a new colonial administration headed by retired admiral Saitō Makoto, the old policy of authoritarian "military rule" (*budan seiji*) was officially rejected in favor of a new "cultural" or "enlightened" (*bunka*) policy of conciliation, and a number of reforms were announced. The post of governor-general was in principle opened to civilians as well as to military men, the gendarmerie was replaced with a regular civilian police force, more Koreans were to be recruited into the bureaucracy, and Koreans were to be permitted to publish their own privately owned newspapers and magazines.[59]

The change to a "enlightened" policy did not, of course, mean a change of Japanese objectives. The fundamental imperialist goal of controlling Korea for Japanese national purposes remained unaltered. While the new regime sought to mollify Korean public opinion and anger, it nevertheless rejected the basic Korean demand for political independence that had been the hallmark of the March First movement.[60] Nor did the Saitō administration's new policy mean a complete abandonment of coercive tactics. Security measures under the Saitō regime were increased and the government continued to deal ruthlessly with those Koreans who openly defied state power. Though the overt threat of force had retreated to the background — symbolized by the police being forbidden to carry rifles or swords in public and the government bureaucrats no longer wearing uniforms — it was nevertheless always there, and Koreans remained aware of it.[61]

On the other hand, the Saitō administration represented a crucial turning point in Korean colonial history, and the importance of the change in policy should not be underestimated. While the Government-General after 1919 never hesitated to apply force whenever other means of persuasion failed, the basic method of rule, at least in regard to the bourgeoisie, shifted from coercion to a more subtle strategy of cooptation. The offensive stick was hidden away, and out came the carrots to distract and seduce. Nowhere was this new tactic more evident than in the Saitō regime's efforts to involve Koreans in the more diversified economic development program discussed earlier.

The March First movement had been a shocking and unnerving experience for the Japanese. It had presented them with the unprecedented spectacle of a Korean people united in spirit and action against Japanese rule. Before 1919 the maintenance of security had been relatively easy. The Japanese had had little difficulty rounding up individual agitators, and the Korean terrain had proved basically inhospitable to effective guerrilla activity. But controlling an entire nation united in hostility was another matter. The gendarmerie's official reports on the demonstrations and its subsequent interrogations of Korean prisoners left no doubt that the independence movement had cut across all existing class lines in Korean society and had even included some members of the nobility and aristocracy who had earlier assented to the annexation. Korean "businessmen and women" and a variety of merchants and artisans had constituted about 13 percent of the total number of Koreans arrested by the Japanese police, and many merchants had closed their shops during the demonstrations as a sign of sympathy with the movement.[62]

Bourgeois participation, moreover, had not been limited to small shopkeepers. Even more substantial bourgeois elements like the Kim family and their associates had lent their support either directly or indirectly,[63] and afterward, in the lingering atmosphere of anti-Japanese bitterness, turned the situation to their advantage by calling for boycotts on Japanese goods and the development of Korean industry by native entrepreneurs.[64] From the Japanese perspective, such people were particularly dangerous because their family and educational backgrounds gave them the prestige and financial resources to lead a mass-based nationalist movement. Indeed, it was just such a potent combination of class forces that had characterized the March First movement, and the Japanese were determined to prevent such a coalition from ever coming together again.

The strategy finally adopted by the Saitō regime toward the nationalist phenomenon was the time-honored one of "divide and conquer," but it had a very definite twentieth-century twist. In the decades since the Restoration, the Japanese had seen their own defensive, unifying nationalism, epitomized perhaps in the wars against China and Russia, give way to increasingly bitter internal class divisions and struggles in the wake of industrialization. They reasoned quite logically that the same phenomenon would also occur in Korea as economic development proceeded. The Korean case, however, was different from the Japanese in one crucial respect: it was Japan—an alien power—and Japanese capitalism that were initiating industrialization on the peninsula. The class divisions in Korean society could develop to Japan's benefit only if a Korean bourgeoisie was somehow brought into the development process as a kind of junior partner. Such class-based cooperation between Japanese and Koreans would be doubly useful. First, it would secure native assistance in constructing an economy in line with Japanese imperial goals. Second, and more important, it would promote class differentiation and conflict in Korean society and thereby destroy the frightening unity of the nationalist movement.

Within several months after assuming power, the Saitō administration had compiled an extensive policy dossier on the question of how to deal with the Korean nationalist movement. There had been some encouraging signs that at least a portion of Korea's propertied elite was wavering in its enthusiasm for what had developed into a violent (and potentially revolutionary) mass nationalism, and one of the papers in the dossier was entitled "The Cooperation of Japanese and Korean Capitalists." It set forth precisely those objectives mentioned above:

Wealthy Koreans have recently grown extremely fearful of the radicalization of popular sentiment. Therefore, we must help them gain a means of self-protection. At the same time, to give substance to the [the concept of] Japanese-Korean harmony (*Nissen Yūwa*), we should endeavor to make [cooperation between Japanese and Korean capitalists] a reality. [To this end], we should have [some of] our supporters in the private sector establish an organization and move about actively between Japanese and Korean capitalists. To the Koreans let [these people] emphasize the future trend toward confrontational relations between capitalists and workers and between landlords and tenants; to the Japanese, let [them] stress the fact that cooperation between Japanese and Korean capitalists is extremely important, both for the development of Korea and for the resolution of the Korea problem.[65]

This new policy of cooperative capitalist development was subsequently reflected not only in the abolition of the Company Law in 1920,[66] but also in the Government-General's industrial commission of September 1921, a comprehensive conference of high-ranking bureaucrats and businessmen that set the agenda of development for the following decade. Japanese-Korean harmony and cooperation in the development of the peninsula was, in fact, an integral theme of the meeting; Korean businessmen were invited to attend as official participants, and the Government-General permitted them to speak freely, present petitions, and offer amendments to the government's proposals.[67]

Much of the language of harmony and cooperation that recurred throughout the discussions and often found its way into the commission's final report — the emphasis, for example, on industrial development through a "great, hundred-year policy of national unity involving both Japanese and Koreans, both high and low, both government and people," and the frequent references to Japanese-Korean "coexistence" (*kyōson*), "co-prosperity" (*kyōei*), or "common welfare" (*kyōdo no fukuri*)[68] — has the hollow ring of similar or identical pronouncements heard later in connection with the Greater East Asia Co-Prosperity Sphere. But to dismiss all such talk about cooperative development as mere rhetoric would be a mistake, especially in the light of the actual class-based cooperation that did take place after 1921.

The Japanese were not, of course, about to give the Korean bourgeoisie nearly as much of a role as it wanted, but there is no question that they desired some Korean involvement in the development process. Concern for economic efficiency made such participation desirable, and the political situation demanded it. Saitō had been welcomed to Seoul in September 1919 by a terrorist bomb attack that had only barely missed killing him and his wife,[69] and two years later, on the eve of the opening of the industrial commission, another bomb had destroyed a portion of the Government-General building where the delegates were to meet.[70] Rhetoric notwithstanding, the Government-General was clearly conscious of the need to defuse the unstable political situation with more than words. The inclusion of Koreans in the industrial commission of 1921 was thus one of the first Japanese moves in a determined effort to check the nationalist movement, and it opened the door to a limited but real efflorescence of Korean industrial capitalism.

The Emergence of an Industrial Bourgeoisie

The pace and scope of the industrialization that took place in Korea after 1919 should not be exaggerated. Before the 1930s the Government-General's main economic concern remained the development of agriculture. In that sense, the Saitō administration's interest in industrialization represented only a modification of the earlier "agriculture first" policy in response to postwar economic changes in Japan proper and, to a lesser extent, a growing recognition by colonial authorities of the utility of Korea as an economic springboard for imperial ambitions on the continent. As such, the new policy was but a tentative first step in the direction of an industrial economy. The Government-General's major thrusts toward industrialization came somewhat later, the first after the establishment of Manchukuo in 1932, and the second, rapidly and deliberately, after the outbreak of the Sino-Japanese War in 1937. Even then, as Bruce Cumings has noted, Korea's industrialization by 1945 was far from complete.[71]

On the other hand, such industrialization, while incomplete, was nevertheless impressive and represented a sophisticated method of exploitation far beyond the simple extraction of raw materials classically associated with colonialism. In the 1930s Korea's unusual position as a partially industrialized colony even allowed the peninsula to acquire a certain elevated status within the empire vis-à-vis newly acquired and relatively undeveloped peripheries like Manchuria and north China.[72] The statistics of growth show us the industrial trend quite clearly. In 1910 the manufacturing share in net commodity-product was only 3.3 percent, and with the Company Law in effect during this period, the manufacturing sector actually shrank to 2.9 percent by 1914. By 1929, however, this figure had risen to 12 percent and by 1940 had reached nearly 22 percent. If one includes other industrial sectors besides manufacturing, the share of industry in total production by 1940 was close to 40 percent. The rapid expansion of war-related industries in the 1930s, moreover, meant that by 1940 about half of the total industrial production was concentrated in the heavy and chemical areas.[73] Without condoning Japanese imperialism, one may say that the forty years of Japanese occupation left both halves of postwar Korea with a substantial material base for subsequent industrial development.

Such statistics are fairly straightforward and hardly new. The material legacy of Japanese rule is, in fact, relatively easy to assess. Far more difficult is the question of the extent to which Korean capitalism may be said to have participated in the colonial industrial development. Virtually all writers on this subject, Korean or non-Korean, have tended to stress the barriers to such Korean participation and to interpret the available statistics in the most negative light in order to expose the exploitative character of Japanese imperialism.

It is certainly important that people be informed and reminded of the nature of imperialism, whether Japanese or American. One problem, however, is that the theme of Japanese exploitation per se has acquired a certain hackneyed quality over the years, especially in Korean scholarship. Who today, for example, would seriously deny that Japanese imperialism in Korea or elsewhere was basically exploitative? Indeed, is it not in the nature of imperialism—whatever the nationality of the imperialist—to be so? The Japanese were not running Korea for the sake of the Korean people, but as a colony in the furtherance of Japanese interests. In 1944, when Andrew Grajdanzev's now-classic exposé of Japan's administration of Korea first appeared, his book was a refreshing and necessary corrective to decades of glowing Japanese reports about the beneficence of colonial rule. But today, some forty years later, many Korean scholars who work on the colonial period seldom go beyond the same themes articulated by Grajdanzev decades ago. Indeed, many of the works by Korean scholars have a certain surreal quality: Japan is condemned first for turning Korea into a colony and then once again for developing its colony according to Japanese rather than Korean needs. However, in such works logic seems to be less important than the emotional satisfaction derived from the denunciation of Japanese behavior.

Beyond the ennui invariably produced by such scholarship lies a more serious problem: the narrow and exclusive focus on exploitation often leads to an avoidance or neglect of more complex and difficult questions about the nature and legacy of Japanese colonialism. The conventional treatment of Korean capitalism during this period is a case in point. The usual emphasis on the exploitation of the Korean people as a whole tends to obscure the differential class treatment the Japanese accorded to Koreans. The Korean bourgeoisie thus becomes only another group to have suffered from Japanese domination, and the subject of Korean capitalism is approached negatively from the perspective of barriers and restrictions rather than from the point of view of growth and development.

Barriers to Korean Capitalism

That there were barriers to Korean capitalist growth is undeniable. Korea was, after all, a Japanese colony. But even so, as already noted, such barriers were not totally insurmountable. The most important barrier of all, the political barrier, was substantially reduced after 1919, when the Japanese authorities took it upon themselves to cultivate a small Korean bourgeois class as an ally and safety valve. Even during the wartime mobilization and consolidation after 1938, when many small and medium companies were merged into larger enterprises, care was taken to preserve a small niche for independent Korean firms. Grajdanzev, who encountered this phenomenon in his own work in the 1940s, but did not have access to the official documents that would have explained it, was nevertheless able to grasp the key point when he wrote: "The fact that the Japanese have not squeezed the Koreans completely out of industry which they could easily do, may be due to political considerations."[74]

Economic barriers also existed to impede the formation of a Korean bourgeoisie, but their importance has been considerably overestimated. In his well-known study of the colonial economy, for example, Sang-Chul Suh stated that "native industries failed to receive financial support from the financial institutions, and the large Korean landlords did not have any incentive for financing native industries."[75] Suh offered no evidence for the first half of his statement, and, indeed, to procure such evidence would have been difficult, for—as we shall see in the next chapter—his statement about financing is simply not correct.

The second part of Suh's statement, that is, that Korean landlords had no incentive for investing in industry, requires qualification. As evidence for this claim, Suh cited the comparative rates of return on investment in land (both paddy and dry) and in common stocks, which he had computed himself from surveys taken by the Chōsen Industrial Bank (Chōsen Shokusan Ginkō) in 1931 and 1937. In all cases, the rate of return on common stocks is lower. The differences, however, are not as great as Suh's statement would suggest. At most they do not exceed 2 percent and are usually much lower. In 1931, for example, the difference between the rate of return on paddy as opposed to common stocks was only 0.8 percent according to his figures.[76]

Even these figures, however, are misleading. Suh's figures for common stocks represent an average of the common stock dividends listed *by industry* by the Chōsen Industrial Bank. As such, they are an average of other averages and do not tell us anything about the rates of return for specific industries or companies. If we examine Suh's original sources, that is, the fairly comprehensive statistics compiled by the Industrial Bank, it becomes clear that landlords did indeed have considerable incentive for specific nonagricultural investments. In 1937, for example, the average dividend rates for commercial (*shōgyō*) enterprises, as well as for the brewing and electric industries, were all several tenths of a percent higher than the figure of 8 percent cited by Suh for rate of return on paddy. For the ceramics and lumber industries, the dividend rates were averaging as high as 10 percent and 10.6 percent respectively.[77]

Many individual companies, moreover, were declaring dividends comparable to or higher than the average of the highest paying industries. Nearly half of the forty-nine commercial firms listed by the Industrial Bank at the end of 1937, for example, were paying dividends of 10 percent or more—some as much as 18 percent or 20 percent. Company dividends in the brewing industry tended to run as high as 22 percent. Even those industries whose average dividend rates were lower than the rate of return on land included companies with dividend rates that were competitive or higher than the returns from land.[78]

It is also important to point out that dividend rates alone do not tell the whole story in regard to incentive for nonagricultural investment. Along with the dividend rates, the Industrial Bank also listed the average profits per industry against paid-in capital. Of the thirty separate categories of investment (encompassing 318 companies) included in the bank's survey for the latter half of 1937, only real estate management showed a profit/capital ratio of less than 10 percent. Most were much higher. Textile profits, for example, were averaging about 19 percent, and they were by no means the highest. Dividends tended to be temporarily low only because the industrial economy was starting to boom as a result of the Sino-Japanese War, and many companies were setting aside large amounts of capital for reinvestment. About 36 percent of the textile industry's profits went into retained earnings in 1937. Chemicals, one of the most rapidly developing industries at the time, showed an average dividend rate of only 3.7 percent, but the profit/capital ratio for the industry was nearly 30 percent, and over 90 percent of its profits were being retained for future expansion by the various companies involved.[79]

Far from being a discouraging time to invest in industry, the end of 1937 was, thus, an excellent time to acquire growth stocks at still relatively low prices. This is precisely what Kim Yŏnsu and his family did, both in Korea and in Manchuria. For various reasons, including, perhaps, security and the sheer inertia of habit, many Korean landlords did continue to keep their wealth in the land, but many others, like the Kims, were also attracted by the prospects of a more diversified investment portfolio. In any case, there is no solid evidence for saying that Korean landlords were without any economic incentive for industrial investment.

The Korean Share

In conventional scholarship on the colonial period, the emphasis on barriers to Korean landlord investment in industry is invariably followed by a recitation of statistics to the effect that the Japanese controlled around 90 percent of the total paid-in industrial capital of the country by the end of the colonial period.[80] The point here, of course, is that the Japanese dominated the economy and Koreans were left with only a small portion of the whole for themselves.

The very high figure of 90 percent does indeed indicate an over-whelming Japanese predominance. Statistics, however, are Janus-faced. If we shift our focus from a simple critique of Japanese exploitation to the question of Korean capitalist growth between 1910 and 1945, we can say in a more positive sense that by the end of the colonial period 10 percent of the paid-in industrial capital of the country was Korean. Put this way, the same statistic becomes infinitely more inter-esting. That the Japanese dominated the economy and thereby re-stricted Korean capitalist development is hardly surprising given the colonial setting. On the other hand, that the Japanese did not squeeze the Koreans out completely — as Grajdanzev observed — and that a Korean bourgeoisie was able to account for as much as 10 percent of the total paid-in industrial capital at the end of the colonial period suggests that the Saitō administration's strategy of cooperative capital-ist development had been implemented and subsequently maintained by succeeding regimes.

The commonly quoted figure of roughly 10 percent, in fact, undoubt-edly represents an underestimation of the actual capitalist participa-tion of Koreans in the colonial economy. The information available refers only to corporations and to subscribed capital, whereas many Korean establishments were unincorporated, and corporations tend-ed to have high debt-equity ratios. By 1945, for example, Kyŏngbang's loans amounted to more than twice the amount of the company's paid-up capital.[81]

More significant is that the figure of 10 percent does not take ac-count of joint Japanese-Korean companies, which may well have gar-nered the lion's share of Korean capital. Such mixed companies were an ideal form of cooperative capitalism from the perspective both of the Government-General and of the Korean businessmen involved. For the government, such companies represented active Korean bourgeois participation in colonial development goals in a way that placed Ko-rean capitalists under the careful watch and guidance of Japanese na-tionals without overt government interference. For Koreans, on the other hand, such companies opened the door to the lucrative profits of the growing industrial economy with a minimum of risk and effort. Such being the case, it is not surprising that the share of joint compa-nies in the total amount of paid-in colonial capital tripled in the decade after 1919.[82] Even later, when the colony's large-scale industrial plans required the induction of huge amounts of *zaibatsu* capital from Japan proper, the Government-General often insisted that Koreans be in-cluded as stockholders in *zaibatsu* projects and even be given seats on the board of directors of the new companies.[83] While it is clear from colonial newspapers and business directories that mixed Japanese-Korean companies continued to be a feature of the Chōsen economy right down to 1945, we do not, unfortunately, have official statistics on this subject after 1929. The figures for that year are nevertheless suggestive: over 30 percent of the total paid-up corporate capital in 1929 was listed as belonging to joint Japanese-Korean firms — quite apart from the figures cited separately for specifically Korean-run enterprises.[84]

None of these statistics adequately measures the significance of Korean capitalist participation in the colonial industrial economy. In regard to the formation of a modern Korean bourgeoisie, the amount of capital contributed by Koreans was less important than the numbers of Korean merchants and landlords who made the transition — wholly or partially — to industrial capitalism during this period. A casual look through any of the many colonial business magazines and directories reveals a world densely populated with Koreans as well as Japanese. Following the repeal of the Company Law in 1920, many landlords and wealthy merchants began to invest in small-scale factories, especially in such areas as cotton spinning and weaving, knitwear, rubber goods, alcoholic beverages, and rice cleaning and polishing.[85] By 1937 there were over 2,300 Korean-run factories throughout the industrial spectrum, and about 160 of these establishments employed over 50 workers. The names of many other Koreans can be found on the lists of the stockholders of both Japanese and Korean industrial companies.[86]

While such investments were generally small in comparison with similar Japanese investments, they were nevertheless often crucial first steps into the world of modern commerce and industry for many Koreans. The late Yi Pyŏngch'ŏl, for example, the founder of the Samsung (Samsŏng) Group and a figure whose name today has much the same legendary ring of great wealth for South Koreans as the name "Rockefeller" does for Americans, was originally a South Kyŏngsang landlord's son who (together with two other landlords) invested part of his inheritance in a small rice mill in Masan in the 1930s and later branched out into international trade and brewing in Taegu.[87] Ku Inhoe, another small landlord's son from South Kyŏngsang and the eventual founder of the Lucky Group in South Korea, was involved in the textile industry during this same period and was an active member of the Chinju Chamber of Commerce and Industry. Hyundai's founder, Chŏng Chuyŏng, also had a small but prosperous machine and automobile service shop by the end of the colonial period.[88] Measured solely in terms of his respective capital contribution to the colonial economy, none of these men was particularly important. The total paid-in capital of Yi's rice mill in Masan, for example, was only 30,000 yen, of which Yi provided only one-third; Ku's first commercial venture was even more modest—a partnership with his younger brother capitalized at only 3,800 yen; Chŏng's initial investment was less than 2,000 yen.[89] From the perspective of Korean socioeconomic history, however, the appearance of such men was indicative of a growing native bourgeois class, for which colonial Korea was in retrospect a training ground and crucible.

Small-scale Korean entrepreneurs like Yi, Ku, and Chŏng, in fact, comprised the broad base of what may be described as a pyramid of Korean bourgeois interests that ultimately reached into the most exalted echelons of the colonial business community. It is the top of the pyramid, however, that ultimately draws our attention. Korean entrepreneurship at that level represented not only the most advanced form of Japanese-Korean cooperative development to be found during the colonial period, but also the highest development of Korean capitalism itself before 1945— and possibly before the 1960s. The Koch'ang Kims were among its most able practitioners, and the business activities of the family, centered on the Kyŏngsŏng Spinning and Weaving Company, give us a good idea of the surprisingly complex and sophisticated form that Korean capitalism was able to attain even within the colonial setting.[90]

The Kyŏngbang Chaebŏl

When Kim Sŏngsu returned home from Tokyo in 1914, he was intent on helping to create in Korea a version of the modern capitalist society he had seen in Japan. Like his father and uncle, his main interest was in education rather than industry, and his first investment in 1915 was in a school.[91] As noted above, however, his acquaintance with Yi Kanghyŏn, the cotton textile engineer and strong advocate of industrial development, quickly led Kim to take an interest in industry as well.

Yi had his eye on the Kyŏngsŏng Cord Company described earlier. The company had been suffering from a sluggish and limited market and from serious internal management problems, and in spite of an apparent attempt to salvage the situation by promoting exports to China, the firm was on the verge of bankruptcy.[92] Because the owners were anxious to cut their losses and sell, the company could be acquired at a good price and converted into a more modern cotton manufacturing facility.

In addition to the low financial risk and the advantage of taking over a factory already in existence, the timing for such a business move was also auspicious. The demand for machine-made cotton cloth in Korea was greater than ever because of the war, and the Government-General was already beginning to show signs of relaxing its restrictive Company Law. In 1917, the Chōsen Spinning and Weaving Company, capitalized at five million yen, was thus formally established in Pusan, and in that same year Yi Kanghyŏn, who had only limited funds of his own, was able to persuade Kim Sŏngsu to take over the failing Kyŏngsŏng Cord Company.[93]

At first Kim and Yi concentrated on expanding the company's production of cloth through the importation of new machinery. It quickly became apparent, however, that the production of the increasingly popular cotton broadcloth required a separate and full-scale facility similar to the one being built in Pusan. Thus, in August 1919, with the abolition of the Company Law in the offing and a new governor-general in office anxious to placate the Korean elite with an offer of cooperative development, the final decision was made to establish a new company devoted exclusively to the manufacture of machine-made cotton yarn and cloth. Official permission to set up the new company was granted in October 1919, even before the formal repeal of the Company Law,[94] and the first general stockholders meeting of the Kyŏngsŏng Spinning and Weaving Company, Ltd., was held at 1:00 P.M. on Sunday, October 5, in the Myŏngwŏlgwan restaurant in Seoul with 130 stockholders (or proxies) in attendance.[95]

Despite conventional scholarly claims to the contrary, it is clear from the records of this first general meeting that the new company, though for the most part owned by Koreans, had Japanese stockholders from the beginning and was thus one of the first important concrete examples of the new Government-General's evolving policy of cooperative capitalist development.[96]

The subsequent growth of the company also followed a course that was in accord with official colonial development policies. We shall examine this growth in detail in later chapters, but for now let us simply note the following general pattern of cooperation: from the outset the company devoted much of its attention to the continental export trade to avoid friction with cotton manufacturers in Japan who were exporting to Korea, and its period of greatest corporate expansion came in the 1930s in conjunction with the Government-General's full-scale development of Korea into an industrial supply base for Japanese economic and military aggrandizement in Manchuria and China.

And the expansion was impressive, incomprehensibly so if one subscribes to the notion that the company was a victim of Japanese imperialism. Between 1919 and 1945 the paid-in capital of the firm went from 250,000 to 10,500,000 yen. The number of company looms grew from 100 to 1,080, and spindleage increased from 21,600 in 1935 to 30,200 by the end of the colonial period. These figures, however, applied only to the company's facilities in Korea. Kyŏngbang also owned and operated a separate spinning and weaving factory of comparable size in Manchuria and maintained business offices in Osaka and Peking and even deep in the interior of central China.

By 1945, moreover, the company had developed from a simple cotton weaving factory into a complete vertically integrated cotton textile operation. This included three separate ginning factories (two in Hwanghae Province and one in P'yŏngyang), the spinning and weaving facilities in Seoul (Yŏngdŭngp'o) already mentioned, a large bleaching and dyeing factory in Sihŭng, and a clothing factory, also in Seoul (Ssangnimdong). In addition, Kyŏngbang's acquisitions included a major rubber goods factory in Yangp'yŏngdong (formerly the Kyŏngsŏng Cord Company) and a silk thread and cloth factory in Ŭijŏngbu.

This was only the most visible part of what eventually developed into a sprawling complex of business activities. Sŏngsu's real interests lay in education and publishing, and when his younger brother Yŏnsu returned to Korea with a degree in economics from Kyoto Imperial University, Sŏngsu gradually turned the actual management of the textile company over to him.[97] Eventually Yŏnsu and his side of the family came to exercise a controlling ownership, and Yŏnsu became president of the company in 1935. Either personally or through the company, Yŏnsu eventually extended his business interests, directly and indirectly, into a wide variety of areas that encompassed Korea, Manchuria, and China. In addition to the areas already mentioned, these included (in no particular order) the manufacture of ball bearings, rolling stock, and fishing nets, the production of gas and hydroelectric power, hemp spinning and weaving, brewing, gold mining, banking, international commerce, real estate and development, transport, shipbuilding, the aircraft industry, metal refining, oil refining, heavy and chemical industries, and railroads. Sŏngsu, moreover, continued to support Kyŏngbang both financially and in an advisory capacity,[98] and his ownership of one of the country's major newspaper firms and private colleges enhanced the power and prestige of his younger brother's industrial interests. Long before 1945 it was clear that the Kims had made brilliant use of the economic opportunities afforded their class by colonial rule; they had, in fact, managed to create one of Korea's first great business groups or *chaebŏl* (in Japanese, *zaibatsu*), a term that Korean reporters were applying to the family's rapidly multiplying entrepreneurial interests at least as early as 1932.[99]

North
Hamgyŏng

South
Hamgyŏng

North
P'yŏngan

South
P'yŏngan

East Sea
(Sea of Japan)

Hwanghae

Kangwŏn

Kyŏnggi

•Seoul

Yellow Sea

North
Ch'ungch'ŏng

South
Ch'ungch'ŏng

North
Kyŏngsang

North
Chŏlla

Chŏngŭp
•

South
Kyŏngsang

South
Chŏlla

Pusan
•

MAP 1. Provinces (*to*) of Korea

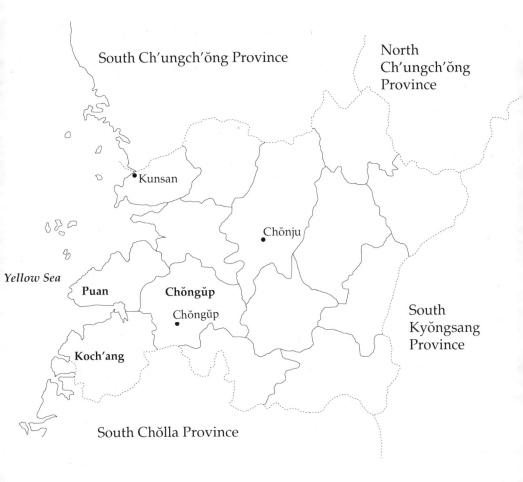

South Ch'ungch'ŏng Province

North Ch'ungch'ŏng Province

Kunsan

Chŏnju

Yellow Sea

Puan

Chŏngŭp

Chŏngŭp

South Kyŏngsang Province

Koch'ang

South Chŏlla Province

MAP 2. North Chŏlla Province by counties (*kun*)

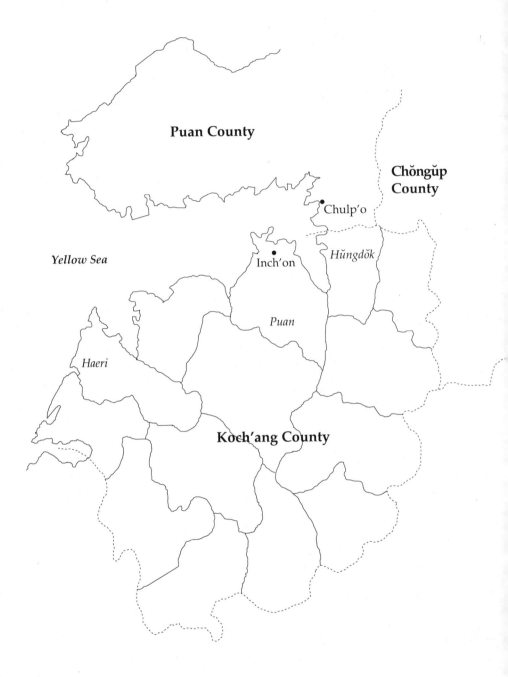

Puan County

Chŏngŭp County

• Chulp'o

Yellow Sea

• Inch'on

Hŭngdŏk

Puan

Haeri

Koch'ang County

MAP 3. Koch'ang County by townships (*myŏn*)

MAP 4. Location of Kyŏngbang's factories and offices in 1945

PART II

THE PATTERNS OF GROWTH

The growth of the Kyŏngsŏng Spinning and Weaving Company represented the pinnacle of Korean capitalist development before 1945. The company's achievements belie the common notion that the sprouts of capitalist growth, first seen in the seventeenth and eighteenth centuries, were virtually stamped out by Japanese imperialism after 1876, only to reappear again after 1945. That the roots of Korean capitalism can be traced back to the pre-1876 period is, I have suggested, a product of wishful academic thinking, but there is no doubt that from 1876 on Korea saw the emergence of a native entrepreneurial class that eventually turned its attention to industry. Far from stifling such growth, colonialism advanced it: for both the economic and political reasons already noted, the Japanese permitted and abetted the development of a native bourgeois class.

To say this is in no way to offer an apology for Japanese imperialism. The purpose is rather to clear away one of the many myths surrounding the colonial period that continue to inform much South Korean scholarship. It is possible — indeed, probable — that the Koreans, left to their own devices, would have produced a capitalist class entirely on their own. But that is not what happened: colonialism was the setting in which Korean capitalism experienced its first real surge of growth. Although this was certainly unfortunate, and is perhaps embarrassing or distasteful for many Koreans to admit, it is nevertheless a fact.

Having acknowledged Korean capitalist development during the colonial period and examined the extent of such growth, it is now necessary to explore the nature of the phenomenon. So far I have been using the term *capitalism* to refer to an industrial or industrializing society characterized by a market economy and private ownership of property. While this definition has been useful in helping to locate and describe the origins and development of a nascent Korean bourgeoisie in general terms, it actually tells very little about the particular capitalism that developed in Korea. What were the economic patterns that characterized Korean capitalist growth? More specifically, what was the role of the state in such development? What, moreover, was the nature of the relationship between the new and growing capitalism of the colony and the capitalism of the Japanese metropole?

An examination of these questions is essential if we are fully to understand the legacy of colonial capitalism, but such study brings us into direct conflict with another of the enduring myths about the colonial period: the notion that Korea's bourgeois development before 1945 may be characterized as "national capital" (*minjok chabon*).

I have already noted in part 1 that conventional South Korean scholars like Cho Kijun reject the idea of any significant Korean socioeconomic development under Japanese auspices. But what about the native capitalist development—epitomized by the Kyŏngsŏng Spinning and Weaving Company—that so obviously did take place? How can such growth be explained without acknowledging colonial influence?

In the concept of "national capital," Cho and others have found an ingenious solution to this apparent contradiction. Like many historical terms used in South Korea today, this expression has Marxist-Leninist roots. In a strict sense, it refers to the small (petty) native bourgeoisie in a colonial situation who compete with and oppose both the dominant imperial bourgeoisie of the metropole and the big native bourgeoisie (the "comprador" bourgeoisie) aligned with imperialism.[1] North Korean scholars have continued to employ and refine the distinction between "national" and "comprador" capital in their writings, and this has given their work on capitalist development in the colonial period—in spite of its tedious encomia to Kim Il Sung (Kim Ilsŏng)—a certain analytical clarity and depth that the south has only recently begun to match. Before the 1980s little distinction was made in the south between national and comprador capital; in general all Korean capital was referred to without differentiation simply as national capital.[2]

And here we arrive at the crux of the myth. Since, according to this hoary view, all Korean capital in the colonial period was national capital, it was also by definition anti-Japanese and existed in opposition both to the colonial power structure and to the capitalist system in Japan itself. Cho Kijun, perhaps South Korea's most venerable authority on Korea's capitalist development, writes as follows in describing the achievements of Kyŏngbang—his premier example of national capital during the colonial period:

Kyŏngbang was operated solely on the basis of Korean capital [*minjok chabon*] and Korean technology. It was difficult for a Korean company to continue to exist under colonial rule without any financial support from the ruling country and without collaboration with Japanese private capital. But Kyŏngbang was one of the few Korean enterprises founded and operated entirely by Korean capital. . . . As for technicians and management — companies in late-developing countries normally employ at least some foreigners on their staff, but Kyŏngbang consciously avoided this.[3]

The question of how this extraordinary feat was accomplished, i.e., how the company was able to obtain the necessary financing, secure required raw materials and technology, establish a market network that encompassed not only Korea but stretched into Manchuria and China as well, all in total isolation or even in defiance of the colonial power structure and the capitalist system in Japan, clearly presents a challenge for even the most imaginative of scholars. But the question is never really posed. Cho, for example, merely notes that under Japanese colonial rule, "it was certainly not an easy thing to lead a company to success in competition with big Japanese capital," but Kyŏngbang's remarkable achievement was the result of the "rational management skills" of its managers.[4]

Like all myths, this one too contains a kernel of truth. It is true that the majority of stockholders in Kyŏngbang were Korean. It is also true that the company used Korean technicians whenever possible. No one who has studied the company, moreover, would deny the managerial talents of Kim Yŏnsu and his subordinates. Nevertheless, to argue that a company of Kyŏngbang's size and strength could ever have developed and survived without close cooperation with the colonial authorities and Japanese private capital is to controvert reason and common sense. Indeed, it is a serious question whether anything approximating Korean national capital ever actually existed (or even could have existed), at least for any length of time, within the framework of Japanese political and economic control.[5]

When we turn from myth to fact, the Kyŏngbang story loses its mystery but gains in interest and significance. Far from standing in isolation from the colonial power structure or in opposition to Japanese capitalism, Kyŏngbang developed in close relation to both, becoming by 1945 an integral part of an imperial economic nexus that stretched from Japan across Korea to the Asian continent. In chapters 3 and 4 we shall consider the relationship between government and business in the colonial context through a study of Kyŏngbang's financing and management; in chapters 5 and 6 we shall examine the relationship of Korean capitalism to the core capitalism of Japan and to the imperial system as a whole.

CHAPTER 3

Class and State

The Financial Nexus

The focus here and in chapter 4 is on the Korean bourgeoisie's relationship with the colonial state. But it was the state, not the bourgeoisie, that set the basic terms of the relationship, and it is therefore with the state that we must begin.

If Karl Wittfogel had studied Korea instead of China, he would surely have found the term "Oriental despotism" inappropriate. The traditional Korean state had been very weak, sharing power in a kind of equilibrium with a well-entrenched landed aristocracy and an aggressive bureaucracy. The aristocracy, moreover, had consolidated its power through control of the examination system (and hence of the key bureaucratic posts) and also through strategic marriage alliances, which included the provision of royal consorts for the king. In contrast to the typical Ming or Ch'ing despot, the Korean monarch was at best only another aristocrat, slightly more exalted, perhaps, but essentially a *primus inter pares* figure, who, if clever enough, could hope to exert some authority by playing off various power factions in the court and bureaucracy against one another. At his weakest, the Korean king was a pathetic pawn of the other parties contending for power. Early in the 508-year history of the Chosŏn dynasty a Korean king once attempted to exceed the tacit limits of authority that circumscribed his office. He was eventually deposed and degraded for all time in the historical record with the title of "prince" (*kun*) even though he had been a reigning monarch—a potent admonition to future Korean kings not to step out of royal bounds.[1]

What had been in some ways a positive check against despotism in the traditional polity proved, however, to be an obstacle in the late nineteenth century as Japanese imperialism forced Korea to open its ports to the modern world of international commerce. Korea's backward economy required a strong, centralized, growth-oriented state that could assume the risks and burden of development and permit the country to survive as an independent nation in a highly competitive world economy.[2] The Yi state was incapable of meeting such a challenge. To do so would have meant a complete disruption of the equilibrium of power that had characterized the dynasty since the sixteenth century, an assertion of royal power that had always been both morally and practically impossible in the society.

When nascent bourgeois families like the Koch'ang Kims were making their first tentative moves from land to industry around 1920, the old Yi state was gone, and in its place was something entirely different. The new colonial state had everything the Yi state had lacked to give Korea a modern economy: a strong governor-general (sōtoku) instead of a feeble monarch hedged in by tradition and aristocratic-bureaucratic restraints, an efficient and docile bureaucracy to carry out orders instead of Chosŏn's factious and censorious officialdom, and, above all, an orientation toward economic development, or more accurately, exploitation.

In carrying out their economic plans, the Japanese transferred to Korea many of the patterns and techniques of development that had been successful in Japan, including a pattern of close government-business interaction. But Korea was not Japan, and the relationship between government and business assumed a somewhat different cast.

The Government-General was basically a dictatorship administered through a large bureaucracy, and the governor-general's word, in the form of executive ordinances (furei or seirei), was quite literally law.[3] Before 1919 he had been responsible only to the emperor himself, and shortly after annexation the Diet had confirmed the right of the colony to make laws independently of Tokyo. It was not until 1942 that Tokyo succeeded in bringing the colony within the legal jurisdiction of the home government by officially placing the governor-general under the Home Ministry. In actuality, however, nothing changed, because the move had been undertaken mainly to promote a psychological sense of wartime unity between colony and metropole rather than specifically to curtail the powers of the governor-general.[4]

The colonial state was not merely a dictatorship but a military dictatorship, reflecting the strategic significance that Japan had attached to the peninsula since the late nineteenth century. Before 1919 only active-duty generals had held the post of governor-general, but in 1919, in a belated concession to Korean opinion following the March First demonstrations, the position had been made a civilian appointment. Once again, however, no substantive changes occured. All sōtoku appointed between 1919 and 1945 were top-ranking military figures in mufti, and only one was not an army general.[5] The colony was handled much like an army fief, passed on from illustrious general to general as each moved upward within the stratosphere of the army command. General Ugaki Kazunari, for example, who became governor-general in 1931, had been minister of war before moving over to Korea. He was followed in the ministry by General Minami Jirō, who several years later went on to succeed Ugaki as governor-general. Minami was in turn succeeded by General Koiso Kuniaki, a junior officer to both Ugaki and Minami who had served as chief of staff of the Manchurian Army and commander-in-chief of the army in Korea.[6]

Like other elements of Japan's complex bureaucratic system, the Japanese army was by no means a monolith, and attitudes toward private enterprise among army officers varied. For army extremists, many of whom had been strongly influenced by the ideas of Kita Ikki, capitalism was a national cancer that required radical surgery in the form of widespread nationalization of commerce and industry, that is, through the establishment of a fully bureaucratized command economy that left virtually no space for private enterprise.[7]

In Japan itself the army was never able to carry out such a program. Business interests were too entrenched in the society and also far too important for the army's own development plans to be treated in so highhanded a fashion. The *zaibatsu* insisted on their own prerogatives, one of which was a major voice in the overall management of the economy. Even at the height of wartime mobilization and controls, Premier Tōjō was forced to appoint a cabinet advisory board composed of financial and industrial magnates and to reshuffle the cabinet itself to appease business interests. As T. A. Bisson noted shortly after the war, government controls in Japan "fell considerably short of applying a thorough scheme of state regimentation to the basic industries and the great business monopolies."[8]

In Manchuria, however, on the fringes of the empire and in territory the army regarded as its own special domain, the national socialist vision of Kita Ikki was able to blossom unchecked. Apart from the South Manchuria Railway Company (Mantetsu), there were no established business interests that could counteract the Kwantung army's authority, and even the Mantetsu was eventually forced to accommodate itself to the army's attempts at total bureaucratic control.[9] With the establishment of the puppet state of Manchukuo in 1932, the army had a perfect vehicle for implementing its economic plans, and Manchuria became a magnet and training ground for upwardly mobile bureaucrats, both civilian and military, who were attracted by the concept of a state-run system.[10] Eventually, as Manchukuo's grand development plans began to show signs of faltering, the army was forced to retreat from its initial stance of extreme anticapitalism and allow some concessions to private enterprise, but Manchukuo's economy continued to be planned and largely controlled by the state until its collapse in 1945.[11]

Korea's military rulers, on the other hand, were inclined to take a more moderate or realistic approach to the question of state control of the economy. In general, they were either part of or closely affiliated with the so-called Control Faction (Tōseiha) of the army, which ran the War Ministry and "believed in the wisdom of cooperating with capitalists and politicians."[12] Under General Ugaki, for example, Korea saw its first great influx of Japanese private capital, including the expansion of the enormous complex of interests centered on the Japan Nitrogenous Fertilizer Company controlled by Noguchi Jun. This was the same period in which Japanese spinning giants such as Tōyōbō and Kanegafuchi, closely affiliated with the *zaibatsu*, opened up large-scale factories on the Korean peninsula with an eye to continental markets.[13]

General Minami, who succeeded Ugaki as governor-general, was equally anxious to draw Japanese capital into Korea to develop the colony's industry. Like his predecessor, who had encouraged private investment with tariffs, surtaxes, and subsidies to raise market prices and protect domestic companies, Minami also offered a variety of economic incentives to private investors — including, for example, low-interest financing, expanded limits on company bond issues, assistance in the expropriation of land for industrial use, and generous tax rates.[14]

While thus not hostile to capitalism, Korea's military rulers nevertheless firmly believed, like their Manchurian colleagues, in the basic creed eventually set forth in *Kokutai no hongi* that public interests took priority over private:

Our national economy is a great enterprise based on His Majesty's great august Will to have the Empire go on developing for ever and ever, and is a thing on which the subjects' felicity depends; so that it is not a disconnected series of activities aimed at fulfilling the material desires of individual persons, a doctrine expounded by Western economists. It is a thing in which the entire nation joins the Way of *musubi*, each person fulfilling his duties according to the part he has been assigned to play . . . . The attitude of mind which is based on the spirit of *musubi* and puts public interests before private ones, paying full attention to one's alloted duties and to being in harmony with others, has been an attitude toward industrial enterprises in our nation; and it is a basic reason for the rise of a strong impetus in the world of industry, for encouraging initiative, stimulating cooperation, greatly heightening industrial efficiency, bringing about the prosperity of all industries, and for contributing toward the increase of national wealth. In our economic activities, we must in the future become fully awake to this particular attitude of mind toward industries, and with this consciousness strive more than ever to develop them. In this manner will economy conform with morals, and develop industries that are based on the Way and not on material profit and be able to enhance the glory of our national entity in our economy.[15]

Such a view was reflected in Governor-General Minami's exhortation to colonial businessmen in 1936 to eschew "capitalistic profits and commercial self-interest" and to consider the economic "mission" of Korea from the standpoint of the "national economy."[16] Not a condemnation of capitalism *per se*, Minami's statement—like *Kokutai no hongi* itself—was basically an assertion of the superior and overriding claims of the state. General Koiso expressed a similar attitude toward the state at his war crimes trial in 1947: "The Japanese way is that no matter what our personal opinions and our own personal arguments may be, once a policy of State has been decided upon, it is our duty to bend all our efforts for the prosecution of such policy. This has been the traditional custom in our country."[17]

Sentiments such as these led Korea's colonial rulers from the beginning to regard capitalism essentially as an instrument of state policy. To insure such subordination, the Government-General kept a tight rein on the colony's financial structure, and ambitious companies like Kyŏngbang more often than not found themselves either directly or indirectly locked in a complicated financial embrace with the government. Corporate management was similarly dominated by the Government-General, which indirectly fixed the contours of corporate policy through its establishment of colonial industrial policies.

State domination was complex and often very subtle, involving considerable overlapping and interaction of the public and private spheres. For if *Kokutai no hongi* preached subordination of the capitalists to the state, it also advocated the nurturing of harmony between the two through the cultivation of the spirit of *musubi*—a notoriously imprecise term, but one that basically suggests a "connecting" or "joining." If businessmen were to be subordinated to the state, they were also to be incorporated into it as an integral part of a great and stern patriarchy. Indeed, the image of the policy as the family writ large, with the ruler as "father," pervades *Kokutai no hongi* and gives its vision of a corporatist political economy a distinct Confucian tint.[18]

And while the businessmen may not have entirely approved of the inferior status accorded them by such thinking, in general they shared — Koreans and Japanese alike — a common Confucian ideological heritage with their rulers that made such status tolerable and interaction with the government a natural mode of business activity. Both Korean and Japanese businessmen, for example, were wont to refer in public to the Governor-General as "a loving father" (jifu), and Tsuda Shingo, president of the Kanegafuchi Spinning Company, remarked with some pride at a Government-General industrial conference in 1936 that "As everyone knows, the political economy of Japan has taken the form of 'familialism,' and its historical development is entirely different from that of the West. Western capitalism has developed generally on the basis of individualism and for that reason is bound to reach an impasse."[19]

Interests as well as ideology served to drive businessmen and bureaucrats into each other's arms. If the requisites of corporate finance left companies like Kyŏngbang in thrall to the Government-General, it was nevertheless a profitable arrangement for everyone concerned, businessmen and bureaucrats as well. A fusion of the public and private spheres in corporate management was similarly beneficial to both parties. By incorporating the businessmen into the policy-making process on both formal and informal levels, the state insured a smoother working of the economy than would otherwise have been the case. And what businessmen lost to the state in the way of autonomous corporate management, they made up for magnificently by way of corporate profits.

With these images of the colonial state in mind, let us then begin our analysis of the government-business relationship with a look at the structure of Kyŏngbang's financing. Money, profits aside, flowed into the company in essentially three ways: from the sale of corporate shares to the public, from subsidies, and from bank loans. The argument for Kyŏngbang as "national capital" notwithstanding, the Government-General, either directly or indirectly, was involved in all three areas.

Equity Capital

The concept of a "joint-stock company" (chusik hoesa) was not new to Koreans in 1919, the year Kyŏngbang was founded, but had been around for some time. As early as 1882, Yu Kilchun had introduced Korean readers to it in his *Regulations for Commercial Firms*, and in October of the following year, the *Hansŏng sunbo*, in an article entitled "On Companies," stressed the importance of business corporations in building up a nation's wealth and power, and explained the meaning of various common articles of incorporation.[20] One may also speculate that even before the 1880s — with the opening of the country in 1876 and the gradual penetration of Chinese, Japanese, and Western merchants — Koreans had undoubtedly had some opportunity to observe the new forms of business directly in Korea itself.

With the abolition of official monopoly privileges and the new government encouragement of private industry through the Kabo Reforms, from the late 1890s Korean business began to assume a more modern, Westernized look. Traditional types of commercial association like *kaekchu* gradually gave way to various Western forms of business such as limited (*hapcha hoesa*) and unlimited (*hammyŏng hoesa*) partnerships, and, of course, the joint-stock company as well.[21] Kyŏngsŏng Chingnyu, the company taken over by Kim Sŏngsu in 1917 and two years later reestablished as Kyŏngbang, had originally been founded as an unlimited partnership in 1910 but was converted into a joint-stock company only one year later.[22]

While Koreans were thus not unfamiliar with the concept of corporate investment in 1919, those with something to invest, for the most part landlords and urban merchants (especially in the port cities), continued to prefer to put their money into land, which had always been the preeminent Korean investment. Japanese policies since the annexation had confirmed the existing Korean landlord system and preserved land as a safe investment, whereas the Company Law in effect from 1911 had made investment in nonagricultural industry — particularly for Koreans — difficult and precarious.

Land was also extremely profitable. One tends to think of the Kanghwa Treaty in 1876 as opening up Korea to international commerce. This is true, but at the same time the treaty also served to open Japan up to Korea as an enormous new market for Korean grains (especially rice). Enterprising Korean landlords and merchants made fortunes from the rice trade between 1876 and 1919, which they used to increase their landholdings even further. As we have seen, Kim Sŏngsu's family, situated in the great Honam Plain of North Chŏlla near the ports of Chulp'o and Kunsan, was among the first Korean landlord families to observe and grasp the epochal changes and opportunities that the new market economy offered for commercial agriculture. In 1876, Kim Sŏngsu's grandfather started out as the third son in a relatively poor landlord family, known more for its scholarship than its wealth. By 1924 the family was the third richest in Korea. It had multiplied its holdings over eight times and as a unit controlled around two thousand *chŏngbo* (about five thousand acres) of land — most of which was paddy. The Government-General's initial policy of developing Korea as a simple agricultural colony, together with high rice (and, correspondingly, land) prices in effect during the First World War, also helped to keep Korean money firmly tied to the land.[23]

We must also note that investment in land was relatively effortless. Even the least enterprising landlords could expect good profits simply by collecting rents, and even that task was normally delegated to stewards. Rents were high, ranging between 30 and 90 percent of the crop, with the average hovering above 50 percent. Land was scarce and tenants cheap. If for some reason a tenant didn't meet his obligations, he could be (and often was) quickly replaced. It was the tenant, moreover, who usually wound up paying the land tax, although it was legally the landlord's responsibility. The tenant was also subject to a variety of other levies from landlords and was himself financially responsible for the actual delivery of the rice to the landlord's granary.[24] Given such circumstances, it is not surprising that many wealthy Koreans chose land as the easy and secure route to profit.

This was still true in 1919. Kim Sŏngsu had to travel all over the country before he found enough subscribers for the first sale of Kyŏngbang shares. The company's authorized capital had been fixed at one million yen, and the first sale brought in only a quarter of that amount. A second sale was held in January 1922, at which time the price per share was reduced from 12.50 yen to 7.50 yen, but even then the response was poor. By 1925 the total number of shareholders had declined by nearly one-half. Subsequent sales were held again in 1928, 1931, and 1933.[25] It thus took Kyŏngbang a total of fourteen years to become paid up. During these early years difficulty in obtaining equity capital was a recurring topic of concern and discussion at company board meetings.[26]

Even the Kims were cautious in making their move from the land into industrial capitalism. Company histories and official biographies stress Kim Sŏngsu's "nationalism" in establishing Kyŏngbang from the beginning as a joint-stock company — in which a large number of Koreans could participate — rather than as a strict family enterprise.[27] It must also be pointed out, however, that by doing so the family was minimizing its personal risk.

Considering the enormous assets available to the family, even to Kim Sŏngsu alone, its initial stake in the company seems quite conservative. Kim Sŏngsu himself, whose personal income from land rents in 1919 exceeded 3,000 *sŏk*—roughly 50-70,000 yen in 1919 rice prices—made an initial investment of only 200 shares, amounting at most to only about 5 percent of his landed income for that year.[28] It was his father (adoptive) and uncle (his real father) who were the biggest family shareholders at the time of the founding of the company, but their respective investments were also small in proportion to their assets. On the basis of available documents, the family's total income from rents in 1919 exceeded 450,000 yen. Sŏngsu, together with his father and uncle, purchased a total of 3,000 of the original 20,000 shares, an investment of 37,500 yen—only 8.2 percent of the family's total landed income in 1919. The remaining shares were widely held by nearly 200 other investors, mainly other large landlords and wealthy merchants.[29] Land was still king in 1919.

Times were beginning to change, however. A drop in the price of rice and land after the war and the new governor-general's policy of supporting some economic development in addition to agriculture had made investment in industry more appealing than before. It was no accident that Kyŏngbang was founded just at this time. As the colonial period wore on, particularly in the 1930s with the Japanese invasion of Manchuria and development of Korea into an "advance military supply base" (*zenshin heitan kichi*), industry seemed more and more of a safe and lucrative investment. In 1937 the rate of return on paddy was about 8 percent. Profits for the textile industry as a whole, on the other hand, were around 19 percent and rising.[30] By 1938, Kyŏngbang was registering profits in the neighborhood of 30 percent and paying dividends of as much as 12 percent per year. Thereafter the company's dividend was never less than 8 percent per year and usually higher.[31]

Under such conditions Kyŏngbang was able to obtain equity capital more easily than before. The company increased its authorized capital in 1935 from one to three million yen, one million of which was paid in within a year and the remainder by the end of 1940—about one-third the time it had taken to sell the sum of its old stock issue. In 1942 the company again increased its authorized capital by five million yen, half of which had been paid in by the end of the colonial period. By 1945 the total paid-in capital had multiplied some fortyfold since 1919 to ten and a half million yen.[32] The number of shareholders, moreover, had more than doubled since 1919, and the Kim family, especially the family of Kim Yŏnsu, who became Kyŏngbang's president in 1935, continued to increase its holdings in the company. In 1919 both branches of the family together had held only about 15 percent of the stock.[33] By 1944 the family stake had risen to over 30 percent.[34] The Kims' early diffidence about industrial investment had gradually been replaced by confidence.

Not only Koreans found Kyŏngbang an increasingly attractive prospect. More and more Japanese were also buying shares in the company. Many South Korean historians, for whom Kyŏngbang is the prime example of "national capital" during the colonial period, have been wont to stress the "pure" Korean nature of the company's financing. This view has even found its way into academic works published in English in the United States by American-educated South Korean scholars. In an article entitled "Nationalism and Korean Businessmen," Daniel S. Juhn writes:

The most outstanding example of an expression of nationalistic sentiment through industrial enterprise is the case of Kyŏngsŏng Textile Company and its founders, whose basic motivation was to found a Korean-owned and Korean-operated industrial enterprise to promote Korean economic independence. Such nationalistic sentiment was expressed in company policies, including the policy of exclusion of Japanese as employees and stockholders.[35]

While Kyŏngbang may have preferred Korean investors, it certainly did not exclude Japanese from its ranks of shareholders. "No one spits on money," says an old Korean proverb,[36] and indeed, whatever its source, money was most welcome at Kyŏngbang. By 1945 Japanese constituted over 13.6 percent of the total number of stockholders, and their combined stock represented 5.6 percent of the total 260,000 shares.[37]

Such Japanese interest indicated, on the one hand, how popular Kyŏngbang had become as an investment prospect by 1945. Whereas Koreans in some cases might be willing to buy stock in the company to support what they considered a nationalist enterprise, Japanese were likely to be more strictly concerned with the bottom line on the company's balance sheet. On the other hand, Japanese investment may also signify the limits of equity financing available to Kyŏngbang from purely Korean sources. In any case, the importance of equity to the company's development should not be overemphasized. In the early years, when the company desperately needed regular inflows of capital to survive, its inability to attract sufficient equity was a major problem. Later, as Kyŏngbang began to prosper and expand, it required greater and greater sums of money, sums that equity alone could not provide. To overcome these problems, the company turned increasingly to the government and the banks for support.

Subsidies

Kyŏngbang's beginning was marked by many difficulties. Partly, at least, these were due to inexperience and just plain bad luck. Yi Kanghyŏn, the company's chief engineer and factory manager, who had been so instrumental in persuading Kim Sŏngsu to invest in the textile industry, proved to be a far better technician than businessman. In 1919, shortly after its establishment, the company had sent Yi to Nagoya to purchase Toyoda looms for the new factory. Having placed his order, Yi then went on to Osaka to secure a supply of cotton yarn. There he became aware of the financial windfalls that clever dealers could reap in the Sampin, Osaka's great market for cotton, cotton yarn, and cotton cloth. Without any previous experience in commodities transactions, and apparently quite unaware of changing market conditions after the First World War, Yi ended up losing much of the company's available cash reserves by speculating in futures. As a result, the company had to suspend its factory construction and postpone the purchase of machinery.[38]

A second major disaster came in 1925, just as the company was beginning to recover from Yi's mistake. This time, however, no one was to blame. In July of that year heavy rains in Korea resulted in catastrophic floods that claimed the lives of hundreds of people and injured hundreds more. In all, nearly three hundred thousand Koreans were afflicted in one way or another. In Seoul the usually quiet and shallow Han River became a raging torrent that poured into Yŏngdŭngp'o and flooded Kyŏngbang's offices, dormitories, and factory, saturating and muddying the company's equipment, raw materials (yarn), and goods on hand.[39]

Natural disasters and errors in judgment, however, were the least of Kyŏngbang's difficulties in the early years. Far more serious was the problem of establishing a viable cotton textile firm in a market already dominated by Japanese imports.

Here the statistics are eloquent in conveying the situation Kyŏngbang faced in 1919. Machine-made foreign cotton goods had begun to penetrate Korea after 1876 and to drive out native handicraft cloth. The process, however, was quite gradual, and it was not until sometime between 1895 and 1904 that foreign cloth came to assume an important place in the Korean market. Thereafter foreign imports continued to rise. Between 1893 and 1919 the quantity of imported unbleached sheeting—the most popular cloth among Koreans and the type that Kyŏngbang itself would begin producing in the 1920s— increased fourfold, from about 500,000 to nearly 2 million rolls (*tan*).[40]

It was Western (particularly British) cloth that initially captured most of the profits. At the outbreak of the Sino-Japanese War, Japanese merchants in Korea were still for the most part selling Western cotton goods. Afterward the situation changed rapidly as Japan fought and defeated first China (1895) and then Russia (1904–1905), in each case consolidating its victory with a firmer control over Korea's politics and economy. Annexation in 1910, of course, gave Japan total control over the country, but because of an understanding with the Western powers that required maintenance of the existing Korean tariff rates for ten years, Japanese cloth imports still continued to face some competition from Western products until the 1920s.

In 1893 Western cotton fabrics constituted 100 percent of Korea's imports of unbleached sheeting. The following year Japanese cloth began to penetrate the Korean market and accounted for 2.5 percent of the total sheeting imports.[41] In 1896, the year after the Sino-Japanese War, this figure had jumped to nearly 8 percent. By 1904, the first year of the Russo-Japanese War, it had more than quadrupled to 33 percent. Only two years later, and one year after the establishment of a Japanese protectorate over Korea, Japanese sheeting imports for the first time surpassed Western imports, accounting for about 53 percent of the total. Thereafter Japanese sheeting quickly drove its Western competition out of the market. In 1910 it amounted to some 63 percent of the total; by 1915 its share was over 97 percent; and by 1919, the year Kyŏngbang was founded, the Japanese imports had virtually eclipsed the Western products, accounting for 99.6 percent of the total unbleached sheeting imports. The Japanese cloth, moreover, was highly regarded by Korean consumers. Even after similar machine-manufactured sheeting began to be produced in Korea itself by Kyŏngbang and others at a slightly lower price, Korean buyers initially continued to prefer the Japanese imports for their reputable brand names and higher quality.[42]

This dismal situation was compounded for Kyŏngbang by the general economic recession that followed the First World War. Prices had been generally high during the war, and, because of the Western powers' preoccupation with the conflict on the European continent, Japanese textile manufacturers had been able to move into markets in China and Southeast Asia previously dominated by the West. Cotton textile exports had boomed, and new spinning and weaving facilities had mushroomed in Japan. After the war, when prices dropped dramatically and the Western powers reasserted their authority in their former markets, Japanese textile firms were forced to curtail production and dispose of excess stock as best they could. As a result, they sold their higher quality goods in Korea at prices more or less comparable with similar Korean-made goods. For producers in Korea like Kyŏngbang, the recession thus had the effect of a double blow. On the one hand, it kept prices so depressed that it was difficult to realize profits substantial enough for growth. On the other hand, it intensified the threat of competition from Japanese textile companies who were dumping their popular cloth on the Korean market.[43]

The new Government-General headed by Admiral Saitō that took charge of Korea in 1919 was aware that unless some sort of special protection was offered to fledgling industries on the peninsula, they would not be able to survive the competition from Japanese imports. The issue was made all the more urgent at the time because tariffs between Japan and Korea were about to be abolished, thus creating a free economy between the two countries in which Japanese manufactured products would clearly overwhelm goods produced in Korea. Subsidies had already been granted earlier to a sugar manufacturing company in P'yŏngyang and to the Chōsen Spinning and Weaving Company (Chōbō), established in Pusan by Japanese capital in 1917. Chōbō, in fact, had been guaranteed a 7 percent dividend by the Government-General. At the industrial commission of 1921, convened by the new Government-General to discuss and formulate the colony's future economic policy, officials acknowledged that plans for additional industrial subsidies had already been decided.[44]

The question remained, however, of who would be the beneficiaries of such subsidies, and, more to the point, whether Korean entrepreneurs would also be granted such special government protection. As we saw in chapter 2, at least as early as the beginning of 1920, the new Saitō government was groping for a resolution of the "Korean problem" that had burst forth anew in 1919 by contemplating the forging of a new cooperative relationship between Japanese and Korean capitalists. A year later the Japanese had taken an important step in this direction by inviting Korean businessmen to participate in the industrial commission. There, in the course of five days of free discourse with the top officials of the Government-General and high-ranking bureaucrats from Japan, together with Japanese businessmen interested in Korea, the Koreans were permitted to present petitions and express their opinions on every aspect of Korea's future industrial development.

The Koreans were not passive observers at the conference. They were vehement about their role and position in the new economic development plan being discussed and insisted that they be treated as equal partners and given the same rights and privileges as Japanese businessmen. From the Korean perspective such equality naturally included a protective policy for native Korean industry equivalent to the one already in effect for certain key Japanese-owned companies operating in Korea like the Chōsen Spinning and Weaving Company. In a petition read aloud to the general assembly of delegates on the final day of the conference, the Koreans called for the expansion of industrial education facilities to upgrade Korean technology and for "subsidies (hojo) and protection (keigo) for industrial companies managed by Koreans."[45]

Japanese delegates to the industrial commission generally supported the Korean position in principle. It was, after all, in accord with basic Government-General policy to establish a link between Japanese and Korean capital. The conference, however, left the question of equality ambiguous. While the Koreans wanted a full partnership, including financial aid and protection for their own companies, some Japanese delegates felt that a partnership and government support were fine, but that Koreans should perhaps confine themselves to industries "for which they are most suitable," such as handicrafts and agriculture. As of September 1921, the issue of government subsidies for a major Korean manufacturing venture like Kyŏngbang was still not completely resolved.[46]

Within nine months, however, it was. On June 11, 1922, the *Tonga ilbo* published the following report:

By their [very] nature, manufacturing firms . . . are very important to Korea's industry and economy, so it is natural that the government should give them special protection. For that reason, it has been arranged for the Chosŏn Spinning and Weaving Company, established in Pusan by Japanese capitalists, to receive subsidies from the Government-General amounting to a 7 percent dividend on shares. The Kyŏngsŏng Spinning and Weaving Company, which is operating the same kind of business, has also had hopes of being granted subsidies in the manner of the Chosŏn Spinning and Weaving Company, and company managers have for some time been engaged in repeated negotiations with officials of the Government-General. As a result [of these discussions] and with the understanding of the authorities concerned, the company has already formally submitted a petition. If it is arranged for the company to receive subsidies as it [now] commences production, it is expected that this will gradually strengthen the company's foundation.[47]

What had happened? First, it is important to emphasize that the new Japanese policy had aimed from the beginning at some kind of reconciliation with the Korean business elite. The decision to extend government protection to Kyŏngbang was ultimately a logical outgrowth of such thinking. Then there was the glaring precedent of Chōbō, exactly the same kind of company as Kyŏngbang. It was difficult for the Government-General to convince Korean businessmen that it was serious about its avowed policy of cooperative development so long as it was granting its favors only to Japanese companies.

Finally, it is most important to remember the highly charged atmosphere in which all this took place. The intense nationalism of the March First independence movement that had provoked this major shift in colonial policy was still seething beneath the surface of Korean society. Only three days before the opening of the industrial commission of 1921, for example, two bombs had been hurled into the central offices of the Government-General itself.[48] Korean entrepreneurs like Kim Sŏngsu and his associates at Kyŏngbang were taking full advantage of the still fierce anti-Japanese sentiment in Korea to pressure the Government-General into carrying out its 1921 promise of a more liberal attitude toward native enterprise. Kyŏngbang was, of course, a major supporter—and beneficiary—of the Association to Promote Korean Goods launched originally in P'yŏngyang in July 1920 by Cho Mansik and others. Kim Sŏngsu's newspaper, the *Tonga ilbo,* also founded in 1920, continued to criticize the Government-General for attempting to eradicate the Korean nation through economic policies that gave control of the economy to the Japanese.[49]

Given such circumstances, it was clearly in the Government-General's interest to take Kyŏngbang under its wing. Official government patronage of the company would provide strong cement for the new link between Japanese and Korean capital. It would be a sign to the Korean business community that the Japanese were sincere in their talk about cooperation. Most important of all, it would weaken a volatile and dangerous nationalist movement by siphoning off a wealthy and influential segment of its leadership. It would, after all, be harder for people like Kim Sŏngsu to attack the government for its economic policies if those very policies were supporting their personal business activities.

The first subsidy, received in February 1924, was used to offset losses from the previous fiscal year and amounted to about 4 percent of Kyŏngbang's paid-in capital at that time. This was, of course, less than what Chōbō was receiving, but Chōbō was a much larger company with five times Kyŏngbang's authorized capital. The subsidies continued every fiscal year thereafter (with the exception of 1932–33) down to 1934–35. In all, they amounted to over one-fourth of the company's paid-up capital in 1935.[50]

Such figures, however, while impressive, do not tell the full story of how important these subsidies were to Kyŏngbang at the time. It is no exaggeration to say that without regular government assistance in its early years of existence Kyŏngbang would probably never have survived. Even with official help, the company operated at a loss until 1925. It did not declare a dividend until 1927, and even that was possible only because of the government subsidy received that year.[51] It was not until the 1930s that the company's financial position was finally stabilized and subsidies were no longer necessary. By then, in any case, Kyŏngbang needed much more money than could be obtained through subsidies. From the mid-1930s the company underwent a significant expansion that required massive new funding. Only the banks could provide that.

Loans

Kyŏngbang's early period, between 1919 and 1935, when the company was struggling to maintain itself and carve out a market, was characterized by slow — initially halting — but steady growth, dependent more on gradual accumulation of equity and regular government subsidies than on substantial loans. During this period only about 25 percent of the company's funding came from loans.[52]

Like the subsidies, however, these loans were crucial to the new company in its infancy. Subsidies did not begin to flow into the company coffers until 1924, but Kyŏngbang had already long since started taking out loans. Indeed, the company was in debt right from the beginning. The management's first plan had been to build the factory in Noryangjin, though this was later changed to Yŏngdŭngp'o. A suitable site in Noryangjin, however, had originally been selected and purchased for about 16,000 yen with a bank mortgage on the property.[53]

In 1920, after factory manager Yi Kanghyŏn's disastrous speculation in Osaka, the company suffered a major financial crisis. Over half of the paid-in capital had been lost in the Sampin. Construction of the new factory in Yŏngdŭngp'o had to be halted, and the machinery ordered from Nagoya could not be paid for. The company was virtually without operating funds. Once again, a bank loan was necessary. Using his father's land deeds as collateral, Kim Sŏngsu obtained an 80,000-yen loan from the Chōsen Industrial Bank.[54]

Even after the company was finally under way and producing cloth for the Korean market from 1923, lack of sufficient working capital continued to be a concern. The problem was not sales alone. Sales were difficult, especially at first, but the market was there. The company was discovering new markets in both Korea and Manchuria, and sales were finally beginning to bring in some income. With a little time and experience, Kyŏngbang could eventually hope to produce goods of a quality to rival the Japanese imports from Tōyōbō and at a competitive price.

But the company was caught in a kind of bind. It had to continue to increase its sales to pay costs, but it could only hope to sell more if it could produce more. Producing more meant more investment in facilities, raw materials, and labor, which, in turn, meant an ever-growing need for capital. Between 1923 and 1935 Kyŏngbang increased the number of its looms from 100 to nearly 900, and in 1931 it enlarged its factory to accommodate the new machinery. In 1919 the company employed about 40 workers.[55] By 1932 this figure had risen to 500.[56]

The money for this expansion came from bank loans. Throughout this period Kyŏngbang continued to have difficulty selling its shares to the public. The government subsidies were a blessing, of course, but they were meant only to keep the company afloat, not to finance growth. In 1929 the board of directors voted to take out a long-term (ten-year) loan for 250,000 yen from the Chōsen Industrial Bank to help pay for new construction and looms. By the autumn of 1931, the factory addition had been completed and the looms installed, but the public sale of shares with which the company had also expected to help finance the project had been very disappointing. In September of the following year the board therefore decided to take out yet another long-term loan from the Industrial Bank, this time for 500,000 yen.[57]

Dependence on the banks was thus growing even in the early years of the company's history, but it was not until after 1935 that

Kyŏngbang began to develop into a large-scale enterprise. This was the period that saw the company become a totally integrated textile firm, capable of transforming raw cotton through ginning, spinning, weaving, bleaching, dyeing, and stitching into completely finished products. It was also the period in which the company expanded its textile interests to include silk and hemp as well as cotton and began to move into nontextile areas as well. It was, of course, also during this period that Kyŏngbang established a huge Manchurian subsidiary, capitalized at ten million yen.

All of this activity required a large outlay of funds. The subsidies were discontinued in 1935, but Kyŏngbang's stock was now selling much better than before, and by 1945 the company's paid-in capital had reached 10,500,000 yen. By far the larger portion of funds for expansion, however, was supplied by the banks. Large, long-term loans were becoming a matter of regular policy. In March 1935, Kyŏngbang's directors approved a 1,000,000-yen loan from the Industrial Bank. Less than a year later, they voted for a 695,000-yen loan from the same bank to help finance the company's new spinning facilities. In 1937, the company took out yet another large loan, this time for 1,500,000 yen. This trend continued. By the end of May 1945, the long-term debt of the company had climbed to nearly 22,000,000 yen, twice the amount of total paid-in capital.[58]

Short-term loans to cover regular business activities also became more important and frequent over time, especially as Kyŏngbang became a more complex company with many affiliates, each with its own expanding volume of business. The demand for such short-term financing became particularly acute with the outbreak of the Sino-Japanese War in 1937 and later during the Pacific War, when the whole colonial economy went into high gear and Kyŏngbang and its affiliates became increasingly involved in producing goods for military use. The financing of the whole group of companies and foundations became extremely complicated and entangled as each unit—the Chungang Commercial and Industrial Company, the Tonggwang Silk Company, the Samyang Company, et cetera—borrowed from the banks and, in turn, borrowed and lent to each other in a dizzying display of internal financing that kept the accountants hopping on a daily basis.

Such bank loans were not always for small amounts, but tended to be quite large, running into millions of yen. This is not surprising, since they were subsequently lent out in smaller portions—16,000 yen, 30,000 yen, 40,000 yen, 93,000 yen, et cetera—to a whole host of affiliates. Bank loans were generally for a period of about sixty days, but in many cases they were repeatedly extended so that they became in effect long-term loans. Such extensions were necessary to cover the internal loans to affiliates, which ranged from periods of only six days to nearly one year.[59]

Over the years Kyŏngbang thus became more and more dependent on bank loans to maintain its increasingly complex business. By 1945 such loans had become the very lifeblood of the company. This fact in itself, however, tells us very little about the underlying dynamics of the company's involvement with the colonial political structure. To answer that question, we must look more closely at the various sources of the loans and the terms under which they were negotiated.

The Sources of the Loans

In prewar Japan much of the strength and power of the great business combines or *zaibatsu* came from their control of the country's banking and credit institutions.[60] In colonial Korea, however, it was the government that dominated the credit market through its ownership or supervision of the leading banks and financial organizations. It was thus more or less to the government that private companies like Kyŏngbang had to turn for their borrowed capital.

The two main government financial organs were the Bank of Chōsen and the Chōsen Industrial Bank. It was the latter that came to play a pivotal role in the colony's economic development because of its special function as the government's key financial organ for implementing official industrial policies. Beginning in 1918 with an authorized capital of twenty million yen, its main business as the successor to the old Bank of Agriculture and Industry was agricultural development. This was an activity in which it continued to be of major importance until 1945—not least through its close relationship with the Chōsen Federation of Financial Cooperatives (Chōsen Kin'yū Kumiai Rengōkai).[61]

As the Government-General's policies gradually shifted toward a more diversified economy, the Industrial Bank similarly branched out into a variety of other areas. By the 1940s, the Industrial Bank's paid-in capital was over fifty-two million yen—twelve million more than the Bank of Chōsen—and it was involved either through direct investment or indirectly (through its funding) in the whole gamut of Korea's commercial and industrial development, from silk cocoons to textiles and heavy industry. It was, in effect, a kind of *zaibatsu* itself. People at the time commonly spoke of such companies as the Seoul-

Ch'unch'ŏn Railway or the Han River Hydroelectric Company as belonging to the Industrial Bank Group (Shokuginkei) in the same way one would speak of Japanese companies belonging to Mitsui or Mitsubishi. In 1942 the Industrial Bank Group represented about 7.5 percent of Korea's total corporate capital. Its indirect control or influence over many other companies through its loans, however, would undoubtedly raise that figure considerably.[62]

The Industrial Bank was not a private company in the same sense as Mitsui or Mitsubishi, for it had been established by the Government-General for the express purpose of "serving as a financial instrument by which the government could carry out its plans for the industrial development of Korea." The government was to provide "support, protection, and special consideration" as well as "to exercise strict supervision" over the bank's management.[63] Like any other colonial official, the bank's president was also appointed by the Government-General.[64] Between 1919 and 1945 this post was held by two men, both of whom were civil servants who had moved up the ladder of the colonial bureaucracy. Hayashi Shigezō, for example, who succeeded Aruga Mitsutoyo as the bank's president in 1937, had passed the Higher Civil Service Examination in 1912 and been sent to Korea to work in the Government-General in 1914. After serving in a variety of posts, including as supervisor (*kanrikan*) of the Industrial Bank—an official liaison position between the bank and the government—he eventually became director of the Financial Affairs Bureau in the Government-General before taking over from Aruga in 1937.[65] The Government-General was also a major shareholder in the bank, even though the circumstances under which the bank operated obviated the need for direct ownership to secure government control.[66]

There were, to be sure, private banks owned and managed by Koreans throughout most of the colonial period. Some, like the Hansŏng Bank or the Tongil Bank, had been founded by Koreans before or shortly after the turn of the century, before annexation and the promulgation of the Company Law made the establishment of new Korean companies more difficult. Others like the Haedong Bank or the Honam Bank had been founded later, in the efflorescence of Korean business activity that followed the March First movement of 1919 and the subsequent abolition of the Company Law in 1920.[67] By 1933, there were seven such banks with branches throughout the country, together accounting for about 19 percent of the colony's deposits and nearly 16 percent of its loans.[68]

As individual banks, however, they were extremely weak compared with either the Bank of Chōsen or the Chōsen Industrial Bank. They competed for regular deposits not only with each other but also with the Industrial Bank and even with the Bank of Chōsen, which functioned as an ordinary as well as a central bank.[69] Their capital was extremely limited. The Tongil Bank, the largest of the seven, had only about 14 percent of the paid-in capital and less than 10 percent of the deposits of the Industrial Bank, and the latter could also easily raise additional capital when necessary by floating bonds in Japan.[70] There was no way the Korean banks could offer the kind of large, long-term financing for business expansion that was the Industrial Bank's specialty.

Given such circumstances, it is hardly surprising that from the very beginning Kyŏngbang looked to the Industrial Bank for financial assistance. It is impossible to give an exact figure or percentage, but the available documents leave no doubt whatsoever of Kyŏngbang's heavy and consistent use of the bank's services for all manner of financial transactions, including the sale of Kyŏngbang's corporate shares, the discounting of its promissory notes,[71] and above all for its loans, especially those loans most clearly associated with the company's development, such as the financing of new spinning and weaving facilities in the 1930s and the construction of its giant subsidiary in Manchuria in the 1940s.[72] The bank regarded its role in the company's expansion as one of its proudest accomplishments, and the Shokugin's official twenty-year history, published in 1938, devoted an entire page of photographs to Kyŏngbang as one of the bank's most successful industrial projects.[73]

The importance of the Industrial Bank in Kyŏngbang's development is even more striking when we recall that the company had a bank of its own. In 1927 Kim Yŏnsu had taken over the Haedong Bank in Seoul, which had been founded in 1920 by a group of Korean aristocrats, including Sin Ch'ŏlhun, Yun Tŏgyŏng, and Sim Sangik. Internal bickering among the directors and economic recession after the First World War had left the bank in an enfeebled condition, but by 1934 Kim had succeeded in turning the bank around and that year even opened a branch in Haeju.[74]

The bank was essentially a family-owned enterprise, with Kim Yŏnsu, his father, wife, and children holding the majority of shares,[75] and one might well have expected it to become a financial mainstay and springboard for the Kim brothers and their various enterprises, just as the Mitsui Bank was serving the Mitsui *zaibatsu*'s sprawling interests in Japan and around the world.[76] Certainly many Koreans at the time regarded the Kims' investment in banking as a step in that direction and were watching to see what would happen. In 1932, for example, *Samch'ŏlli*, one of the colony's most popular Korean-language magazines directed toward the growing Korean urban business and professional elite, featured an article on Korean banking that emphasized the role of banks in the development of two of Korea's most prominent business groups, including that of Kim Sŏngsu: "The Tongil and Haedong banks are worthy rivals in many respects.... Competition between these two banks may be seen as a struggle for supremacy between the forces of Min Yŏnghwi and Kim Sŏngsu, the peninsula's two *chaebŏl* magnates. Since the main power of these two *chaebŏl* is concentrated in their banks, there is unusual public interest in the respective fortune and standing [of these banks] in the future."[77]

It was not really true, however, that the Kims' financial power was concentrated in their bank, and, in any case, the Haedong Bank proved to be inadequate for Kyŏngbang's business activities. In 1933 its paid-in capital was only 800,000 yen, and its deposits were less than 2 percent of the deposits in the Chōsen Industrial Bank. Its total assets, in fact, amounted to only slightly more than 3,000,000 yen.[78] On the other hand, during the period in which Kim Yŏnsu was managing the Haedong Bank, Kyŏngbang was undergoing a major expansion and the Industrial Bank was supplying the company with millions of yen in long-term loans. As Kim Yongwan, a brother-in-law and business associate of the Koch'ang Kims during the colonial period,[79] told this writer in 1984: "Haedong was a small bank. It didn't have many customers and had only a small amount of deposits. So Kyŏngbang couldn't operate using only Haedong Bank. It was too small. So we inevitably did business with the Industrial Bank."[80]

Kyŏngbang did not even use the Haedong Bank extensively for more regular financial transactions, such as the discounting of the promissory notes it received from its customers. Between February and September of 1934, for example, just when the Haedong was showing signs of a bright future, it was only handling about 52 percent of Kyŏngbang's daily business. Most of the rest was being transacted through the Industrial Bank. By May 1936, well over 90 percent of the company's regular business was being entrusted to the Industrial Bank.[81] Shortage of capital continued to be a major problem at the Haedong, and the high hopes that Kim Yŏnsu had had for the bank in 1927 had vanished by the late 1930s. The bank had become instead a virtual white elephant, and it was with pleasure and relief that Kim relinquished it to the Hansŏng Bank in 1938.[82]

The Chōsen Industrial Bank was thus Kyŏngbang's main source of capital as well as its chief financial agent during the company's rapid expansion in the 1930s and 1940s. Indeed, as we have seen, the company had been involved with the Industrial Bank from the beginning, at least as early as 1920, when Kim Sŏngsu obtained an 80,000-yen loan to help cover Yi Kanghyŏn's loss of company funds in Osaka.

The question remains, however, as to the terms of the numerous loans that the company had taken out from the Industrial Bank. For it is only in looking at the various interest rates that the company was paying over the years that we can grasp the real significance of the loans. The history of Kyŏngbang's loans was, in a larger sense, the history of the company's increasing integration into the colonial political structure. In general, the early years may be regarded as a trial and adjustment period, during which the company gradually cemented its relationship with the banks and colonial authorities. By the mid-1930s Kyŏngbang had become an accepted and active participant in the colonial economy. This change was reflected in the interest rates the company was charged for its loans.

The Terms of the Loans

Authoritative information on the early loans is scant at best. Unfortunately for the historian, the ravages of time and war have done their damage, and, apart from the information already cited, there seems to be little detailed record of the company's loans before the 1930s. In the minutes of a board meeting held in September 1924, however, we catch a glimpse of the prohibitive cost of loans for Kyŏngbang in the 1920s. As noted above, the company had originally purchased land in Noryangjin for its new factory but later decided to build in Yŏngdŭngp'o instead. The land had been very expensive—nearly 16,000 yen (about 1 yen per *p'yŏng*)—and by 1924, paying off the bank mortgage on it had become a drain on the company's finances. Yi Kanghyŏn informed the board that he knew of someone willing to buy the land for about 14,500 yen and recommended that they sell it, even at a loss. The board agreed.[83]

The reason the company was so anxious to get rid of the land as quickly as possible, even at a net loss of about 1,500 yen, was because of the high interest it was having to pay on the mortgage. As Yi pointed out, the income from the land was only about 700 yen per year. The interest on the mortgage, however, was close to three times that amount or about 12 percent per year.[84] The minutes do not tell us exactly which bank was involved, but one may speculate that it might well have been the Chōsen Industrial Bank, for the mortgage was fixed at just about the same time that Kim Sŏngsu had taken out a loan from the Chōsen Industrial Bank to extricate Kyŏngbang from the Sampin crisis. In any case, the Industrial Bank was the colony's most active investment bank, and one may reasonably assume that other banks followed a similar interest policy. In 1919, the Industrial Bank interest rates ranged between 7 and 12 percent, depending on the customer.[85] Thus at 12 percent Kyŏngbang was paying the maximum for its mortgage. It is not surprising that the board quickly agreed to dispose of the land—even at a loss—as soon as it had found a buyer.

By the latter half of the 1930s, perhaps even earlier, Kyŏngbang's position in regard to interest rates had changed dramatically. This was due at least in part to a new low interest policy in effect in both Japan and Korea from 1932 on. Interest rates in Korea, moreover, as reflected in the Chōsen Industrial Bank, had been steadily declining since the 1920s, from a peak of 13 percent in 1921 to slightly under 7 percent in 1937.[86]

Even given the reduced rates, however, there was still plenty of room for special consideration to favored customers. The rates cited were for the Industrial Bank's high-interest loans. The bank had a different policy for "special low-interest loans" (*tokubetsu teiri kashitsuke*). In 1937, for example, the interest on such special loans ranged from about 5.0 to 6.8 percent.[87] In addition, the bank could of course lessen the burden for privileged clients even further by agreeing to a comfortably long repayment period and also by permitting a grace period of one or more years before any interest payments on the principal were due.

How then was Kyŏngbang treated by its main banker in the 1930s and 1940s? Here we are fortunate in having more documents from which to piece together the story, and they all show conclusively that the company was indeed a "special" customer of the Industrial Bank.

We note from the company's extant expense records, for example, that between May 1938 and May 1939, it was paying a regular monthly interest of 6,875 yen on a loan from the Industrial Bank. We also note on subsequent ledgers that by the end of 1939, the payments had been reduced to 6,690.46 yen, and by the summer of 1940, reduced again to 6,500.86 yen.[88] Although the expense ledgers do not specify when the loan was taken out, the amount of the principal, or the exact terms of repayment and interest, this information is in a 1944–45 ledger, in which many of Kyŏngbang's outstanding loans at that time are recorded in more detail. For the loan in question there is even a complete repayment schedule of both principal and interest covering the entire period of the loan, along with all the pertinent terms and conditions.

From this document we learn that the loan was for 1.5 million yen and was originally taken out from the Industrial Bank on June 13, 1937.[89] The loan ledger makes no mention of the use to which the loan was put, and there is also no reference to it in the minutes of any of the company board meetings around this time. It was just about this time, however, that Kyŏngbang was adding 4,000 spindles to its new spinning factory and setting up a cotton ginning mill in Hwanghae Province, so we may hazard a guess that the money may have gone to pay for these new facilities.[90]

The terms of the loan were excellent, well within the category of special low-interest loans that the Industrial Bank provided for its best customers. The interest rate was fixed at 5.5 percent per year, and the principal was to be repaid over thirteen years. The bank also gave Kyŏngbang an added benefit in the form of a two and one-half year grace period, so the first semiannual payment of principal and interest was not due until December 1939.[91]

Even short-term loans from the Industrial Bank were granted to Kyŏngbang with favorable conditions. Most were originally taken out for a period of about two months, but extensions were routine, and the loans became, in effect, a kind of tacit long-term financing. Interest on these loans was computed according to a daily rate, which tended in the early 1940s to be about 1.4 sen per hundred yen.[92] This was a good rate: the bank's average daily charge per hundred yen on short-term loans in 1941, for example, was 1.7 sen.[93] The rates were so good that Kyŏngbang could not match them in its internal loan transactions with its own affiliates. Whenever it borrowed from an affiliate like Samyang or loaned to another like the Tonggwang Silk Company, it consistently paid or charged a slightly higher rate of interest than it was paying to the Industrial Bank.[94]

The Loans in Perspective

Why was Kyŏngbang given such preferential financing by the Industrial Bank? One factor, which I shall discuss in detail in chapter 4, was that the loans were for projects strongly encouraged by the government. There were other reasons, however, which had to do with the commitment of the bank itself to Japanese-Korean cooperative development in general and to Kyŏngbang in particular.

First, we must recall that there had been a major shift in Japanese colonial policy with the accession of Governor-General Saitō in 1919. For political reasons, as well as for the sake of a more efficient development of the economy, the colonial authorities after 1919 were anxious to cultivate a Korean business elite whose class interests would be in harmony with Japanese imperial goals. Financing for Korean companies was a critical aspect of the problem that needed to be worked out. Korean businessmen who participated in the Government-General's industrial commission of 1921 had complained that the banks had discriminated against them in the past and presented a petition calling upon the Japanese to facilitate the financing of Korean companies.[95]

The change did not come overnight. As we have seen, Kyŏngbang was being charged a very high rate of interest for a mortgage in 1924. On the other hand, financing was now easier for those Koreans who could afford it, and the Japanese were slowly and cautiously admitting Koreans into the higher echelons of the colonial economy.

The Chōsen Industrial Bank played a key role in this process. It is hardly an accident that Kim Sŏngsu turned to the Industrial Bank for help in 1920 when the company was in danger of failing. It was not simply that the Shokugin was the colony's most active investment bank. The close relationship that was forged between the bank and Kyŏngbang had much to do with the general policy of the bank itself toward Koreans, and this, in turn, was a reflection of the change in colonial policy and the attitude of the new bank president, Aruga Mitsutoyo.

Aruga, who had a crucial role in implementing the Government-General's new policy of cooperative development, began his career in Korea as a government bureaucrat in the Tax Supervising Office during the protectorate, rose to the head of the Customs Office, and later became chief of the Finance Section of the Bureau of Financial Affairs of the Government-General. In 1918 he left official government service and joined the newly organized Industrial Bank as a director. The following year he was selected by the Government-General to succeed Mishima Tarō, the bank's president, who had died suddenly. For the next seventeen years Aruga presided over the bank's affairs, and even after his retirement, he continued to take an active part in Korea's development. Both during and after his tenure as bank president he was a towering figure in the colonial economy, commonly regarded as the "founding father" of the Korean business world.[96] A 1940 biographical sketch in a popular Korean-Manchurian business encyclopedia gives us some idea of Aruga's immense prestige among his contemporaries:

> It is well known that Mr. Aruga's contributions to the [shaping] of the Korean financial world of today are beyond measure. . . . In 1936, his goals achieved and his fame secure, he relinquished the presidency of the Chōsen Industrial Bank to a younger man and returned to Japan. But his legacy of accomplishments as the founding father (*umi no oya*) of the peninsula's business world, which has recently experienced a surge of growth, has again forced him to take part in the Korean business world.[97]

In this powerful colonial bureaucrat and financier Korean businessmen had a friend. Like his colleagues in the Government-General, he was, to be sure, an imperialist. His interest was not in helping Koreans per se but in developing the economy as he was appointed to do. At the same time, however, he was a true believer in the efficacy of Japanese-Korean economic cooperation. As Kim Yongwan said of him in an interview:

> As president of the Industrial Bank, Aruga's purpose was to develop the Korean economy, so ultimately he had to encourage economic activity among Koreans. . . . That was his philosophy. He believed that the economy could be developed quickly only if Koreans and Japanese worked together. . . . Moreover, Aruga believed that even though Korea was a colony, it was more in Japan's interest to treat Koreans equally and develop the country together rather than rely on oppressive controls. That was his way of thinking.[98]

As Kim pointed out, Aruga was aware of the value to Japan of "treating Koreans equally," and in his position as head of the government's most important financial organ of economic development, he tried to put this policy into practice. First of all, he attempted to reduce discrimination between Korean and Japanese employees within the bank itself in regard to salaries, expense accounts, and promotions. According to Kim Yongwan:

> At that time there was a lot of discrimination against Koreans. . . . Salaries, for example. If Japanese were given 100 yen, Koreans were given only 60 yen. This was true in all the government offices as well. Aruga did away with all this. It didn't matter whether one was Korean or Japanese—each received 100 yen. The same was true for business traveling expenses, lodging, and so

forth. In the government, Japanese were allowed larger expense accounts. Aruga made them equal, raising the Korean expense accounts to the Japanese level.[99]

The same policy was gradually applied to Korean businessmen who required the services of the bank, especially loans. In 1934, for example, Aruga personally approved a large loan to Pak Hŭngsik, who needed the money to finance a chain of department stores throughout the country. As for Aruga's relationship with Kyŏngbang—even before he came to know any of the Kims personally, Aruga was well versed in the family's background and financial standing through a study of Korean property undertaken by the Industrial Bank. From the beginning, therefore, he was disposed to regard Kyŏngbang as a sound investment, and, in the words of Kim Yongwan, "he helped us just as if we were a Japanese company."[100]

The bank policy initiated by Aruga Mitsutoyo was a key factor in Kyŏngbang's ability to obtain financing. In a sense, it opened the door to everything else that was to follow. Again, however, one must stress that the process was gradual. In the 1920s, with the change in colonial policy and with Aruga's personal attitude, the company was able to get its foot in the door of the colonial economy and to keep pushing. By 1945, the door was wide open, and Kyŏngbang was firmly inside. Between these two periods lay a span of about twenty-five years, during which Kyŏngbang became ever more integrated into the existing political and economic structure. Here, in this increasingly intricate net of personal and corporate connections that eventually came to constitute the colonial political economy in 1945, it is possible to find a second element in the company's success in securing bank loans: by 1945 Kyŏngbang had virtually become a member of that group of banks and companies that together comprised the so-called Kingdom of the Industrial Bank (Shokugin Ōkoku).[101]

We must begin here by putting the relationship between Kyŏngbang and the bank into its proper context. To understand the incestuous tangle of people and companies that lies at the heart of the relationship, we must remember that we are dealing with a time and place where the very concept of "antitrust" was foreign and impractical. In threading their way through the labyrinth of documents confiscated from the *zaibatsu* in 1945, American occupation authorities noted with great understatement that "the concept that interlocking directorates or intercorporate stockholdings may be potentially dangerous is foreign to Japanese thought."[102] It was equally foreign to the thought of Japanese colonialists in Korea and to the Koreans who cooperated with them. We would be well advised to keep in mind the image of "one trust" that Japan evoked for General Secretary Pearse of the International Federation of Master Cotton Spinners and Manufacturers Associations in 1929.[103] For colonial Korea, where the power of the state was even greater than in Japan, such a metaphor was all the more apropos.

In attempting to describe the many personal and corporate threads that linked Kyŏngbang to the Industrial Bank and vice versa, it is difficult to know where to begin. What is certain, however, is that a connection between the two existed from the very start in the person of Pak Yŏnghyo (1861–1939), and it is perhaps best to begin our discussion with a fresh look at this famous figure of modern Korean history.

Pak is best known for his role as one of the leaders of the abortive Kapsin Coup of 1884, which attempted to reform the traditional Korean state along lines inspired by the model of Meiji Japan. After the failure of the coup, he escaped to Japan, returning again in 1894 to serve briefly in the new Kabo reform cabinet established under Japanese tutelage. In 1895, when the Japanese decided to abandon their support of the reforms in the wake of foreign pressure, especially from Russia, Pak again fled to Japan. After the Russo-Japanese War had placed Korea firmly within the Japanese orbit, he returned again to his homeland, where he served as a royal minister in the cabinet of Yi Wanyong. With Japan's annexation of the peninsula in 1910, Pak, who had married into the Korean royal family, was given a marquisate and became a member of the Japanese House of Peers.[104]

And so the story of Pak Yŏnghyo ends in most Korean history books. In fact, however, Pak was only forty-eight years old in 1910, and he continued to live an active life in Korea for nearly thirty more years, until his death in 1939. For much of that time, between 1919 and 1935, he was Kyŏngbang's first president.

Pak was a perfect choice to head the new company in 1919. First of all, there was his indirect affinity with the Kim family. Like the Kims, Pak's geographical and familial roots lay in the Chŏlla provinces,[105] and one can imagine Kim Sŏngsu—or, more likely, his father—reminding Pak of common Honam ties and affections in persuading Pak to assume the company presidency. Moreover, as noted in chapter 2, from early on the Kim family had been strongly influenced by and sympathetic to the ideals of national development put forward by the Kaehwa or "Enlightenment" party, in which Pak had been a key figure.

More important to the company's existence and growth, however, was Pak's status within the imperial social and political structure. In 1919 Kim Sŏngsu was a mere twenty-eight years old, hardly an age to inspire respect in a society where "seniors" ruled while "juniors" listened and obeyed. He was only about four years out of college and his career was still ahead of him. Pak, on the other hand, already had a long and well-known personal history as a major political figure who had been willing at least on occasion to cooperate with the Japanese. Such political considerations were uppermost in the minds of the Kyŏngbang shareholders who selected Pak as company president. As the official Kyŏngbang history notes:

The company's first president, Pak Yŏnghyo, was an important statesman of the late Chosŏn dynasty. Although he never invested in the company, he continued to hold the company presidency until 1935 because of his great help during this period in resolving any difficulties with regard to government permits and company operations. The reason for keeping such a person in the presidency for so long—someone who neither attended meetings of the board of directors nor intervened in the operation of the company—was to mitigate the various regulations of the colonial government authorities.[106]

Pak could do more, however, than "mitigate government regulations." Even before he became Kyŏngbang's president in 1919, he was already closely associated with the Chōsen Industrial Bank. Cho Kijun, in his well-known history of Korean capitalism, has written that "from the beginning the Chōsen Industrial Bank thoroughly excluded Koreans from participation in its management."[107] This is not true. Along with Aruga Mitsutoyo, who joined the bank at its inception in 1918 and very shortly thereafter became the bank's president, Pak was an original member of the bank's board of directors. Like Aruga, he was appointed to the board on October 1, 1918, and he remained in that capacity after Aruga had become bank president until the end of 1930. Even after his official retirement from the board, he continued to play a role in the bank's affairs as an adviser (komon) until his death in 1939.[108]

We have no evidence linking Pak to any specific Kyŏngbang loan from the Industrial Bank, but his close association with the bank from its foundation in 1918 and, indeed, throughout his tenure as Kyŏngbang president, certainly did not adversely affect the company's relationship with the bank. On the contrary, given the company's success in even its early years in obtaining loans from the bank, one suspects that Pak's seat on the bank's board was very useful indeed. Given his age and status, Pak was in a position to deal with top bank officials, including Aruga himself (who was twelve years younger and not given a peerage until 1934), on a relatively equal basis.[109] Kyŏngbang, in any case, did not have any doubts about Pak's utility. He was kept on as president for sixteen years.

By the 1930s, however, the Kim brothers—and especially Yŏnsu— were well on their way to becoming notables of the colonial business world in their own right, and they were no longer so much in need of distinguished surrogates to help them in their dealings with the colonial authorities and the banks. Kim Yŏnsu himself now participated directly in the Industrial Bank's myriad financial activities. Along with other prominent Korean businessmen, including Han Sangnyong, Pak Yŏngch'ŏl, and Min Taesik, he was involved (as an auditor) in the Chōsen Trust Company, a major subsidiary of the Industrial Bank. He also held an auditorship in the Chōsen Savings Bank,[110] another Industrial Bank affiliate, that in 1943 owned the largest block of Industrial Bank shares.[111] In addition, he was a trustee of the Chōsen Industrial Promotion Foundation, which had been set up by the bank in commemoration of its tenth anniversary in 1928 to provide financial support for commendations, leadership, and programs in connection with the increase and improvement of Korean products.[112]

Kim Yŏnsu's position in such companies was a reflection of the increasingly comfortable relationship that was developing between Kyŏngbang and the Industrial Bank. Consider, for example, the situation in regard to bank and company shares. In the name of various mutual aid organizations such as the Friends of Kyŏngbang, the Friends of Chungang Commercial and Industrial Company, or, later, the Samyang Foundation—all controlled by Kim Yŏnsu—the company held blocks of stock in a wide assortment of colonial enterprises. Included among such foundation property were shares in both the Industrial Bank proper and its major financial subsidiary, the Chōsen Savings Bank.[113] In turn, the Industrial Bank and its various affiliates and foundations—Chōsen Trust, Chōsen Savings, Friends of Chōsen Savings—together held about 6.4 percent of Kyŏngbang's total stock by the end of the colonial period.[114] This was the largest single block of shares in the company apart from that held by the Kim family itself. Not surprisingly, Kim appointed one of the bank's most trusted officials, Nakatomi Keita (himself a shareholder in the company), to serve as an auditor of the company from the end of 1939 to August 1945.[115]

Nakatomi's overlapping role as Kyŏngbang stockholder and career employee of the Industrial Bank was by no means unique. A closer look at the company's Japanese stockholders shows that many of them were in one way or another associated the the Industrial Bank. Their names are now, of course, all long forgotten and not to be found in any of the history books. At the time, however, they were among the most well-known and influential men in Korea's banking circles. Shiraishi Jinkichi, Tanegashima Shigeru, Terada Kazuichi, and Hayashi Yutaka, for example, were managers of some of the bank's most important provincial branches in (respectively) Pusan, Taegu, Wŏnju, and Sinŭiju.[116]

Other bank officials who held Kyŏngbang stock were men like Nakatomi, who worked in the main office in Seoul, often presiding over the bank's key financing divisions such as the Commercial Finance Section or the Industrial Finance Section, through which Kyŏngbang contracted many of its bank loans.[117] Some, like Watanabe Toyohiko, were officials of the Government-General whose work brought them into contact with the bank. Watanabe, for example, was concurrently a director in the Government-General's Chōsen Forestry Development Company and, along with Kim Yŏnsu, a trustee in the bank's Chōsen Industrial Promotion Foundation.[118]

The extent to which Kyŏngbang was considered part of the bank's charmed circle of favored companies is further illustrated by the high rank of the company's stockholders at the Industrial Bank. Provincial branch managers and head office section chiefs were, in fact, among the lowest-ranking bank officials on the company's list of shareholders. Above them were a number of present and former members of the bank's board of directors. Noda Shingo, for example, rose up through the bank's hierarchy of branch managerships to the main office, where he headed a number of key sections, including the commercial and industrial financing sections. He went on to represent the bank at its most important branch office in Osaka, afterwards returning to Korea to join the bank's board of directors in 1934. He later became president of the Hansŏng Bank after its merger with the Haedong. Like many of the bank's highest officials, he also served as a trustee of the bank's Chōsen Industrial Promotion Foundation.[119]

Another Kyŏngbang stockholder was Hayashi Shigeki. Before joining the bank he had been a civil servant in the Government-General.

He began his career in Korea by working his way through various sections in the Bureau of Financial Affairs, the Monopoly Bureau, and the Railway Bureau. In 1929 he moved into provincial government, becoming governor of North Chŏlla, the home province of the Kim family. Later that same year he was appointed governor of North Kyŏngsang and afterward returned to Seoul, where he served as the head of the Government-General's Education Bureau. In 1933 he moved over to the bank, beginning his career there at the top, as a member of the board of directors. In 1937 he served briefly as president of the Hansŏng Bank, where he was instrumental in effecting the merger with the Haedong Bank owned by Kim Yŏnsu. He later went on to serve as executive director of the Han River Hydroelectric Power Company and as president of the Seoul-Ch'unch'ŏn Railroad, two of the Industrial Bank's large affiliates.[120]

Last, but far from least, were Imori Meiji and Hayashi Shigezō. Imori had originally been with the old Bank of Agriculture and Industry before it was superseded by the Industrial Bank in 1918. He stayed with the new bank, where he held a number of important posts, including manager of the bank's branches in Mokp'o and P'yŏngyang. He then moved into the head office, where he was put in charge first of the Commercial Finance Section and later of the Industrial Finance Section. In 1930 he was given a bank directorship. His crowning achievement came in 1934, when he was appointed president of the Chōsen Savings Bank, the Industrial's most important bank affiliate, which controlled the single largest block of shares in the Industrial Bank itself. He continued to hold this position for over ten years, until the end of the colonial period.[121]

If any further proof were needed of close personal connections between Kyŏngbang and the Industrial Bank, the name of Hayashi Shigezō would fulfill that purpose admirably. With 1,200 shares, Hayashi was one of Kyŏngbang's biggest individual Japanese investors. His real importance to Kyŏngbang, however, lay elsewhere. As Aruga Mitsutoyo's successor, he was also the *tōdori* or president of the Industrial Bank, its highest official. Like many Industrial Bank officers, he had had his early training in the Bureau of Financial Affairs of the Government-General, rising to the top of the bureau's hierarchy before being appointed to succeed Aruga in 1937. He remained head of the bank until the colony came to an end in 1945, and it was during his tenure as bank president that the relationship between Kyŏngbang and the Industrial was to blossom into full maturity, producing so many of the special low-interest loans mentioned earlier.[122]

It was also during Hayashi's tenure as *tōdori*, moreover, that the company became more and more of an integral part of the Industrial Bank's financial "kingdom," not only feeding off its generous mother lode of financial resources, but taking an increasingly active role as a junior partner in a number of the bank's affiliated business enterprises. Again using the Samyang Foundation as a vehicle for channeling company funds into other investments, Kim Yŏnsu acquired thousands of shares in at least three of the Industrial Bank's major industrial subsidiaries: the Chōsen Smelting Company, which was capitalized at ten million yen and owned a total of thirteen private gold and silver mines in Korea and Japan (eleven in Korea); the Seoul-Ch'unch'ŏn Railroad, also capitalized at ten million yen and run by Hayashi Shigeki, the former Industrial Bank director and Kyŏngbang shareholder; and the Han River Hydroelectric Company, a huge corporation with an authorized capital of twenty-five million yen, whose president was none other than Aruga Mitsutoyo, still busy with the bank's business even after his formal retirement in 1936.[123] Kyŏngbang also invested directly in the enormous Chōsen Aircraft Company (capitalized at fifty million yen in 1944),[124] in which the Industrial Bank may also have been involved.[125]

In view of all this, it does not seem entirely inappropriate to characterize Kyŏngbang in its full colonial flowering as a company whose personal and corporate connections placed it comfortably within the orbit of the Chōsen Industrial Bank. It was, in effect, part of the great "trust" that constituted the bank's "kingdom," less formally connected than other members of the group, perhaps, but a member nevertheless. One can hardly doubt that such membership was an advantage in obtaining soft loans.

In placing Kyŏngbang within the kingdom of the Industrial Bank, moreover, we find that we have also placed the company securely within the bosom of the state itself, for, as we noted earlier, the Industrial Bank was the Government-General's main financial organ for funding its colonial development programs. Kyŏngbang's relationship with the bank represented a considerable development of the government-business relationship beyond the straightforward pattern of subsidization seen in the 1920s and early 1930s. Through the bank the relationship had expanded by 1945 into a tangle of personal and corporate interests that had turned Kyŏngbang for all practical purposes into a quasi-governmental company, privately owned, to be sure, but with a financial structure intimately and intricately linked to the state.

CHAPTER 4

Class and State

Partners in Management

The blurring of public and private spheres that we have found in Kyŏngbang's financial structure may also be seen in the actual management of the company. Even though Kyŏngbang was managed on a mundane level in the office and factory by its own board of directors, corporate policy in a wider sense was determined at the top of the colonial bureaucratic structure through the formulation of official industrial policies. In that sense, corporate policy was largely an extension of official industrial policy into the private sector, and one may say that the Government-General was the ultimate manager of Kyŏngbang and all other private colonial firms.

As with financing, however, subordination to the state in corporate management was subtle and complex. The establishment of official policy was by no means a simple, unilateral affair. Nor did the rewards of official policy accrue to the Government-General alone. Various kinds of formal and informal interaction between the state and private enterprise characterized the process of policy making, and the policies so determined were in the end beneficial to both parties. Kyŏngbang, for example, discovered that serving the state could be very profitable.

The Making and Implementation of Policy

Industrial commissions — *iinkai* or *chōsakai* — convoked by the governor-general were the most formal and infrequent form of collaborative policy making between government and business. They were, however, extremely important, not only because they constituted industrial policy making at the very highest level, but also because they established the broad framework in which colonial development would take place over the next several years or even the next decade. In that sense at least, they were similar to meetings held today in developing countries to devise long-term economic strategy in the form, for example, of the so-called five-year plans regularly announced by the government in South Korea. The colonial conferences were not held on a regular basis, but were special commissions designed to restructure colonial policy in accordance with significant new domestic and / or international conditions.

Between 1910 and 1945 three such conferences were held. The first was in 1921, in the wake of the March First movement and the economic readjustment following World War I. The second was convened fifteen years later in 1936 to reassess Korea's role vis-à-vis the new state of Manchukuo in the light of the growing international trade war and unstable situation in China. The third was held in 1938 to bring Korea fully in line with the intensive Japanese military mobilization under way. Thus, although held in Seoul under the leadership and sponsorship of the Government-General and concerned primarily with specific Korean problems, the conferences were at the same time imperial assemblies, providing a forum for discussion and formulation of Korea's economic position and role within the Japanese Empire. In keeping with this spirit, delegates from Korea were joined by participants from all over the imperium.[1]

Prominent Koreans from various walks of life, including Korean businessmen, participated in all three conferences. In 1921 the Koreans' position was still insecure. The policy of the new Saitō regime supporting the limited growth of a Korean bourgeoisie was still being formulated, and Korean entrepreneurs were unsure as to where exactly they stood with the Government-General.

This uncertainty was reflected in their petitions and discussion, both of which were centered on the demand for a fair share in the proposed economic growth. Both Kim Sŏngsu and Kim Yŏnsu were, of course, still too young and undistinguished to be invited to the first conference, but one of the Korean petitions presented there calling upon the Government-General for support and protection had been drafted by the Congress of Korean Industry (Chosŏnin Sanŏp Taehoe), a Korean group organized by Kyŏngbang's nominal president Pak Yŏnghyo.[2]

By the time of the second and third conferences, the Koreans had become a more integral part of the economic system. If there was any tokenism in the Japanese decision to invite Koreans to the first conference in 1921, it had greatly diminished by 1936 and 1938. At the second conference, in 1936, Kim Yŏnsu bluntly criticized what he considered exorbitant Manchurian tariffs and the proposed policy of government economic controls—sentiments shared and echoed by all the Japanese spinners on the peninsula.[3] He was speaking less as a Korean than as president of one of the colony's major textile firms. In 1938, Kim was invited again, not only as the head of Kyŏngbang, but as chairman of the Chōsen Spinners Association, that is, as the chief representative of the peninsula's cotton textile manufacturing industry.[4]

The development programs produced by such conferences were comprehensive, touching on virtually all aspects of political economy — on agriculture, commerce, and industry, to be sure, but also on problems of labor, education, and ideology. Considering their lengthy agenda, it is not surprising that the conferences lasted for several days. They were opened with welcoming and exhortative speeches to a general assembly of delegates by colonial officials, including the governor-general and the vice-governor-general, who acted as the chairman of the conference. These were followed by a brief general session of free discussion, after which the delegates were divided into separate committees to consider specific areas and problems in detail. On the last day of the conference all delegates reassembled for a final general session and closing speeches.

The combination of both larger and smaller sessions allowed businessmen to comment not only on subjects about which they were particularly concerned but also on all the major issues of colonial economic development. In 1936, for example, Kim Yŏnsu attended the general sessions and also participated in the "Raw Materials and Industry" committee. This group considered, in addition to textiles, such industrial areas as metal refining, gold mining, shipbuilding, aircraft, machine tools, and coal liquefaction, as well as questions related to the problem of economic controls and labor policy.[5] Each committee was provided by the Government-General with detailed studies, reports, and statistics related to the particular discussion topics, and in each case the Government-General's highest-ranking bureaucrat answered any questions that might arise in the course of discussion. Businessmen were thus given more or less full access to the economic data of the colonial administration and urged to speak their minds.

We must not forget, however, who was really in charge. It is well to keep in mind General Koiso's comment that "once a policy of State has been decided upon, it is our duty to bend all our efforts for the prosecution of such [a] policy."[6] In retrospect, it now seems clear that by the time the Seoul conferences were held, the basic policy had already been more or less "decided upon" by the Government-General. Delegates were presented with a complete draft proposal by the Government-General that became the basis for their discussions. They were, of course, theoretically free to make any changes they wanted by proposing and voting on amendments,[7] but such alterations as they did make usually amounted to little substantive change in the basic government draft. In general, the drafts were left largely intact, and businessmen confined themselves to questions about what all the rather obfuscatory government language really meant and how it was going to be translated into action. Even when the businessmen were clearly opposed to certain major policies in the draft, as in 1936 when one after another — Kim Yŏnsu included — bewailed the projected imposition of government controls on production, in the end they tended to resign themselves to the basic outline of state policy as it had been set before them.

The importance of the conferences, nevertheless, should not be underestimated. They did provide a role, however minor, for the business community in the highest echelon of the formal policy-making process. Even if policies were not always to their liking, businessmen could feel that they were part of the colonial "family," with privileged access to the power structure and a voice that would be heard by the proper officials, including the governor-general himself. While they may have fallen short of the perfect harmony envisioned in *Kokutai no hongi,* the conferences at their best were impressive displays of *musubi* in action, helping to establish a bonhomie and sense of cooperation between government and business leaders that facilitated the implementation of specific policies later.

Formal conferences were not the only kind of cooperative policy making. Far more common were small, informal sessions between business leaders from a particular company or industry and the responsible government officials. At least eight months before the commission of 1936, for example, Kim Yŏnsu and other colonial textile manufacturers were holding round-table meetings with Government-General bureaucrats on the "control of the cotton spinning industry in Korea, as well as the maintenance of harmony with the industry in Japan."[8]

Policy making, moreover, continued in informal fashion long after the industrial commissions had formally drawn up their development programs. In the final reports of the commissions only the broad, general direction of policy was set forth, leaving the timing and specific methods of implementation largely to the discretion of the Government-General. In this ongoing process of policy formulation and implementation, the colonial bureaucracy was careful once again to include the business community. The necessity of consultation with the business leaders was explicitly recognized in the industrial commission's report of 1936. With regard to the question of industrial controls, the report enjoined the Government-General "to take into consideration all the various Korean domestic conditions . . . and the interests of Korea's domestic producers and consumers."[9]

Before the late 1930s the government interfered relatively little with market forces or in the concrete implementation of official policy at the company or factory level. In that respect, one can agree with Cho Kijun's characterization of Kyŏngbang as an essentially private, Korean-managed company. Company officials were free to purchase raw materials, set production goals, expand facilities, and distribute their goods themselves in accordance with the market's demand — within, of course, the broad framework of policy devised by the Government-General.

From the late 1930s, however, the exigencies of wartime mobilization took precedence over everything else, and the economy was gradually subjected to a wide range of government controls, most of which were adaptations of controls also in effect in Japan. Through a combination of successive imperial decrees (*chokumei*), as well as colonial ordinances (*furei*) and notices (*fukokuji*), Korea was gradually converted into something more closely resembling the "bureaucratic command economy" mentioned earlier.[10] Economic journals at the time spoke of a "reconstitution" (*saihensei*) of the colonial economy from a capitalistic system to a "bureaucratically controlled industrial structure," in which military priorities set by the government determined virtually all aspects of the production process.[11]

Wartime Controls

The controls put into effect were extensive. Industrial raw materials were rationed, with priority being given to war production. Those that had to be imported — such as Indian and American cotton — were carefully controlled through a licensing system, not only to insure sufficient and appropriate quantities for both military and civilian use, but also to regulate the outflow of precious foreign exchange, so vital to the empire for its purchase of basic war materials from abroad. Further, exports were subjected to a licensing system to control and coordinate trade within the empire and also to promote trade with countries outside the Yen Bloc to garner more foreign exchange. Capital was mobilized for wartime purposes and financing strictly controlled to channel investment into strategic industries. Restrictions were placed on the expansion of facilities as part of this effort and also to coordinate the overall wartime production process. Eventually a rationing system with prices set by the government was extended over the entire range of company management, from the purchase of raw materials down to even the lowest levels of distribution of manufactured products. An "economic police force" (*keizai keisatsu*) was also set up within the Bureau of Police to make sure all the various controls were enforced.

The way in which the new, "reconstituted" system worked was through a network of cartels and subcartels established by the Government-General as a result of the industrial commission of 1936. Through these organizations (usually called *rengōkai* or *kumiai*) the Government-General brought all the companies within a particular industry or trade into a single association. For example, the entire textile industry — embracing the whole range of textile products and processes — was eventually brought under a single amalgamated control organization, the Chōsen Textile Industry Association (Chōsen Sen'i Sangyōkai).[12]

The ostensible reason for the establishment of such cartels was to benefit small and medium enterprises through a cooperative pooling of resources and facilities with the bigger companies.[13] The result was the same as in Japan itself: the absorption and control of the smaller firms by the larger. Oligopolization of the economy actually made for a more efficient utilization of scant resources and also made overall control of the industrial structure by the Government-General more effective. Not surprisingly, the government, as in Japan, actively promoted company mergers through "business reorganization" to enhance the coherence and strength of the system as a whole. It was as a result of such measures that Kyŏngbang in 1944 expanded its operations to include the manufacture of silk products through the absorption of the Tonggwang Silk Company.[14]

The Government-General ran the economy by issuing directives to the various control organizations, generally on a monthly or semiannual basis. As noted above, the official penetration of the production process was deep — generating, one suspects, enough red tape to satisfy the most dedicated of bureaucrats. Consider, if you will, the government's role in the cotton textile industry in 1943, from the allocation of raw (seed) cotton to the distribution of finished cotton cloth.[15] In the allocation of raw cotton grown in Korea, production quotas and other instructions (such as the amount of staple fiber to be mixed with pure cotton in yarn production) were sent out to the Chōsen Spinners Association (Chōsen Bōseki Kōgyō Kumiai), which in turn would decide the production quota for each of its member companies. Before the Spinners Association could obtain the necessary raw cotton, however, the government also had to issue a directive to the Chōsen Cotton Association (Chōsen Menka Dōgyō Kumiai), which, in turn, also had to hand down quotas to its own member companies.

Once the cotton had been spun into yarn, it was sold to the main wholesalers' control association at prices set by the government. The main wholesalers' control association then distributed the yarn to its members, who resold the goods—again with a profit margin fixed by the government—to the control association of the middle wholesalers. This group distributed the yarn once again among its members, and they, in turn, sold it at official prices to the members of the various industrial associations (e.g., the Chōsen Dyers' Association and the Chōsen Towel Association), to individual companies like the Chōsen Electric Cable Corporation, to government bureaus (e.g., the Bureau of Railways), and to other industrial consumers, all of whom had been separately informed of their purchase quotas by the Government-General.

The next step was to weave the yarn into cloth. Since the major cotton spinning companies were also the major weavers, it was not necessary for them to obtain yarn through the wholesalers to make cloth. All they had to do was wait for instructions from the government. The Government-General formulated a production policy for each fiscal period (six months) that established the production and distribution quotas for each type of cloth. The plan was then implemented through the various producers' and consumers' associations, each of which was separately informed of the amount of cloth it could purchase—always, of course, at officially regulated prices. Standards for the quality of cloth produced were similarly set by the Government-General.

What is especially interesting here is that in spite of all this ponderous effort to erect a consciously bureaucratic economy during the war, the Government-General continued, as before, to provide some room for the business community in both the making and implementation of policy. This was particularly true of the cotton textile industry, which, because of its enormous capital resources (due to the investments in Korea of such leading Japanese firms as Tōyōbō and Kanegafuchi) and its establishment of an effective nationwide distribution cartel as early as 1920, was able to maintain a certain degree of autonomy even in the midst of all the wartime controls.[16]

Even at the height of the Pacific War, for example, the Chōsen Spinners Association—composed of the colony's seven largest cotton textile firms and headed by Kim Yŏnsu of Kyŏngbang—was to a considerable extent self-governing. There were directives from the Government-General, but the assignment and enforcement of individual production quotas for each of the major firms was delegated to the association. The Government-General, moreover, continued throughout the war to observe the injunction in the 1936 industrial commission's report "to take into consideration the interests of Korea's domestic producers and consumers." In the case of cotton cloth, controls were decided and executed not by the Government-General alone but in cooperation with a twenty-five member Cotton Cloth Controls Committee (Mempu Tōsei Iinkai), composed of "representatives of the producers, wholesalers, and major consumers, along with the appropriate government officials."[17]

The Social Nexus

By far the most informal and perhaps most effective interaction between government and business in what was essentially a continuous process of policy making and implementation took place in a way that mixed business with pleasure. Unfortunately, since so much of this personal interaction was necessarily private, the historian can do little more than guess at the extent or substance of it. But not to mention it at all would surely be an egregious omission, for if the present is any guide to the past, we can hardly doubt that many colonial business deals were struck between businessmen and bureaucrats over drinks in the relaxed and convivial atmosphere of a good wine house or restaurant.

We learn, for example, from associates who knew him well that Kim Yŏnsu enjoyed more than just an occasional cup of wine.[18] We also learn from his official biography that Kim was accustomed to dining and drinking with high-ranking colonial bureaucrats in connection with his business activities. This same biography even provides us with a detailed description of two such evenings at the Hŭirak Restaurant in July 1939, when Kim discussed his textile business in Manchuria with Matsuzawa Tatsuo, chief of the Foreign Affairs Section of the Governor-General's Secretariat, and the two men came to an understanding that affirmed the Government-General's support for Kyŏngbang's new factory, under construction at the time near Mukden.[19]

One wishes there had always been on hand at these affairs a consci-

Part of the Kim family compound in Inch'on, as it looks today. The building in the photograph was originally the reception quarters of the Kim Kijung household. The gateway on the left leads to the household's family quarters, the roof of which is visible in the background.

Kim Kijung.

Kim Kyŏngjung.

Kim Sŏngsu (*left*) and Kim Yŏnsu as schoolboys in Tokyo.

Kim Sŏngsu in 1921.

Kim Yŏnsu in 1921.

Pak Yŏnghyo

Saitō Makoto

Aruga Mitsutoyo

Downtown Seoul (Namdaemun-no) in the 1930s. Partially visible on the extreme left and right are, respectively, the Bank of Chōsen and the Seoul Post Office.

entious scribe with a sense of history who stayed sober and took copious notes. In such matters, however, discretion was usually paramount, and these occasions were rarely recorded. As the ITT lobbyist Dita Beard said in 1972: "I don't put anything in writing. If it's important enough, you shouldn't, and if it is not important enough, why bother?"[20] Still, those government-business tête-à-tête's like the one mentioned above of which we have some knowledge suggest that such private meetings were then as now an important element in the overall dynamics of state-company policy formulation and implementation.

There were other, better-documented occasions in which the state and bourgeoisie came together in a way that mixed business with pleasure on a regular basis. These occasions were provided by business associations such as the Chamber of Commerce and Industry (Shōkō Kaigisho) and the Chōsen Business Club (Chōsen Jitsugyō Kurabu). In many ways the organizations were similar. Both had Koreans as well as Japanese in their membership and sponsored similar activities: luncheons or dinners featuring a variety of guest speakers, including Government-General bureaucrats or visiting officials from other parts of the empire; symposia on current problems or topics of interest; and publication in a monthly journal of useful economic information and statistics, including an assortment of pertinent articles and speeches by government officials, businessmen, and scholars.

Both were also to a certain extent official organizations and in that sense they represented a coalescence of business and bureaucracy from their inception. This was more obviously true of the chamber, which had been legally established by the Government-General in 1915 to absorb and replace already existing similar business associations founded and run separately by Koreans and Japanese.[21] The impetus for the formation of the Business Club had come from a section of the business community itself, but honored guests and speakers at the club's founding luncheon included members of the bureaucratic elite such as Minobe Shunkichi, governor of the Bank of Chōsen; Commerce and Industry Section Chief Ikuta of the Government-General's Bureau of Industry; and even Vice-Governor-General Mizuno himself.[22]

The club's membership also gradually came to encompass not only businessmen from the major banks and companies but also top-level colonial government officials, military officers, and educators. The membership list of July 1936 reads like a *Who's Who* of colonial Korea, and includes most of the Chōsen contingent in the industrial commissions later that year and in 1938. Nearly every major bureau of the Government-General was represented in the club by its highest-ranking official, including the Bureau of Police. And in 1936, as in 1920, the vice-governor-general acted as one of the club's advisers.[23]

What is particularly interesting about the Chōsen Business Club, however, is that it was founded and run not by Japanese but by Koreans. The original sponsors and officers of the club were all Korean, among whom the most important was Han Sangnyong, chairman of the club for most of its existence.[24] More and more Japanese were admitted over time, but the club's membership in the beginning was largely Korean, and new Korean members continued to be inducted along with Japanese. In 1929 the club had 169 members, of whom 127 were Korean.[25] By the end of 1936, the membership had more than quadrupled to nearly 700 members, about half of whom were Korean.[26] Kim Yŏnsu joined the club in 1936, just when he was becoming a major colonial business figure as president of Kyŏngbang and head of the Haedong Bank.[27]

The club's purpose was avowedly social. Kim Yongwan, who had himself been a member, made a point, when interviewed, of distinguishing the club from the officially established and more formal Chamber of Commerce and Industry. The Business Club had been, in Kim's words, a private "fraternal organization" (ch'inmok tanch'e), where members could come together on an informal, friendly basis.[28] In 1929, in a speech commemorating the tenth anniversary of the club's founding, Han Sangnyong had said much the same thing: the club had been organized "to encourage friendship among members and increase prosperity through the expansion of knowledge, as well as to promote harmony between the Japanese and Korean business worlds."[29]

The club's facilities were extensive and designed to foster these aims. Centrally located in downtown Seoul near the Government-General's offices, they included a lecture hall, a conference room, a common room, a room for special symposia, a reading room, and space reserved for recreational pursuits such as billiards, go (paduk in Korean), Asian chess (shōgi in Japanese; changgi in Korean), music, fine arts, and Chinese and Japanese poetry. There were also rooms for club discussions, business discussions, and various kinds of small meetings. Members assembled at least once a month for a regular supper meeting that featured distinguished guest speakers from Korea (who were often club members themselves) as well as from Japan and other parts of the empire. The club also helped sponsor special symposia on subjects of topical interest such as "Korean-Manchurian Economy and Industry," and published a monthly journal (in Japanese) that highlighted the recent activities both of the club and of individual members and kept members informed of current economic developments and opportunities on the peninsula and elsewhere.[30]

Unlike the Chamber of Commerce and Industry, the Business Club had no branches outside Seoul. It was really more of an exclusive, metropolitan organization, properly designated a "club" (*kurabu*) and with all the elitist connotations of that term. It was not a place where the common bank teller, merchant, or bureaucrat—Japanese or Korean—would have felt comfortable. Nor would he have been invited to join. Although there were some members from the provinces and Japan, the Business Club was essentially for the people in the capital who were really running the colony—the bank presidents and governors; the chairmen and presidents of the big corporations; the owners of the major newspapers; high-ranking military men, including the chief of staff of the army and the head of the military police; and, of course, the cream of the colonial bureaucracy.

The elitism and "clubbiness" were reflected in the club's social events, such as its exclusive luncheons and fellowship parties (*konshinkai*) for new or departing colonial officials and for retired colonial bureaucrats on return visits to Korea, including former governors-general. In 1935, for example, ex-Governor-General Saitō Makoto—then viscount and Lord Privy Seal as well as former prime minister (1932-34)—returned to Seoul to commemorate the twenty-fifth anniversary of Japanese colonial rule. The Business Club held a "grand welcoming luncheon" for him and his large entourage, which included many former bureaucrats of the Government-General. Speaking on behalf of the club, Chairman Han Sangnyong welcomed the old admiral "home" to his "family." "In inviting Your Excellency [here], our feeling is not at all one of welcoming a distinguished guest from a distant land; we feel [instead] as if we are welcoming a loving father (*jifu*) home from a journey."[31]

The existence of such a business association established by Koreans under Korean leadership shows once again how well integrated into the colonial polity the Korean bourgeoisie had become by the 1930s. In discussing the various interactions between government and business in the making and implementation of policy, we have been concerned, naturally, with the Koreans rather than with the Japanese, but it is striking that there seems to have been little significant difference between the two groups in such interaction, whether formal or informal. The upper echelons of both groups participated in policy making at the highest, most formal level and enjoyed, moreover, a regular informal access to high officials, including the governor-general himself, that was unimaginable to the average resident of the colony—whether Japanese or Korean. In addressing Saitō as a "loving father," Han Sangnyong was not simply being obsequious. His particular choice of words was grounded in his own and other Korean businessmen's personal experience and interaction with Government-General officials and reflected the reality of the government-business relationship in a bureaucratic capitalist state with a Confucian hue.

The Primacy of Interests

When all is said and done, what really cemented the government-business relationship was not so much ideology or personal interaction, but material interest. Collaboration in the formulation and execution of official policy was beneficial to both sides. By treating the business community as a junior partner in the decision-making process, the Government-General made capitalism all the more effective as an extension of state policy.

The business community, on the other hand, found that serving state interests simultaneously insured corporate expansion and profits. Kyŏngbang was a case in point. The company's greatest expansion came between 1937 and 1945, when it served as an obliging and effective instrument of Government-General wartime policy. And at no time during the colonial period were the profits of state service more impressive.

Kyŏngbang: The Wartime Fusion of Corporate and State Policy

From the mid-1930s when Kyŏngbang, under Kim Yŏnsu's leadership, began an expansion that would continue uninterrupted through 1945 and extend the company's interests far beyond the simple cotton weaving operation originally established in Yŏngdŭngp'o in 1919, Korea was undergoing a major and rapid industrial transformation that was aimed at turning the colony into an "advance military supply base" (zenshin heitan kichi) for Japan's penetration of China.

There was nothing new in the idea of Korea serving as an industrial link between Japan and the Asian continent, but the intent of earlier policy seems to have been as much economic as military, at least at first. Wars with China and Russia and participation on the winning side in World War I had secured for Japan not only Taiwan and Korea, but slices of Manchuria, China, and Russia as well. In 1919 Japan attended the Versailles conference as an acknowledged imperialist power. Two years later the Government-General was actively exploring ways of developing Korea as an integral part of the new empire, thus providing Japan with a central artery to the Asian continent in an economic as well as geographical sense. During the industrial commission of 1921, for example, the proposal for "General Industrial Policy" put before the delegates began with a ringing declaration of Korea's imperial status: "Since Korea is a part of the imperial domain, industrial plans for Korea should be in conformity with imperial industrial policy. Such a policy must provide for economic conditions in adjacent areas, based on [Korea's] geographical position amid Japan, China, and the Russian Far East."[32]

With the Kwantung army's invasion of Manchuria in 1931 and the establishment of Manchukuo, the Government-General's policy of economic linkage between Korea and its northern neighbor was reaffirmed and given an even more solid footing. It was also given increased importance as the centerpiece of a comprehensive imperial policy being formulated in Tokyo. Japan's growing ascendancy in international trade (especially in textiles) had been provoking hostile foreign reaction in the form of tariffs, and each of the major imperialist powers was attempting to protect its own trade interests through the establishment of self-sufficient spheres of economic influence. Japan, of course, was no exception, and began to promote the idea of a Japanese-Manchurian Bloc (Nichiman Ittai). This concept became one of the main themes of the Government-General's industrial commission of 1936, which proposed that industrial development in Korea be geared toward "a closer integration of the Japanese and Manchurian economies" in order for Japan "to achieve a victorious position in the international economic war (*sekai keizaisen*)."[33]

International economic competition, however, was not the only, or even the primary, concern of Government-General officials who were promoting such regional economic integration in the late 1930s. At a meeting with his senior bureaucrats soon after taking office, Governor-General Minami used an anatomical metaphor to describe the kind of integration he had in mind: Japan was the "torso" (*dōtai*), Korea the "arm" (*ude*), and Manchuria the "fist" (*kobushi*).[34] Minami's analogy was more suited to a regional industrial structure geared for military aggression than for peaceful economic rivalry, and it is very difficult in retrospect to separate in neat chronological fashion the economic growth of the Korean colony from its development as a supply base for the Kwantung army. The actual term "advance military supply base" was not used in official Government-General policy statements until the 1930s, but Korea's governors-general — all of whom were active or retired high-ranking military officers and all but one of whom was an army general — were not insensitive to the aspirations and needs of Japan's continental forces. More often than not they were sympathetic. As early as 1926, Admiral Saitō encouraged the Japan Nitrogenous Fertilizer Company to begin developing Korea's hydroelectric resources — a project that as Kobayashi Hideo points out, was from the beginning closely related to perceived continental military needs at the time.[35] Even General Ugaki, who had acquired the reputation of being something of a moderate within the army ranks, saw regional economic integration in largely military terms. His cooperation with Noguchi Jun in expanding the hydroelectric power system and building up a heavy industrial structure in the northern part of Korea was part of a coordinated effort with the new state of Manchukuo's own plans for industrial development and became the linchpin for later militarization of the Korean economy based on the electrochemical industry.[36]

In October 1936, eight months before the incident at the Marco Polo Bridge that expanded into the Sino-Japanese War, the Government-General's industrial commission had already called for the "rapid and positive development . . . of key industries from the point of view of national policy and especially national defense."[37] As Miyabayashi Taiji, director-general of the Chōsen Cotton Yarn and Cloth Merchants Association (Chōsen Menshifushō Rengōkai), noted in his remarks at the conference, Japan was in the midst of an epochal shift toward a "semi-wartime economy"; should a "state emergency" arise, both Korea and the Korean textile industry would play a key role as a "commissariat" (heitambu) for the army.[38]

Miyabayashi's words, of course, were prophetic. After the outbreak of the Sino-Japanese War in July 1937, the concept of Korea as an industrial supply base for Japan's military control of the continent became official policy that remained in effect until August 15, 1945, and industrial policy at the Government-General's commission of 1938 was accordingly discussed under the rubric of The Expansion of Military Industry. Among the industrial products the commission decided to develop in connection with Korea's new position as a wartime provisioner were light metals (aluminum and magnesium), coal oil and its substitutes, soda, ammonium sulphate, explosives, machine tools, motor vehicles, railroad rolling stock, ships, aircraft, leather, mining equipment, and hemp yarn and cloth. The Government-General agreed to lend its assistance in the expropriation of land for factory sites and promised to facilitate financing for the war effort.[39]

Kyŏngbang's role in the implementation of wartime policies was multifaceted. First of all, there were the company's various contributions to the national war chest. These involved, for example, large donations ranging from 10,000 to 100,000 yen voted periodically by the board of directors to groups such as the Chōsen Air Defense Association, the Chōsen Mechanized Defense Association, and the Japanese army and navy.[40]

During the war years Kyŏngbang also regularly purchased a considerable number of war bonds. There is no way of knowing the full extent of the company's investment here, but extant ledgers suggest that it was substantial. A total of about sixty separate purchases, most of them made in the 1940s, are still on record of a myriad of bond issues in denominations of 1 to 10,000 yen. Among such investments were China Incident National Treasury Bonds, Greater East Asia War Bonds, National Treasury Bonds for the Greater East Asian War, Special National Treasury Bonds for the Greater East Asian War, and National Treasury Discount Bonds for the Greater East Asia War. Other bond issues purchased by the company included Special National Defense Bonds, Wartime Savings Bonds, and Wartime National Defense Bonds.[41]

The actual number or bonds held by Kyŏngbang was probably far higher than indicated in the ledgers. The bonds listed above were all held either by Kyŏngbang directly or in the name of the Samyang Foundation. Though the records have been lost, one may reasonably assume that Kyŏngbang's various subsidiaries, including the South Manchurian Spinning Company, would have purchased bonds as well.

Either the company or Kim Yŏnsu personally also made substantial investments in the war industries being promoted in Korea by the Government-General. As noted above, one of these industries was the manufacture of hemp yarn and cloth. War had greatly magnified the importance of hemp as a textile raw material both in Japan and Korea. Before 1937, Korea had been importing large quantities of American and Indian cotton, but with the outbreak of the Sino-Japanese War, such imports were drastically curtailed to minimize the outflow of foreign exchange. As the war in China intensified and expanded into the Pacific War, cotton was strictly rationed, with priority given to military use, and cotton spinners were instructed to produce mixed yarns containing 30 percent staple fiber by weight to maximize the efficient use of the raw cotton available.[42]

The Government-General thus turned to hemp as one way to alleviate the raw cotton shortage. Hemp could be grown in Korea, and in addition to pressuring Korea peasants to devote more acreage to it rather than to food production, the government put its efforts behind improving seeds and cultivation methods. Similarly, the Government-General, which was now strictly controlling the growth of all industrial production facilities, gave its wholehearted support — reflected in the report of the industrial commission of 1938 — to the establishment and expansion of new factories for manufacturing hemp yarn and cloth.[43]

As we shall see later, when we look at the company's economic ties to the Japanese metropole, Kyŏngbang had a close and longstanding relationship with the C. Itoh Trading Company, which was the founder and owner of the Kureha Spinning Company in Japan. Like other Japanese textile firms, Kureha was in possession of a good deal of surplus textile machinery, idle for lack of sufficient raw materials and also in danger of sudden destruction by an increasing number of American air strikes against the Japanese homeland. A solution to the dual problem of putting such equipment to good use and removing it from exposure to attack was to move it to Japan's overseas territories like Korea and Manchuria, where it was sorely needed to raise the level of industrial self-sufficiency.

Thus in 1942, with the blessing of both the Ministry of Commerce and Industry and the Government-General, Kureha began to move its excess machinery to Korea. A new company for the manufacture of hemp yarn and cloth was set up in Taejŏn — the Chōsen Kureha Spinning Company — with 20,000 spindles and 500 looms. It was capitalized at 5 million yen (1.25 million yen paid in), of which Kureha contributed 70 percent. The remaining 30 percent was divided equally among three other corporate investors, one of which was Kureha's old friend Kyŏngbang.[44]

Kyŏngbang's investment in war industries was by no means limited to textiles. It extended also to heavy industries such as oil refining and shipbuilding, a trend that was duplicated in Kim Yŏnsu's personal investments (often in the name of his children) in such companies as Kanegafuchi Industry and Kawasaki Heavy Industries.[45]

Both oil refining and shipbuilding were crucial to the war effort and became ever more so in the later years as Japan lost its oil-producing territories and its fleet in Pacific battles with U.S. forces. Korea, of course, had no oil of its own, but it had large reserves of coal in the north that could be converted into oil and into a number of important by-products, such as paraffin, pitch, and asphalt. Kyŏngbang's investment (or what we know of it) in the Chōsen Oil Company in Wŏnsan, which was first established in 1935 and then expanded during the war, came to slightly more than 1 percent of the new company's huge paid-in capital of 22.5 million yen—most of which was supplied by the Japan Nitrogenous Fertilizer Company and Japan Petroleum. This was not an insignificant figure in itself and was almost as much as Kyŏngbang's first sale of shares in 1919. More important, however, was that Kyŏngbang's investment here was in a vital area of war production. A yearbook from 1943 describes the Chōsen Oil Company as "not only the king (*ōja*) of the peninsula's oil world but . . . in fact a contender for first place in Japan's oil industry." One of the refinery's greatest contributions to the wartime economy was its ability to produce high-quality lubricating oil, which Japan had previously imported from the United States.[46]

Kyŏngbang's investment in Chōsen Heavy Industries, Ltd., was another instance of the company's support of heavy industries directly related to war production. Known later in South Korea as the Korea Shipbuilding and Engineering Corporation—a major shipbuilding firm in the 1970s—Chōsen Heavy Industries was founded in 1937 with a paid-in capital of 1.5 million yen. By 1943 this figure had climbed to 7 million yen, most of which came from Mitsubishi Heavy Industries and the Oriental Development Company.

The company was a direct outgrowth of the Government-General's industrial conferences of 1936 and 1938, which had designated shipbuilding as one of the key industries for development in the new "semi-wartime" and later wartime economy. Located in the port of Pusan, the shipyard had two docks, which could accommodate, respectively, 4,500-ton or 7,000-ton commercial and naval vessels for both construction and repair. In addition, the company engaged in salvage work on ships that had been damaged at sea (an increasingly important function of the shipyard as the war wore on).

From the beginning the company was more than a shipyard. It had originally been established through the absorption of two already existing companies, the Saitō Iron Works and the Chōsen Electrolytic Steel Mill, and it continued to fabricate a wide assortment of steel products: bridges, sluice gates, steel towers and beams, containers, as well as steel casting, cast iron, and other alloys. It had a woodworking shop in addition to facilities for electric and gas welding, and it was able to construct and repair all kinds of steam engines, boilers, and equipment used in the mining industry. All of these activities were in accord with the policy established at the Government-General's industrial commission of 1938.

Extant ledgers show Kyŏngbang's investment in the company — 1,000 shares — to have been relatively small, compared, for example, to Mitsubishi's nearly 30,000. Again, however, the size of the investment is less significant than its importance as a contribution to a crucial war industry. Chōsen Heavy Industries was the colony's largest shipyard, and its biggest customer was the Japanese Imperial Navy. After 1940, in fact, the company was placed under the direct supervision of the navy, for whom it produced scores of small naval vessels until 1945.[47]

In addition to diverting some of Kyŏngbang's profits into oil refining and shipbuilding, Kim Yŏnsu joined forces with Pak Hŭngsik and a number of other Japanese and Korean businessmen in the final months of the war to establish a company that would produce the most vital military product of all: airplanes. To appreciate the importance of such a factory, it is necessary to recall the difficult circumstances of Japan in late 1944.

By the end of 1942 in the wake of Guadalcanal, Japan was on the defensive, and there was an urgent demand for more ships and planes. In 1943, the Ministry of Commerce and Industry was reorganized into a Munitions Ministry for maximum mobilization of the wartime economy, and the new ministry, as Bisson notes, quickly became in effect an aircraft production board.[48] On June 15, 1944, Allied B-29 bombers based in China made an historic raid on the Yawata steel plant, and by the end of the year, B-29s of the 20th Air Force in the Marianas began devastating the industrial heartland of Japan around Tokyo, Nagoya, and Osaka. Dispersal of aircraft plants throughout the country and in different parts of the empire (including Korea) — already planned earlier in the year — quickly became a necessity.[49]

Korea was a natural place for such production. It was securely under Japanese control, and of all of Japan's major overseas possessions, closest to the manufacturing centers of Japan itself. Most important, perhaps, it was not included among the targets of Allied bombing raids. The colony's lack of a comprehensive and integrated technological base for the production of fully equipped planes was no obstacle. Korea's factories could concentrate mainly on the production of fuselages and basic aircraft components that could be shipped to nearby Japan. By the end of the war, moreover, little thought was given to advanced technology in aircraft production. The entire industry was bent toward a terrible last-gasp defensive effort: the fabrication of simple trainer planes that could be built by semiskilled labor and would have to be used only once — in *taiatari* or suicide attacks against Allied forces converging on the Japanese homeland.[50]

As early as 1942, Mitsui had extended the production of its Shōwa Aircraft Company to P'yŏngyang. According to the report of a postwar American presidential mission dispatched to investigate Japanese industrial holdings in Manchuria and Soviet-occupied North Korea, the Mitsui plant had been producing, at a rate of fifty per month, army training planes clearly meant for *kamikaze* raids against the U.S. military.[51] Mitsui was joined in this desperate effort in October 1944 by the Chōsen Aircraft Company (Chōsen Hikōki Kōgyō KK), organized by Pak Hŭngsik with the support of the Japanese army. Located on the outskirts of Seoul in Anyang, the factory scheduled its first production for June 1945.[52]

Kyŏngbang, as we shall see shortly, had developed a close relationship with the Japanese army during the course of the war, and Kim Yŏnsu had already put some money into the aircraft industry through his purchase of shares in Kawasaki Heavy Industries, one of Japan's four main aircraft companies. Kim's active participation in the Chōsen Aircraft Company, therefore, was not at all unusual, especially since the impetus for the plant came directly from the native Korean business community, though undoubtedly at the urging of the Government-General. At the founders' meeting held on October 1, 1944, Pak Hŭngsik was elected president of the new company, and Kim was given a seat on the board of directors. The company was capitalized at an enormous 50 million yen. Again we can not be sure of the full extent of Kyŏngbang's financial investment, but the records we do have show a purchase of 8,000 shares for 200,000 yen on June 23, 1945.[53]

Such financial contributions and investments were no more than an extension of Kyŏngbang's productive efforts in its own factories on behalf of what Han Sangnyong and other businessmen were publicly calling the "holy war" (*seisen*).[54] Between 1937 and 1945 the company's spindles and looms turned out unprecedented quantities of cotton yarn and cloth for military use, especially cloth for Japanese army uniforms. By the end of the war Kyŏngbang had become more than a simple spinning and weaving operation producing unbleached "gray goods" for other companies to finish. By August 1945 it had expanded its facilities to include the largest bleaching and dyeing factory on the peninsula, where it produced its own khaki cloth for uniforms, using a company dye made from Amur maple leaves. By that time Kyŏngbang had even acquired a clothing factory, which was officially designated as a "military plant" (*gun no shitei kōjo*). There Kyŏngbang workers were able to cut, sew, and stitch the actual uniforms themselves, using cotton fabric the company itself had ginned, spun, woven, bleached, and dyed.[55]

Uniforms were only part of the story. Kyŏngbang's financial involvement in the Chōsen Aircraft Company in late 1944 was intimately connected with the company's own production for the Japanese army. The army needed not only uniforms, but airplane fabric for the control surfaces of its planes and a wealth of other textile, rubber, and chemical products related to aircraft production that could be produced by Kyŏngbang and its subsidiaries. In its regular semiannual business report for May 1944, the company stated that "just [at the moment] when [we] were hoping to contribute directly to the vital task of increasing the production of airplanes, [we] were given the honor of being designated a collaborative factory of the Army Air Arsenal." In October of that same year, several days after the formal inauguration of the Chōsen Aircraft Company, Kyŏngbang's board of directors also voted to amend the by-laws of the company to permit the production of bulletproof glass and airplane coatings.[56] Kyŏngbang's role in the new and burgeoning Korean aircraft industry thus went well beyond the purchase of aircraft company stock: the company was also directly involved in the manufacture of the airplanes themselves.

Kyŏngbang: The Rewards of Wartime Service

In carrying out the Government-General's policies, Kyŏngbang was not merely serving the government's interest, but was also making money. And this was the glue that really held the relationship together. In its report for the thirtieth fiscal period ending May 31, 1942, Kyŏngbang had informed its stockholders that during the last six months "we have, through [our] production, wholeheartedly devoted [ourselves] to [our] patriotic duty and achieved considerable results."[57] The company was not indulging in the usual hyperbole found in most corporate business reports: war was proving to be extremely profitable. Between 1938 and 1945 Kyŏngbang enjoyed a business boom without precedent in its previous twenty-one years of operation.

Sales were better than ever before. In 1937, a month before the Sino-Japanese War, the gross profit from sales during the previous six months had been around 300,000 yen, the company's second best sales period since 1919. A year later, in the heat of the Japanese military campaign in China, the company's accountants were dealing with figures they had never encountered before. The sales profits for the six-month period ending in May 1938 had doubled to over 600,000 yen. Six months later they shot up to nearly 1.5 million yen, a figure that became more or less the norm for the duration of the war.[58]

The controls that Kim Yŏnsu and other businessmen had railed against at the industrial commission of 1936 turned out to be a blessing in disguise. Gone were the difficult days when Kyŏngbang had to worry about such things as competitive quality and pricing. Cartels had replaced competition with cooperation. Throughout the war the Government-General also continued to lower the minimum quality standards for textile goods, while simultaneously keeping prices high enough to cover the increasing costs of wartime production and insure business profits.[59] The shortage of goods, moreover, created a sellers' market. As Kim Yongwan told this writer in 1984: "As the Japanese continued to make war, goods were in short supply, and it didn't matter whether the quality was good or bad. Whatever you produced you could sell."[60]

The Japanese Imperial Army was also for Kyŏngbang a manufacturer's dream: a captive customer of relatively indiscriminate taste, but with immense resources and an insatiable appetite. The company's wartime business reports are periodically dotted with references to the "markedly increased military demand" or to the company's success in filling orders for "special military goods."[61] Kyŏngbang's importance to the army, whose needs took priority over everything else, also allowed the company to expand its facilities and create an integrated textile operation at a time when funding and construction were being strictly limited by the government. As an integral part of the colonial war "commissariat," Kyŏngbang had no difficulty securing financing from the Industrial Bank or construction licenses from the Government-General: between 1933 and 1945 the company's fixed assets in the form of real estate, buildings, and equipment increased over fifty times.[62]

The company's net profits from the war were considerable. Once again 1938 was the key year, the year following the outbreak of the war in China and the beginning of Korea's transformation into a continental supply depot. Net profits in 1936 and 1937 had been ranging from 60,000 yen to 70,000 yen per six-month period. There was then a dramatic jump in the first half of 1938 up to 220,000 yen. Six months later, in November 1938, the recorded net earnings had shot up again nearly three times to around 600,000 yen. They continued to rise further in 1939, and in the second half of 1940 exceeded 700,000 yen. Another six months later, in May 1941, they passed the 800,000-yen mark and continued to remain at this high level throughout the war.[63]

Where were all these profits going? Some of the money, of course, was being paid out to the company's more than four hundred stockholders. Dividend payments, however, were normally restricted by the government during the war to a maximum 6 percent per year for companies with an authorized capital of 200,000 yen or more, and Kyŏngbang's returns on equity capital were running as high as 32 percent.[64] With Kyŏngbang's financial pipeline to the Industrial Bank, funds for expansion that equity alone could not cover were for the most part obtained through easy loans rather than by dipping into corporate profits—hence the company's staggering debt of 22 million yen by 1945.[65] Such loans, however, had to be paid back, and, in the meantime, there were also regular payments of interest to be taken care of. Nevertheless, as already noted, Kyŏngbang's loans were granted with preferential rates and conditions. This special treatment kept the interest payments relatively small and spread both interest and principal payments out over a decade or more in most cases, with comfortable grace periods added to lessen the burden even further.

Where, then, was the money going? The answer is that much of it was going into the company's own treasury. Such corporate hoarding was deliberately encouraged by the government authorities during the war. The official restriction on dividend payments, for example, was not meant so much to pressure companies into using their profits to pay off their debts as to insure a smooth working of funds through the accumulation of internal corporate reserves, on which the government placed no limitations.[66] Such reserves would generally be placed in the banks as deposits, where they could be loaned out again where needed, or they could be invested directly by the companies themselves, as we have seen, in national bonds and vital war industries. Thus, even with specially approved dividend payments to its stockholders of usually 10 percent (and never less than 8 percent) per year,[67] and in spite of regular outlays of interest and repayment of principal on a debt totaling 22 million yen, Kyŏngbang was able by 1945 to accumulate reserves amounting to almost 40 percent of its paid-in capital. In 1933 Kyŏngbang's reserves were listed at only 4,462 yen. By May 31, 1945, the company's legal reserves alone were 850,000 yen, and its "special reserves" (*betto tsumitatekin*), that is, money set aside at the discretion of the company itself, amounted to an impressive 3 million yen.[68]

Although the whole socioeconomic structure in which the company had waxed and battened would come crashing to the ground in less than three months, in the spring of 1945 the Korean skies were clear of Allied bombs, and all Kyŏngbang's property was still intact. The company had just opened its new bleaching and dyeing factory in Sihŭng, built with funds supplied by the Chōsen Industrial Bank, and operations at its other new factory (rubber goods) in Yangp'yŏngdong were going smoothly: indeed, the military's demand for rubber hose was stronger than ever. Only a few months before, the Government-General had "substantially raised" the price of cotton goods, and although this had fallen short of the kind of "fundamental" price revision desired by the company, another price rise, for rubber hose, was expected soon.[69] Net profits were slightly down as compared to those at the end of 1944, though still comfortably above the magic 800,000-yen figure that the company had first seen in 1941,[70] and Kyŏngbang's treasury was richer than ever before in the company's history. On the eve of Liberation, Kim Yŏnsu and his directors could look back over nearly eight years of uninterrupted and unprecedented prosperity. Peacetime, with all the competition among spinning companies and the higher standards for cotton cloth, had been something of an obstacle to Kyŏngbang's development. The war, on the other hand, had been a godsend.

Summary

The chief feature of the government-business relationship in colonial Korea was the overwhelming dominance of the state. The Government-General determined the basic direction and priorities of economic development through the establishment of official industrial policy and ensured, in large part through its control of the colonial financial structure, that its plans would be carried out in the private sector. Companies like Kyŏngbang, so dependent on funds supplied in one way or another by the Government-General, had little choice but to manage their affairs in accordance with official development goals, for financing was only available for work the government wanted done.

But such subordination was not simply a mechanical function of state power and control, and to concentrate solely on the factor of coercion is to rob the relationship of its great complexity and subtlety.

In a sense, businessmen were not so much subordinated by the political structure as incorporated into it, and, indeed, it is sometimes difficult to see where the state leaves off and capitalism begins. A number of elements, including ideology, personal and corporate interaction, and concrete material interests, all served to blur the distinction between the public and private realms and to fuse state and capitalism into a single, complex whole.

Though all of these factors were important and, in a sense, inseparable, it was above all the material interest both sides had in working together as a unit that served as the ultimate cohesive. In the colonial state, personified to a large extent by the governor-general, the goal was not so much simple economic gain as the augmentation of national (that is, Japanese) power—an expansion of power that would, of course, at the same time, increase the personal power of the men involved. With their military backgrounds and experience, moreover, all Korea's governors-general, to a greater or lesser degree, were wont to identify national power with military imperialism. Thus economic development in Korea tended to be viewed by Korea's colonial rulers (and hence by their subordinates) in military terms and largely in connection with the army's subjugation and exploitation of Manchuria and China.

The interests of the colonial businessmen, whether Japanese or Korean, were less complex. Their paramount concern was with profits for their companies and themselves. While they might have preferred less government direction and interference in the operation of their companies, they accepted, indeed, demanded, as in the case of Kyŏngbang's insistent request for government subsidies, government support and protection in times of difficulty.

The greatly expanded role of the Government-General in the economy during the war did not upset the system, because, first, it was not a simple arrogation of power. Business as well as government recognized the need for official mobilization of resources and production for the war effort. Second, in spite of the imposition of far-reaching bureaucratic controls, the government continued to allow business some part in the making and implementation of policy. Third, and most important, the system continued to work during the war because government controls did not ultimately have an adverse effect on corporate profits. As we have seen in Kyŏngbang's case, such controls turned out to be an unexpected boon. To the very end, the colonial government-business relationship proved to be a mutually beneficial union.

CHAPTER 5

Between Metropole and Hinterland

The Acquisition of Raw Materials and Technology

Fusion with the state was one conspicuous aspect of Korean capitalism during the colonial period. Another no less striking feature was the extreme dependence of Korean capitalism on the larger, more established capitalist firms based in Japan itself, and on the particular imperial socioeconomic structure generated by Japan's military conquests on the Asian continent.

While such dependence manifested itself in economic terms, its underlying cause was essentially political, a logical consequence of Korea's subjugation as a Japanese colony: the Government-General no more contemplated the development of an economically independent Korea than it did the establishment of a politically independent Korean state.[1]

The colonial authorities made this point clear as early as 1921, at the industrial commission convoked that year to discuss the broad contours of Korea's development policy for the post-World War I period. Vice-Governor-General Mizuno and Bureau Director Nishimura (Bureau of Industry) were questioned repeatedly at the conference by delegates from Japan who were concerned about the potential threat that the Government-General's proposed industrial development posed to Japan's own industries and exports. There was no mincing of words.

At the general session on the first day of the conference, one delegate bluntly asked the colonial officials if the new policy was not actually aimed at "rejecting manufactured goods from Japan":

As far as the policy of promoting industry is concerned, I understand almost everything in the policy draft. There is something, however, I think I would like to hear a little [more] about. The policy of [industrial] promotion is centered on the idea of having both raw materials and a production base. This policy seems to take on added importance in view of the forthcoming abolition of duties on imports from Japan. If the raw material and production base are [both in Korea], it seems to me that this will amount to a policy of rejecting manufactured goods from Japan. Is this correct?[2]

Nishimura immediately jumped in to set the record straight. The intent of the Government-General's development of Korean industry, he declared, was in no way to foster the economic independence of the peninsula. On the contrary, the government's goal was to promote a closer and more systematic economic integration of the colony into the Japanese Empire:

In no aspect of the Government-General's management of the industrial [economy] has there been the slightest thought of Korea adopting some kind of discriminatory policy toward Japan. [All the policies] have been conceived with the object [of fostering] a single coexistent, coprosperous Japanese-Korean unit. With respect to the duties on Japanese imports or whatever [other] system, there is no thought of rebuffing Japanese imports and having Korea manufacture [products] on its own. It's just that at present Korea is at a low level of development, and when free competition [is instituted between Japan and Korea], economic growth will not be possible, so [Korea] requires considerable protection. In the future, even if [Korea] concentrates on the agricultural sector, that alone cannot achieve economic development. Therefore in Korea too, gradual industrial growth is not only necessary but must also be planned. First of all, what [industries] are we planning to develop? Those [industries] which, for example, have some current experience in Korea or for which raw materials can be easily obtained in the future. That's what [we] meant [here in the policy draft]. In no way [are we] presuming to reject Japanese imports or compete [with Japan] as a separate country.[3]

As we have seen, such integration was to include the unequal but concerted cooperation of Japanese and Korean capital in the development process, an effort that would help stabilize the political situation on the peninsula and secure the collaboration of a nascent Korean bourgeoisie in colonial policies. The inevitable result of such cooperative development, as the Japanese authorities undoubtedly foresaw, was the subordination of the Korean bourgeoisie to its Japanese counterpart through the latter's crucial and commanding role in development process, both in regard to the provision of capital itself and the procurement of raw materials and technology, and in connection with the control and exploitation of major markets. To survive and prosper, the Korean bourgeoisie was compelled to work with and through the Japanese capitalist system.

The dependent character of Korean capitalism was reflected not only in its subordination to Japanese capitalism, but also in its structural reliance on the Japanese Empire, which stemmed from the colonial government's vision of Korea as an economic link between Japan and the Asian continent. In 1921 the Government-General was just beginning to formulate such a policy, which reached its full articulation—the concept of industrial development in Korea as part of a three-way hierarchical and complementary economic relationship based on Japan's needs and goals—only after Japan's seizure of Manchuria ten years later.

The establishment of a new Manchurian state under Japanese control and directly bordering on China itself greatly expanded both the actual and potential periphery of Japan's empire, and Korea's role as a burgeoning semi-industrial country within the imperial system was accordingly reaffirmed and magnified. The existence of such new imperial territory ripe for exploitation came to play an important and ultimately crucial role in capitalist growth, as Korean businessmen became increasingly dependent on peripheral raw materials and markets and even became economic imperialists themselves. By 1945 Koreans like Kim Yŏnsu had as much of a stake in the perpetuation of the existing imperial system as the Japanese militarists who had created it.

We have already seen in chapters 2 and 3, though in a different context, how, first, Japanese capital dominated Korean industrialization during the colonial period and, second, how extensively even Korean companies like Kyŏngbang relied on Japanese capital for their expansion. Here and in chapter 6 we shall consider the various ways in which the imperatives of Kyŏngbang's production and marketing kept the company securely bound to the core capitalism of Japan proper and to the imperial system as a whole.

Raw Materials

The production process of any industrial enterprise requires, apart from inputs of capital and labor, the procurement of the raw materials and technology necessary to create the product in question. In a sense, the whole process commences with the acquisition of raw materials, and it thus seems appropriate to begin our study there. Kyŏngbang's raw materials consisted of cotton yarn in the early years when the company was only a weaving factory. In the 1930s, when it expanded into a combined spinning and weaving operation, it was capable of producing its own yarn, but to do so, it needed a steady and inexpensive supply of raw cotton.

Cotton Yarn

From its inception in the early 1880s the cotton textile industry in Japan was characterized by operations that combined both spinning and weaving. Although some cotton yarn had to be imported at first, the industry was exporting yarn in less than a decade. Cotton was thus the primary raw material required by the Japanese textile industry even before the turn of the century.[4]

In contrast, Kyŏngbang did not even begin producing its own cotton yarn until 1936, seventeen years after the founding of the company. The company's charter of 1919 makes it clear that spinning was conceived as an eventual goal from the beginning by the company's promoters,[5] but Kyŏngbang's shortage of capital and limited technology in its early years restricted its field of activity. Even the Chōsen Spinning and Weaving Company in Pusan, established in 1917 by Japanese investors as a joint spinning and weaving operation, had to rely on imported yarns to a certain extent at first.[6]

These yarns were coming for the most part from Japan. As we have seen, by 1920 Japanese textile goods had largely displaced Western products and were in a position to dominate the Korean market. To obtain its yarn Kyŏngbang thus had to look across the East Sea. In 1932, for example, in an interview with a reporter from the *Chōsen jitsugyō kurabu*, Kyŏngbang's business manager Yi Sangu remarked that the company purchased its raw materials chiefly from Japan.[7] Such dependency left Kyŏngbang in a distinctly disadvantageous position vis-à-vis Japanese spinning and weaving companies exporting to Korea like Tōyōbō and Kanegafuchi.

There was, first, the expense of the yarn itself, to which had to be added the cost of brokerage, tariff duties, and transport from Japan. The necessity of such transport presented its own special problems because it took between two and three weeks, and there was always the possibility of delay. In the repeated loading and unloading between train and ship, moreover, the yarn was often damaged. The company tried to reduce the transport time and minimize expenses and the risk of damage by using the Ozaki Steamship Line, which had a branch office in Inch'ŏn, and to some extent it was successful. Under the new arrangement, delivery to Inch'ŏn took only three days, and the shipping charges also decreased by about one-half.[8]

There was still no guarantee, however, that the goods would arrive intact, and, in addition, there was another problem — the quality of the yarn itself. As long as Kyŏngbang continued to use yarn spun by a factory located far away in Japan, it was dependent on that factory's goodwill and attentiveness to quality control in obtaining decent yarn. This problem continued to plague the company until Kyŏngbang set up its own spinning factory in 1936. It became such a matter of concern that Kyŏngbang eventually began to dispatch its own personnel to the Dai Nippon Spinning Company's factory in Akashi to make sure the quality of the yarn it was purchasing would be satisfactory.[9] After 1936 this problem gradually faded away as Kyŏngbang began to produce more and more of its own yarn, but the company's new and ever increasing demand for raw cotton now created other problems and gave rise to another, more complex form of dependency on Japan. Before we consider the various elements of Kyŏngbang's cotton dependency, however, let us note how the procurement process itself worked to tie the company into the Japanese metropolitan economic structure.

The Procurement Process

Whether the item sought was cotton yarn or cotton itself, the company obtained its raw materials for the most part through Japanese trading firms.

It was not necessary, of course, for Kyŏngbang to have done so. The company could have chosen, and occasionally did so choose, to deal directly with the actual producers or their agents. In general, however, there were powerful economic reasons for the company to work through the large, established Japanese trading companies.

One crucial reason was that such dependency helped to minimize the risks involved. To keep the factory operating on a smooth and regular basis, the company had to insure that it always had stocks of raw materials on hand, taking into account such factors as delivery time and the possibility of receiving damaged goods. Futures trading in commodities, whereby a company agreed to purchase a certain quantity of goods at current prices for a specified future delivery, was thus very common in the textile industry. The market price of raw cotton (and, correspondingly, cotton yarn) was, however, notoriously unstable, fluctuating as much as 30 percent in the course of a normal year.[10] Success in the futures market required not only a comprehensive and detailed knowledge of the market for the commodities involved, but also immense cash reserves as a hedge against sudden, unpredictable price falls. An unwary speculator with limited capital could easily push his company to the brink of bankruptcy in the course of futures trading. As we have seen, this is exactly what happened to Kyŏngbang in its first year of operation when the company delegated Yi Kanghyŏn to purchase yarn directly through the Sampin in Osaka.

The large Japanese trading companies, on the other hand, were in a position to dominate the textile commodities trade. By the time Kyŏngbang was founded, they had already enjoyed decades of experience and profit in the business. The Oriental Cotton Trading Company (Tōyō Menka KK), for example, which was formally established as a separate company by Mitsui in 1920, had been operating as a textile department within the great Mitsui Bussan since the 1880s.[11] In 1929 Arno S. Pearse from Manchester noted that a total of only three firms — the Japan Cotton Trading Company (Nippon Menka KK), the Oriental Trading Company, and the Gōshō Merchants Company (Gōshō KK) — together controlled about 80 percent of Japan's imports of raw cotton and a similar percentage of the sales of all cotton goods manufactured in Japan. Each had a subscribed capital of tens of millions of yen, equally enormous reserves, and offices in all the cotton centers of the world.[12] There was really no good economic reason for Kyŏngbang to try to establish a separate international procurement network of its own. All Kyŏngbang's purchaser had to do was take a short walk over to Tōyō Menka's branch office in Seoul[13] and place his order, probably over a refreshing cup of hot green tea.

There was another reason for Kyŏngbang to work through the Japanese trading firms. Especially in its early years when the company was first getting started and its sales were sluggish, cash flows were a major problem. Even as sales improved there were still difficulties because it was customary in Korea for merchants in the textile trade to defer payment on goods received for up to forty days.[14] To compensate for this, Kyŏngbang had to find some way of postponing its payments for imported raw materials without disrupting the flow of raw materials itself. With their great reserves and large turnover, the Japanese trading firms were able to offer excellent terms to their customers, especially to smaller, struggling companies like Kyŏngbang in the 1920s, for whom such credit could mean the difference between continued growth and bankruptcy. In an interview with this writer in 1984, Kim Yongwan still spoke of one of Kyŏngbang's main suppliers of yarn during the colonial period, the Yagi Trading Company (Yagi Shōten) of Osaka, with respect and gratitude. The people who ran Yagi, said Kim, were much like the people who ran Kyŏngbang itself — from high-born families, honest, active, interested not only in profits but also in the people with whom they did business. Most important, they were willing to give Kyŏngbang a line of credit: "So, if Kyŏngbang was short on money, they would sell and deliver to us on credit. Whenever we had problems, they would help us. The owner of the company was extremely kind to us."[15]

The relationship with Yagi also allowed Kyŏngbang to purchase its raw materials at favorable prices. For the same reasons that they could provide excellent credit terms, the large Japanese trading houses could also offer their best customers the benefits of their speculations in the futures market.[16] Such consideration was more than a blessing for Kyŏngbang in its early years: it was a necessity if the company was to survive in the face of competition from Japanese exports. In 1932 a reporter asked Kyŏngbang's business manager Yi Sangu how the company had been able to meet the challenge of Japanese exports to Korea. Yi replied that one crucial factor had been the company's ability to purchase raw materials at low prices.[17]

With so much to offer, the Japanese trading firms proved irresistible. Kyŏngbang's relationship with the Yagi Trading Company remained close throughout the colonial period. Yagi opened a branch office in Seoul in 1933, and Yagi's branch manager Ikeda Torazō was a Kyŏngbang stockholder.[18] Kyŏngbang also purchased raw materials through a number of other Japanese companies, including Nippon Menka and Tōyō Menka.[19] In each case the connection with Kyŏngbang was strengthened by these trading firms not only handling Kyŏngbang's procurement of raw materials but also—as we shall see in more detail later—acting as the company's sales agents.

Kyŏngbang was thus deftly enmeshed in a tangle of commercial ties that intimately linked it to the Japanese capitalist core. The company was in that sense really no different from any of the Japanese textile factories operating in Korea or in Japan itself: they too all depended on one or more of the large Japanese trading firms for their raw materials.

Raw Cotton

After 1936 Kyŏngbang had its own spinning facilities, and its interest in raw materials shifted from yarn to raw cotton itself. This change had the effect of gradually drawing the company even deeper into the Japanese economic nexus and ultimately giving Kyŏngbang a stake in the maintenance of the imperial economic system itself.

To understand the origin and dynamics of this relationship between company and empire, it is necessary to know a few facts about the cotton industry in Korea. Korea's land and climate are well suited to cotton cultivation and the country was capable during the colonial period of producing much of the total raw cotton it needed for domestic use. In 1941, for example, the monthly journal of the All Japan Cotton Spinners Association (Dai Nippon Bōseki Rengōkai) made the following comment on the rapid development of the Korean textile industry since the 1930s: "It goes without saying that the reason the spinning industry in Korea has been able to achieve rapid development during the past several years lies in the fact that Korea is to a great extent self-sufficient in the basic raw material: cotton."[20]

Korea was, in fact, able to grow a native cotton in all but one of its thirteen provinces and had been doing so for centuries. Most of the cotton was produced in Korea's southern provinces, especially in South Chŏlla. At the end of the Chosŏn dynasty, a well-defined cotton trade network encompassing the whole country had existed through which the most prominent cotton-producing regions could exchange goods with regions specializing in other products.[21]

Under Japanese rule Korea's cotton production was improved and expanded. Like the Koreans, the Japanese had been growing native cotton for centuries—since the end of the Muromachi Period (1338–1573)—and had even exported 15,000 bales of cotton to England during the American Civil War. In general, however, Japan's climate was less suitable to cotton cultivation than Korea's, and once the Meiji leaders had initiated industrialization, they quickly realized that it was cheaper simply to import raw cotton from overseas. Import duties on raw cotton were thus abolished as early as 1896.[22]

The first imported cotton came from China, but there was also considerable Japanese interest in Korea as a source of raw cotton even before the annexation in 1910. In 1904 the Japanese consul in Mokp'o introduced American upland cotton[23] to Korea for the first time, and in 1905 the Japanese Cotton Spinners Association financed an organization in Korea to promote production of the plant on the peninsula. This organization, the Association for the Cultivation of Cotton, distributed the superior American upland cotton seeds to Korean peasants free of charge and taught them advanced methods of cultivation to increase yields.

In 1906 the Japanese spinners also established the Korean Cotton Corporation in Osaka with a branch office in Mokp'o. The corporation advanced loans to Korean peasants who mortgaged their cotton crops to the company, thus allowing the Japanese spinners to maintain control over much of the raw cotton produced in the peninsula's southern cotton belt. The corporation also sent agents over to Mokp'o to purchase cotton through local brokers from peasants who had not mortgaged their crops. A local history of the Mokp'o area published in 1918 notes the existence of some eighty local cotton brokerage houses in the city who were working with the Japanese agents. The corporation was so anxious to obtain Korean cotton that it sent some of its agents deep into the tiny cotton-producing villages of the area to buy cotton directly from the individual Korean cultivators.[24]

After 1910 the Government-General also took an active part in promoting cotton production. In 1912 the authorities in Seoul launched a six-year plan that aimed at increasing the amount of land for cotton cultivation to 120,000 *chŏngbo* (100,000 *chŏngbo* of American upland cotton, 20,000 *chŏngbo* of Korean native cotton). By 1918 the results were encouraging, and the government wished to develop cotton production even further.

In 1933, Governor-General Ugaki announced a second plan that called for "cotton in the south, sheep in the north." The goal was to raise the amount of land set aside for cotton production to 500,000 *chŏngbo* by 1953. This plan was later revised upward twice to accommodate an ever-growing demand for raw cotton, especially after the outbreak of the Sino-Japanese War in 1937. Actual results, however, fell far short of the government's ambitious targets. Nevertheless, Korea's cotton production capacity had expanded considerably since 1904. In 1935, for example, the country was able to produce an amount of raw cotton equal to nearly 90 percent of its total domestic consumption. This figure fell to between 60 and 64 percent in subsequent years as Korea's textile industry rapidly expanded with the influx of Japanese capital and the establishment of large-scale combined spinning and weaving operations in Korea by Tōyōbō, Kanegafuchi, and other huge Japanese companies, but by 1939 the peninsula was once again producing an amount equal to nearly 90 percent of the total domestic consumption.[25]

The phrase "equal to" used above is deliberate and important. Even though Korea was producing nearly enough for its own domestic needs, it was not consuming all that it produced. The country was in the anomalous position of exporting somewhere between 20 and 50 percent of its yearly cotton crop even though it was producing slightly less than the amount it needed each year for domestic consumption.

To make up the difference, Korea was forced to import cotton from abroad. Imports continued to increase even as domestic cotton production was expanding and reaching a peak. The figures from any year will do to demonstrate the pattern at work here. In 1935, for example, Korea produced 86.5 percent of the cotton it needed to fulfill its domestic needs. It then exported 34.2 percent of its own production and wound up importing a total of no less than 43 percent of its domestic needs. In 1936, Korea only produced about 60 percent of its domestic needs, but because it exported about 50 percent of its production that year, it ended up importing 70 percent of the total required amount.[26]

What was going on? Why was Korea, itself not entirely self-sufficient in cotton, exporting up to 50 percent of its crop and then turning around and importing much larger amounts than it would have needed if it had not exported so much in the first place?

These seemingly improbable figures only begin to make sense when we examine Korea's position in the Japanese imperial division of labor. While the actual functioning of the system was, of course, more complex than the theory behind it, there was nevertheless a real attempt to put the theory into practice. In general, Japan was to be the producer of the sophisticated manufactured goods that required advanced technology, Manchuria and later China were to furnish many of the industrial raw materials, and Korea was to specialize in basic, unsophisticated industries requiring unskilled or semiskilled labor.[27]

What this meant to the textile industry was that Japan would concentrate on producing high-quality yarn and fabric for more expensive tastes in the West, while Korea would focus on simple, coarse materials for what we would today call the Third World. Manchuria and especially China would help provide the raw cotton and wool. At the industrial commission of 1936, Miyabayashi Taiji, a longtime resident of Korea and director-general of the Chōsen Cotton Yarn and Cloth Merchants Association (Chōsen Menshifushō Rengōkai), characterized Korea's role as follows:

In the Japanese spinning and weaving [industry] the machinery has become increasingly sophisticated, and [the industry] has been concentrating on producing only goods of high quality. [The industry thus] seems to be advancing even to the point where it is following in precisely the same [dangerous] footsteps as England's Manchester. If that's the case, the question of where the production of coarse cloth should be apportioned is an important matter for the fate of the spinning and weaving [industry] in Korea. The total world population is about 2.3 billion people, and of these, 400 million are still completely naked and 400 million are still half-naked. They are starting out by wearing the cheapest coarse material. However, when it comes to supply

sources for such [coarse cloth], the Indian spinning and weaving [industry]—
which until now has been our customer—is aggressively moving under orders
from England, the home country, to export to those places where Japan has
been trying to export. As you might expect, China is also promoting its spinning and weaving industry with the same intention. For the purpose of confronting and overcoming this [kind of competition], Korea, through the export
of Korean-made products, has come to assume a very important role in place
of Japan. In view of this, I fervently believe that it is an absolute necessity
from the point of view of the state to nurture industry all the more in Korea
in order to produce in Korea many inexpensive goods that are impossible
to produce in Japan—to make it a policy to manufacture in Korea things
[we] can't make in Japan.[28]

Korea's position in the imperial textile industry depicted by
Miyabayashi was clearly reflected in the type of yarn and cloth the
peninsula was producing. Shortly after Miyabayashi made the remarks
quoted above, Kim Yŏnsu himself decided to say a few words. In the
course of his speech, he described in detail the specific products the
Korean cotton industry was manufacturing in 1936. He noted that
there were basically two kinds of cloth being produced: coarse and
fine. The coarse cloth or "sheeting" was made from a thick number
14 yarn. What Kim called "fine cloth," moreover, was only fine in
comparison to the Korean sheeting. The Korean "fine cloth," according to Kim, was made from number 20-25 yarns, which are normally
classified by textile experts as "coarse" or possibly "medium." Korea
was thus producing very simple, thick fabric—exactly the kind
of cheap and durable cloth most popular in prewar Seoul, Mukden,
and Peking, but, then as now, not very exportable to New York or
Sydney.[29]

The unsophisticated quality of Korean production may be emphasized further by a comparison with Japan. By 1936 Japan had entered
its golden age of prewar textile production. In its volume of cotton
yarn and cloth production, it had already surpassed England and was
ranked second (after the United States) in the world.[30] In addition,
as Miyabayashi pointed out, Japan was concentrating more and more
on the production of high-quality goods. In 1929, for example, when
Arno S. Pearse from Manchester made his tour of Japanese and Chinese mills, Japanese factories were already spinning out a wide variety
of yarns with counts running as high as 120.[31]

At the time of the industrial commission of 1936, furthermore,
Japan was engaged in increasingly bitter disputes with the United
States, Australia, and other advanced industrial nations over its textile

exports to those countries. Only about two months after Miyabayashi and Kim Yŏnsu attended the conference in Seoul, Claudius T. Murchison, president of the American Cotton Textile Institute, declared, in a speech at the Textile Square Club in New York, that "Japanese imports will constitute a genuine menace to the American industry before the passage of another year." On the same day Lawrence Richman, treasurer of the Crompton Company of Warwick, Rhode Island, told the Tariff Commission in Washington, D.C., that Japanese competition threatened to drive American manufacturers of cotton velveteen and corduroy out of business and asked for respective tariff increases of 62.5 and 50 percent.[32] Japan had become a major supplier of manufactured products to the very country that had first forced it to open its ports to international trade.

In the unsophisticated nature of Korea's textile production within the imperial industrial structure, we find an explanation for the incongruous pattern of the colony's raw cotton trade. Cotton textile manufacturers naturally did not use the same kind of cotton for all grades of cloth. High-quality cloth demanded a high-quality cotton blend and vice versa. The Japanese had been promoting the cultivation of high-grade American upland cotton on the peninsula since 1904, but much of this cotton was intended for export at low prices to Japan's own spinning mills. Korea retained some of its cotton for use in its own factories but also imported (at great expense) a certain amount of high-grade cotton from the United States to compensate for the exports. At the same time a much greater amount of inferior Indian cotton was also imported to be mixed with the American variety to create a blend appropriate for the production of Korean coarse cloth.[33] The need to apportion raw cotton in accordance with Korea's particular role in the imperial production of textiles was the motivating force behind the initially puzzling cotton import-export pattern described earlier.

Given Korea's subordinate economic position within the Japanese Empire, this pattern was not at all unusual but was duplicated in other industries during the colonial period. Hundreds of thousands of tons of Korea's abundant high-grade anthracite coal, for example, were shipped every year to Kyūshū, from which Korea then imported an inferior bituminous coal, which was supplemented by other bituminous imports from Manchuria. At the industrial commission in 1936, Kim Yŏnsu himself complained about the situation in the coal industry and advocated a less expensive policy of "using Korean coal in Korea."[34] With cotton as with coal, however, satisfying the needs of colonial businessmen was less important to the Japanese authorities than maintaining a hierarchical division of labor within the empire.

As the war went on, the vision of an economically interdependent and hierarchical Yen Bloc became more and more impractical as enemy forces destroyed Japanese ships and disrupted shipping lanes, and each of Japan's overseas possessions was forced into a certain amount of economic self-sufficiency. By then, however, the already established pattern of dependency and apportionment of production made autarky on the peninsula impossible. Even at the height of the Pacific War, Korea was still exporting its American upland cotton to Japan in exchange for Japanese stocks of Indian cotton.[35]

In the end, the Korean textile industry's dependency on raw materials was not only limited to supplies of inferior Indian stock from Japan: by 1945 the Korean industry had become dependent on the maintenance of the imperialist system as a whole—especially on Japan's continued occupation of China.

As Japanese influence and control spread across Asia, public and private interest in developing a convenient continental source of raw cotton for Japan's ever expanding spinning industry grew accordingly. We have already seen how this interest was manifested in Korea; similar efforts were made in both Manchuria and China.

In Manchuria the South Manchuria Railway Company and later the Manchukuo authorities tried to foster cotton production, but most of the country lay too far to the north to be suitable for the cultivation of high-grade cotton. The native Manchurian cotton had to be mixed with American upland cotton in order to be spun. In general, however, it was used for padding in winter clothes, and Manchukuo continued to import large quantities of raw cotton from abroad. F. C. Jones has noted that as late as 1937 the production of cotton in Manchuria for the modern textile industry had scarcely gone beyond the experimental stage. The Manchukuo authorities continued through 1945 to promote cotton cultivation by a mixture of "inducements and threats," but the results were not very satisfactory.[36] After 1937, earlier hopes of turning Manchuria into a cotton belt for Japanese industry were superseded by the economic opportunities presented by Japan's invasion of China. In the end it was China that was designated to become the main source of supply of cheap cotton for the Greater East Asia Co-Prosperity Sphere.

As noted above, Meiji Japan's first imports of raw cotton had come from China. As the Japanese textile industry grew and became more and more sophisticated, shifting from coarse to medium to fine yarns and cloth, it gradually abandoned Chinese cotton for superior grades of raw cotton—first from India, later from the United States and Egypt.[37] The wartime necessity of curtailing the outflow of foreign exchange for cotton imports from the United States and elsewhere after 1937, however, made Japan look once again to its newly conquered territories in China as a source of raw cotton. Although the quality of Chinese cotton was inferior to that produced in the United States, it could, as in Korea, be improved with better seeds and cultivation methods, and China's immense cultivation area looked extremely promising to the empire's cotton-starved militarists and textile magnates.[38] Under wartime conditions, moreover, quality, as we have seen, was less important than the simple maintenance of production.

Even before Japanese troops on the continent swept south in 1937, Japan had already been importing about 2.4 percent of its yearly raw cotton needs from China.[39] Once the war had given the Japanese army control over large sections of the country itself, plans were quickly laid by Japanese officials to transform vast tracts of land south of the Great Wall into cotton-producing areas.

Given Korea's geographical proximity to China, the colony's bureaucrats and businessmen were among the empire's most ardent supporters of such exploitation. The report of the Government-General's industrial commission of 1938, for example, included a special section on "The Use of Cotton from North China in the Spinning and Weaving Industry." The report called for the replacement of raw cotton imports from the United States and India by a combination of Korean and Chinese cotton. American imports were to be replaced by an increase in the cultivation of American upland cotton in Korea itself.

As a producer of coarse yarn and cloth, however, Korea only used 40 percent of the higher grade American cotton in its particular blend for yarn: a full 60 percent of the blend consisted of Indian cotton. The industrial commission was not disconcerted. Cotton production in north China, the commission noted, had been about five million piculs in 1936; this was already more than six times Korea's total cotton consumption, and the prospects of increasing production even further (now that Japan was in control of the area) were "extraordinarily bright." The delegates therefore called for all Indian cotton imports to be replaced by imports from north China, and the Korean textile industry suddenly found itself dependent for much of its basic raw materials on the Japanese army's continued control of Chinese territory.[40]

The great expectations of the Government-General and the colonial textile industry in regard to China and Chinese cotton turned out to be far too sanguine. China was never able to produce enough cotton to satisfy all imperial needs, and regular transport became more and more of a problem as the war went on.

Nevertheless, it is clear from Kyŏngbang's own business reports that the company was depending on Chinese as well as Korean cotton to keep production going during the war. As noted earlier, Korea's own plans for increased cotton cultivation fell far short of the projected goals. Unexpectedly cold weather during the growing season also took its toll on some of the cotton crops. Kyŏngbang mentioned such problems in its wartime business reports to stockholders — while also making enthusiastic comments concerning the arrival of Chinese cotton for "special use," that is, for authorized nonmilitary production.[41] Quite apart from the company's interest in the Japanese army as a valuable customer, such dependency on China as a source of raw cotton for its civilian production clearly gave Kyŏngbang a vested interest in Japanese militarism on the continent through 1945 and strengthened the company's ties to the imperial system as a whole.

Technology

The myth of Korean "national capital" discussed earlier holds that Kyŏngbang relied entirely on Korean technology for its operation and development during the colonial period. Common sense alone suggests that this could not have been the case. Nevertheless, while such historical distortion is unfortunate, it does at least serve to emphasize the important role that technology inevitably plays in the production process as well as in permitting a developing nation to achieve a certain economic autonomy. Before we examine the technological situation that prevailed in colonial Korea, let us for the sake of comparison consider the way in which Japan was able to overcome an initial dependency on foreign technology and establish its own national technological base.

Technology as it concerns us here really has two aspects. One is the actual machinery and equipment required by any particular industry, the other is the technical knowledge and skill needed to produce or operate such machinery. Late developing countries have a certain advantage over their predecessors in that they can borrow or purchase the most advanced technology available at the time. No country that has followed in Britain's wake, for example, has had to "reinvent" the steam engine. Until a country manages to establish facilities within its own borders for producing industrial machinery and training technicians, however, it will invariably be dependent for its industrial equipment and technical expertise on another country that has already done so. Depending on the national aspirations of the country concerned, such reliance on foreign help may be considered demeaning. It is certainly expensive and renders the country vulnerable to outside forces.

Like all late developing countries, Meiji Japan also began industrialization dependent on foreign technology. In the cotton textile industry, for example, Japan naturally turned to England as a model. In the 1880s Meiji Japan's leading textile firm, the Osaka Spinning Company, conscientiously followed a standard British design for its own mill, even to the point of using Lancashire red brick for the factory facade. All machinery, accessories, and parts were ordered from England, and all were identical down to the smallest specification to equipment being used in British mills. As late as 1909 nearly 90 percent of Japan's total spindleage was supplied by Platt Brothers of Oldham, England.[42]

British technicians also played a prominent role in the establishment of Japan's modern textile industry. One scholar notes that "during at least the first seven years and very possibly the first thirty-five years of the firm's (Osaka Spinning Company's) existence, English technicians were never very far away." Not surprisingly, it was Platt Brothers who also provided the Japanese with technicians as well as with mill designs and machinery. Many new companies continued to retain Platt Brothers technicians as consultants after their mills had been built and the machinery installed, and in the period before the First World War a small group of Platt Brothers representatives "serviced the entire industry."[43]

It was not long, however, before Japanese firms began to produce domestic versions of imported textile machinery. As early as the 1870s, Japan was capable of producing its own spinning machinery, and the Japanese textile industry had its own hank-cop reeler even before the country had a constitution.[44] In spite of many such cases of Japanese firms displaying the technical expertise to produce import substitutes, the textile industry in general continued to prefer foreign machinery until the First World War.[45]

The war proved to be a stimulus to the technological development of the industry. Preoccupied with fighting in their own part of the world, the Western powers abandoned their Asian markets to Japan, and the Japanese textile industry boomed. During the war, however, it became extremely difficult for Japanese textile manufacturers to obtain equipment and parts from abroad, and the industry was forced to fall back on domestic producers. The result was a collaborative effort between the textile and machine industries that continued to flourish even after the war came to an end.[46]

After the war the Japanese went on to produce precision textile machinery that by the late 1920s was as efficient and competitive as anything that could be produced in either England or the United States. As far as weaving technology was concerned, the Japanese had actually surpassed the Western countries with the invention of the Toyoda Automatic Loom in 1926.

Toyoda's new loom and the technical expertise that obviously lay behind it created something of a sensation within the international textile community, many of whose members in the West had blithely underestimated Japan's technological capabilities. The loom was an apt symbol of the enormous strides made by the Japanese in the development of industrial technology since the Restoration. It allowed factory managers to assign as many as sixty looms to a single worker, whereas before the average number of looms per worker had been six. Every part of the loom, including the screws, was fabricated at Toyoda, and the market price in Osaka was about four hundred yen cheaper than the American standard automatic loom.[47] Western technical and commercial experts like Arno S. Pearse who came to Japan to see the new loom in operation and to have a firsthand look at the industry that had produced it were astonished by what they saw. As Pearse quickly realized, the Toyoda Automatic Loom was only the most visible part of a broad and creative national technological base. After a visit to the Toyoda Automatic Loom Works in 1929, Pearse wrote: "The writer when visiting the Toyoda Automatic Loom Works was surprised to find that many automatic machine tools are used. The foundry is on the latest model of the textile machinists in the U.S.A. Besides having the latest moulding machinery they use a very modern chromium-plating plant, in order to make all bright parts rustless, which is a great advantage in the fog-bound weaving sheds of the Far East."[48]

Pearse also noted that in addition to the Toyoda Automatic Loom, the Japanese were producing a number of other looms—all of which, Pearse added with emphasis, were "their *own* inventions." In fact, Pearse observed, very few foreign looms were now being sold in Japan and even used Japanese looms were fetching higher prices than comparable secondhand European machines. The perfection of the Toyoda Automatic Loom, Pearse concluded, demonstrated the progress of Japanese technology: "Even today, with the exception of the mule (and that is no more considered an essential machine), one can buy all other machines of Japanese make. . . . Japan has made such progress in engineering that within a few years very little textile machinery will be imported from Europe."[49]

As far as textile technology was concerned, by 1930 the Japanese had little if anything to learn from the West. In fact, the situation was now reversed. Westerners were now touring Japan to try to understand the secret of Japan's success. In his report of 1929 Pearse stated bluntly that Europe could learn an important lesson from Japan in weaving,[50] and the following year saw a watershed in that regard. In December that year Platt Brothers, the English machinery firm that had supplied Meiji Japan with so much of its first textile technology, signed an agreement with Toyoda giving Platt the exclusive right to manufacture and sell Toyoda looms in Britain (including British possessions in Africa and Asia) and on the continent. In January 1930, Toyoda technicians left for England to instruct and train Platt engineers in the Toyoda manufacturing process.[51] The able student was now teaching the teacher—a good indication of the high level and prestige that Japanese textile technology managed to attain before 1945.

William Lockwood has described the success and impact of the Toyoda loom as an "exceptional" case in the history of prewar Japanese technology, and it is true that in other industries—especially those like aeronautics requiring advanced engineering skills—Japan lagged behind the West in the pre-1945 period.[52] In the textile industry, however, Japan could justly claim equality and in some respects superiority vis-à-vis the West. And if prewar Japanese technology suffered somewhat from comparison with the West, it nevertheless towered like Mount Fuji over the abject state of technology in colonial Korea.

Machinery

When the Japanese decided to permit some industrial development in Korea after 1921, they naturally had no thought of simultaneously developing a technological base within Korea itself.

There would have been no point to such an undertaking. First, the colonial government's initial conception of industrial development for Korea was extremely narrow, and a broad and sophisticated technological infrastructure in Korea would have been superfluous. The Government-General's focus, of course, was entirely on Japan's own needs. As Vice-Governor-General Mizuno noted at the time, what Japan required from Korea were those products Japan could not produce itself, especially industrial raw materials. In addition to the development and exploitation of Korean natural resources, the Saitō government proposed a limited development of light industry, especially textiles, for which there was a sufficiently large market both in Korea and on the Asian continent so as not to interfere unduly with exports from Japan itself.

The Japanese also regarded Korea as an extension of Japan proper and saw no reason why a second and possibly competitive technological base should be established in Korea. Korea could obtain all the technology it needed from Japan. This dependency was also facilitated by the abolition of all tariffs except on liquor and textiles between Korea and Japan in 1923.

At first such an arrangement seemed both reasonable and adequate given Japanese goals and Korea's low level of technology. Even the Korean bourgeoisie, which had been brought into the policy-making process, raised no objections at the time to the idea of dependency on Japanese technology. In his various comments at the Government-General's industrial commission of 1921, Han Sangnyong, for example, accepted dependency on Japanese capital and technology as a natural condition of Korean industrial development and focused his concern instead on insuring a role in the development process for the Korean business elite.[53]

Later, as Japanese aims on the peninsula became increasingly militaristic and Korea came to be seen as an "advance military supply base" for continental aggrandizement, the policy of technological dependency proved to be shortsighted. Plans were subsequently made at the industrial commissions of 1936 and 1938 for rapid expansion of the machine and tool industries in Korea in conjunction with the development of a military-oriented heavy industrial base.[54]

Some progress was made, but it was a case of too little too late. The machine and tool industry (including vehicles and vessels) constituted only 2.3 percent of Korea's total industrial production as late as 1938, and the country continued to import virtually all of its important capital goods from Japan through 1945.[55]

The problem was complicated because Korea's technological dependency on Japan was not limited to machinery and tools but included accessories and spare parts as well. Even the nuts, bolts, and washers for the industrial machinery had to be imported from Japan. Everyday light bulbs, so basic to modern life, provide a good case in point. Korea was rich in the tungsten needed for the filaments used in the bulbs, and the bulbs were actually fabricated in Korea. The filaments, however, were manufactured in Japan. Japan imported Korean tungsten and then exported it back to Korea in the form of filaments.[56]

Korea's dependency on Japanese technology is well documented in Kyŏngbang's papers. In 1922 the company installed its first power looms, which were purchased from Toyoda,[57] and the relationship between Kyŏngbang and Toyoda continued to deepen throughout the colonial period. In addition to looms, Toyoda provided Kyŏngbang with various kinds of spinning equipment, including such things as weights for rings, creeper lattices, hopper bale breakers, hopper openers, lattice feeders, hopper feeders, clearer cages, dust trunks, exhaust openers. scutchers, and drawing frames.[58]

Kyŏngbang used many other Japanese suppliers as well. In 1933 the company imported 224 Nogami automatic looms, the newest and best equipment available at the time.[59] For basic machinery, as well as for accessories and parts, Kyŏngbang often dealt directly with the particular manufacturer, but there were also many instances of the company's purchase of equipment through Japanese commercial houses such as Takashimaya's Osaka branch or the Osaka-based Murakami Shōten, which acted as an agent for Toyoda. Other Japanese companies with which Kyŏngbang did regular business included such firms as Nippon Machine Industry Company KK, Nōsawa Machinery KK, Bandai Trading Company KK, and Ōnishi Shōten KK.[60]

The use of non-Japanese equipment by Kyŏngbang was exceptional but not unheard of. In 1936, for example, the company installed 21,600 Swiss spindles in its new factory.[61] In general, however, Kyŏngbang placed its orders with Japanese companies, and even the Swiss spindles were probably ordered through a Japanese trading concern.

Given Japan's proximity and its special relationship with Korea, the preponderant use of Japanese technology was not surprising. The Japanese companies, moreover, gave Kyŏngbang excellent terms. Payments were often spread out over a decade or more, and yearly amortization ran as low as 7.4 percent in many cases. In May 1937, for example, Kyŏngbang purchased thirty drawing frames for its spinning department directly from Toyoda for a total of 57,000 yen. The initial amortization was 7.4 percent per year paid in semiannual installments. The yearly rate of amortization rose slightly to 9 percent and later to 11.2 percent as the debt was gradually reduced, but eight years later when the colonial period suddenly came to an end, Kyŏngbang still owed over 40 percent of the original 57,000 yen to Toyoda.[62]

Even Kyŏngbang's small orders were given favorable treatment by Japanese suppliers. In May 1937, for example, Kyŏngbang purchased a single ring grain balance from the Matsui Company. The total amount involved was only 70 yen, yet even this order was paid off over a period of two years at a rate of 8.8 percent. At the same time Kyŏngbang also acquired an item from the Sugihara Company that cost only 120 yen. After eight years of semiannual payments of between 3 and 5 yen, the company still owed Suihara 46 yen as of May 1945.[63]

Many such transactions can be found on the thousands of pages of Kyŏngbang's extant records and vouchers. Such papers eloquently confirm the almost total dependency of the company on Japanese technology. As Kyŏngbang expanded in the many directions indicated earlier, the need for Japanese equipment naturally increased dramatically. Eventually, in 1942, the company even established a formal representative office in Osaka to facilitate such procurement.[64]

The most telling evidence, however, of the scope of Kyŏngbang's dependency lies less in the volume of its purchases from Japanese companies than in the orders themselves. In addition to relying on basic Japanese machinery, the company also depended on Japan for nearly all of its accessories and spare parts. It is difficult, for example, to think of a more simple and basic accessory in the spinning process than the bobbin on which the yarn is wound, but even bobbins, at 4 sen apiece, were ordered from Osaka or Kuwana.[65] And bobbins were only one of the many accessories and parts Kyŏngbang imported from Japan. A single invoice from Takashimaya's Osaka branch dated June 8, 1942, lists fifteen different accessories or parts, including such items as knobs, caps, catches, blades, and springs used in the spinning and weaving processes. The invoice even includes orders for studs and washers.[66] Virtually all of the company's machinery right down to the screws themselves were coming from Japan.

Technical Expertise

Colonial Korea's technological dependency on Japan was not only manifested by machinery and parts. Equally important was the dependency on Japanese technical knowledge and skills. It did no good to have the latest equipment from Nagoya if one did not know how to operate it properly or repair it when it broke down. Such expertise was based on a certain level of technical study and training in the textile field that necessitated an industrial educational and training establishment that colonial Korea simply did not have.

Once again Korea's backwardness may be emphasized by a brief comparison with Japan itself. From the beginning the Meiji government took an active role in the acquisition of Western technical knowledge and in the development of a comprehensive industrial educational system in Japan. In addition to sending technical missions and individual students to the West for observation and study, both the government and private industry hired hundreds of foreign technicians to instruct and train Japanese in Western technology.

More important, perhaps, was the attention given to national education. In 1871 a Ministry of Education was inaugurated, and a national system of education based on French models was established that gave ample regard to the needs of industry. By the turn of the century nearly 30,000 six-year elementary schools were providing millions of Japanese children with the basic education essential to any industrial society. Beyond this elementary level, a structure of secondary and higher technical education was gradually developed — including extensive facilities for advanced scientific and engineering research — that eventually won Japan international recognition and prestige. The combination of such policies was so successful that Japan was able to replace most of its foreign technicians with native Japanese by the 1920s,[67] and by the late 1920s Toyoda was actually dispatching its own Japanese technicians to England to teach and train British engineers in the manufacture of the company's own patented automatic loom.

In Korea the Japanese implemented a very different policy of industrial education. In Japan itself their goal had been to develop a comprehensive system of technical education that would produce not only a diverse labor force with the necessary knowledge and skills to handle various levels of technical work but a core of scientists and engineers who could perfect and advance the current state of technology. Korea's colonial government, on the other hand, was interested mainly in insuring the existence of a labor force in Korea that possessed the rudimentary education required to carry out orders from factory managers who were for the most part Japanese.

There was, in fact, more than a little concern among the Japanese that too much education for the Korean working class might be potentially dangerous to Japanese colonial interests. At the industrial commission of 1936, colonial Korea's biggest single private investor and employer, Noguchi Jun of Nippon Chisso, whose various enterprises in Korea accounted for over 40 percent of the peninsula's total paid-in industrial capital at the time,[68] suggested that the higher common or middle school system for Koreans be restructured so as to concentrate more on vocational education and simultaneously preclude young Koreans from receiving a more expansive general education that might lead to an interest in communism:

When I first began my [business] activities in Korea, the Koreans I employed as workers were generally graduates of higher common school. But Russian communism was rampant in North and South Hamgyŏng Provinces, and scores of arrests were carried out around this time. On each such occasion many of the criminals came from my factory. All of them were graduates of higher common school. I decided from that time on never to employ any higher common school graduates in my factories. I would imagine that those who engage in [industrial] work in Korea in the future will have the same experience [as I did]. As it seems, the higher common schools are spending a good sum of money on producing people not very useful to business — although one shouldn't generalize [because some useful men may emerge from the existing school system]. What I would like to suggest, therefore, is to take the standard five years [of education] in the higher common or middle schools and assign the first two years to general education and the following three years to vocational education in such [areas] as industry and commerce.[69]

Before 1936, when the Government-General first began to lay plans for the transformation of Korea into a military supply base, the Japanese had shown little interest in developing even industrial education for Koreans beyond the most elementary level. At the time Noguchi made the remarks quoted above, there was only one professional technical school — the Keijō Higher Industrial School — in the entire country, and its curriculum left much to be desired. Noguchi himself suggested that its limited course offerings made it only "half a school."[70]

At the university level, the situation was even more dismal. An imperial university had been established in Seoul in 1925, but it had no engineering college until 1938, and Han Sangnyong noted at the 1936 conference that although one could find Korean bureaucrats in the colonial government who had become provincial governors and heads of bureaus, the colony did not have even one Korean professor in a technical field.[71]

In the late 1930s the Government-General attempted to rectify this situation as Korea's crucial role in the anticipated continental war became increasingly apparent. The industrial commission of 1936 called for a general expansion of vocational and technical education at all levels along with an effort to foster apprenticeship training below the secondary level. Noguchi Jun must have been pleased with the commission's final report. Although the commission advocated the establishment of advanced industrial courses at the university level together with the spread of professional and higher industrial schools, major emphasis was placed on the intensification and redirection of elementary and secondary education specifically in conjunction with the Government-General's new industrial goals.[72]

Such, at least, was the commission's plan and hope. To translate such goals into reality would have taken far more time and money than the Japanese had left. One does not create or transform an entire educational system overnight, nor is industrial expertise acquired simply by attending school. In the nine years that remained of Japanese colonialism in Korea after 1936, new educational facilities were opened, and more Koreans than ever before received some basic primary and vocational education.[73] In general, however, after 1936 Korean companies like Kyŏngbang continued to be dependent on Japanese technical skills.

It seems to have been company policy for Kyŏngbang to use Korean technicians whenever possible, and it is at least partly because of this avowed aim, repeatedly emphasized in the company's advertising and official histories, that the myth of Kyŏngbang's reliance solely on Korean technology appears to have taken such firm root. Even as early as 1932, Kyŏngbang's business manager Yi Sangu proudly told a reporter from the *Chōsen jitsugyō kurabu* that the company's personnel were entirely Korean and that they were "in no way inferior to Japanese or other foreign workers or technicians."[74]

While Kyŏngbang's technical experts indeed proved themselves to be able textile engineers, they were not all Korean. Some were Japanese. Given the undeveloped state of Korean technology and technical education, it is difficult to see how the company could have avoided using Japanese engineers somewhere along the way.

The company was, in fact, compelled to make numerous exceptions to its much publicized nationalistic policy. When, for example, the Kims converted the old Kyŏngsŏng Chingnyu Company into a rubber goods factory after Kyŏngbang's new facilities had been built, the entire operation, from preliminary design to initial production, was entrusted to a Japanese engineer.[75] Both the Yagi Trading Company and C. Itoh, Japanese textile firms with whom Kyŏngbang enjoyed a particularly close relationship, also regularly supplied the company with Japanese technicians at Kyŏngbang's request.[76] And in the 1930s, when Kyŏngbang first expanded its operations to include spinning as well as weaving, it was a Japanese engineer with C. Itoh named Kirita who was Yi Kanghyŏn's first choice to supervise the construction of the new factory.[77]

While Kyŏngbang could not entirely escape a dependency on Japanese technicians, the company nevertheless made a conscious and determined attempt from the beginning to train its own personnel. Funds were regularly set aside by the board of directors for such purposes. Even as early as October 1919 at its second formal meeting, the board voted to budget 2,400 yen (nearly 10% of the company's paid-in capital at the time) "for the training of technicians."[78]

Such efforts by the company to create its own core of technicians, however, in the end only emphasized Korea's dependency on Japan. Kyŏngbang's technicians could of course obtain some basic technical education in Korea itself, but they invariably found it necessary to pursue advanced study or training in Japan. Yi Kanghyŏn, the company's first and foremost technician, was himself a graduate of the Tokyo Higher Industrial School (later Tokyo Industrial College). Yun Chubok, whom Kim Yongwan chose to manage the new factory of Kyŏngbang's affiliate, the Chungang Commercial and Industrial Company, was a graduate of Kyūshū University.[79] With so many of its own personnel the products of a Japanese technical education, it is not surprising that in 1940 the company donated 10,000 yen to Kyoto University's Chemical Research Institute to encourage the university's work in textile technology.[80] A financial contribution of such magnitude epitomized the company's attitude and position with respect to Japanese technology.

It was, in fact, regular company practice for Kyŏngbang to send its new technical personnel to Japan for training.[81] In turn, this desire to give its technicians the best training available in Japan also served to cement the company's ties with Japanese textile firms and thus in a larger sense to strengthen the bond between Korean and Japanese capital.

Kyŏngbang's relationship with the C. Itoh Company was a case in point. Now one of the largest general trading companies in Japan, C. Itoh originally began as a textile wholesaler in Osaka and eventually became one of the major prewar international textile trading companies with assorted other interests as well, including agricultural products, machinery, iron and steel products, and automobiles. Once Japan's political predominance in Korean affairs was stabilized with the transformation of the country into a Japanese protectorate in 1905, the company moved quickly to establish a direct export line to Korea by opening a branch office in Seoul in 1907. Although C. Itoh subsequently diversified its products and expanded its markets to many other areas as well, the company continued to play an important role in Korean trading circles.[82]

Pak Sŭngjik, whose enterprise in the textile trade stretched back to the late Yi dynasty and whose son later went on to establish one of South Korea's largest business groups (Tusan), was originally responsible for bringing Kyŏngbang and C. Itoh together. The contact proved to be the beginning of an amiable and mutually profitable relationship, and personal and business connections between the two parties continue to be strong even today.[83]

During the colonial period C. Itoh became involved in several crucial aspects of Kyŏngbang's business. In addition to supplying Kyŏngbang with raw materials and machinery at good prices, the company also acted as a sales agent for Kyŏngbang's cloth. In the late 1930s it also helped Kyŏngbang set up its spinning and weaving factory in southern Manchuria, and Kyŏngbang returned the favor several years later by joining C. Itoh in a new textile venture in Korea (Taejŏn).[84]

What interests us here, however, is C. Itoh's role during the colonial period as one of Kyŏngbang's main sources of Japanese technology. As noted, Kyŏngbang would ask C. Itoh and other companies to furnish Japanese technicians when needed. This was only part of the story. Kyŏngbang recruited many of its young Korean engineers from the Keijō Higher Industrial School in Seoul, whose students entered the school after passing through five years of middle or higher common school.[85] The course of study at Keijō Higher Industrial took three years, and students in the textile department could take beginning, intermediate, and advanced classes in a variety of subjects, including spinning, weaving, and dyeing. The school also offered classes in mechanical design, mechanical principles, industrial organization, figured weaving, principles and testing of raw materials, and fabric analysis and design. In spite of the school's rather impressive textile curriculum, Kyŏngbang nevertheless found it necessary to supplement the education available in Korea by sending those graduates the company hired to Japan, where they received an additional year's on-the-job training at one of the various factories owned by the Kureha Spinning Company, a subsidiary of C. Itoh.[86]

It was a convenient and valuable arrangement for both firms. C.

Itoh enjoyed the long-term use of Korean personnel free of charge and was simultaneously rewarded with regular business from Kyŏngbang in orders for raw materials and equipment as well as contracts and fees for handling the sale of Kyŏngbang's cloth. For Kyŏngbang the arrangement was even more advantageous. In addition to learning something of the ruling metropolitan language and culture, Kyŏngbang's young engineers in their year at Kureha were given a taste of the international textile trade at one of its major centers and, most important, exposed at the factory level to the best and most recent technology that the Japanese textile industry could offer.

For Kyŏngbang on its own to have provided its new technicians with a Japanese education and experience of such depth would probably have been impossible. It would certainly have been expensive. With the Kureha connection, Kyŏngbang obtained this training gratis. Each month the company received a bill from Kureha to cover the cost of its trainees' food, living allowances, and bonuses—a good part of which cost Kyŏngbang would have been paying even if the trainees had never left Korea. For the training itself, however, there appears to have been no charge.[87]

In 1984 Kim Yongwan told this writer that Kureha Spinning had been "a good friend" to Kyŏngbang.[88] In a sense he was correct. For its own reasons Kureha had indeed been kind to Kyŏngbang, but there was much more to the relationship than friendship. Important interests had been at stake on both sides. Among other things C. Itoh had wanted to keep a good customer. For Kyŏngbang the relationship had been far more serious and important—Kureha had provided the company with a direct and inexpensive channel through which Kyŏngbang had been able to obtain the essential technical expertise so lacking in Korea itself.

CHAPTER 6

Between Metropole and Hinterland
The Quest for Markets

Production in itself involves only expense. To transform debits into credits, production must be complemented by marketing, which involves two different though related areas. The first concerns the distribution channels through which any company sells its products. The second refers to the market structure itself — the particular pattern or configuration of the company's sales, that is, what the company is selling to whom and why.

Marketing in this dual sense was to mean for Kyŏngbang a deepening of that dependency relationship with Japanese capitalism already seen in the company's procurement of raw materials and technology. In the end, moreover, the marketing of its goods led Kyŏngbang into active collaboration with Japanese imperialism in Manchuria and China and greatly increased the company's tangible stake in the perpetuation of the empire.

Distribution

It would be wrong to suggest that Kyŏngbang was totally dependent on Japanese trading companies for the marketing of its yarn and cloth. The reality was much more complicated. Ultimately the company did turn to Japanese firms, but both before and afterward it utilized other marketing methods as well. The crucial concern of the company was to sell its goods — a need that approached desperation in its early years — and any and all means deemed useful were employed.

The Government-General proved to be helpful in a number of ways. We noted earlier that the government's subsidies to Kyŏngbang were a key factor in the company's ability to survive in the midst of competition from Japanese exports in the 1920s. The colonial authorities also sponsored periodic trade fairs to promote Korean products.[1] Either directly or indirectly, through such semiofficial organizations as the Seoul Chamber of Commerce and Industry, the government also organized fact-finding missions to explore potential new markets; Kim Yŏnsu, for example, participated in such a mission to Manchuria (sponsored by the P'yŏngyang city government) in 1921.[2]

After Manchuria became an independent state under Japanese tutelage, such tours became even more frequent, and the Government-General, as part of its general policy of building a Japanese-Manchurian economic bloc, made a point of assisting any companies that were interested in the Manchurian market. Thus shortly after the establishment of Manchukuo in 1932, the Seoul Chamber of Commerce and Industry arranged a fact-finding trip across the Yalu in which Kyŏngbang participated.[3] Several years later the Government-General lent its full support, financial and otherwise, to Kyŏngbang's efforts to establish a new spinning and weaving facility in Manchuria itself.

While government encouragement was valuable, it was also limited and occasional, at best a useful supplement to the company's regular marketing activities. In Kyŏngbang's early years the distribution of goods was handled for the most part by the company itself. It was an arduous process. Even though Kyŏngbang's prices were slightly lower than those of similar goods imported from Japan, the quality of the company's cloth was also somewhat inferior. Compared to the well-known Japanese brands like the "Triple A" exported by Tōyōbō, moreover, Kyŏngbang's cloth was virtually unknown.

For such reasons Korean merchants at first refused even to carry Kyŏngbang's goods. The company poured almost 10 percent of its operating expenses into sales and sent its salesmen throughout the Seoul area virtually begging the merchants to handle its cloth, but the merchants generally declined. They were not even willing to sell Kyŏngbang's goods on a commission basis lest the company's unpopular cloth take up space that could be more profitably occupied by Japanese imports. Outside Seoul the situation was similar. The company became so desperate that it eventually dispatched its salesmen to local periodic markets, where they were forced to hawk the company's wares in competition with a host of other peddlers.[4]

Such measures were not entirely without effect. At the very least they helped introduce Kyŏngbang's cloth to Korean consumers. At the same time the quality of Kyŏngbang's cloth improved as the company became more experienced. Kyŏngbang was also fairly successful in its appeals to nationalistic sentiment among Korean consumers, especially in the northern part of the peninsula.[5] In attempting to persuade potential customers to try its goods, the company focused its advertising on Kyŏngbang's unique position as a large-scale textile factory owned and operated by Koreans. Kyŏngbang's New Year's advertisement in the January 1924 issue of Sanŏpkye—the official journal of the Association to Promote Korean Goods—is a good example of the kind of appeal the company was making. The first lines of the advertisement call upon all Koreans "who love Korea" to use only Korean products, "starting with the material for clothes—broadcloth produced for the first time with Korean capital and technology."[6]

In time the company was able to persuade Korean merchants to accept its cloth, and Kyŏngbang eventually began to consign its goods to selected Korean merchants as "special sales agents" (t'ugyak p'anmaejŏm) on a regular basis. By the 1930s the company had established scores of such relationships with small and medium wholesale and retail shops.[7] Of these many contacts, two in particular proved to be especially significant and enduring in the history of the company. The first was with Pak Sŭngjik.

Pak was born in 1864, the third of five sons, to a peasant family living in the Kwangju area of Kyŏnggi Province. He spent his childhood and adolescence at home helping his family work the land, but a fascination with commerce led him to join the Kyŏnggi merchants involved in the foreign cloth trade through Inch'ŏn. By 1898 he had accumulated enough capital and experience to open his own dry-goods shop at Chongno Sa-ga in Seoul, and within several years he had established a reputation that attracted attention in the highest official circles in the capital. After 1905 those circles were dominated by the Japanese, whose attitude toward Korean merchants was generally condescending or even contemptuous, but even they were impressed. Itō Hirobumi, for example, Korea's first resident general, noting that Pak and another Korean were "effective and promising" merchants in the textile business, instructed the governor of the Bank of Korea to give them his support.[8]

Pak, on the other hand, had no qualms or lack of confidence about working with the Japanese even though he had never learned their language and had to operate through interpreters.[9] In 1907 he and a number of other Koreans joined a Japanese businessman named Nishihara in setting up a new joint venture textile trading firm, the Kongik (Kōeki) Company (literally, "common benefit"), that made history by establishing a direct import line with Japanese trading companies in Japan, thereby breaking the strangle hold of Korea's predominantly Chinese middlemen. Pak went on to become one of the most important and respected businessmen in colonial Korea, and his descendants today control one of South Korea's largest business groups.[10]

When Kyŏngbang was just beginning to produce its first cloth in the 1920s, Pak was already a key merchant in the Korean textile trade. The Kongik Company had expanded from an unlimited partnership with a capital of only about 21,000 yen into a joint-stock company capitalized at 1 million yen in 1921. It had gradually set up branch offices throughout the country and extended its activities to major cities in Manchuria as well.[11]

Pak's influence was enhanced further by his position of leadership among both Korean and Japanese textile merchants. In 1918 he had organized Seoul's Korean cotton cloth traders into a citywide association over which he presided as chairman.[12] At the same time his role as stockholder and president of Kongik made him a pivotal figure in the establishment of a similar association in Seoul dominated by Japanese merchants that was eventually transformed into the Chōsen Cotton Yarn and Cloth Merchants Association. When the association was established in 1920, Mitsui Bussan's Seoul office assumed the chairmanship, and Pak was given a seat on the board of directors. In 1929, on the eve of the tenth anniversary of its founding, the association published a detailed history of the cotton textile trade in Korea in which Pak was specially commended as a "pioneer in Japanese-Korean cooperative enterprise."[13]

Through Pak Sŭngjik, Kyŏngbang gained entry to a wide network of yarn and cloth distribution channels, including direct access to major Japanese trading companies. Kyŏngbang's formal introduction to the C. Itoh Company, for example, was arranged by Pak, who was particularly close to the famous Osaka firm because of its substantial equity investments in Kongik beginning in 1910.[14] Even after Kyŏngbang's operations had significantly expanded and the company began to make extensive use of the major Japanese trading firms, the relationship with Pak was maintained, and Kyŏngbang continued to take advantage of Pak's connections with the Korean merchants in Seoul.[15]

A similarly close and mutually beneficial relationship developed between the Kims and another Korean merchant: Pak Hŭngsik. In 1926, just as Kyŏngbang was finally starting to make a dent in the market with Pak Sŭngjik's help, Pak Hŭngsik made his first appearance in Seoul as a brash young businessman from the north. Like Pak Sŭngjik, he came from commoner stock and was a self-made merchant who had started out at the bottom as a teen-ager in his home province.[16] Pak had entered the Chinnamp'o Commercial and Technical School, but he had quit almost immediately to return home and take care of his mother.[17] Like Pak Sŭngjik, lack of higher education proved to be no obstacle to success in business. Whereas the Kim brothers relied on the immense resources of their family and their first-rate Japanese education, Pak Hŭngsik made his way to the top of the colonial business world through a potent combination of determination, inventiveness, forcefulness, and bravado.

And, of course, Japanese help. Even the Kims with all their inherited advantages could not have done so well had they not consciously and assiduously cultivated the colonial power structure. More than the Kims, however, Pak was an ideal candidate for the cooperative capitalist development deliberately encouraged by the Japanese colonial authorities after 1919. He was, first, a naturally gifted entrepreneur — both creative and aggressive — while the Kims tended to be more industrious than creative and were inherently more conservative. Such a contrast was not surprising given the very different perspectives of the two families. For the Kims the goal was to protect and embellish a great fortune already in hand. Pak's ambition and talents, on the other hand, were to a large extent the fruits of deprivation, and he brought to his enterprise the hunger and zeal of a bright but poor young man on the rise.

Such a background also left Pak with few, if any, sentimental feelings about Korea's precolonial independence. Unlike the Kims, who were never able quite to forget their tenuous yangban heritage, Pak seems to have looked entirely to the present and future for his identity. The Yi dynasty had denied his family a place in the sun, but the colonial system offered new opportunities to the clever and able. To some extent the Kims had to be coaxed into cooperation with Japanese promises and subsidies; Pak, on the other hand, leaped into it at the first opportunity. He was exactly what the Japanese were looking for.

Pak's chance came with his move to Seoul in 1926. He had already made a name and some capital for himself both in Chinnamp'o and in his hometown of Yonggang in the rice and paper trades, respectively. Before moving south he had also set up a company in Yonggang that provided financing, warehousing, marketing, and transporting of various products, including raw cotton, and had established a kindergarten and agricultural school there as well. Once in Seoul, his career began to soar. He began with a paper goods company and made a point of developing good relations with the Japanese merchants who controlled the market. By 1932 he had become a major supplier of newsprint with sales of around three million yen per year, and the Government-General was one of his biggest customers. Eventually his markets included both Manchuria and China.[18]

Pak Hŭngsik's business activities were so diverse and extensive that his career could easily be the subject of a separate study itself. Like the Kims, he became deeply enmeshed in the colonial economic and political structure and enjoyed close business and personal relationships with the Japanese elite. He owned stocks and sat on the boards of many Japanese companies operating in Korea, including the Ōji Paper Company's huge pulp plant in North Hamgyŏng[19] and the Oriental Development Company.[20] His numerous Japanese friends and acquaintances included Aruga Mitsutoyo, president of the Chōsen Industrial Bank, who supplied him with many of the funds for his various projects, and Governor-General Ugaki, who saw to it that Pak was included in the Ōji Paper Company's expansion into Korea.[21] In a newspaper interview in 1942, Pak felt at ease referring to Governor-General Minami and his wife as "a loving father and mother." He was also one of the very few Korean commoners ever to be admitted into the imperial inner sanctum: on an official business mission to Japan in December of that same year, Pak was welcomed at the Imperial Palace and given an audience with the Japanese emperor.[22]

Our main concern here, however, is with Pak Hŭngsik's involvement in Kyŏngbang's sales operation. In 1931 Pak bought out a department store in Seoul called Hwasin from the store's founder, Sin T'aehwa. He turned the store into a corporation, forced a leading Korean competitor out of business, and eventually built Hwasin into one of the five main department stores in the city. Several years later he also set up Hwasin Chain Stores as a separate corporation with, initially, 350 shops throughout the country joining the organization on a voluntary basis. Distribution centers were established in Seoul, P'yŏngyang, Wŏnsan, Kunsan, and Pusan.[23] Among the goods Hwasin sold was Kyŏngbang's cloth.[24]

This was only the beginning of the relationship, however. In 1938 Pak established a foreign trade department in his Hwasin corporation to take advantage of the new markets being opened up by the Japanese army in China. Several months later this department was superseded by a new and separate trading company,[25] which in 1941 was amalgamated with several other Hwasin companies into the Hwasin Trading Company, Ltd. (Hwasin Sangsa CH), capitalized at five million yen.

Textile products were among the major items handled by the firm: Kyŏngbang held shares in the company; and Kim Yŏnsu was on the board of directors.[26]

During the war, when all textile goods were being rationed through specific trading companies designated by the government, Kim and Pak also collaborated on a joint-venture trading firm called Taedong Cloth, Ltd., which specialized solely in textile goods. Pak served as president of the company, and Kim took a seat on the board.[27]

Like other Korean and Japanese wholesalers who handled the Kims' cloth, Pak also purchased shares in Kyŏngbang, both personally and in the name of his companies. By 1945 Pak was one of Kyŏngbang's largest shareholders apart from the Kim family and the Chōsen Industrial Bank, and he also served on the company's board of directors.[28]

Kyŏngbang's special marketing connections with Pak Hŭngsik were buttressed by Kim Yŏnsu's participation with Pak in a number of other business projects outside the textile industry, such as the Chōsen Aircraft Company, of which Pak was president, and the Chōsen Oil Company in Wŏnsan.[29]

Although relationships such as Kyŏngbang enjoyed with Korean traders like Pak Sŭngjik and Pak Hŭngsik were important to the company's growth, they were exceptional: Kyŏngbang continued to maintain contact with a considerable number of Korean textile merchants, but the total volume of its business with the Koreans was relatively small. The great bulk of the company's cloth was distributed through the larger Japanese trading firms. These included such already-familiar names as Yagi, C. Itoh, Japan Cotton (Nippon Menka), Oriental Cotton (Tōyō Menka), Mitsui Bussan, and Gōshō. Other Japanese companies regularly used by Kyŏngbang were Katō, Marumiya, Takase, and Mataichi.[30]

Consider, for example, the sales record of the company's twenty-fifth fiscal period, between May 31 and November 30, 1939. Gross sales amounted to about 4 million yen. About 61 percent of this total went to Japanese trading companies, with Mitsui Bussan heading the list at 723,000 yen, followed by Kyŏngbang's old friend Yagi Shōten (519,000 yen), Tōyō Menka (462,000 yen), and C. Itoh (450,000 yen).[31]

These figures are even more impressive when one remembers that Kyŏngbang at the time had its own trading company (Taedong Cloth, which Kim Yŏnsu had established with Pak Hŭngsik), and that the company also made use of one of its subsidiaries (the Chungang Commercial and Industrial Company) as a sales vehicle as well. Of the four million yen in sales collected in the latter half of 1939, Taedong accounted for about 25 percent and Chungang for only about 10 percent. Even after 1941, when Kim Yŏnsu had set up yet another trading company on his own with himself as president, Kyŏngbang continued to depend heavily on the Japanese merchant houses listed above.[32]

Such dependency, of course, made perfect economic sense. It was common practice even for the major Japanese textile manufacturers during this period to market their goods through the big Japanese trading companies. For Kim to have insisted on using only Korean companies, even companies controlled by himself, would have spelled disaster for Kyŏngbang's business. Kyŏngbang naturally had to pay the Japanese companies for their services (usually in the form of rebates proportionate to the volume of goods sold)[33] but such charges were more than offset by the advantages that a major Japanese trading house could offer. No Korean trading firm in the colonial period, for example, could even have begun to compete seriously with a company like Mitsui Bussan in capital, experience, and sales channels, especially in Mitsui's own Asian backyard.

Extensive sales networks, moreover, were only part of the total package offered by the Japanese firms. As we have already seen in Kyŏngbang's relationships with Yagi Shōten and C. Itoh, the Japanese trading companies were in a position to be of immense assistance to manufacturers in the procurement of raw materials and technology. The Japanese-run Chōsen Spinning and Weaving Company in Pusan, for example, experienced many of the same initial marketing problems faced by Kyŏngbang, but once Chōbō turned the distribution of its goods over to Tōyō Menka, the company saw a dramatic expansion of its returns on sales, in no small part because the relationship with Tōyō Menka allowed Chōbō to obtain imported raw cotton expeditiously and at a good price.[34] In return for such consideration, the Japanese trading companies naturally expected to be rewarded with, among other things, regular sales contracts and/or agency agreements from the firms they were helping. If Kyŏngbang had refused to sell its cloth through the Japanese, it would have jeopardized its entire business operation. But no such irrationality was ever contemplated. When Kyŏngbang's connection with Pak Sŭngjik presented the company with an opportunity to establish a good relationship with C. Itoh, the Kims were grateful and ready to take advantage of it.

The Market Structure: Manchuria and Beyond

Hemingway's famous short story, "The Snows of Kilimanjaro," begins with a parenthetical but suggestive note about the mountain itself. "Kilimanjaro," Hemingway writes, "is a snow covered mountain 19,710 feet high, and it is said to be the highest mountain in Africa. Its western summit is called the Masai 'Ngage Ngai,' the House of God. Close to the western summit there is the dried and frozen carcass of a leopard. No one has explained what the leopard was seeking at that altitude."[35]

In the summer of 1946, Edwin M. Martin, an economist on the general staff of the United States Reparations Commission, was inspecting former Japanese industrial property in Korea and Manchuria. On June 13, near Mukden, Martin picked his way through the charred and rusted remains of what only ten months before had been a large new spinning factory with 35,000 spindles, over 1,000 looms, and some 3,000 workers. The Chinese authorities had reported that the Soviets had removed $45 million worth of materials from the plant before setting fire to it. Martin seemed somewhat surprised to learn from a Korean guard still at the site that the factory had been built with Korean rather than Japanese or Manchurian capital and noted in his report that this fact "could not be checked."[36] Like Hemingway pondering the dead leopard so seemingly out of place on the summit of Mount Kilimanjaro, Martin may well have wondered to himself what the victims of Japanese colonialism were doing way up in Manchuria with a multimillion dollar textile plant.

The ruined factory Martin found in 1946 was the residue of Kyŏngbang's subsidiary, the South Manchurian Spinning Company (Namman Pangjŏk CH). In one sense there is really no mystery as to what the Koreans were doing there. Hemingway's leopard may well have been seeking God, but the Koreans were looking for corporate profits. The larger story of how and why the company became so deeply involved in Manchuria, however, is complex and fascinating. The answer lies in Kyŏngbang's particular market structure, and the pattern we find there is, in turn, largely the result of Korea's economic position within the Japanese imperial system.

Secondary Factors

There were, of course, secondary factors as well. Before we examine the structural characteristics of Korea's role in the Japanese Empire that led to Kyŏngbang's involvement in the Manchurian market, let us consider some of the other forces that contributed to the company's presence in Manchuria.

The geographical and political aspects of Manchuria—its contiguity with Korea and, especially after 1931, its domination by Japan—made it a logical area of interest to businessmen in colonial Korea. Manchuria was also a land of special concern to Koreans. By 1940 there were about 1.2 million Koreans living there,[37] and they were regarded by Korean businessmen in Korea as a natural market and source of commercial connections. And vice versa: it was not uncommon for Korean residents of Manchuria to extend their activities to Korea itself. Kyŏngbang, for example, did business with a Manchurian-Korean cloth merchant named Kang Chaehu. Kang's Yongjŏng Trading Company, in turn, was based in Chientao but had a branch office in Korea (in Ch'ŏngjin), and the company was a Kyŏngbang stockholder.[38]

There was also a compelling personal reason for Kim Yŏnsu's interest in Manchuria: land. After the seizure of Manchuria in 1931 and the establishment of Manchukuo in 1932, the Japanese began to promote large-scale subsidized land reclamation through the use of Korean immigrants. The policy solved several problems in one stroke. First, it alleviated population pressure and its attendant political problems in Korea by disposing of great numbers of impoverished peasants unable to meet the exorbitant colonial tenancy rates. An agreement was eventually reached between the Manchurian authorities and the Korean Government-General that provided for a yearly immigration of 10,000 Korean families into Manchuria.[39]

Such a policy was also an inexpensive method of clearing the land for eventual Japanese colonization while at the same time limiting the spread of Chinese settlements, which posed a potential threat to Japanese economic and political control of the country.

Korean migration north also contributed in no small degree to the production of rice for Japan's growing population as well as for Japanese troops stationed on the continent. Unlike the Manchurian-Chinese, who were not rice growers, the Manchurian-Koreans were skillful in the cultivation of paddy and became Manchukuo's foremost rice producers. In 1936, for example, the Manchurian-Koreans were responsible for almost 90 percent of Manchukuo's total rice crop.[40]

During this period the Samyang Company, which controlled and managed Kim Yŏnsu's extensive landholdings in Korea, began to expand its activities across the Yalu and Tuman (Tumen) rivers, acquiring huge tracts of uncleared land from the government or from private owners—both Chinese and Japanese—and turning them into large agricultural estates (*nongjang*) populated by Korean immigrant-tenants. The company opened a representative office in Mukden in 1936, and the clearing of land for the company's first Manchurian *nongjang*, the Ch'ŏnil Estate, located across the Liao River from Yingkow, began in February 1937. Land reclamation for a second estate (Pansŏk) northwest of Mukden was begun around the same time. Thereafter until the end of the colonial period Kim Yŏnsu continued to create such estates: Kyoha and Kudae in 1938, Maeha in 1939, and Ch'abung in 1942.[41]

The amount of land involved was prodigious. Even before Kim set up the South Manchurian Spinning Company in 1939, he was already in possession of thousands of acres of Manchurian land. The scale of the Ch'ŏnil Estate alone was impressive. Its original area in 1937 was about 1,500 acres, but by the end of the colonial period it had grown to about 4,400 acres.[42]

The other estates were also huge: Pansŏk began with about 1,700 acres, Kyoha and Kudae together amounted to about 1,000 acres, Maeha was another 900 acres, and Ch'abung was the smallest with about 400 acres.[43] In 1939, moreover, Kim purchased a firm called Samch'ŏk Enterprises for one million yen from another Korean entrepreneur, Kim Yŏbaek. With the company came the rights to over 70,000 acres of virgin forest in northern Chientao that Kim Yŏbaek had acquired from the government for reclamation and settlement.[44] By 1945 Kim Yŏnsu's total landholdings in Manchuria had reached nearly 90,000 acres. With such vested personal interests in Manchuria, it is not surprising that Kim Yŏnsu looked to the north as an area of expansion for his rapidly growing textile firm.

Colonial Policies

The main force behind Kyŏngbang's Manchurian connection, however, lay in a market structure largely determined by Japanese imperial policies. In general these policies had two major aims. The first was negative: to develop Korean industry in such a way as to avoid competition with the *naichi* or imperial metropole. Korea's rulers wished to open the colony up to industrial development in 1921 to increase Korea's value as a Japanese possession, but such development was to be consistent with Korea's subordinate status with respect to Japan proper. The idea of Korea eventually exporting sophisticated manufactured products to Japan, for example, was so far beyond the imagination of Japanese colonial thinking that it was never even seriously discussed at the industrial commission of 1921.

What did concern many Japanese delegates to the conference, however, was the possibility that the lucrative Korean market for Japanese exports might eventually be taken over by Japanese or Korean companies operating in Korea itself. Textiles were, of course, a major bone of contention. The Government-General's support and subsidies for the Chōsen Spinning and Weaving Company stirred up a storm of protest at the time from cotton manufacturers in Japan who saw a threat to their Korean markets,[45] and the colonial government's proposed plans for additional encouragement and subsidies for the textile and other industries in Korea was a major issue at the conference in 1921.

It was the Government-General's belief, on the other hand, that some protection had to be accorded such companies as Chōbō or they would simply be overwhelmed by Japanese exports and never reach the point where they could stand on their own. Colonial authorities in 1921 were particularly concerned about the effect that the imminent abolition of tariffs between Korea and Japan would have on Korea's nascent industries, which they feared would drown in a flood of Japanese goods.

Manchuria offered a solution to the thorny problem of development without competition. First, there was the great potential of the continental market, which by its very size could help resolve the inherent contradiction of simultaneous industrial development in both Japan and Korea. One of the best exponents of this view, which eventually became policy, was Kada Naoji, a colonial bureaucrat-turned-expatriate businessman who later became president of the Chōsen Chamber of Commerce and Industry.[46] Speaking at the industrial commission of 1921, Kada rejected the idea of many Japanese at the conference that the Government-General's decision to develop the colony's industrial base would threaten Japan's exports to Korea. Among other things, Kada had his eyes on the Manchurian market. It was, he believed, big enough to accommodate colony and metropole both:

I believe there's no need to think in terms of competition [in Korea between Japan-based industries and Korea-based industries] and that [we] must advance [together] in coexistence and harmony. When [we] look at the trade situation with Manchuria and Siberia, moreover, the potential market for industrial products is enormous. And so there too I think that only when Japan and Korea—Japan-based industry and Korea-based industry—eschew competition and strive for concerted, sound development, will [they] see steady progress through the opening of trade in these areas.[47]

Scale was not the only attraction of the Manchurian market. The character of the market was also important. To avoid conflict with the metropole, colonial authorities from the beginning advocated development that would complement rather than compete with Japanese industry.

What this amounted to was an apportionment of production according to each country's respective level of technology. As noted earlier, Korea's role in the imperial textile industry was to produce cheap, coarse cloth for unsophisticated markets while Japanese companies in Japan concentrated on high-quality cloth for export to more advanced countries. As the Japanese textile industry grew increasingly proficient technologically, Korea was to assume the burden of producing "many inexpensive goods that are impossible to produce in Japan."

As peripheral areas of the Japanese Empire populated mainly by poor people with simple tastes, Manchuria and inland China were ideal markets for colonial Korea's manufactured goods, especially textiles. They became even more important and attractive as markets to colonial exporters as Korea's own markets became increasingly sophisticated and dependent on higher quality goods from Japan and after Japan had established firm political control in Manchuria.

Even as early as 1921, the Government-General explicitly recognized the utility of such markets as an outlet for Korean goods and as a safeguard against competition between Korea and Japan over markets in Korea itself. At the industrial commission that year, for example, Vice-Governor-General Mizuno noted how Korea's technological inferiority to Japan would preclude competition between colony and metropole and enhance the importance of peripheral regions as export markets for Korea:

Overlapping and mutual competition between products of Korea and Japan may seem to be a good thing, but from a larger perspective, I don't think it's appropriate. There's no need to promote [production] in Korea that is well-developed and has a solid foundation in Japan and to supply [Korea] beyond [what Japan is supplying]. Similarly, Japan as well should not oppose, or deliberately compete with, special industries in Korea that are exceedingly well-suited to Korean [conditions]. [Our] desire is to avoid such contradictions and conflicts through careful consultation with the Ministry of Agriculture and Commerce [in Tokyo]. In my view, what [we] seriously need to promote in the future [here in Korea] are [those goods] which are needed but unobtainable in Japan, but which can be [obtained] in Korea. [We] must pursue a course of supplying Japan with those much-needed [goods], such as raw materials, which are not produced in Japan but which can be produced in Korea. On the other hand, there is no need to abandon developed industries which exist both in Japan and Korea, and so, as I mentioned earlier, [we] also hope to export likely goods to such places as China and the Russian Far East after an investigation of export channels [in these areas].[48]

The second major aim of Japanese policies dealing with Korea's economic role in the empire was positive rather than negative. While on the one hand the Government-General wished to forestall competition between colony and metropole, it also wanted to promote commercial ties between Korea and Manchuria to strengthen the bond between Japan and its growing continental empire. Because of its geographical position, Korea was regarded as a natural link in the imperial economic chain connecting Japan with Manchuria and China.

The concept of a Japanese-Manchurian economic bloc did not reach its full flowering in Government-General policy until 1936, but a tendency toward such thinking by Korea's rulers was evident decades before. Shortly after the annexation in 1910, for example, the Bank of Chōsen initiated an economic advance into Manchuria that was eventually to make the bank the "spearhead of Japanese penetration in Manchuria, the Russian Far East, and China." From 1917 until 1937 Bank of Chōsen notes were the sole legal tender in the Kwantung Leased Territory and the South Manchuria Railway Zone, and were widely circulated throughout Manchuria. The bank had branch offices in all the major commercial centers of continental East Asia, and as early as 1921 its Manchurian loans were considerably in excess of its loans in Korea itself.[49]

Private commercial contacts between Korea and Manchuria also received the Government-General's blessing during this period. In 1917, for example, the Hansŏng Bank sponsored an economic mission to Manchuria and China that lasted nearly two months. The mission produced a 288-page report that stressed the economic opportunities available to Korea with the continent's increasing economic and political integration into the Japanese Empire.[50]

In 1921 the Government-General went much further in its official encouragement of Korean-Manchurian economic ties. In the final report of the industrial commission held that same year in Seoul, the Government-General explicitly linked its proposed industrial development of the peninsula not only with Japan but with China (including

Manchuria) and the Russian Far East as well, declaring that any plans for industrial development "must be predicated on . . . the economic conditions in these adjacent areas."[51]

The establishment of Manchukuo in March 1932 affirmed and enhanced Korea's position as an industrial link between Japan and the continent. With Manchuria now firmly under Japanese control, the "enormous" market that Kada Naoji and the Government-General had contemplated in 1921 was finally thrown open not only to Japan but to Japan's increasingly industrialized colony south of the Yalu as well. The Government-General moved quickly to take advantage of Korea's unique geographical position. As soon as the smoke from the guns had cleared—and even before the new state had been officially proclaimed—the Government-General dispatched a general fact-finding mission on a tour of the country from Mukden to Dairen.[52] Several months later the Government-General began planning the establishment of trade agencies (*assen kikan*) in all the major centers of Manchuria to facilitate the "advance of Chōsen commerce and industry into Manchuria and Mongolia."[53] In February 1933 the Chōsen Trade Association (Chōsen Bōeki Kyōkai) was inaugurated with government support as a central organization in the official promotion of trade with Manchuria.[54] Key bureaucrats in both the Government-General and the new Manchukuo government contributed articles to Korea's business journals and made themselves available to interested businessmen for lectures and symposia.[55] By 1936 the concept of a Japanese-Manchurian Bloc had become a central theme of imperial policy. At the Government-General's industrial commission that year plans were laid for a rapid development of Chōsen industry aimed at enhancing Japan's position in international trade and building up Japanese military strength. Such development was to be accomplished in close collaboration not only with Japan but "with respect to [Chōsen] industries which have a relationship with Manchuria," by "giving consideration to coordinating [our efforts] with Manchurian industry."[56]

The commission of 1936 also advocated increased trade with Manchuria—including transit trade—and called for the rapid completion of various port facilities and the establishment of free port systems in such key northern transit cities as Ch'ŏngjin, Najin, Unggi, and Chinnamp'o. The Government-General was requested to work together with the Manchurian authorities toward a restructuring of the existing tariff system between the two countries, including a mutual reduction of tariff rates.[57] With the outbreak of war in 1937 and the

Japanese army's seizure of additional territory on the continent, the Government-General's efforts to foster foreign trade with Manchuria and other areas was, of course, greatly intensified and expanded.

Such encouragement evoked a warm response from colonial private enterprise. With the Bank of Chōsen leading the way, both Japanese and Korean companies based in Korea had already begun to establish branch offices throughout Manchuria soon after the annexation. Pak Sŭngjik's Kongik Company, for example, had branches in Mukden, Ch'angch'un (later Hsinking), Antung, and Harbin by 1919.[58]

Not surprisingly, Japan's invasion of Manchuria in 1931 was greeted with great enthusiasm and interest by the colonial business community. In May 1932, the Chōsen Business Club sponsored a major symposium at the Chōsen Hotel in Seoul on "The Promotion of Korean-Manchurian Trade" that brought together over thirty of the colony's leading Korean and Japanese businessmen and bureaucrats.[59] The following month the Seoul Chamber of Commerce and Industry invited Government-General officials from the Bureau of Industry to its general meeting "in order to solicit their expert opinions on [the question of] export trade with Manchuria—[a subject that is] at present the focus of attention of people in commerce and industry throughout the country."[60]

Such symposia and meetings became a regular feature of business life in the colony from 1932 on. The anniversary of the Manchurian Incident was officially commemorated in Seoul each September 18, and businessmen like Han Sangnyong regularly delivered panegyrics on the event that were later published in the leading business journals —one indication of how important the colonial business community regarded the Manchurian market.[61]

Korean businessmen in particular were excited by the prospects of Manchuria under Japanese rule. In addition to the opportunities afforded by the new market, the subjugation of Manchuria offered Koreans a certain psychological satisfaction that made Japanese control of Korea itself somewhat more palatable. Korea's industrial growth since 1921 had done little to raise the colony to equal economic status with Japan, but in relation to Manchukuo, Korea in the 1930s was relatively developed—capable, for example, of exporting textiles and other manufactured goods to Manchuria in return for raw materials and foodstuffs. This was, of course, a pattern that Japan had been practicing on Korea for decades, and the existence of Manchukuo as a new periphery that Koreans themselves could exploit hand in hand with the Japanese gave Koreans a new, elevated image of themselves—especially with respect to the largely Chinese population of Manchuria. At a symposium on "Chōsen-Manchurian Economy and Industry" jointly sponsored by a number of business and research organizations in 1937, Kim Sayŏn, chairman of the Chosŏn Malt Company, and later an auditor of Kyŏngbang's South Manchurian Spinning Company, articulated the new Korean attitude that had been developing since 1931: "Recently," Kim said proudly,

Korea has seen remarkable industrial and economic development, and a spirit of rapid advance has quite taken hold. Certain areas of business are more developed than [those] in Japan, and there are also quite a number of facilities [here] which are superior to [those found in] the business world of Japan. Manchuria, on the other hand, seems to me to be in all respects—and especially when it comes to the question of industry—still in a period of infancy. It is therefore my very firm view that while Korea and Japan are largely equal in terms of ethnic and economic [development], Manchuria, on the other hand, is entirely different from Korea in these respects.[62]

The new feeling of superiority was all the more gratifying in view of the longstanding animosity that many Koreans had for the Chinese —stemming in large part from friction between Manchurian-Koreans and Manchurian-Chinese over land and water rights.[63] Shortly after the state of Manchukuo was officially proclaimed, for example, Han Sangnyong, who had just returned from an observation mission there on behalf of the Government-General, wrote that for Manchuria's Korean population, which had been suffering under the yoke of Chinese officials, bandits, and landlords, Japan's new imperial protection promised "great happiness."[64]

Such feelings, of course, played directly into the hands of the Japanese, who were quick to use Korean enthusiasm about Manchukuo to draw the Koreans ever deeper into a compact with imperialism. Thus for political as well as practical reasons, the Japanese found it convenient to accommodate Korean hopes and expectations about Manchuria to some extent. Koreans were indeed accorded a certain preferential treatment in Manchuria, at least in relation to the dominant Chinese population. Korean immigrants were settled on reclaimed land from which the Chinese were excluded or on land that had often been unfairly or forcibly acquired from Chinese owners. In the event of any trouble from Chinese peasants, Korean immigrants could count on the support of the Japanese police. The Japanese, in fact, employed large numbers of Koreans in the Manchurian police force itself and also made extensive use of Chinese-speaking Koreans in the Manchurian bureaucracy, especially as interpreters.[65]

Korean businessmen were similarly able to take advantage of their special position and join the Japanese in the development of the Manchurian economy at the expense of Chinese native capital. Kim Yŏnsu's personal investments in major Manchurian corporations included, for example, a block of shares in the Yingkow Spinning and Weaving Company, which had originally been established with Chinese capital before 1931 to help counteract the influx of Japanese textiles, but from 1933 on had been gradually taken over by the Chōsen Spinning and Weaving Company of Pusan.[66] In short, Manchukuo gave Koreans the opportunity to engage in the same kind of economic exploitation of the Chinese that Koreans had been suffering under the Japanese since 1905.

The colonial authorities did their best to promote such surrogate imperialism. Articles describing the "ancient remains of Korea in Manchuria" not only lent spurious respectability to Japanese political claims to Manchuria as an historically justified extension of their Korean colony; they also encouraged Koreans themselves to think of Manchuria in imperialist terms as Korea irredenta.[67] Korean immigrants who were sent north to clear the forests both for themselves and for Japanese colonists were commonly referred to as the "pioneers of Manchuria." Korean businessmen interested in expanding their operations to Manchuria were assured of the full support and mediative power of the Government-General.[68]

In the end the Government-General's efforts to direct colonial industry toward the Manchurian market proved to be successful not only in minimizing competition with the Japanese metropole and advancing imperialist goals, but also in generating a large volume of trade for Korea. The Japanese seizure of Manchuria was naturally a great help in giving substance to such policies. With the establishment of Manchukuo, Korean exports enjoyed a boom that eventually allowed Korea to move from an almost total trade dependency on Japan to a more diverse trade structure. In 1929 Korea's total foreign trade with countries other than Japan had reached 35 million yen. By 1933, one year after the founding of Manchukuo, it had climbed to 52 million yen. In 1937 it was more than double that figure at 113 million yen, and by 1939 it had more than doubled again to 269 million yen—a nearly eightfold increase since 1929. Most of this trade involved exports to Manchuria: 77 percent of the total in 1933, 63 percent in 1937, and 76 percent in 1939.[69]

Korea's cotton textile industry was, of course, a major participant in the Manchurian boom. In 1937, for example, cotton cloth exports accounted for about 16 percent of the total foreign trade. The effect of the establishment of Manchukuo on the industry was immediate and dramatic. In 1931 Korea had exported only about 7 million square yards of cotton cloth abroad (not including Japan). The following year saw this figure leap to over 36 million square yards — more than a 500 percent increase. By 1938 it had reached nearly 93 million square yards. In August 1938, cotton cloth exports to Yen Bloc countries were restricted to increase the inflow of foreign exchange through textile exports to countries outside the bloc, and the Manchurian export boom came to an end for the Korean textile industry.[70] By that time, however, colonial spinners were already establishing factories in Manchuria itself, and Kyŏngbang was one of them.

Kyŏngbang in Manchuria

Kyŏngbang's own market structure developed in almost perfect conformity with the policies of the Government-General described above. Consider, for example, the question of competition between colony and metropole. Conventional Korean histories that portray Kyŏngbang as a model of "national capital" stress the company's gallant efforts to oppose Japanese capital during the colonial period. While a certain amount of such competition was inevitable once Kyŏngbang began to sell its cloth in the Korean market, there is no evidence whatsoever that Kyŏngbang ever seriously sought to challenge or block Japanese metropolitan textile capital in any way. Indeed, all the evidence points toward just the opposite conclusion — that from beginning to end Kyŏngbang chose the safer, officially sanctioned course of accommodation and cooperation over confrontation.

In part, Kyŏngbang's avoidance of confrontation was due to the company's initial poor showing in the Korean market. Early attempts to compete with Tōyōbō's well-established and popular Triple A brand imported broadcloth nearly drove Kyŏngbang into bankruptcy. To begin with, price differences between the two companies' products were slight. Even as late as 1929, for example, one roll of Tōyōbō's 17-pound Triple A cloth was selling for 13.50 yen. A similar cloth sold by Kyŏngbang under the T'aegŭksŏng [Star of the Great Ultimate] label was only 50 sen cheaper. Price was not the only factor: even if Kyŏngbang's cloth was somewhat less expensive, many Korean consumers still preferred Tōyōbō's higher quality and famous name.[71]

Virtually from the beginning, moreover, the company pursued a marketing strategy that eschewed confrontation. Far from attempting aggressive competition with the Japanese, Kyŏngbang deliberately relinquished the wealthy and populous southern part of the peninsula as a market to Tōyōbō and other Japanese companies and concentrated instead on selling its goods in the northern part of the country, especially in the P'yŏngyang and Wŏnsan areas. There, where the people tended to be poorer—and therefore more inclined to buy a less expensive cloth—and also more susceptible to Kyŏngbang's promotion of itself as a "nationalist" enterprise (the Movement to Promote Korean Goods had originated in P'yŏngyang), Kyŏngbang enjoyed some success and was able to dispose of the stocks that had been piling up because of sluggish sales in the south. The decision to abandon the southern market was made very early (shortly after the company first began selling its cloth in 1923) and was the idea of Kim Yŏnsu himself.[72]

By that time the company was also well on its way to discovering other promising markets even farther north in Manchuria. The Kims, of course, were well aware not only of the Government-General's distaste for any friction between colony and metropole but also of the government's hopes for Korea to become an economic steppingstone to the continent, and Manchuria was on their minds from the very beginning. In applying for a charter from the Bureau of Industry in August 1919, the Kims specifically stated that they eventually intended to export to Manchuria.[73] Kim Yŏnsu had scarcely completed his university education in Japan and returned home to Korea before he was off on an inspection tour of Manchuria—just prior to his formal appointment as Kyŏngbang's managing director in 1922.[74]

Kyŏngbang's cloth quickly became a popular item in Manchuria. Even when the company was still only testing out markets in border cities like Ŭiju, Sinŭiju, and Manp'ojin, investigations revealed that much of its cloth was being purchased by visiting Manchurian-Chinese merchants.[75]

Such popularity was not surprising. As the Government-General had foreseen, Kyŏngbang's technological level was ideally suited to the Manchurian market. When the Japanese textile industry was developing its expertise to a level that would allow it to threaten American textile manufacturers' own domestic market, Kyŏngbang was instead concentrating on the production of its own brand of the thick and cheap coarse sheeting in forty-square-yard rolls (*tan*) that was most in demand in Manchuria.[76] The name of the fabric, Pulloch'o, which meant "Herb of Eternal Youth" in Chinese characters, was also particularly appealing to Chinese customers.[77]

The Japanese seizure of Manchuria came at an excellent time for Kyŏngbang. By 1931 the company had over ten years of experience in the textile industry and the early period of fumbling was over. Kyŏngbang, moreover, had found a market in Manchuria for its Pulloch'o brand cloth that looked very auspicious indeed. At the time of the invasion in September 1931, the company had just completed an expansion of its factory in Yŏngdŭngp'o and installed 224 new looms to keep up with the Manchurian demand.[78]

The establishment of Manchukuo threw the northern market wide open, and Kyŏngbang wasted no time in taking advantage of the opportunity. Even as early as 1932 about 26 percent of the company's total sales came from Manchurian exports. In 1933 the company added another 224 looms to its factory in Yŏngdŭngp'o.[79] That same year Kyŏngbang participated in extended trade fairs in Dairen and Mukden, where the company hosted exhibitions demonstrating exactly how the popular Pulloch'o cloth was made with Toyoda looms. A large advertising balloon — at the time still largely a curiosity — was floated in the air above the company's exhibits to attract spectators. In the end, Kyŏngbang sold far more cloth at the fairs than it had anticipated, and the following year the company opened its own representative office in Mukden.[80]

Kyŏngbang had every reason to establish its own office in Manchuria. Sales were booming — and not only at the trade fairs. Gross sales for 1932 were double the previous year and climbing. In 1931 they had been only about 1.4 million yen; by 1934 they had reached a new peak of nearly 4.5 million yen. Kyŏngbang's cloth became so well known in Manchuria that the Chinese commonly referred to the company simply as the Pulloch'o Hong. Hsinking wholesalers who continued to purchase the cloth in large quantities were unable to satisfy the consumers' requests, and a black market Pulloch'o trade flourished. Orders increased to the point where the company could not even handle all of them by itself and had to resort to a subcontracting arrangement with one of the Dai Nippon Spinning Company's branch factories in Tsingtao.[81]

To keep up with the feverish demand, Kyŏngbang added still another 224 looms to its weaving factory in 1936 and for the first time also began to spin its own yarn with 21,600 newly installed spindles (4,000 more spindles were brought in the following year). Even as Kyŏngbang was opening its new spinning factory in 1936, the company was al-

An aerial view of the Kyŏngsŏng Spinning and Weaving Company in Yŏngdŭngp'o in the 1930s.

Kyŏngbang's board of directors in the 1930s. *Top (from left to right)*: Kim Chaesu, Yi Kanghyŏn, Ch'oe Tusŏn, Yun Chubok. *Bottom (left to right)*: Min Pyŏngsu, Hyŏn Chunho, Kim Yŏnsu, Pak Hŭngsik.

Cotton spinning at Kyŏngbang (1930s).

Cotton weaving at Kyŏngbang (1930s).

Calisthenics at Kyŏngbang's South Manchurian Spinning Company (1940s).

The industrial commission of 1938, officially called the Chōsen Government-General Commission on Policy for the Current Situation.

Sekiya Teizaburō

Kim Yŏnsu (*left*) hosting a luncheon to celebrate the tenth anniversary of the founding of Manchukuo (March 1942). Kim was the Honorary Consul-General of Manchukuo at the time.

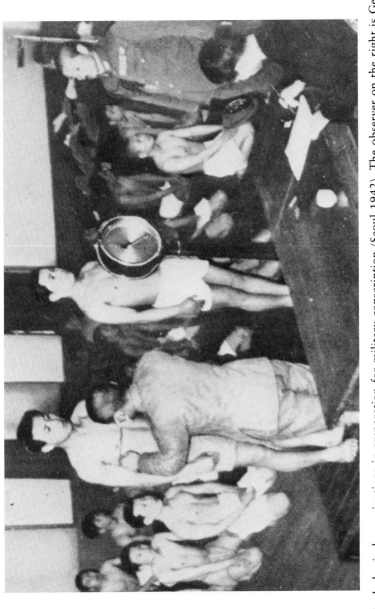

Required physical examinations in preparation for military conscription (Seoul 1942). The observer on the right is General Takahashi, Chief of Staff of the Chōsen Army.

A Korean student soldier (*hakpyŏng*) about to enter the Japanese army.

Training and "spiritual mobilization" in the Naisen Ittai period.

ready laying plans for the construction of another new spinning facility in Sihŭng.[82]

The Manchurian door, however, was beginning to swing shut. In the early 1930s, Manchukuo's authorities had avoided precipitating a conflict with the textile industry in Japan by continuing to rely on Japanese and Korean imports for more than half the total domestic demand.[83] In July 1933, for example, the high Chinese tariffs that had annoyed Japanese textile exporters in Korea like Miyabayashi Taiji were reduced, and Manchukuo's market was opened to foreign and especially Japanese goods, including cotton textiles.[84]

But the military leaders who ran Manchukuo soon began to devise their own plans for the country's development into a continental war base, plans that necessitated a certain degree of self-sufficiency in textiles and other industries. Thus even before the Sino-Japanese War made such policy all the more imperative, Manchuria saw a significant expansion of its textile industry through the investment of Japanese capital both in already existing mills and in new factories. In 1933, for example, Kanebō took over a factory that had been confiscated from the old government as enemy property in 1931. Other Japanese factories already in operation like Naigai and Fukushima enlarged their facilities while Dai Nippon and Oriental Cotton built new plants. As noted earlier, even the Chōsen Spinning and Weaving Company of Pusan acquired control of a former Chinese spinning company in Yingkow and expanded it into a substantial subsidiary.[85]

To protect its own growing textile industry, in November 1934 the Manchukuo government revised its tariff rates upward for cotton yarn and piece goods, and the Korean textile industry received a major jolt.[86] The volume of cotton cloth exports to Manchuria in 1935 fell by almost 35 percent from the previous year.[87] Kyŏngbang's gross sales declined by an even greater percentage. In 1934 they had been at a record high of nearly five million yen. The following year they dropped to about three million yen, and by May 1936 they had fallen again to about two million yen—a drop of 60 percent within two years. The need for a general reduction of the Manchurian tariff became a major topic of concern and discussion among colonial businessmen, and the industrial commissions in both 1936 and 1938 enjoined the Government-General to work toward this goal.[88]

None of Korea's cotton manufacturers was more concerned about the tariff problem than Kim Yŏnsu. By the mid-1930s Manchuria had become the centerpiece of Kyŏngbang's marketing strategy. All the company's grand plans for expansion were predicated on the continued existence of an open market to the north, and now the market was closing its doors.

There was nowhere to go. The Korean market for cotton textiles was full. In the early 1930s several of Japan's largest spinning companies had set up their own mills in Korea to escape the restrictions of the factory laws and take advantage of Korea's location as a gateway to the new continental market. Tōyōbō had led the way in 1933 and was followed soon after by Kanegafuchi, Dai Nippon, and others.[89] With such competition on the peninsula itself, even the small market in the northern half of the country that Kyŏngbang had carved out for itself was shrinking.

Unlike most of the other manufacturers, whose main factories were in Japan and for whom Manchuria was only one of several markets, Kyŏngbang produced essentially only one type of cotton cloth and was dependent almost entirely on Manchuria as an export market. Chōbō, of course, was also as dependent as Kyŏngbang on the Manchurian market, but unlike Kyŏngbang in 1936, the Pusan firm had a large subsidiary in Yingkow.

At the Government-General's industrial commission of 1936, Kim Yŏnsu listened as Tsuda Shingo (the president of Kanebō) and others bemoaned the imposition of government controls on an expanding colonial textile industry. The normally reticent Kim finally gave vent to his frustration. The problem, he declared, was not just controls but tariffs—the Korean textile industry was being blocked in all directions:

What happens when [we] export to Manchuria? As everyone knows, the Manchurian tariff rate is high. At present [we] are exporting [there], but it is not profitable. [We] are [simply] exporting [there] out of necessity. The tariff is 30 yen per bale. Our factory and business costs, including both direct and indirect expenses, for manufacturing [one bale of] sheeting out of raw cotton do not even come to 30 yen. But when we export [that same bale to Manchuria], the tariff is more than the cost of production. That's why the spinning companies in Manchuria are thriving today.[90]

In the end the tariff problem lost its urgency for Kim Yŏnsu and other colonial manufacturers with the outbreak of the Sino-Japanese War in 1937 and a consequent demand for supplies by the Japanese army that could not be adequately met in Manchukuo itself.[91] In spite of an avowed policy of self-sufficiency with protective tariffs for its own textile industry, Manchukuo found itself ordering more cotton cloth from Korea than ever before. In 1937 the volume of Korea's cotton cloth exports to Yen Bloc areas doubled from the previous year and rose by another 14 percent in 1938.[92]

In 1938, however, a more serious obstacle to the continental export trade arose. In dire need of foreign exchange to pay for its imports of war materials, Japan began to restrict the exports of cotton goods to Yen Bloc countries. The effect on the Korean textile industry's export trade was catastrophic. By 1940 the volume of trade in cotton cloth had decreased by 97 percent from the 1938 peak and was actually below the volume recorded for 1931.[93]

The Pacific War would, of course, eventually render such restrictions obsolete, but Kim Yŏnsu and his associate at Kyŏngbang did not know that in 1938. What they did know was that the China Incident was giving every indication of dragging on for some time, and that they had suddenly lost their best market for Pulloch'o cloth. The only way to retrieve it seemed to be to move Kyŏngbang's production into Manchuria itself.

The South Manchurian Spinning Company

The Government-General was also in favor of such a move. With the establishment of large-scale factories on the peninsula by the major Japanese spinners, Korea now had enough facilities to take care of its own domestic needs, and the government was curtailing any further increase in spindles. Kyŏngbang was advised to abandon its plans for a new spinning factory in Sihŭng and instead to construct a new plant in Manchuria, where the Manchukuo authorities were promoting a program of national self-sufficiency. The Government-General assured Kim Yŏnsu, moreover, that it would give Kyŏngbang its full support and assistance, which meant, among other things, the benefit of its good offices in negotiations with the Manchurian government.[94]

There were risks, of course. The building of a new factory in Manchuria would signify for Kyŏngbang both a direct and substantial material investment in Japanese imperialism that required a good deal of faith in Japan's future. According to family members, Kim Sŏngsu was apprehensive about the project. His younger brother, who was running the company, however, was confident. In December 1939, the South Manchurian Spinning Company (SMSC) was formally inaugurated and Kim Yŏnsu was elected president. Three years later the factory was completed and producing its first commercial yarn and cloth.[95]

The establishment of the South Manchurian Spinning Company represented the first example of large-scale Korean industrial capitalist expansion outside Korea itself. It was, however, not so much a sign of the maturity of Korean "national capital" as a crowning achievement of the policy of cooperative capitalist development launched by Governor-General Saitō in the 1920s and an indication of the extent to which Korean capital had become an integral part of the Japanese capitalist system.

All the various threads that linked Kyŏngbang to colonial policy and the Japanese metropole were called into play to make the factory a reality. Personal relationships were clearly among the most important of such ties. A grateful letter from Kim Yŏnsu to House of Peers member Sekiya Teizaburō dated September 25, 1939, suggests, for example, that Kim's personal connections with older, well-placed Japanese, some of whom, like Sekiya, had once held key posts in the Government-General, was a crucial factor in obtaining a permit for the factory from the Manchurian authorities on September 18 of that year.[96] The Government-General also kept its promise to Kim and not only assisted Kyŏngbang in obtaining financing through the Chōsen Industrial Bank and its counterpart in Manchuria but also made sure the company was able to acquire the necessary raw materials for construction. Kyŏngbang's close associate, the C. Itoh Company, helped relieve the burden of investment by contributing equity. Toyoda, which had furnished Kyŏngbang with so much of the machinery for its factories in Korea, pulled out all the stops for its old customer—not only granting exceptionally generous sales terms but also arranging for the new machinery to be built at a Toyoda branch factory in China rather than in Japan, and delivered in a way especially convenient for Kyŏngbang.[97]

The scale of the project necessitated such assistance. In 1939 Kyŏngbang's authorized capital was five million yen, and it had taken the company nearly twenty years to build up a plant in Korea with about 25,000 spindles and 900 looms. In contrast, the SMSC's authorized capital was fixed at ten million yen—about 11 percent of the *total* authorized textile capital in all of Manchuria in 1938.[98] When the SMSC was completed in 1942, the wall around it encompassed over 100,000 *p'yŏng* (about 80 acres), and the factory itself had 35,000 spindles and over 1,000 looms—more than Kanebō's mill in nearby Mukden. By 1944 the total number of workers and staff in all of Kyŏngbang's Korean factories numbered approximately 3,500. The SMSC alone, on the other hand, employed some 3,000 people.[99] In addition to the factory buildings, the plant included a warehouse, a boiler room, dormitories for both male and female workers, private family housing and bachelor quarters for staff, dining facilities, lecture halls, and a hospital.[100]

The SMSC also demonstrated that the Koreans could be as hard-headed and effective as the Japanese when it came to the techniques of economic imperialism. Indeed, in some respects the SMSC represented a refinement of those techniques. In Korea, for example, new companies established by Japanese capital often included Koreans as shareholders or members of the board of directors. In Manchuria the Kims were less subtle. No Chinese equity was sought in setting up the SMSC. Most of the stock was held by Kyŏngbang itself, and the board of directors was entirely Korean.[101]

Even the composition of the labor force reflected the company's imperialist attitude. Korean businessmen in Korea had often criticized the Japanese for using Japanese workers when Korean labor was abundantly available. At the industrial commission of 1936, for example, Pak Yŏngch'ŏl, president of the Chōsen Commercial Bank, rose to give an impassioned speech against what he considered Noguchi Jun's discriminatory hiring policy.[102] In Manchukuo, however, the SMSC followed a deliberate policy of hiring only Korean labor. Workers were recruited whenever possible from the Korean population in Manchuria itself, but this often proved difficult. To supplement the Korean labor force drawn from Manchuria, Kyŏngbang even brought in labor from Korea. At the time of Liberation, the company had more than 1,000 teen-age peasant girls recruited from Korea working in its factory in Manchuria. Like Noguchi Jun, Kyŏngbang's executives were uncomfortable with an alien native labor force over which they could exercise only limited control.[103]

Kyŏngbang's new venture in Manchukuo led Kim Yŏnsu to take a more general interest in the development of the Manchurian economy. Indeed, not only the SMSC's scale but its very location placed it in the center of such development. The factory was situated in Suchiatun, where the South Manchuria trunk line that ran all the way to Dairen divided to form the Mukden-Antung branch to the Korean border and eventually on to Seoul.[104] Only ten miles to the northeast, in the center of the fertile Manchurian plain and near the coal fields of Fushun and Penhsihu, lay Mukden, Manchukuo's largest city (over one million people in 1940) and the heart of the country's growing industrial base.[105] In 1939, when Kyŏngbang was just beginning to set up the SMSC, Mukden's western suburb of Tiehsi was undergoing a rapid transformation into the country's largest industrial complex. Already Tiehsi had expanded to five square miles with 107 factories in operation and over 80 more under construction or consideration. Textile companies like Kanebō had already moved into the area and more were to come. In addition, Mukden was rapidly becoming a center of the metal, machine, and chemical industries.[106]

Once Kyŏngbang had secured a foothold in the region, Kim Yŏnsu began to purchase stocks in Mukden companies. One of his first investments was in the Mukden Bank of Commerce and Industry, Manchukuo's largest ordinary bank, and one, moreover, that was particularly involved with financing in the Mukden area.[107]

In 1941 he also bought a block of shares in the Mukden-based Manchurian Real Estate and Development Company.[108] Riding the wave of the city's remarkable expansion, this company was specializing in the development of residential areas, the construction and financing of homes, stores, apartments, and office buildings, and in hotel management. At the time Kim invested in the company, it was managing the leases on 63 rental homes, 79 stores, 235 apartments, and 2 hotels, including one of Mukden's finest, the 321-room Taisei.[109]

Other Mukden companies in which Kim purchased shares included the Manchurian Paper Company and the Manchurian-Mongolian Woolen Company, which was Manchukuo's principal woolen manufacturer and had close ties to the Korean Government-General through the Oriental Development Company, one of its major stockholders.[110]

Mukden was not the only Manchurian city in which Kim Yŏnsu developed an interest. As noted earlier, Kyŏngbang's old rival, the Chōsen Spinning and Weaving Company of Pusan, had taken over the Yingkow Spinning and Weaving Company from Chinese native capital in 1933 and expanded its facilities. By 1940 the company had about 56,000 spindles and was still growing.[111] Kim was also attracted by the prospect of a spinning mill with good access to port facilities and a convenient location just across the Gulf of Pechili from China. Wartime controls in Korea had eliminated even the vestiges of the limited competition among textile companies that had characterized the 1920s. Kim himself was head of the Chōsen Spinners Association, a government-sponsored cartel of the colony's seven major cotton manufacturers, who cooperated in pooling their various resources, and Kyŏngbang or its affiliate, the Samyang Foundation, eventually came to hold shares in most of these companies, including Chōbō.[112] It was therefore quite natural in 1939 for Kyŏngbang to acquire stock in Chōbō's textile company in Yingkow.

Kim also personally invested in the Dairen Machine Works,[113] the South Manchurian Gas Company, also located in Dairen,[114] and the Manchurian Bearing Company in Hsinking.[115] In addition, his interest in breweries, which had placed him on the board of directors of Mitsubishi's Shōwa Kirin Beer company in Korea, was now also extended to Manchuria. In 1940 Kim acquired the Oriental Beer Company in Harbin from a previous Korean owner, Kim T'aebong, who had fallen into financial difficulties. He retained the German technician who had been working there and stabilized the company's financial situation. Eventually the company was producing about 150,000 bottles of beer per month for the Harbin area.[116]

Kyŏngbang in China

Through personal and corporate investments beginning with the South Manchurian Spinning Company in 1939, Kim Yŏnsu and Kyŏngbang became deeply involved in the Manchurian economy by 1945. Manchuria, however, was not the only area outside Korea in which Kyŏngbang developed an interest. The company's Manchurian connection, which had begun in the 1920s as a marketing strategy largely imposed from above, eventually drew Kyŏngbang deep into the interior of China itself.

As noted earlier, China and Manchuria had been linked together as marketing areas for Korean products in official Government-General policy as early as the industrial commission of 1921. Even before that, of course, there had been considerable public and private interest in the China market in Korea. Japan's seizure of German possessions in China during the First World War, for example, had stimulated both businessmen and bureaucrats in the colony to take a fresh look at the China market. The Hansŏng Bank's economic mission headed by Han Sangnyong in 1917 had toured not only Manchuria but traveled extensively throughout northern and central China as far south as Changsha and Siangtan. In his report Han took note of Korea's unique geographical position relative to China and the beneficient economic effect of the world war on trade between Korea and China: "In a geographical sense Korea is extremely close to China. Particularly with the European War, Japanese-Chinese trade has developed all the more, and, accordingly, commercial transactions between Korea and China have become more frequent as well, [thus] enhancing more and more the degree of closeness [between the two countries] in an economic sense."[117]

Japanese claims to Shantung, however, were not supported by international opinion after the war, and Japan was forced to return the territory to China in 1922. Massive Chinese boycotts of Japanese goods and the Kuomintang's establishment in 1928 of a government in Nanking with a policy of high tariffs made the Chinese market increasingly difficult to penetrate, and Japan and Korea subsequently concentrated their continental marketing efforts on Manchuria and the South Seas.

All this notwithstanding, China was, of course, never entirely forgotten. At the industrial commission of 1936, for example, Tsuda Shingo, president of the Kanegafuchi Spinning Company, issued a clarion call for Japan's penetration of the China market. Tsuda warned his fellow delegates that unless Japanese officials stopped trying to control the Korean textile industry (to protect textile interests in Japan and Manchuria) and paid more attention to promoting Korea's economic expansion in China, the Chinese themselves and other foreigners would eventually develop a spinning industry in Asia that would threaten Japanese interests:

It's a great mistake to think only [in terms of] Japan and Manchuria, forgetting the fact that in China the labor force is extremely abundant and cheap. Nowadays there is constant discussion even among businessmen in Japan about the spinning industry expanding in all directions. If [we] hold back, hesitating [to expand], the result will be the development of the Chinese spinning [industry]. In considering the future of China with its cheap, 400 million-plus labor force, [we] dare not take only a narrow view of things. In fact, speaking on the basis of recent circumstances, talk is flourishing among British spinners about the necessity of countering this [development in China] by transferring factories to Asia, whatever the cost. Recently a decision has already been made [by the British spinners] to build spinning factories in Australia, as a way of protecting their own country's industry by shifting [their] spinning factories to Australia. Similarly, the United States, in order to check the advance of the Japanese spinning [industry], is also embarking on a scheme to construct factories in the Philippines and obstruct [our] industry. England is again trying to counter Japan by bringing spinning and weaving machines into China as well. So if [we] internally suppress Japan's advance into foreign areas, you can bet that the result will be the expansion into Asia of other countries' factories. [In other words], in trying to protect ourselves, we'll be hurting ourselves. So we must think [carefully]. This question [of controls on industry] has different implications for each of twenty-odd industries. So what needs to be done [here], I think, is to adopt different approaches in each case, accommodating the wishes of the industrialists as well as domestic and foreign conditions, while also considering Korea's own unique position.[118]

For the Government-General and businessmen like Tsuda, the outbreak of the Sino-Japanese War nine months later was probably the best thing to happen economically since Japan's invasion of Manchuria. Once again a coveted market on the continent was opened to Japanese penetration.

In 1938 the final report of the Government-General's industrial commission cited the "Promotion of Trade with China" as a major item in the government's overall encouragement of overseas trade. In line with this new policy, Korea's southwestern ports were to be renovated and expanded to facilitate commerce between Korea and such Chinese ports as Tientsin, Tsingtao, and Shanghai. The Government-General was exhorted to assist colonial businessmen in their search for markets by expanding its research and administrative facilities to provide reliable information on local customs, trading conditions, commercial practices, and other business intelligence, including basic details about shipping methods, transport charges, and tariff rates. The Government-General was also called upon to help promote Korean products among Chinese consumers through the use of newspapers, magazines, pamphlets, and films in the Chinese language and to encourage visits to Korea by influential continental merchants.[119]

The report also emphasized the economic potential of Inner Mongolia, only recently secured by Japanese forces, as a new export market for Korean goods "on the basis of complementary trade." "Complementary trade," of course, meant such trade as was appropriate between a new periphery and Korea's growing industrial economy; the report specifically noted, for example, that Korea could import basic raw materials such as wool, leather, and coal from Inner Mongolia and export such items as cotton cloth. Since the Japanese army was still continuing its "pacification work" (*sembu kōsaku*) in Mongolia, the report also urged the Government-General to make the necessary arrangements for Korea to become a supplier of military goods to Japanese troops operating in the region.[120]

As in 1931, the colonial business community was caught up in a buoyancy of expectation about the new market that was reflected in a flurry of meetings, symposia, and articles centered on the Korea-China trade.

And once again, Korean businessmen were among the most enthusiastic participants in all this activity. In the March 1938 issue of the *Chōsen jitsugyō kurabu*, Kim Yehyŏn wrote that Koreans joined their "Japanese brothers" (*Naichi dōhō*) in exultation over every report of victory in the "holy war" against China. Kim noted, furthermore, that "once the war thus comes to an end [with a Japanese victory], it is not difficult to imagine that we Koreans as well, openly advancing into northern or central and southern China, can reap various benefits as the third party."[121]

As one might have predicted, Han Sangnyong made another of his observation tours of the continent the following year and concluded an optimistic report on the trip with a hope for future investment of Korean capital and human resources in China:

In conclusion, having made the observation trip to north China, I feel not only very happy but also very expectant of the future. My only [additional] hope is that Japanese and Chinese in the north China area be strongly encouraged to renew their appreciation of Korea. Furthermore, I think it is desirable to have Koreans and Japanese invest considerable capital from the peninsula and to encourage [them] to do business [in north China]. And in terms of human [resources] as well, I hope that the peninsula will be encouraged to make a substantial contribution [to north China].[122]

Kyŏngbang, of course, had not waited for a recommendation from Han Sangnyong before making its move into China. The Japanese invasion had not only pierced the tariff wall but had thrown the local Chinese factories into chaos. As a result, Kyŏngbang's market for Pulloch'o cloth was expanding with every thrust of the imperial army, and the company did indeed have good reason to rejoice in each new report of a Japanese military triumph. Even before the final decision was made to establish a factory in Manchuria, Kim Yŏnsu was exploring the possibility of a textile venture in north China.[123]

Only months after the outbreak of hostilities, Kim dispatched two Kyŏngbang men to north China to investigate the war's effect on the Chinese market and also to choose a site for a new factory. The men initially recommended Tungchow, just twelve miles east of Peking, but the company hesitated to take action until the area was completely secure.[124]

While Kyŏngbang's executives were vacillating about Tungchow, another opportunity arose for the company to expand into China in the form of an offer from Toyoda to join the famous manufacturer in a joint-venture gossamer spinning plant in Changte, Honan Province. Kyŏngbang decided to accept the proposition and made plans to arrange for a seven-million-yen investment, but after a preliminary inspection of the site, Kyŏngbang's agent reported once again that ongoing military conflict made the location unsafe.[125]

Kyŏngbang received yet another offer from a mill in Tientsin with 40,000 spindles owned and operated by Chinese capitalists. The factory was under the jurisdiction of the Japanese army, who had already made plans to turn it over to Japanese corporate management. In an attempt to forestall confiscation, the Chinese owners tried to persuade Kyŏngbang to come into the company as a partner and operate the factory together as a joint venture. Kyŏngbang initially agreed but withdrew from the deal when it discovered the machinations behind it and found itself in confrontation with the army. The company finally gave up its plans to acquire or build a factory in China itself and decided instead to construct the SMSC in Suchiatun.[126]

The Chinese market, however, was by no means abandoned. As the war spread into the Pacific, and Japanese forces overran Southeast Asia and the South Seas, the original Chinese market burst its national boundaries and came to fascinate businessmen like Kim Yŏnsu more strongly than ever. Chŏn Sŭngbŏm, a member of the Chōsen Industrial Bank's Research Department, expressed this feeling well in an article for the Chōsen Business Club journal in 1942:

The Korean economy has been playing an important role as a link and forward base in the construction of the Japan-Manchuria-China economy, and this function will by no means be diminished by the addition of the natural resources of the southern regions to the coprosperity sphere. On the contrary, with the acquisition of new raw materials, Korea's abundant electric power and excellent technology give promise of the rise of new industry. And not only that. This [promise of new growth] has further vitalized the already established various heavy and chemical industries which [must] act as the propeller of this [new] growth. What is more, with the acquisition of new markets in the southern regions, the future of Korea's light industries has also begun to brighten.[127]

Kim Yŏnsu eventually came to the conclusion that the expanded Chinese and Asian market was important enough to warrant the formation of a special trading company over which he could exercise control, and he thus turned to his friend and associate, Pak Hŭngsik.

Like Kim, Pak had been excited by the trading prospects opened up by the Sino-Japanese War. In 1938 he had set up a new foreign trade department in his Hwasin company, and the following year he had expanded the department into a separate company. In 1941 it was reorganized into the Hwasin Trading Company, Ltd. (Hwasin Sangsa CH), capitalized at five million yen. Kyŏngbang helped contribute to the company's equity, and Kim Yŏnsu took a seat on the board of directors. Textiles were, of course, one of Hwasin Trading's main export items, and by 1943 the company had representative offices in Tientsin and Shanghai.[128]

In the end, moreover, Kyŏngbang actually did manage to set up shop directly in China, though not on the scale it had originally envisioned. By early 1943 the company had established a representative office in Peking. It had even opened an office some 320 miles to the south in the Japanese army's Number 2 Factory in the city of Changte (now Anyang), north of the Yellow River in Honan Province.[129]

It is not clear exactly what Kyŏngbang was doing in Honan. It is possible that the company may have had some financial stake in the Changte factory. On the other hand, the Changte factory was spinning gossamer thread,[130] a product with which Kyŏngbang was unfamiliar, and the company may simply have been acquiring the technology and experience to launch a similar project in Korea—yet another reflection, perhaps, of Kim Yŏnsu's extensive participation in war-related industries between 1938 and 1945. In any case, there is no question that by the end of the colonial period the demands and opportunities of Kyŏngbang's complex market structure had taken the company far indeed from its main base in Yŏngdŭngp'o—not only across the Yalu into the heart of Japan's military establishment on the continent, but even to the warring outer reaches of the empire in occupied China.

Summary

When Korea's colonial rulers extended the offer of cooperative development to the Korean bourgeoisie in 1921, they surely knew that such development would effectively bind Korean capitalism to its counterpart in Japan and to Japanese imperialist goals.

And so it was. As we have seen, the requisites of production (raw materials and technology) and marketing led Kyŏngbang to form personal and corporate connections with the metropolitan capitalist system that by 1945 had made the company an integral part of that system. Where the inherent logic of capitalist production failed to create such dependency or actually threatened to spawn competition rather than cooperation, as in the case of potential marketing conflicts between colony and metropole, the Government-General was quick to implement policies to rectify the situation.

In the end the combination of natural capitalist development and government policy worked not only to subordinate Korean capital to Japanese capital but to enmesh Korean capitalism in the imperial economic structure on the continent. In the 1930s, when the periphery of the Japanese Empire was expanded through military conquest to include vast new blocks of economically undeveloped territory in Manchuria and China, this connection was reinforced and deepened. By 1945 Kyŏngbang looked on the empire's hinterlands not only as a source of raw materials but also as an important market and area for corporate expansion.

PART III

CLASS AND SOCIETY

Between 1919 and 1945 the Korean bourgeoisie developed a dense and wide-ranging web of ties with the colonial state and Japanese private capital that greatly helped to propel Korean capitalist growth. The bourgeoisie's relationship with Korean society, however, was far more problematic. The new Korean bourgeois newspapers and magazines of the 1920s and 1930s, including Kim Sŏngsu's *Tonga ilbo*, portrayed businessmen like the Koch'ang Kims and their associates as part of a new "core class" in modern Korea,[1] and such self-perception was not without foundation. Korea was experiencing the beginning of an historic shift from an agrarian to an industrial economy, and the Korean bourgeoisie was certainly in the forefront of such change. Nevertheless, even as Korean capitalists prospered in an economic sense with the expansion of the colonial industrial structure, their political position within Korean society grew increasingly tenuous.

As Gramsci and others have suggested,[2] the stability and longevity of capitalist societies have depended to no small degree on the ability of the bourgeoisie in each case to transcend its own narrow economic perspective and a reliance on force and to achieve a position of leadership or "hegemony" based on broad popular consent. This has required an ability or willingness on the part of the class itself — or failing that, the state (often acting against the short-term interests and over the protests of the bourgeoisie) to grant a variety of economic and political concessions to other·classes, and especially to the working class. By giving the workers a definite material stake in capitalist society, concessions such as universal suffrage and the right to organize and strike for better wages and working conditions have served to diminish the natural class antagonism between capital and labor and thereby to reduce the bourgeoisie's need for intimidation and force as a means of maintaining its privileged economic position.

Historically, moreover, the establishment of bourgeois hegemony

188

has also required that the capitalist class in each case assume and sustain a position of moral-cultural leadership in the civil society by conceiving and pursuing its own class interests in terms of universal values around which other classes have been able to rally, and which, in time, have become so socially diffused as to attain the status of conventional wisdom or "common sense" in the society as a whole. Thus capitalist classes in the West have been able to capture the imagination and sympathy of other classes by articulating and pursuing their interests in terms of the principles of freedom and equality associated with economic laissez-faire and liberal democracy. In England, for example, the bourgeoisie's key role in the popular struggle for political reform in the nineteenth century firmly established the class's reputation as a preeminent force of social progress, even though the struggle for reform actually served fundamental bourgeois economic interests at the time.[3]

In part because of the nature of the colonial political and economic structure, and in part because of myopic self-interest, the Korean bourgeoisie offered few material concessions to the working class during the colonial period. Official colonial industrial policy was predicated on the exploitation of a cheap and subservient labor force without legal or political rights, and the colonial bourgeoisie, whose ear was so finely attuned to the nuances of bureaucratic suggestion and command, was thus free to develop a chronic deafness to the most basic demands of a growing Korean working class. As a result, the relationship between Korean capital and labor during the colonial period tended to assume the character of a stark confrontation between two warring camps. Strikes were frequent and often violent, and the Korean bourgeoisie came to rely heavily on the support and intervention of the Japanese police to maintain the status quo.

The colonial Korean bourgeoisie was also never able to achieve a position of ideological leadership in Korean society. While England's capitalists had found themselves at the head of a democratic movement because democratic principles and politics meshed well with a bourgeois desire to force political and economic concessions from a reluctant aristocracy, democracy was never a factor in Korean capitalist development. One reason for this was that the bitter European class struggle between aristocrats and industrialists that had turned the latter into democrats never really materialized in Korea. As we saw in part 1, Korea had no bourgeoisie to speak of before 1876, and even after that capitalism had developed very slowly over some forty years, with the core of the nascent Korean bourgeois class coming from a progressive element within the old landed elite itself. Class transformation rather than class conflict thus characterized the rise of a Korean bourgeoisie during this period.

Equally important, however, was the pattern of class-state interaction described in part 2. In 1919, when a Korean industrial bourgeoisie was just beginning to emerge, an authoritarian state structure geared to economic development was already firmly in place. As we have seen, it was under the aegis of this authoritarian system — essentially a military dictatorship operating through a civilian bureaucracy — that Korean capitalism experienced its first surge of growth between 1919 and 1945. Democratic politics had no part whatsoever either in the functioning of the system as a whole or in the pursuit of capitalist interests within the system. On the contrary, bourgeois political activity, such as it was, consisted exclusively of official or private interaction with the bureaucracy and was an accepted and integral part of the existing authoritarian political structure. The main facets of this interaction have already been discussed in detail in chapters 3 and 4, and there is no need to reiterate them here. Suffice it to say that Korean capitalism was comfortably authoritarian from the beginning.

While democracy was thus irrelevant to Korean capitalist development in the colonial setting, nationalism, on the other hand, seemed to offer a more natural basis on which to fashion a popular bourgeois ideology of leadership. The managers of Kyŏngbang liked to stress the Korean character of their company and from the beginning made use of nationalist themes in their advertising. For a variety of reasons, however, including the dependence of Korean firms (and especially larger companies like Kyŏngbang) on the colonial political and economic structure, the Korean bourgeoisie's commitment to nationalist principles was in fact weak to nonexistent. Where it did exist at all, as in the case of Kyŏngbang, it never posed a serious challenge to basic Japanese policies. Indeed, in the late 1930s, Korean capitalists even cooperated with the Government-General in its implementation of a ruthless wartime policy of assimilation that aimed at the virtual eradication of Korean culture. By 1945 the bourgeoisie had become a class in conflict with its own society on ideological as well as material grounds.

CHAPTER 7

"Without Any Trouble"

Capitalist Views and Treatment of the Working Class

Andrew Grajdanzev has described colonial Korea's labor conditions as constituting a "paradise for Japanese industrialists."[1] He was not exaggerating. Although the Japanese were fond of characterizing the Korean worker as unambitious, physically and intellectually lazy, and irresponsible, they were also quick to point out that Korean labor was "abundant" and "cheap."[2] The steady impoverishment of the peasant population that was the hallmark of the colonial rural economy forced thousands of Koreans to seek employment in the cities, and this labor surplus, together with the generally low standard of living, made the cost of labor in Korea about one-half that in Japan.[3]

But Korean labor was not merely cheap; it was also bereft of any kind of political or legal protection. In Japan itself, where labor conditions were also far from pleasant, the state had at least passed a universal male suffrage law and factory legislation designed to curb some of the worst abuses of the industrial system, especially in regard to juvenile and female workers. These laws did not automatically apply to the colonies, and, indeed, colonial industrialists remained completely unencumbered with such measures throughout the pre-1945 period.[4] For Japanese spinning giants like Kanebō and Tōyōbō, 80 percent of whose work forces consisted of young, unmarried girls between the ages of fourteen and eighteen,[5] the factory law, revised in the 1920s, was a particular nuisance and a major factor in the decision to establish new factories in Korea in the early 1930s. Note, for example, the following statement by the All Japan Cotton Spinners Association in 1941:

As a modern factory industry in terms of capital investment as well as factory size and facilities, the cotton yarn spinning industry in Korea is quite impressive. Indeed, the cotton spinning industry was inevitably destined to thrive [there]. For, as noted above, Korea is well-suited for cotton cultivation, and

191

the authorities, moreover, have been encouraging the expansion of such production, with the result that the volume of [cotton] produced has been gradually increasing. Not only that, [Korea] also offers many favorable conditions
for factory management. [It] has an abundance of labor power and on its
borders the vast consumer markets of Manchuria and China. *Furthermore,
[it] lies outside the jurisdiction of the Factory Laws.* (Italics mine)[6]

Korean businessmen, of course, also enjoyed the benefits of this
reservoir of cheap and unprotected labor. There is no evidence to suggest that labor conditions in Korean-owned factories were any better
for the average worker than in those run by Japanese. They were,
in fact, generally worse, because most Korean establishments lacked
the scale and capital reserves of the larger Japanese enterprises.[7]

The simple fact was that all colonial companies, regardless of the
nationality of their ownership, were part of the same economic system,
and even if Korean owners had been interested in giving their workers
better treatment than they could receive under the Japanese—a suppo-
sition for which there is again no evidence—it would have been difficult for them to do so and survive as businessmen. Even in a company
like Kyŏngbang, which was far larger than the average Korean firm
and also made a point of stressing its "nationalism," workers suffered
from the same low pay, long hours, and generally uncomfortable and
restrictive conditions that characterized Japanese-run companies like
Chōbō in Pusan.

The colonial industrialist's "paradise" was, in fact, all too often a
"living hell"[8] for the Korean workers. Conditions varied, of course,
depending on the type of industry and the skills of the particular individual in question, but even in our special area of interest, the cotton
textile industry, which was by no means the worst in terms of labor
conditions, it takes little effort to imagine that one of the main things
that kept the workers in the factories was the even bleaker prospect
of starvation in their home villages.[9]

Working Life at Kyŏngbang

Kyŏngbang employed both men and women, some of whom were married and had children, but the vast majority of workers (around 80
percent of the total) were poor, unmarried peasant girls in their early
to late teens. In the early years the company generally recruited its
labor from the Seoul-Yŏngdŭngp'o area, but as the company expanded

and the demand for workers increased, recruitment officers were appointed to scout the countryside, and eventually Kyŏngbang set up permanent local recruitment offices in the provinces. Not surprisingly, many of the girls who joined the company came from the Honam area (North and South Chŏlla) that was home to the Koch'ang Kims themselves, and it seems a reasonable assumption that a certain number of these girls were daughters of the family's numerous tenants.[10]

The Honam connection was not just a matter of convenience in recruitment. Throughout the colonial period, except during the war years, when the Government-General allowed companies to draft workers as needed, the company had a constant problem recruiting labor. In part this was because the girls were needed at home in the fields, but there was undoubtedly another reason as well. Poor as they were, the Korean peasants, like parents everywhere, were loath to send their daughters away from home to a distant factory. When they did so, it was generally an act of desperation—because food was scarce, because extra money was needed for living expenses, or because the girl herself needed some kind of dowry to get married.[11] Under such conditions, traditional or regional bonds with the employer, however tenuous, must have been reassuring to the concerned parents.

And, indeed, there was good reason for the parents to be concerned. First of all, the working hours at Kyŏngbang were grueling. In Japan, the revised factory law had abolished night labor (between 11 P.M. and 5 A.M.) for female and juvenile workers (fourteen years and under) —thus, in effect, reducing each work shift to 9 hours (Japanese textile companies commonly operated on a two-shift system). Since the law also prescribed thirty minutes of rest time when the shift exceeded 6 hours, the actual Japanese work day was, in fact, only 8½ hours.[12]

In Korea no such laws were in effect, and Kyŏngbang operated on a twenty-four hour basis, with two shifts of twelve hours each (6 A.M. to 6 P.M. and 6 P.M. to 6 A.M.). The company allotted each shift a total of forty minutes rest time (including the time taken for meals), thus making the actual work day for each girl more than eleven hours,[13] and there is no indication that juvenile workers were given any special consideration in terms of working time, although they were paid considerably less than adults.[14] Also in contrast to Japan, where the factory law stipulated that each worker had to have two rest days per thirty-day month, Kyŏngbang's workers could be compelled to toil through their eleven-hour workdays up to thirty days a month.[15]

The sheer number of hours the company required of each girl was exhausting in itself, but the nature of the work and the conditions under which it was carried out undoubtedly made the hours seem even longer than they were.

Since the girls were for the most part recruited from the peasantry, they were no strangers to a poor and harsh existence, but they were also accustomed to the fresh air, slow pace, and extensive human interaction of the villages and rice paddies. Now, however, they suddenly found themselves confined for hours on end to a hot, stuffy, and windowless room filled with deafening machines demanding their constant attention and making communication with fellow workers all but impossible — machines, moreover, that could easily cost a careless or tired girl a finger.

Everywhere — in the machines, on the floor, in the air, and, inevitably, in the girls' hair, eyes, ears, nose and throat — the factory dust continued to accumulate: tiny particles of cotton fiber that made it difficult to breathe for all and for the unlucky led to serious bronchial troubles or byssinosis.[16] When the Hanyang Women's Association visited Kyŏngbang's factory in 1936, the sight of the company's young girls at work made some of Seoul's more privileged women realize, perhaps for the first time, how fortunate they themselves indeed were. The association chairman, Yi Chaegon, later wrote: "When [we personally] witnessed the frail young girls in the dust working away for all they were worth, we truly felt pity for them. At the same time, we all reflected on how we had been carelessly wasting what [they] had been producing with such backbreaking effort. We all came away with the deep feeling that we should not waste even a strip of cotton cloth."[17]

The girls' existence at the factory was made even more uncomfortable by the company's intense labor supervision and control. Kyŏngbang regarded the factor of labor control as so crucial to its production that when the company expanded its operations to Manchuria in the late 1930s, it deliberately used Korean labor — even to the extent of transporting over a thousand girls from the peninsula itself — rather than drawing its workers from the indigenous Chinese labor market.[18] It was easier, to be sure, for Korean managers in Manchuria to supervise production in their own language, but there was certainly no dearth of Chinese-speaking Koreans around to act as interpreters, and Chinese workers, moreover, were more readily available and less expensive than imported Korean labor. The Chinese, on the other hand, as natives of the area and victims of what they undoubtedly regarded as joint Japanese-Korean imperialism, were potentially more troublesome than young Korean girls totally dependent on the company in a foreign country.[19]

The pressure of controls began, in a sense, almost immediately, with the signing of a contract that tied each girl to the company for a period of at least three years.[20] Since each girl was required to turn over a certain portion of her monthly wage to the company as "compulsory savings" (*kangje chŏgŭm*) to be kept for her until she completed her three-year term, she could break her contract only at the risk of forfeiting some of her hard-won earnings. The company was free, of course, to fire the girls at will and could use always use the threat of dismissal to keep them in line.[21]

Inside the factory itself the discipline was severe. While the white-collar staff was permitted during working hours to take time out for a cigarette, a cup of tea, or a chat with visitors, the girls tending the spindles and looms were not allowed to receive visitors and could only leave their place of work with special permission. Even the married women on the payroll with newborn infants were not free to nurse their children without consent from their supervisors. Indeed, surveillance seems to have been constant and harsh—so much so that the girls complained of "being watched like cattle or horses" and of "abusive language" from superiors. In addition, the girls were subject to a "penalty system" (*pŏlgŭm chedo*), by which they were held personally liable for any damages to the cloth or machinery under their care.[22]

The company's controls extended even into the girls' personal lives after they had completed their daily shifts. Such concern on the company's part is usually depicted in the official company histories and biographies as an implicitly moral attitude in accord with traditional paternalistic values.[23] In fact, the company was not so much a stern, benevolent "father" with its "children's" interests at heart as a competitive business with rigorous production schedules and quotas, and it had a vested interest in regulating any personal behavior on the part of its workers that might interfere with the smooth and efficient operation of the factory.

Self-interest could often take the appearance of paternalism. In his more traditional role as landlord, for example, Kim Yŏnsu set up "model villages" on his agricultural estates in which tenants were summoned to work each morning by the clanging of a bell and where drinking, gambling, and early marriage (men under the age of twenty) were strictly forbidden.[24] While such injunctions may be seen as a slightly updated version of traditional Korean paternalistic enlightenment of the masses by the educated elite, it is also true that they served to promote Kim's interest in a punctual and sober agricultural work force whose marginal subsistence (and marginal docility) would not be upset by physical or financial indulgence.

Drinking and gambling, of course, were not matters the company had to worry about with its teen-age girls, and, indeed, the girls did not have a great deal of time for any kind of leisure at all. Apart from holidays, they had only twelve hours of nonworking time every day. Two of these twelve hours were allotted for education provided by the company[25] and one may surmise that about eight hours were spent in grateful sleep, thus leaving each girl only about two hours per day of private recreational time. With the "compulsory savings system" in effect, moreover, they had little money to spend on extra-company activities.

Nevertheless, one can hardly doubt that the girls looked upon their daily two-hour respites and holidays as precious moments of freedom from the company regimen. Here, at last, was a chance to wash off the cotton dust, put on clean clothes, and perhaps—if they were not too tired or too sick—to get out of the company compound altogether. In addition, perhaps, to a chance for a brief encounter or flirtation with an exotic city boy, such freedom offered the girls, reared in mud-hut villages, the opportunity to explore the fascinating big city itself —with its royal palaces and parks, paved streets and automobiles, great stone office buildings, coffee houses, movie theaters, department stores (including Pak Hŭngsik's famous Hwasin) and glimpses of people dressed in the latest Tokyo fashion streaming in and out of the Chō-sen[26] and other major hotels.

From the company's perspective, however, such curiosity and personal freedom represented a possible threat to productive efficiency. Once outside the company gates, the girls could easily lose track of time and wind up reporting late for work. They could expend their limited energies, which the company would rather see applied to spindles and looms, on personal pleasures. They could become entangled in emotional relationships that diverted attention from their exacting factory tasks. They could be corrupted by "evil ideological elements"[27] interested in fomenting labor unrest. Or, worst of all, they could run away from the factory altogether, and the company would have to replace them.

The company's solution to such potential problems was to house its young, unmarried female workers in dormitories within the factory compound. The dormitory system was by no means unique to Kyŏngbang or to colonial Korea. It had long been standard practice in Japanese textile companies, and the Japanese themselves had originally been inspired by the dormitory system in the mills of Lowell, Massachusetts, and other early nineteenth-century American textile towns.[28] On the one hand, the dormitory system provided the girls with relatively inexpensive accommodations and helped to persuade parents reluctant to part with their young daughters that the company would be assuming the role of a surrogate parent. Most important, however, the system allowed the company to extend its control of the workers beyond the workplace itself.

Kyŏngbang's girls were bound by contract to live in the dormitories (strategically located next to the factory itself) throughout their three-year term, and it was through this provision that the company was able to restrict the girls' movements after working hours. Once the girls had finished their work and had their meal, they were expected to return to the dormitory and remain there unless they obtained specific permission from the company to do otherwise. Visitors from the outside were similarly monitored.[29] The system resembled nothing so much as that in effect at a low-security prison or in the military, and, indeed, the term used for outside visitations — *myŏnhoe* — was (and still is) the same in all three cases.

How then did the company compensate its young female workers for such drudgery and personal deprivation? Kyŏngbang's girls were paid at most only about one-half the corresponding rate in Japan. In the late 1920s, for example, Japanese female cotton textile weavers received an average of between 30 and 50 yen per month. In contrast, Kyŏngbang's best-paid weavers, who put in far more hours each month than their Japanese counterparts, were struggling with the company at that time to keep the wage at 21 yen per month,[30] and even as late as 1936 the highest monthly wage a Kyŏngbang girl could expect to receive was only 30 yen. It is necessary to stress that this was a maximum wage: most of Kyŏngbang's female workers received far less for the same number of hours and days. Those girls with less experience, and also juvenile workers, for example, were paid as little as 20 to 30 sen per day — 6 to 9 yen per month.[31]

Such low wages, as noted earlier, were normal in colonial Korea. In fact, both Kyŏngbang's minimum and average daily wage for adult female workers seem to have been somewhat higher than for such workers in other industries, and its minimum wage was comparable to that of Japanese-run cotton textile companies in Korea. The company's maximum daily wage around 1930 (about 70 sen), however, fell far short of the highest daily wage (2.50 yen) paid to adult female workers employed in the rice mills in 1931 and was even slightly lower than that of Japanese textile companies like Chōbō.[32]

For young girls whose future happiness beyond the factory hinged almost exclusively on the ability to acquire a satisfactory husband, a major impetus for joining Kyŏngbang was the hope of accumulating an attractive dowry. It is difficult to see, however, how such wages could have contributed to a dowry that was anything more than a pittance. While our figures can be no more than approximate, let us assume that around 1930 the average Kyŏngbang girl made about 50 sen per day or 15 yen per month. Of that amount, each girl paid 4.50 yen per month to the company for food.[33] Based on a 1929 report of the Japan Cotton Spinners Association, we may make a conservative estimate that each girl spent about 5.25 yen per month on various personal necessities such as towels, soap, tooth powder, clothes, shoes, and so forth, including various items required in the factory itself.[34] According to such calculations, the average girl's net earnings were thus about 5.25 yen per month. After three years at that rate she would have accumulated a total of 189 yen—enough for a family of five to subsist on a diet of barley and millet for about nine to thirteen months.[35]

One can argue about whether such an amount of money would have constituted an enticing dowry. It should be noted, however, that rice, not barley or millet, was the preferred Korean staple and that such a budget takes nothing into account besides food. Still, the average Kyŏngbang girl would most likely have been pleased if she could have counted on a full 5.25 yen per month for her dowry. The actual amount she was able to save was probably far less.

The figure of 5.25 yen per month is, in fact, an ideal estimate. It assumes, for example, that the girl never left the factory, that she never treated herself or her friends to any snacks—indeed, to luxuries of any kind, however insignificant, that she never got sick, and that she was never assessed any fines by the company. It also assumes, equally unrealistically, that she was paid a consistent daily wage. In fact, one of the major complaints of the female workers at Kyŏngbang in 1931 was that they were paid according to a "contract wage system" (*togŭpche*) based on production quotas determined by the company rather than a "daily wage system" (*ilgŭpche*) which would have guaranteed them a regular daily wage.[36]

But even supposing that through heroic self-sacrifice and phenomenal luck a girl was able to achieve the 5.25-yen ideal, how much of it could she reasonably have hoped to keep for herself? Once again the question is debatable, but it is difficult to escape the conclusion that a certain (if not a major) portion of her earnings would have gone to her family in the countryside. The Government-General's "typical" five-member family was, in fact, another idealization of reality. The absence of effective birth control methods, the age-old desire of Korean parents for a comfortable supply of sons, and the customs of concubinage and widower remarriage all combined to make the traditional Korean family as large as possible (both Kim Sŏngsu and Kim Yŏnsu had thirteen legitimate children). In all likelihood, our average Kyŏngbang girl was probably helping to support at least one younger brother or sister back home at a minimum cost of 3 yen per month (the Government-General's estimated minimum cost of food for one family member in a five-member family).[37] If we subtract this amount from the girl's ideal monthly net earnings of 5.25 yen, we have a net savings of 2.25 yen per month and a projected total dowry of 81 yen—enough only to feed a family of five for four to five months on the same unpalatable diet of barley and millet.

Apart from their beggarly wage, the girls appear to have received little additional compensation for their hard work.[38] There was, of course, the assurance of regular meals and a place to sleep. But room and board at the factory, though comparatively cheap, was by no means free: directly or indirectly, the girls paid at least part of the total cost of each. The company meals, in fact, seem to have been surprisingly expensive for institutional fare. In Japan, for example, cotton textile workers paid for about one-third of the cost of their meals; the company itself subsidized the rest. At Kyŏngbang, the ratio seems to have been reversed; the girls were paying exactly the same amount of money for food each day as their Japanese counterparts, although the standard of living was much lower in Korea.[39]

The quality of the room and board provided by the company left much to be desired. The Kyŏngbang dormitory had sixty-eight Korean-style *ondol* rooms that functioned as the girls' living and sleeping quarters. As in Japan, each of the rooms had an area equal to fifteen mats (each mat measuring one by two yards). In Japanese companies, however, it was customary for eight to ten (or fewer) girls to share a room (Osaka's municipal regulations even stipulated that each girl be allotted a minimum space of one and one-half mats). At Kyŏngbang, on the other hand, twelve to thirteen girls were crowded into a single room. The absence of adequate recreational and sanitary facilities in the dormitories was also a problem. Indeed, in the early years of operation, according to the company's own official history, the dormitory "functioned solely as a place to sleep."[40] By 1936 the Hanyang Women's Association noted the existence of "a splendid rec-reation room" in the dormitory, but the workers themselves seem to have been less impressed with what the company was providing—one of the first demands they made after Liberation was, in fact, for "full recreational and sanitary facilities."[41]

As for food, low-grade rice and a paucity of fish or meat were com-mon features of the daily fare in colonial Korea's textile factories, and there is no reason to think Kyŏngbang's meals were exceptional. One must acknowledge, however, the possibility that Kyŏngbang's food may have been on the whole somewhat better than the usual factory meals, perhaps because of the company's access to cheap rice from the Kim family's granaries. In the early 1930s, for example, when many of Kyŏngbang's workers were demanding changes in regard to wages, hours, and restrictions on personal freedom that were identical to those being voiced by workers at Chōbō, they did not, as did the latter, specifically cite the quality of the food as a grievance.[42]

On the other hand, during the years following the outbreak of the Sino-Japanese War in 1937—and especially during the 1940s—both the quality and the quantity of the food provided by the company to its workers deteriorated greatly. Even the official company history acknowledges that the food problem during this period was so terrible as to be "utterly beyond description" and provides a few details that confirm its own assessment: "From 1944 on, as the signs pointing toward Japan's defeat became stronger day by day, [the company] was unable to continue even the 3.3 hap [1.27 pint] daily food ration of 70 percent-plus mixed grain (millet, beans). The best [the company] provided was bean cake and rice husks on the verge of turning bad, and jet-black wheat flour."[43]

What the company history fails to point out, however, is that the food situation was "utterly beyond description" primarily for the workers. It is important to recall, first, that this was the period in which Kyŏngbang was enjoying an unprecedented boom in sales and profits. Second, although it is true that the Government-General implemented an official rationing system during the war that affected everyone in some way, it is also true that the system did not affect everyone in the *same* way. In an explosion of pent-up bitterness after Liberation, Kyŏngbang's workers not only demanded "better food" but accused the company management during the war of having practiced "discriminatory rationing" at the expense of workers who had been "collapsing from overwork and malnutrition."[44]

A word or two should also be said about the company's educational program for its young female workers. In addition to training the girls in those skills required for factory work, the company also provided two hours of "dormitory education" each day, which included a certain amount of instruction in elementary reading, writing, and arithmetic. While the value of such instruction should not be underestimated — many of the girls who entered Kyŏngbang during the colonial period were virtually illiterate even in *han'gŭl*, the simple native Korean phonetic script — it is important to see the company's educational program in its proper perspective.

First, its purpose was not simply (or even primarily) humanitarian, as the company histories suggest. The existence of such a program, like the dormitory system itself, was extremely useful in helping persuade reluctant parents to turn their children over to the factory for three years in the belief that they would be well taken care of.

And again like the dormitory system, the educational program functioned in part to reinforce the company's control over the girls. Basic instruction in the liberal arts, for example, constituted only about one-third of the curriculum. Another one-third was devoted to the girl's future duties as a wife — handicrafts, knitting, sewing, flower arranging, and so forth — all of which served subtly but effectively to emphasize her subordinate role in the scheme of things to men in general and, by extension, to the company management in particular. The final one-third of the company's educational program was even more directly related to social control. Here the stress was on "moral cultivation," including such subjects as "general etiquette" and "the rules of factory life."[45]

Second, it is important to consider how much reading, writing, or arithmetic a tired girl could have absorbed after eleven hours of virtually continuous work in the factory. Such subjects, moreover, do not just require mental alertness; they also presuppose a modicum of study and preparation for which the girls had neither time nor energy. In any case, Kyŏngbang's workers found the company's program lacking and called for the establishment of "full educational facilities" in 1945.[46]

Resistance and Repression

In his 1929 report on the Japanese cotton industry, General Secretary Arno S. Pearse cautioned the International Federation of Master Cotton Spinners and Manufacturers Association that

> when investigating conditions in the Far East, one has frequently to regard them with Eastern and not with Western spectacles, and particularly in the case of wages, hours of work, food, amusement, housing, so-called restraint of liberty, etc. . . . Discipline and order are, of course, essential when one has to deal with thousands of young girls, and this means some restraint of liberty, which most will agree is a good thing for the girls at that age; but *this limitation of freedom is no great hardship to the women of the East* [italics mine], for here they do not enjoy as many privileges as in the West. . . . Though the writer was unable to speak with the girls in their own tongue, he could see that most of them carried about an expression of cheerfulness.[47]

Pearse's statement is a revealing expression of class, gender, and racial bias but a poor depiction of the realities of the labor situation in prewar Asia. The truth is that Pearse himself was not regarding Japanese factory conditions with "Eastern spectacles." If he had been more interested in researching labor problems or been able or willing to interview workers in an informal atmosphere outside the factory compounds, he would have found a work force that was considerably less content than it appeared, superficially and only momentarily, to foreign visitors.

Indeed, at the time of Pearse's visit, Japan was on the eve of some of the most prolonged and violent labor disputes in its history. Even the "cheerful" girls of Kanebō, the largest and most consciously "paternal" of all prewar Japanese cotton textile firms, were rioting en masse against the company's wage cuts only months after the publication of Pearse's report.[48] And if there was labor unrest in prewar Japan, there was certainly no lack of it in colonial Korea, where wages and working conditions were far worse.

Labor disputes in Korea did not, of course, begin suddenly with the annexation in 1910. As early as 1888, demands by miners in Kangwŏn Province for higher wages and better working conditions had led to rioting and widespread violence, and some of the earliest examples of concerted strikes by Korean workers were carried out by disgruntled stevedores in Mokp'o between 1898 and 1903. But it was not until the peninsula began to experience industrialization under Japanese colonial rule in the 1920s and 1930s and saw the emergence of a distinct working class that labor problems became a common feature of Korean urban life. In 1912, for example, the Government-General recorded a total of only 6 labor disputes; by the 1930s the country was seeing an average of about 170 strikes a year.[49]

The Government-General's response to such incidents was essentially twofold. First, it showed utter indifference to the root cause of the disturbances, for example, the terribly low wages and poor working conditions of the laboring class.

That such an attitude was deliberate and not the result of bureaucratic incompetence can hardly be doubted. In Japan itself, Meiji and Taishō bureaucrats had demonstrated a keen and early awareness of the need to mitigate the social conflicts of industrialization by progressive social and political legislation—even at the risk of antagonizing the bourgeoisie. As early as 1881, for example, the newly inaugurated Ministry of Agriculture and Commerce had begun to investigate the possible application of factory legislation to Japanese industry, and by 1887 the ministry had completed an initial draft of a factory law with forty-six articles.[50]

Such official attention to labor problems was, to be sure, motivated more by a pragmatic interest in social control than by a genuine concern for the plight of the working class. In 1891, for example, Kanai Noboru, a distinguished academic economist whose creative interpretations of the German historical school had inspired many of the early Meiji bureaucrats, had warned that "if workers are treated like beasts, then after several decades unions and socialism will appear."[51] Nevertheless, such thinking led in time to the passage of some important legislation, including the Factory Law of 1911 and the Universal Manhood Suffrage Law of 1925 that together gave Japanese workers at least a modicum of legal and political protection.

In contrast, the Government-General did nothing really significant to ameliorate the harsh conditions of colonial labor in Korea. Only after 1938, when the need arose to mobilize the Korean masses for intensive wartime production and sacrifice, did the government finally show even a nominal interest in the problem.

And, indeed, it was only a nominal interest. A colonial version of Japan's Sampō or Industrial Patriotic movement (Sangyō Hōkoku

Undō) was set in motion to "eradicate the idea of confrontation" and promote "harmony and unity between capital and labor." Much as in Japan itself, however, the Government-General's Sampō movement emphasized "spiritual strengthening" and the cultivation of friendly relations between workers and managers (through the establishment of factory councils or committees, i.e., *kondankai* or *iinkai*) at the expense of the material issues that were the real crux of the capital-labor problem. Businessmen, for example, were exhorted by the Government-General in 1938 "always to be mindful of improving wages and working conditions," but they were under no official compulsion to *do* anything for their workers. As the war dragged on, moreover, the Government-General actually instituted controls that were designed to keep wages artificially depressed,[52] and general working conditions in the factories—as with Kyŏngbang—degenerated to a new low.

While the colonial authorities paid little attention to the basic problems that were provoking labor unrest, they did not remain indifferent to any overt expressions of such discontent. Korean workers had none of the limited political or legal rights of their Japanese counterparts, but they were subject to a full battery of prewar Japanese security measures and criminal laws, including the Public Order and Police Law and the Peace Preservation Law.[53]

As in Japan, such laws were aimed at curbing the growth of radical labor organizations—the Peace Preservation Law of 1925, for example, expressly prohibited the formation of any organization that "sought to change the national polity (*kokutai*) or repudiated the system of private property"[54]—but they could, of course, also be used by the police to smash unions or strikes whose radical content and connections were highly tenuous. As Grajdanzev noted in 1944, attempts to form trade unions in Korea were "suppressed with an energy equal to that used in the suppression of Communism and the eradication of 'dangerous thoughts.' " Even when a strike evinced no signs of radical influence whatsoever, strikers could still be forcibly detained or arrested at the discretion of the police simply for "obstruction of business."[55]

In general, the colonial authorities allowed and encouraged factories to resolve their own labor problems, but each neighborhood police station meticulously monitored every dispute or strike in its particular area. If there was any hint of radical influence within the striking labor force, if the strike threatened to get out of hand and spread to other factories, or if the strike simply looked as though it might go on indefinitely, the police intervened—swiftly, decisively, and often violently.

All in all, it was a simplistic, crude approach to social control, a striking contrast, indeed, to the Government-General's far more subtle and careful handling of the Korean bourgeoisie. Perhaps such inflexibility was inevitable given the nature of Japanese rule. The Korean bourgeoisie was, after all, a relatively small group, and its class interests were not ultimately in conflict with Japanese goals; there was little room, on the other hand, for any kind of meaningful compromise with the Korean masses, on whose backs the whole system of colonial exploitation rested.

The Government-General's reactionary attitude toward labor emboldened colonial businessmen, whether Japanese or Korean, to be as cavalier and callous as they wished toward their own workers. Armed with the assurance that the government and its police were ultimately on the capitalist's side in any labor dispute, a colonial manager tended to adopt an uncompromising stance toward virtually any demand his workers might put forward. Such rigidity naturally provoked anger among the workers and enhanced their determination to achieve their goals—which, in turn, stiffened a manager's resolve not to give way. A vicious circle of spiraling resentment was created, only to be broken, more often than not, by the police, on whom the management had been counting from the beginning.

The Kyŏngbang strikes of 1926 and, especially, 1931 were examples of just such a pattern of interaction among management, labor, and police. They also provide compelling evidence of the Korean bourgeoisie's reliance on state intimidation and force.

The Kyŏngbang Strike of 1926

The Kyŏngbang strike of 1926 involved two separate but related issues. One was the question of radical tendencies among the Kyŏngbang workers.

As disillusionment over the failure of the March First movement deepened, and many Koreans who had been profoundly impressed by the ideals and success of the Russian Revolution returned home from study in Japan and Russia in the early 1920s, there was a rich and intense flowering of Marxist- and Leninist-inspired writing and activity in Korea. The nascent labor movement, which had begun in 1920 with the formation of the Korean Workers Mutual Aid Society (Chosŏn Nodong Kongjehoe), was naturally a major focus of attention for young Korean radicals. Their influence was soon being felt in the Kongjehoe — originally religious and reformist in character — and even before the official inauguration of the Korean Communist party in 1925, they had succeeded in giving the labor movement a definite Marxist bent by organizing the Korean Worker-Peasant League (Chosŏn Nonong Ch'ongdongmaeng) in 1924.[56]

The league advocated "the liberation of the working class and the establishment of a completely new society," and it vowed "to struggle unceasingly with the capitalist class until the attainment of ultimate victory." By 1926, the league had become an important vehicle of the Korean Communist party and had affiliates all over the country, with a total membership exceeding 50,000.[57] One of those affiliates was the Sihŭng Workers and Friends Mutual Aid Society (Sihŭng Nou Sangjohoe) in Yŏngdŭngp'o. Numbered among the Sihŭng Nou Sangjohoe's affiliates, in turn, was an in-factory *sangjohoe* that had been organized by Kyŏngbang's workers in the winter of 1925.[58]

Quite apart from the possible threat of radicalism, however, there was another even more basic issue involved in the dispute over the Kyŏngbang Sangjohoe: the simple question of the workers' right to organize themselves for their own protection.

Aside from its formal tie to the Worker-Peasant League, the Kyŏngbang Sangjohoe does not appear to have been a particularly radical association. One of its original purposes seems to have been to block the company's practice of precipitate dismissal of workers. Even during the strike itself, the demands put forward by the Sangjohoe had no radical content whatsoever, but may be seen, rather, as the natural and limited claims of a group of workers who were dissatisfied with the treatment they were receiving at their particular factory. Such claims included the restoration of workers who had been fired, better remuneration for female workers, the abolition of the penalty system, the improvement of working conditions, and an apology from the factory technician. In addition, the Sangjohoe also demanded the resignation of the company's board of directors and insisted that the company recognize the workers' right to form unions and engage in strikes.[59]

All these requests were radically unpleasant as far as the management was concerned, but they were, objectively speaking, hardly subversive in a political sense. There was, for example, not even the slightest echo in such demands of the Worker-Peasant League's call for "liberation" of the working class and life-or-death "struggle with the capitalist class." In the final analysis, the Kyŏngbang Sangjohoe's link to the Worker-Peasant League appears to have been little more than a formality—a judgment supported by the eventual release by the police of most of the Sangjohoe's leaders on the company's recognizance.[60]

It is difficult to say which distressed the company more: the possibility, however slight, of radicalism within its own ranks, or simply the threat that a workers' union might pose to company policies.

There is no reason to doubt the company's genuine fear of radicalism. Like the police itself, the Kyŏngbang management tended to see any expression of labor discontent in terms of Communist agitation. When asked by this writer, for example, to explain the sudden explosion of labor discontent at Kyŏngbang almost immediately after Liberation, Kim Yongwan promptly proceeded to equate the company's labor problems with communism and recalled the efficiency of the colonial regime in keeping such matters under strict control: "The Communists stirred everything up. It wasn't really a labor problem. During the Japanese occupation the Communists were totally overwhelmed and couldn't budge. So the work went very smoothly."[61]

Nevertheless, the company's preoccupation in 1926 seems to have been as much or more with restricting the workers' attempts to organize per se as with quashing Communist activity. In none of the company's official statements at the time, for example, is there any mention of a radical challenge from the Worker-Peasant League; newspaper accounts, on the other hand, clearly reveal the company's antipathy toward the Sangjohoe's pledge to stand behind fired workers.[62] In any event, since "mutual aid" among the workers was linked, however peripherally, to radical unionism, it rendered the Kyŏngbang Sangjohoe vulnerable to the police and ultimately worked to the company's advantage. In the end, the company was able to see two undesirable birds killed with one stone.[63]

The stone was thrown by Kyŏngbang's management in early May, 1926, when the company demanded that the Kyŏngbang Sangjohoe sever its connection with the Worker-Peasant League. When the Sangjohoe refused, the company ordered its workers either to withdraw from the existing Sangjohoe and form a new association or to leave the company—a clear attempt on the company's part either to end or to control unionism under its own roof.[64]

This hostile attitude of the company toward the Sangjohoe brought many of the workers' latent grievances to the surface. They promptly submitted a petition (in the name of the Sangjohoe) that contained the demands cited above, and, on the morning of the seventh, 180 male and female workers (of about 400 total) walked off their jobs.[65]

The company refused to compromise on the question of the Sangjohoe and turned its back on the demands of the strikers. The only way for the problem to be resolved, insisted Executive Director Yi Kanghyŏn, was "for all the regular workers, before anything else, to come out to the factory as soon as possible and work."[66]

Such intransigence stemmed from a number of factors, all of which we shall see again in the strike of 1931. First, we may note the company's attitude of moral self-righteousness. "The nature of our company," Yi declared,

is [that] of a profit-oriented organization, but in fact [we] haven't paid a single dividend to [our] shareholders in the last eight years because [the company] was established on the unusual principle of Koreans making everything on their own. When you think of other profit-oriented companies, [such a thing] is really incredible. We've [always] given a high priority to the question of wages for [our] regular workers, and to other matters, such as the workers' freedom. As the party of responsibility [here], the company considers it regrettable that, with sudden raising of all kinds of demands [by the workers], this kind of extraordinary situation has arisen out of a trivial problem.[67]

Yi's depiction of the strike as a "trivial problem" expanded to "extraordinary" proportions reflects a second factor at work, one which can only be described as a disdain on the part of the company's management toward its own workers. If Japanese capitalists looked down upon Korean workers because they were Korean, Korean capitalists seem to have looked down upon them because they were workers, or uneducated peasants one step removed. In this view, workers or peasants were at best "simple" or "naïve" — recurring adjectives in the official company histories — but at worst they were "stupid" or emotionally unstable. Yi Kanghyŏn, for example, accused the Kyŏngbang strikers of "misunderstanding" the company's motivations and of letting themselves be "blindly carried along by shallow emotions." "I just hope," he told a reporter from the *Tonga ilbo*, "the various workers presently on strike will see the light and return to work without any trouble."[68]

The obverse of such condescension was an elitist view of the capitalist role in the economy. As Michael Robinson has suggested, men like Kim Sŏngsu and his associates tended to regard themselves as part of a new "core class" in Korean society, a modern version, as it were, of the old Confucian literati.[69] From such a perspective, the role, indeed, the *duty*, of labor was quite simply to serve its capitalist superiors, even to the point of self-sacrifice.

Korean businessmen never wearied of voicing moral indignation over what they considered the Government-General's favoritism to Japanese business concerns, even when they were making comfortable wartime profits in the 1930s. Further, we have already seen in chapter 3 how insistent the Kims and their newspaper, the *Tonga ilbo*, had been about the Government-General's responsibility to provide subsidies to Kyŏngbang in its early years of operation. Consider now the attitude of the *Tonga ilbo* toward the labor movement. The following editorial was written in regard to a general strike involving more than a thousand workers in the Korean-dominated knitwear industry in P'yŏngyang in 1925, two years after Kyŏngbang had begun receiving official subsidies from the Government-General. The knitwear workers were protesting against the lowering of their wages and the Korean manufacturers' policy of using even less expensive Chinese labor.[70] In a remarkably explicit justification of bourgeois class interest, the *Tonga ilbo* came to the manufacturers' defense: "The circumstances of Korean-run industry are that we are located next door to the cheap labor force of China and, on the other hand, have to compete without any protection whatsoever with goods from Japan, where factory industry is developed. Thus, to the extent that [Korean-run] industry itself is unstable, the workers movement in it will have to be content with a less than satisfactory standard."[71]

Self-righteousness, a patronizing attitude toward the working class, and capitalist elitism notwithstanding, what ultimately led Kyŏngbang to take so uncompromising a stance toward the demands of its own workers was the company's certainty of government and police support. Soon after the strike commenced in May 1926 — before the *Tonga ilbo* had even published any news of the strike itself — the Yŏngdŭngp'o police moved in to take eleven of the Sangjohoe's leaders off to the station for interrogation.[72]

The company publicly denied any responsibility for the police intervention,[73] and in a narrow sense this may have been true. But, as the company management surely knew, the police did not require a formal request from any business firm to become involved in a labor dispute — especially one that had the slightest tinge of radicalism about it.

The workers, in any case, seem to have had no doubt about the company's accountability for the police involvement, and even the company was quick to parlay its influence with the police as a bargaining chip in getting the workers to return to the job. "Several workers have been taken to the police station," noted Yi Kanghyŏn on the third day of the strike, "but this [problem] too will be satisfactorily resolved only when all the workers return to their jobs without any trouble."[74]

"Without any trouble," of course, meant without any conditions that the company found objectionable. And so it was. In the end, the tacit partnership of company and police proved overwhelming. The Kyŏngbang management did finally agree to a few minor demands, including the reinstatement of workers who had been fired, and it also promised to "make an effort to secure the release of workers held by the police." But the real victory clearly went to the company. The Sangjohoe was dissolved, and the workers returned to their jobs under most of the same conditions as before the strike. Thanks to the police, Kyŏngbang had been able to thwart unionism before it really took hold without making any major concessions to its workers. Moreover, the whole affair had interrupted only four days of the company's production.[75]

The Kyŏngbang Strike of 1931

In both its pattern of development and final denouement, the Kyŏngbang strike of 1931 was very similar to the one in 1926, but it was decidedly more violent. Let us pause for a moment to consider the setting in which it took place.

The Setting. The main cause of the strike was Kyŏngbang's decision to reduce wages by 20 percent in May 1931. In an interview with the *Tonga ilbo* on May 30—three days into the strike—Yi Kanghyŏn defended the company's actions as inevitable, a simple question of corporate survival:

That the problem has come to this makes [us] feel sorry, both for the workers and also, truly, for society in general. But with the recent worldwide depression and, moreover, the unspeakable impoverishment of Korean villages, general consumer buying power has hit bottom, and all manufacturing companies are in a state of uncertainty as to whether or not they can go on. So in our company, too, in order to economize, both the business and the factory management took a voluntary reduction in total income from April, but [we] continued to maintain the existing industrial wage [level] for the workers. Inevitably, however, we temporarily stopped night work and continued to operate only during the day. And then . . . as the people responsible [for the company], [we] had no choice but to reduce wages to some extent, even though it was not [our] original intention.[76]

There was some truth to Yi's statement. As noted in chapter 2, the 1920s had been a period of severe depression in the agricultural sector both in Japan and Korea and the "worldwide depression" of which Yi spoke had thus intensified an already bad situation. In 1929, for example, C. H. Stephan, the American vice-consul in Seoul, had sent the following report to the commercial attaché in Tokyo:

General economic conditions throughout Chosen during the first half of 1929 continued to be affected by the poor crops in 1928. Prolonged and excessive dryness during May and June threatening the possibility of another poor crop year added to the anxiety of the masses whose purchasing power was reported to have reached its lowest degree. The general depression and pessimism prevailing in commercial markets and commercial spheres generally was accounted for accordingly. . . . The demand for cotton and hemp textiles was also very poor due to the depression in all the farming villages.[77]

Throughout the 1920s Kyŏngbang had been attempting to cope with these adverse circumstances in a variety of ways, including, among other things, the exploration of new markets in the north (especially Manchuria) and experimentation with different sales techniques.[78] Limitation or reduction of labor costs — which for some cotton textile companies could run as high as 48 percent of the factory production cost[79] — was naturally also of prime concern to the company management.

In fact, 1931 was not the first year Kyŏngbang had attempted to lower wages. Only three years earlier the company had installed some new labor-saving machinery (presumably warp-stop motion) that allowed a girl to weave twice as many rolls of cloth in the same amount of time. The company then fired about sixty girls in the weaving department and instituted a new wage system that effectively cut wages by as much as 21 percent — even though the girls who were allowed to stay on were now doing twice as much work as before.[80]

A strike had ensued on May 29, 1928, but it began to fizzle out almost immediately. On June 5 the *Keijō nippō* reported that the strike was having "no effect," because the company, in the midst of a slack season and already operating on only one shift per day, could easily afford a temporary slowdown or even a halt in production.[81]

Given this situation, police intervention proved unnecessary. After only three days, many of the girls returned to work. The company subsequently agreed to maintain the old wage for the most experienced workers and promised that any wage reductions would be in proportion to the number of rolls of cloth produced.[82]

Thus by June 7 the strike was over, and, as in 1925, Kyŏngbang had clearly been the winner. The workers who had been laid off were not rehired; the company's right to reduce wages had been upheld; and even though some of the girls had managed to keep their old wage, to earn it they now had to do twice the amount of work they had done in the past.

During the strike in 1928 Yi Kanghyŏn had made essentially the same public plea for understanding that he would make in 1931, that is, that the situation was inevitable: to survive, the company had no choice but to lower wages. While such a statement must have been difficult for the workers to accept even in 1928 (only three months before the wage cut, for example, the board had voted an 8 percent yearly dividend to its stockholders),[83] it was surely more plausible in 1928 than it was in 1931.

Thanks in part to Government-General subsidies, the company had continued after 1928 to declare 8 percent yearly dividends down to the eve of the strike in 1931,[84] and, furthermore, sales had been steadily picking up between 1928 and 1931 with Kyŏngbang's gradual penetration of the Manchurian market. Signs of the company's growing prosperity and optimism must have been obvious to any worker in May 1931; all he or she had to do was look around at the new factory construction that was going on at the time. Yi Kanghyŏn's lament about the company's urgent circumstances notwithstanding, the truth of the matter was that the company was cutting its wages by another 20 percent just as it was undertaking a major expansion. These two actions were not merely coincidental.

The year 1931 was an excellent time for expansion. While on the one hand the general depression was keeping cloth prices low, it was also reducing dramatically the costs of construction and new machinery. For those companies with an eye to the future and access to funds, the idea of expansion in the midst of depression was not only feasible but compelling. Thus, in Japan itself, many textile companies, including Kyŏngbang's close associate, the C. Itoh Company (Kureha Spinning), were taking advantage of the bleak economic situation created by the world depression and Japan's return to the gold standard to increase their fixed capital and enhance their productive facilities. On September 3, 1930, for example, *The Japan Chronicle—Weekly Commercial Supplement*, published in the heart of Japan's Osaka-

Kobe textile region, carried the following report on "spinning mill extensions":

Spinners are active in extending their mills, as machinery, land, and buildings do not cost much. The whole installation, as a matter of fact, costs only 45 yen—sometimes 40 yen—per spindle as against 70 yen two years ago and 100 yen at the time of the war boom. With such a small investment, spinners are in a position to carry on business on a lucrative basis. The Kureha Spinning commenced production only in September last year and yet declared an 8 percent dividend in May. Seeing this, the Toyama Boseki owned by the same capital group has decided to establish a 36,000 spindle mill and also extend its existing mill by 96,000 spindles. The Temma Spinning Company is to create a new 30,000 spindle mill in Toyama. Among those planning extensions are the Toyo, the Dainippon, and the Fukushima Spinning Companies.[85]

At Kyŏngbang too, the notion of expansion had been in the air for some time. At a corporate board meeting held on May 29, 1930, Yi Kanghyŏn—in a private description of Kyŏngbang's economic situation that was strikingly different both in content and tone from his public pronouncement justifying the 20 percent wage reduction a year later—enthusiastically advised that the company take advantage of the current depression and enlarge its factory. Yi's recommendation was recorded in the board minutes for that day as follows:

Regarding the factory extension and the additional installation of looms: according to the [acting] board chairman [Yi Kanghyŏn], the statistics of the past several years [show that] while the present consumption of cotton cloth in Korea amounts to about 66-plus million yen, the amount being produced [inside the country] is no more than about 22-plus million yen. Most of the difference is being supplied by imports. A look at the company's achievements [show that] everything in general is proceeding smoothly. There have, moreover, been frequent occasions every year during the period of demand when the goods in stock have not in themselves been sufficient to fill the orders received, and [Yi] has the strong feeling that our production is falling short [of demand]. And so, because the future prospects of the industry are extremely bright, and also because—owing to the fall in prices—construction costs and machinery costs are about 20 percent lower, [Yi] explained that [now] is the most appropriate time for expansion . . . and recommended an increase of 224 looms and a factory extension to accommodate them.[86]

The board agreed with Yi and voted unanimously to go ahead with the proposed expansion. By September 1931 the factory addition had been completed and 224 new looms installed.[87]

What interests us here, however, is not so much the expansion per se as where the money for the project ultimately came from. Even though construction and machinery costs were lower than normal in 1930 and 1931, they still had to be paid, and it is very clear that such payments were not being covered by the company's profits. Profits during this period (even with the Government-General's subsidies figured in) were still too small in themselves to finance any major expansion. And, in any case, they were being entirely consumed — except for a small amount the company was required by law to place in reserve — by the 8 percent dividends mentioned earlier.

Kyŏngbang was, in fact, hard pressed for capital to fund the new construction. In January 1931 the company held a fourth sale of corporate shares, which increased its paid-in capital by 250,000 yen.[88] But this new equity was by itself insufficient. At a board meeting in September 1932, Yi Kanghyŏn noted that the expansion of facilities had been forcing the company to dip into its "working capital" and recommended that Kyŏngbang apply to the Chōsen Industrial Bank for a 500,000-yen loan.[89]

It is in this context of a cash flow crisis generated by Kyŏngbang's new construction between May 1930 and September 1932 that the company's decision to reduce wages by 20 percent in the spring of 1931 assumes its true character. While Kyŏngbang's managers were eventually compelled to take out a loan to help finance a project that equity alone could not handle, their first response to the cash flow problem had been to reduce operational expenses, that is, to lay off workers and cut wages. Corporate expansion, not corporate survival, had been the chief factor at work here.

Seen in this light, Kyŏngbang's action seems clearly one-sided, if not exploitative. The company was financing its expansion in the midst of a severe depression at the expense of those who could least afford it. And as if to emphasize who was to bear the brunt of the burden for the project, the board of directors not only declared an 8 percent dividend to the company's shareholders just before cutting wages by 20 percent, it also voted at the same meeting to recommend to the shareholders that the board itself be given a yearly compensation of 6,000 yen for fiscal 1931-32 — an amount equal at the time to more than twenty years of total wages for one of Kyŏngbang's best paid female weavers.[90]

The Workers' Challenge. While the key issue in the 1931 dispute was the 20 percent wage cut (announced in May), the actual strike seems to have been precipitated by Kyŏngbang's abrupt firing of 12 high-level workers on May 26. Taking advantage of the 6 P.M. shift change, about 300 workers (both male and female) held a conference on the twenty-eighth and drew up a petition, which the company promptly rejected. In response, the workers went on strike the following morning.[91]

As in 1926, the workers' resentment about one specific issue — in this case the reduction in wages — immediately mushroomed into a general expression of dissatisfaction with the treatment they were receiving at the company. Beginning with "absolutely no reduction in wages," the workers' petition of May 28 contained a total of 17 different demands that encompassed the whole range of working class life at Kyŏngbang:[92]

1. Absolutely no reduction in wages
2. A minimum wage of 80 sen per day
3. Equal pay for equivalent work for juvenile workers of both sexes
4. Public calculation of wages
5. Payment of living expenses and consolation money to injured workers
6. Absolutely no dismissal of workers [without good reason]
7. Payment of more than 6 months of severance pay to dismissed workers
8. Adoption of an 8-hour workday
9. Adoption of a 6-hour workday for juvenile workers
10. Abolition of the contract wage system and adoption of a daily wage system
11. Freedom of entry and exit for workers on the job and for those workers living in dormitories; also freedom to receive visits from outsiders
12. Abolition of forced savings
13. Elimination of surveillance and abusive language
14. Increase of [total] daily rest time to one hour
15. Freedom of association
16. Abolition of the penalty system
17. Freedom of married workers to breastfeed babies

While all these demands were important to the workers, the points concerning wages and hours were paramount. As Song Kwangmun, one of the striking Kyŏngbang workers told a reporter at the time:

Of our seventeen demands, the [most] important are: absolutely no reduction of wages; establishment of an eight-hour workday; and a change from a contract to a daily wage system. In the past, on a daily wage [system], there was some benefit to us. Now, on a contract wage [system], [our] income has greatly shrunk. At present, with difficulty, the best [pay] is 70 sen [per day], the worst 30 sen [per day]. I'm sure you know that we won't be able to make a living if [they] suddenly cut this. In a word, a person has to be able to make a living, doesn't he?[93]

The Company's Response. Following what was by now a familiar pattern, the Kyŏngbang management treated the strike as a "momentary misunderstanding" on the part of the workers and insisted, as we have seen, that it was the company's survival—not the workers'—that was really at stake.[94] Along with the statement quoted earlier, Yi Kanghyŏn also issued a point-by-point rebuttal of the workers' seventeen demands, which was published in toto by *Tonga ilbo* on May 31.

According to Yi, there was absolutely no room for compromise with the workers' major demands. With regard to the question of wage reductions and a minimum wage of 80 sen per day, Yi declared flatly that "these [demands] involve the life or death of the company and therefore, regrettably, cannot be accepted." The idea of an eight-hour workday (with a six-hour day for juveniles) was similarly unacceptable: "These are targets for the future and presently under study, but they cannot be implemented at this time." As for the workers' desire for a return to the daily wage system, Yi replied that "from the standpoint of operational efficiency, such a change is difficult."[95]

The company was also uncooperative with the secondary demands listed in the petition. The workers' request that the company reveal its method of calculation for wages was, according to Yi, "based on a misunderstanding totally without foundation." A minimum of six months of severance pay was "absolutely out of the question." Freedom of association for the workers was a matter "outside the purview of the company."[96]

In many cases, the company simply refused to acknowledge that a legitimate problem even existed. "There are no cases," said Yi, "where we have ever dismissed workers without reason." Again: "There has never been a case of our managers using impolite language." And again: "There have never been any restrictions on outside visiting or on entry and exit for those living in the dormitories, but we have necessarily had to impose such restrictions on workers during business hours." And finally, in regard to the request that married workers be freely allowed to breastfeed their babies: "I don't think the female workers have expressed any [such] dissatisfaction in the past, and so I do not believe this will be a problem in the future."[97]

On only two of the seventeen points—both of which were relatively minor—did the company show any willingness at all to compromise. One was the demand for the abolition of the compulsory savings system. According to Yi, the system was "being carried out for the sake of [workers] when they leave the company, but if all the workers are against it, its abolition is no problem." The other point Yi was willing to concede was the demand for a total rest time of one hour: "At present it's forty minutes but it's possible to extend it to one hour."[98]

Stalemate. The company's unyielding attitude made serious negotiation virtually impossible from the start, and, as in 1926, only hardened the workers' resolve not to retreat. Not only did the strikers refuse to work; they took over the factory and vowed to remain inside until the company gave in on the key demands. Family members of the strikers lent their support by bringing in food twice a day. Song Kwangmun, the worker quoted earlier, said quite simply, "So long as [the managers] ignore our opposition to a reduction in wages, we will never work or leave the factory." The *Tonga ilbo* reported on May 31 that solidarity among the workers was "firm" and predicted that settlement of the strike "would probably require considerable time."[99]

Time, however, was on the company's side. As in 1926, all the company had to do was wait. Even if the workers did not give up the strike out of sheer exhaustion or from a pressing need to provide *some* income, however unsatisfactory, for their families, the company knew the police would eventually take action to disperse the strikers, either for political reasons or simply because the strikers were "obstructing business."

Radicalism was never really an issue in the strike of 1931. Some of the points in the Kyŏngbang workers' petition, for example, the call for an eight-hour workday, the establishment of a minimum wage, the abolition of wage discrimination against women and juveniles, were also claims being put forward at the time by various Korean Communist groups,[100] but the Communists only seem to have been advocating what many workers themselves, at Kyŏngbang and elsewhere, felt were just demands. The police, of course, were acutely sensitive to Communist activity in any labor dispute, and on May 30, Saeki Tasuke, head of the Higher or Political Police (Kōtō Keisatsu) Section of the Kyŏnggi Provincial Police Bureau, arrived in Yŏngdŭngp'o to investigate the circumstances of the Kyŏngbang strike. There is no indication that he found anything alarming, and on the following day the *Keijō nippō* reported "no evidence of machination by ideological elements" at Kyŏngbang.[101]

In the final analysis, the Kyŏngbang workers appear to have been acting spontaneously and entirely on their own. Indeed, at least one sympathetic student of the radical Korean labor movement at the time regarded the Kyŏngbang strike as one of several sorry instances of leftist inactivity. Despite the readiness of the workers to fight, he wrote, such strikes "had not been duly supported by the left wing and went off without its participation."[102]

Although there was no suggestion of Communist involvement in the strike, the police were still concerned about it dragging on indefinitely and eventually becoming a focus of radical activity or simply an inspiration to workers in other factories—as, for example, in the case of the three-month-long general strike in Wŏnsan in 1929.[103] Still, the police did not immediately rush in and disperse the strikers with force. Indeed, the police seem to have been more interested in a peaceful resolution of the strike than the company itself, and one newspaper even commented that Chief Fujii and his staff at the Yŏngdŭngp'o Police Station were actually "sympathetic" toward the strikers.[104]

Such "sympathy" definitely had its limits, but it is true, nevertheless, that having once ascertained that the strike was free of radical elements, the police initially decided on caution and restraint. They even attempted to act as a mediator to settle the strike through compromise on both sides. Section Chief Saeki of the Kyŏnggi Political Police and Police Inspector Takada visited Kyŏngbang and bluntly told company officials to resolve the strike as quickly as possible, and Chief Fujii finally pressured the company into agreeing to a 10-sen increase in the minimum wage for female workers and to the rehiring of six workers who had been fired.[105]

For the workers, however, who were asking for a 50-sen increase in the minimum wage and much more besides, such concessions were not nearly enough. They continued to occupy the factory, and the strike once again threatened to turn into a protracted stalemate. By now, however, the police were firmly on the company's side. Chief Fujii had accepted Yi Kanghyŏn's declaration that the company could compromise no further, and whatever sympathy he may originally have had for the workers had now turned to impatience and anger in the face of their steadfast defiance.

Police Intervention. The clash came on the morning of the thirty-first—only the third day of the strike. The Yŏngdŭngp'o police positioned themselves around the factory, and Chief Fujii ordered the workers to accept the company's compromise and disperse. Further occupation of the factory, Fujii warned, was "illegal" and would not be tolerated. He gave the workers ten minutes to make up their minds. The workers held firm, and at 9 A.M. Fujii instructed the police to enter the factory and break up the strike.[106]

The forced entry enraged the workers, who continued to resist the order to disperse and fought the police as best they could—some with knives. In a burst of frustration and anger at the company, many workers rampaged through the factory, randomly smashing windows and attempting to damage the equipment and machinery. Those on the outside who had not taken part in the actual occupation of the factory also shouted their encouragement and surged inside to join in the melee.[107]

The workers, of course, did not really have much of a chance against the police, and in the end about forty (both men and women) were arrested and taken off to the Yŏngdŭngp'o Police Station, though not before a contingent of additional policemen had been rushed in from provincial headquarters.[108]

The whole area around the factory became a scene of commotion and extreme tension. In a spontaneous mass gesture of moral support for their fellow workers, those workers who had not been arrested rushed wildly after the police and their prisoners, crying and shouting all the way to the station. When they refused to disband, the police reappeared and finally managed—only with considerable effort—to disperse them by force.[109]

Thereafter the police went on full alert. The factory was shut down, and the immediate area was sealed off tightly. People were forced to stay inside, and even small groups of twos and threes were broken up by the nervous and suspicious police. Many of the workers fled to neighboring districts, where they tried to decide what to do next.[110]

The End of the Strike. There was, in fact, little choice but to accept defeat and return to the factory. Already weakened by the relentless daily regime at the looms, Kyŏngbang's workers, some of whom were still children, had suddenly gone on strike, in some cases without sleep, and had held the factory for sixty-five continuous hours before being swept into a physical battle with the police. They were exhausted.[111]

They were also demoralized. The police had not only smashed the strike but also arrested all its principals, including Song Kwangmun. By June 2, two days after the police intervention, most of the leaders of the strike had been summarily charged with "obstruction of business," convicted, and locked up in Sŏdaemun Prison. On June 4, the *Keijō nippō* reported that "what was left of the strike group was gradually weakening."[112]

Even if the workers had had the energy and heart to continue the strike, they would still have lacked the necessary funds. As noted above, the workers received no assistance, monetary or otherwise, from outside groups such as the Korean Communist party, and, unlike the company, which had access to bank loans and could fall back, if necessary, on the financial reserves of the Kim family, the workers were entirely dependent on their own meager resources. As the factory closure extended into the first week of June, thoughts of continued resistance inevitably began to give way to a more basic concern about subsistence. The hard fact was that the workers needed the company more than the company needed them. The company could always replace recalcitrant strikers with more obedient recruits from the countryside, but the strikers desperately needed the company's wages just to exist. "Weeping bitterly," they slowly began to trudge back to Yŏngdŭngp'o to beg the company to put them back to work as soon as possible.[113]

The Kyŏngbang management hastened this process of capitulation with a threat. Sure of ultimate victory, the company announced that it would resume operations on June 5 and that any and all workers who did not report for work "unconditionally" by 6:30 A.M. the following day could consider themselves fired. Needless to say, most of the workers returned. The company then declared that it would voluntarily raise the minimum wage by 10 sen—as it had promised the police—and "give future consideration" to the various points in the workers' original petition.[114]

The company's triumph was total. *Tonga ilbo*, which had continually understated the seriousness of the strike (in contrast to its coverage of strikes at Japanese companies) and had neglected to mention except tangentially the violence that occurred in the factory during the scuffle with the police, merely noted on June 6 that most of the workers had returned to their jobs. Reports in the Japanese newspapers went more to the heart of the matter. An article in the *Chōsen shimbun* proclaimed "Victory to the Company" in boldface and went on to state that the strike had been "resolved . . . without [the company's] agreeing to a single one of the workers' seventeen conditions." And with equal honesty if less fanfare, the *Keijō nippō* informed its readers that the Kyŏngbang strike had ended in "overwhelming defeat" for the striking workers.[115]

Beyond 1931

As far as is known—though this is by no means definitive—the strike of 1931 appears to have represented the acme of organized and overt resistance by Kyŏngbang's workers to the company's labor policies before 1945.

The apparent docility of the workers after 1931 was due in part, perhaps, to the subsequent expansion of the colonial economy after the Japanese army's seizure of Manchuria in 1931 and the outbreak of the Sino-Japanese War in 1937. The improved business opportunities and conditions that followed such territorial aggrandizement and war may to some extent have helped to diffuse tensions between capital and labor.[116] Wages, for example, at Kyŏngbang and other factories were gradually increased during this period. In 1932, the most a Kyŏngbang girl could hope to receive was eighty sen a day, in 1936, the maximum wage for females was twenty sen higher; by 1945, quite a number of girls were receiving a daily wage of more than one yen, and a few girls were getting over three yen per day.[117]

But we must beware of overemphasis here. The treatment accorded workers at Kyŏngbang and elsewhere in the 1920s and early 1930s did not suddenly or dramatically improve in the midst of greater economic prosperity. Indeed, as in 1931, Kyŏngbang's expansion continued to be based on the assumption of a cheap and strictly controlled labor force, while the benefits of growth went, as always, primarily to the company and to its managers and shareholders. Real wages, for example, that is relative to prices, actually showed a downward trend during the late 1930s, and if Kyŏngbang's best-paid workers were finally receiving more than one yen per day during this period, the lowest-paid workers were getting only twenty sen—actually less than in 1931.[118] The company, on the other hand, was busily accumulating profits and storing up reserves as never before during this same period, and the board of directors was now voting itself an aggregate salary of 20,000 yen per year—in addition to allowances and regular semiannual bonuses of 5,000 to 9,000 yen.[119] Working and living conditions in the factory compound, moreover, not only failed to improve, but in some areas—food, for example—actually worsened during the war years, as has already been noted.

How then do we explain the relative quiescence of Kyŏngbang's workers after 1931 and that the number of labor strikes in general tended to decrease in the late 1930s? The answer seems obvious: the intensification of police control.[120]

Like all other aspects of the economy during the war years, labor was subjected to stringent regulation by the Government-General. The National General Mobilization Law, passed by the Imperial Diet in

1938 and revised in 1941, served as a general enabling act for official control of the economy both in Japan and Korea. Among other things, it authorized the Government-General to "issue necessary orders regarding the prevention or settlement of labor disputes or the closing of plants, suspension of operations, or restriction or prohibition of acts relating to labor disputes."[121]

In the past the police had generally intervened only after the fact in a labor dispute or strike, that is, when the company concerned had found itself unable to resolve the problem on its own. This had clearly been the pattern at Kyŏngbang in 1931 and even in 1926, when there had been some initial suspicion by the police of Communist involvement. After 1938, however, as part of the overall government effort to keep the wartime economy functioning at maximum efficiency, the police found themselves in the business of preventing as well as ending such incidents.

And they were highly successful. Kim Yongwan's recollection that "the work went very smoothly"[122] at Kyŏngbang during the colonial period because of strict Japanese control was, in effect, a testimony to the accomplishments of the Japanese police.

That it was police control and not any improvement in working conditions that permitted work at Kyŏngbang to go "very smoothly" during the last years of the colonial period was amply demonstrated in August 1945. As soon as Liberation swept aside such control, Kyŏngbang's 1,400 workers immediately began to organize themselves and petition the company for reform. By the end of the month the company was engaged in the longest and most serious strike in its twenty-six year history. One leftist, though not specifically Communist, newspaper published at the time by the newly formed National Council of Korean Labor Unions (Chosŏn Nodong Chohap Chŏn'guk P'yŏngŭihoe or Chŏnp'yŏng) reported the strike as follows: "In an attempt to escape from a miserable existence and inhuman exploitation, 1,400 workers at the Kyŏngsong Spinning and Weaving Company's factory in Yŏngdŭngp'o have presented [the company] with [some] just demands and are carrying out a bold struggle on behalf of Korea's entire working class against Kim Yŏnsu, the imperialist lackey and vicious owner of the factory."[123]

For anyone who had participated in or observed the strikes of 1926 and 1931, the burst of organized labor activity at Kyŏngbang in August 1945 must surely have had a touch of *déjà vu* about it. Many of the demands at Liberation, including the call for an eight-hour workday and for personal freedom of movement, were the same claims that Kyŏngbang's workers had been making on and off throughout the colonial period. For nearly two full decades the company had been able to hold its workers at bay—but only with the firm backing of the Government-General and the colonial police.

CHAPTER 8

Class Over Nation

Naisen Ittai and the Korean Bourgeoisie

While the public excoriation of Kim Yŏnsu in 1945 as a "vicious" factory owner underscored the anger and alienation that capitalist treatment of the working class had provoked during the colonial period, his being further denounced at the time as an "imperialist lackey" also signified an ideological dimension to the bourgeois estrangement from Korean society. At the core of this problem was the issue of bourgeois nationalism and the related question of collaboration with the colonial regime and colonial policies, especially during the wartime mobilization of 1937–45.

Nationalism and Capitalism in Korea

Nationalism was the key to ideological leadership in the colonial period, and, indeed, the bourgeoisie in Korea had little else with which to fashion an ideological hegemony. In the West capitalism had developed not only as a specific form of economic activity, but also as a way of life largely separate from, and in opposition to, an existing feudal society. Even before its political triumphs in the eighteenth and nineteenth centuries, it had already acquired a rich ideological heritage of economic and political liberalism that had grown naturally out of its concrete struggles with feudalism. Such liberalism not only provided strong justification for the unfettered individual pursuit of profit, traditionally regarded as one of the seven cardinal sins, its irresistible appeal to other classes chafing under a variety of feudal restrictions also gave the bourgeoisie a position of natural ideological leadership within the growing Western capitalist societies.[1]

In Korea, as we have already noted, capitalism developed under very different historical conditions that had nothing to do with Western liberalism, either in an economic or a political sense. No Korean counterpart to Adam Smith appeared to raise selfishness to the level of a moral principle for colonial Korean businessmen. On the contrary, Korean businessmen were compelled to pursue their interests within a still strongly Neo-Confucian society that regarded business purely for the sake of individual gain at best with suspicion and at worst as an act of moral turpitude. The complexity and contradictions of such a situation were compounded in that many of the early capitalists tended to come from a progressive segment within the old landlord-bureaucratic class, thus leaving the Korean bourgeoisie itself with a certain ambivalence about its own profit-seeking activities. This ambivalence, as well as a clear concern for public opinion, were reflected in the Korean bourgeois press. There the desire to appear virtuous while making money led Korean businessmen to adopt and foster a griffinlike public image of the businessman as Confucian moral paragon—a successful moneymaker who, in fact, cared little for money, but was keenly interested in such things as "humanity" and "righteousness." In an interview for *Samch'ŏlli* in 1935, for example, a reporter asked Kim Sŏngsu if he thought that money was the most important thing in the world. Kim's reply was worthy of Mencius: "Certainly not. What's money [that anyone could ever consider it so important]? There's nothing more vulgar than money, nothing more filthy than money. How could [anyone] ever say that money was the most important thing in the world? I, for one, have never once thought that money was the most important [thing]. More [important] than money are humanity and also righteousness."[2]

Rhetoric of this kind, even if sincere, was hardly sufficient to provide a basis for bourgeois ideological leadership. What was needed was both a philosophical and material commitment on the part of the business elite to an ideal that would not only advance their economic interests but also elicit the genuine support of other classes on the basis of the actual conditions of colonial society. Nationalism was at least potentially such an ideal. Certainly it had shown itself capable of sweeping across class lines, as in the case of the March First movement. It might be argued, furthermore, that the Korean bourgeoisie had a natural interest in overturning a system in which most Koreans, simply because they were Korean, were assigned a permanent second place to Japanese.

But subjunctives, however compelling, are easily deflated by history. The Korean bourgeois commitment to nationalism, such as it was, was in fact a fragile bloom, hedged in by all kinds of constraints. It did not last long beyond the March First movement, and by the late 1930s, most of Korea's major businessmen found themselves actively or passively helping to implement a policy that was aimed at the destruction of a separate Korean national identity.

Before, however, we examine this policy and the Korean involvement in it, including the involvement of the Koch'ang Kims, let us first consider some of the forces that limited bourgeois nationalism and ultimately led to such collaboration. One thinks immediately, of course, of the failure of the March First movement in 1919 and the ensuing feeling of despair that Koreans experienced in the face of overwhelming Japanese military strength and the absence of support from other foreign powers. But not all Koreans subsequently turned to collaboration with the colonial regime. Most simply suppressed their anger and continued to endure as best they could. A good number, moreover, chose to carry on the nationalist movement in more radical and dangerous ways.[3] An explanation of bourgeois collaboration, therefore, cannot be found in the failure of the March First movement alone. Other forces were also at work. One such element, the practice of *sadae*, was far older than the bourgeoisie—as old, perhaps, as Korea itself.

The Sadae Legacy

Scholars today in both North and South Korea tend to interpret all of Korean history in nationalistic terms, but both nationalism and nationalist history are relatively recent phenomena that grew out of a late nineteenth-century reaction to imperialism and were reinforced by the experience of colonialism. Koreans, of course, had always been aware of their ethnic and linguistic differences from the peoples around them and may well have felt a certain loyalty toward the Korean monarch or even the ruling dynasty. But before the late nineteenth century there was little, if any, feeling of loyalty toward the abstract concept of "Korea" as a nation-state, or toward fellow inhabitants of the peninsula as "Koreans." Far more meaningful at the time, in addition to a sense of loyalty to the king, were the attachments of Koreans to their village or region, and above all to their clan, lineage, and immediate and extended family.

The Korean elite in particular would have found the idea of nationalism not only strange but also uncivilized. Since at least the seventh century the ruling classes in Korea had thought of themselves in cultural terms less as Koreans than as members of a larger cosmopolitan civilization centered on China. The Korean king was formally invested by the Chinese emperor, Chinese was the written language of the court and aristocracy, and the Chinese classics of philosophy and literature provided the basis for all education. To exist outside the realm of Chinese culture was, for the Korean elite, to live as a barbarian.

At the beginning of the Yi dynasty this orientation toward Chinese culture took the form of an official foreign policy called *sadae* or "serving the great," where "the great," of course, meant China. In one sense the *sadae* policy represented a brilliant diplomatic strategy by which Korea obtained the good will, protection, and sophisticated culture of a great power — its "elder brother" in the common Confucian parlance of the time. On the other hand, such orientation and deference toward a foreign country greatly weakened any tendency toward nationalism that might have existed among the Korean elite.[4] In the fifteenth century, for example, the attempt to translate a Chinese rhyming dictionary into *han'gul,* the newly created Korean phonetic script, provoked a vituperative memorial to King Sejong from Ch'oe Malli, the highest ranking academician in the prestigious Chiphyŏnjŏn (College of Assembled Worthies). The memorial showed clearly the unabashed, even militant, comopolitanism of the yangban aristocracy. "Although from ancient times," Ch'oe wrote,

customs and local usages have differed within the Nine Isles, there has never been a case of one of them separately making a script based on the local speech. Only types like the Mongolians, Tanguts, Jureen, Japanese, and Tibetans have their own graphs. But these are matters of the barbarians and not worth talking about. It has been traditionally said, 'Change the barbarians using Chinese ways'; we have never heard of changing toward barbarousness. Through the succession of ages, China has always regarded our country as having the bequeathed customs of Kija, but in matters of culture, literary and material, and in ritual and music, we have rather taken after China. To now separately make the vulgar script is to discard China and identify ourselves with the barbarians. This is what is called "throwing away the fragrance of storax and choosing the bullet of the preying [sic] mantis." This is certainly a matter of great implication for our civilization.[5]

Despite the growth of nationalism after 1876, the traditional Korean elite's disposition to find its identity within the framework of an initially alien culture seems to have carried over to some extent into the colonial period, with Japan replacing China as the center of civilization and as Korea's "elder brother." The process had already begun in the late nineteenth century in the midst of the disintegration of the existing Chinese world order, when a reformist element in the Korean elite began to turn away from China and look toward the West and Japan as models of a new world civilization. Although the early yangban reformers who found their inspiration in Japan did not envision any kind of formal political merger between Japan and Korea, an extreme version of the reformist view appeared between 1904 and 1910 in the form of the so-called Advancement Society (Ilchinhoe), which placed Japan at the center of a new anti-Western, Pan-Asian civilization and publicly supported both the protectorate and the annexation.[6]

One finds echoes of this transposed *sadae* attitude in the speeches, writings, and transcribed conversations of Han Sangnyong and other prominent Korean businessmen in the colonial period. The language they used when speaking with Japanese officials and businessmen was often floridly deferential, even by prewar Japanese standards. Even in those cases where a poor command of Japanese left little room for embellishment or subtlety, the old *sadae* attitude of a Confucian younger brother beseeching his elder was still clearly discernible. In the remarks of the least polished speakers, one often finds the most bluntly explicit *sadae* attitude. At the Government-General industrial commission held in 1938, for example, Hyŏn Chunho, the president of the Honam Bank and a close friend and business associate of the Koch'ang Kims,[7] struggled with his imperfect language to persuade the Japanese to be more generous and tolerant toward their less advanced Korean younger brothers:

Think of [us] Koreans as your younger brothers [otōto] or followers [kobun], and be big enough [to accept us as such]. And if we make mistakes, guide [us], teach [us], and forgive [us]. In other words, please be generous. I would hope that Japanese would consider it shameful to quarrel or fight with uneducated people like Koreans and [would instead] deal with [Koreans] with magnaminity. . . . In short, my point here today [is this]: I would like to ask the Japanese to become big brothers [aniki] or patrons [oyabun] and treat Koreans with great tolerance.[8]

The Colonized Mentality

Hyŏn's self-abasing remarks, so painful and embarrassing for Koreans to contemplate today, reflected far more than the practice of *sadae*, which for the yangban had been a symbolic and ritualistic expression of high achievement and status in a universal civilization rather than a mark of Korea's inferiority to China.[9] Hyŏn's comments in fact betrayed a mentality deeply conditioned by the experience of colonialism.

The two forces seemed to interact with one another in the Korean bourgeois mind to produce a particularly intense feeling of love-hate, not only toward the Japanese, but also toward the self and other Koreans.

To understand the complex emotions at work here, we must begin by noting, with Albert Memmi, that racism lay at the heart of every colonial system.[10] Like colonialists everywhere, the Japanese tended to think of Koreans as an inferior people. The economist Takahashi Kamekichi wrote in 1935, for example, that "the Korean worker has no desire to advance, is lazy, has no desire to use intellect in work and has a very weak sense of responsibility."[11] Even a Japanese family who owed their very lives to Korean friends who had smuggled food to them and helped them escape from the peninsula after the Japanese surrender could still speak of Koreans as a whole as "unruly," "vicious," and "stupid" once they were safely repatriated. The Japanese, of course, noted, encouraged, and praised what they considered exceptional behavior on the part of Koreans, but the acknowledgment of such exceptions was only another expression of the racist attitude. The family mentioned above, for example, attributed their Korean friends' kindness and loyalty to beneficent colonial tutelage: "When we think we have loyal friends like that, we believe that we are only fair in saying that we [Japanese] have not done too much wrong [in Korea]."[12]

On the one hand, such racism provoked resentment and strengthened the bourgeoisie's feeling of ethnic solidarity with other Koreans. At the industrial commission in 1936, for example, Pak Yŏngch'ŏl, the president of the Chōsen Commercial Bank, delivered an emotional speech tinged with anger in which he cited the Korean marathon runner Son Kijŏng's victory for Japan in the Berlin Olympics two months earlier as an example of the kind of greatness of which Koreans were capable and entreated the Japanese businessmen present to eschew discrimination and hire as many qualified Koreans as possible in their banks, companies, and factories.[13] Similarly in the transcripts of the industrial commission of 1938, one finds under all the deference and politeness a good deal of bourgeois frustration and bitterness stemming from suspected or actual discrimination against Koreans in colonial society, whether in the hiring of Korean workers, in the relative pay scales of Japanese and Koreans in the colonial bureaucracy, or in the requirement that Koreans obtain transit passes to take the Pusan ferry to Japan.[14]

One the other hand, largely because of their role in the colonial development process, Korean businessmen had been assimilated into Japanese society and culture far more deeply than any other class by the end of the colonial period and had to a certain extent ended up, like Memmi's Frenchified Arabs in Tunisia, by changing their "skin."[15] Assimilation had been facilitated, of course, by a common Chinese cultural heritage and also, in the case of Koreans like Hyŏn Chunho and the Koch'ang Kims, by an early fascination with and admiration of Japan, enhanced by years of education and experience in Japan itself. But assimilation had also occurred on a more mundane level, through the kind of professional and personal interaction described in part 2. At the industrial commission of 1936, for example, Pak Yŏngch'ŏl noted the progress of such assimilation in Korea and re-counted an experience when he himself had mistaken the Korean manager of a power plant for Japanese.

Japanese and Koreans have been in contact and associating [with one another] both in the villages and also in urban areas like this one. By observing [Japanese] etiquette and lifestyles day in and day out, a minority [of Koreans] — not exactly a majority, to be sure — have become extremely well assimilated. . . . Last year in August I went on a visit to the hydroelectric plant on the Pujŏn River operated by Mr. Noguchi. . . . A certain individual acted as [my] guide. Since he and Archives Section Chief Shioda [of the Government-General], who is here [today], appeared together and took me around at that time, I just assumed he was a Japanese. Later, [he] gave me his name card, and [I realized] he was a Korean.[16]

The degree of assimilation varied greatly, of course, even at the elite level. In the matter of language, for example, some Korean business-men, like Pak Sŭngjik, never learned to speak Japanese at all, while others, like Hyŏn Chunho, spoke it poorly in spite of a university education in Tokyo. The Koch'ang Kims, on the other hand, seem to have made the Japanese language their own, and today at the National Diet Library in Tokyo one can see graphic evidence of such mastery in the Kims' extant handwritten letters to various high-ranking Japanese officials. To the uninformed native Japanese reader, the calligraphy, expressions, personal references, and subject matter of such letters give little hint that the people who wrote them were Korean. The letters instead suggest that the writers were educated and well-connected Japanese businessmen residing in Korea.[17]

In adopting the language, manners, and even many of the goals of the Japanese colonizers, the Korean bourgeoisie inevitably found itself to some extent also adopting the very ideology of Japanese colonialism itself, including that aspect of the ideology that denigrated Korean ethnicity. One sees this in Hyŏn Chunho's comments quoted above, where Hyŏn himself conceded the essential inferiority of Koreans to Japanese. At its most extreme, this view could even take the form of a denial of the Korean capacity for nationalism and a total embrace of the Japanese imperial cult. Thus at the industrial commission of 1938, Ch'oe Rin, the president of the Government-General's Korean-language newspaper, the *Maeil sinbo*,[18] could declare:

National character [is something which] has developed from a variety of centers, but in [all] the world, the [only] people to have been formed through the development of a true — an absolutely unchanging — center are the Yamato [Japanese] people. They are a people who have been formed with the eternal, single-family lineage of the Imperial Household as [their] center. Their national character is deep-rooted, strong, and has come down from high above. I do not think, however, that either the Korean people or the Chinese people have been formed from such a center.[19]

Nineteen years earlier Ch'oe had been one of the key figures in the March First movement and one of the thirty-three signers of the Korean Declaration of Independence, which made his statement all the more extraordinary and poignant, underlining the searing effect of Japanese colonialism on the bourgeois nationalist psyche.[20]

The Late Development Effect

There were also material reasons for Korean bourgeois collaboration with the colonial regime. As Alexander Gerschenkron and Ronald Dore, among others, have observed, late-developing countries have had to rely both on the state and on the wealthier, more advanced countries to furnish much of the required capital and technology for industrialization.[21] Colonial Korea's dependence on outside assistance was of course compounded because the state itself was controlled by a foreign power.

Even before the annexation, Korean businessmen like Pak Sŭngjik were looking for Japanese partners to strengthen their companies. Such partnerships were simply good business; there were few Koreans willing to invest in the nonagricultural sector at the time, the Yi state was in financial disarray, and Japanese businessmen represented not only a country that was rich and developed relative to Korea but also one that was geographically close and culturally similar. Although in time more and more Koreans were willing to invest some of their money in commerce and industry, the bourgeoisie's need for public and foreign assistance continued, and colonialism only deepened the dependency on Japan. As Han Sangnyong observed in 1921:

As everyone knows, establishing a business in Korea, where everything, including capital and expertise, is so undeveloped, naturally requires a joint [effort] of Japanese and Koreans. For most of [its] capital and expertise, moreover, [such an enterprise] must depend on the Japanese. When [we] look at the current situation, [we] can say that the paid-in capital of most companies has been induced from Japan. Or, to put it another way, [these companies] have taken on the character of what must be called Japanese-Korean joint-enterprise.[22]

Even Kyŏngbang, despite its avowed policy of "Koreans making everything on their own," was forced virtually from the time of its establishment to turn to the colonial state for financial support, a reliance on Japanese or Japanese-controlled capital that only increased as the company expanded. As we saw in chapter 5, an even greater pattern of dependency was established at Kyŏngbang with respect to Japanese technology. Such structural imperatives originating in the phenomenon of late development and magnified by colonialism gave the Korean bourgeoisie a concrete interest in reaching some kind of accommodation with the colonial authorities.

Economic Cooptation

The policy of cooperative capitalist development initiated by the Saitō regime in the 1920s also tended to dilute bourgeois nationalist sentiment by giving Korean businessmen a certain vested interest in the colonial system.

To be sure, the policy had not turned out to be all that Korean businessmen had hoped it would be at the time of the industrial commission in 1921. While the commission was in session Kim Sŏngsu, using the *Tonga ilbo,* and Pak Yŏnghyo, then president of Kyŏngbang and the chief organizer of a Korean business group called the Congress of Korean Industry (Chosŏnin Sanŏp Taehoe), had peppered the delegates with editorials and petitions calling for a policy of industrial development "centered on Koreans [rather than Japanese]."[23] And even Han Sangnyong, who had made a point of distancing himself from the *Tonga ilbo* position during the commission by openly stating that the Japanese should be the main beneficiaries of industrial development on the grounds that it was they who would be providing most of the capital and technology, had nevertheless made a plea at the time for allowing more Koreans to participate in and profit from colonial development plans.[24]

The Government-General, of course, never considered, let alone adopted, an economic policy centered on Koreans, and even as late as 1938 Korean businessmen were still asking for a larger share in the management and profits of the industrial economy. At the industrial commission that year, for example, Hyŏn Chunho said: "In the area of business too, indeed, in each area of business, especially [in those areas] where lucrative, profitable business is possible, [I] would like to ask [you] to apportion the shares—and beyond that, apportion, for example, even the directors' shares—among Koreans as well [as Japanese]."[25]

On the other hand, although the Korean bourgeoisie did not get all it had asked from the Government-General, it was not completely ignored. Hyŏn's remarks were the complaint of an insider who had already been given a place at the table but who wanted a larger portion of the dinner. They were made in the context of a history of Korean-Japanese economic cooperation developed over the previous seventeen years, and in the hope of even greater cooperation in the future as a result of the expanding wartime economy and the anticipated acquisition of more imperial territory.

As we saw in parts 1 and 2, the policy of cooperative capitalist development after 1919 had gone beyond mere rhetoric. By the late 1930s Korean businessmen had been able to carve out a certain niche for themselves within the imperial economy, and larger companies like Kyŏngbang had acquired this niche with considerable Japanese cooperation and assistance. While such economic concessions and cooperation still left much to be desired from the Korean perspective, they nevertheless made the colonial experience for Korean businessmen far more palatable than for the majority of Koreans and tended to mitigate nationalist resentment by the bourgeoisie toward the Japanese. The following letter from Kim Sŏngsu to Governor-General Saitō, for example, written in 1927, only eight years after the March First movement (and shortly after Saitō's sudden return to Japan for health reasons) suggests the depth of Kim's gratitude to Saitō for his patronage, and, concurrently, the role that such patronage played in facilitating bourgeois accommodation with the colonial government.

Kye-dong, Seoul
December 30 [1927]

The Right Honorable the Viscount Saitō Makoto
Naka-Chō, Yotsuya-ku
Tokyo.

My Lord:

[It has been] oppressively cold recently. Please allow me to inquire if your lordship is [now] on the way to a healthy recovery. I am thankfully getting along fine, so I hope you will put your mind at ease about my unimportant affairs. [I] deeply regret [your] departure from Korea because of [your] ill health. [I] would like to render my heartfelt gratitude for your lordship's many kindnesses, and especially for [your] special patronage of the Kyŏngsŏng Spinning and Weaving Company, which [I] deeply appreciated. As an expression of [my] feelings of sadness at your departure, [I] am sending under separate cover a piece of ceramic ware. It would be the greatest of honors [for me] if [you] were to accept this humble [gift] as a souvenir. I hope that you will take especially good care of yourself in this [cold] season and regain your health as soon as possible. With best wishes, I remain,

Respectfully yours,
Kim Sŏngsu[26]

Cooptation was also substantially advanced in the 1930s by the opening of new economic frontiers in Manchuria and north China that Koreans as well as Japanese could profitably exploit. As Pak Yŏngch'ŏl said in 1936:

To be sure, there has been some unrest [in the past], and there were of course various reasons for it. Whether we call it discontent, dissatisfaction, nationalist ideology, or the skeptical thinking that has been flourishing lately, as a result of such things, there has, [at least] temporarily, been some unrest. Recently, however, in the last four to five years, even Koreans, recognizing the international standing and power of the Empire—especially since the Manchurian Incident—have gradually come to realize that the peace of Asia necessarily depends on the power of Japan, and that the future livelihood of Koreans also depends on the power of Japan.[27]

As we saw in chapter 7, the economic cooptation of the Korean bourgeoisie also stimulated class differentiation and conflict in Korean society. This, in turn, inclined Korean capitalists to think first of their class interests (which made them dependent, like their Japanese counterparts, on the colonial police) and only secondarily, if at all, of a national struggle against the Japanese.

The Passage of Time

One final factor here seems worthy of note: the sheer passage of time. By 1938 Korea had been under Japanese occupation for over three decades, and nearly twenty years had elapsed since the March First movement. A whole new generation of Koreans had been born and come to maturity under colonial rule, and even for those who still remembered the country when it had been independent, colonialism had increasingly become part of the fabric of everyday Korean existence. There was little indication in 1938 that Japan was embarking on a course that would result in the collapse of its empire a mere seven years later. Indeed, the empire had expanded dramatically in the 1930s, and in 1938 Japan seemed to be on the verge of extending its control over much of continental East Asia.

Nationalist resistance, of course, had continued in Korea even after 1919, and the new generation raised under Japanese rule was by no means completely coopted by the authorities. For the bourgeoisie, however, the weight of time tended to interact with those constraints on the nationalist impulse already mentioned so as to magnify doubts about the possibility of Korean independence and to strengthen, in turn, the sense that the only practical course of action lay in taking advantage of whatever opportunities for advancement were offered within the existing system. In 1949, when Yi Sŭngu told a prosecutor at the South Korean National Assembly's antinationalist trials that he had not been able to imagine Korean liberation even in his dreams, he was undoubtedly expressing a feeling that had deeply influenced the bourgeois response to the Naisen Ittai policy a decade earlier.[28]

Naisen Ittai

Between 1919 and 1937, the Government-General tended to follow a policy of moderation with respect to Korean nationalist sentiment. While no nationalist activity that directly challenged the existing political apparatus was tolerated, the authorities did permit a certain "cultural nationalism" to develop within the colonial context. The intent of such policy was not, of course, to encourage Korean nationalism but rather to weaken it — to rechannel, as it were, the fierce and uncompromising political nationalism of the March First movement into cultural areas and activities that did not openly conflict with colonial goals.[29]

The incident at the Marco Polo Bridge outside Peking in July 1937 changed everything. As the incident quickly developed into a war, and the war gradually expanded into Southeast Asia and the Pacific, the Japanese need for manpower as well as materiel steadily increased, and it was not long before the leaders in Tokyo and Seoul not only came to see the Korean peninsula as an advance military supply depot but also began to regard the Korean people themselves as indispensable to the Japanese war machine. The report of the Government-General's industrial commission of 1938 noted that in connection with Korea's special mission as an advance military supply depot for the continent, "the rapid development of material resources on the peninsula" required "the cultivation of human resources."[30]

This sudden new interest in Korean "human resources" by the authorities took many forms, including, ironically, official recognition of the need to improve the general health and physical strength of the people.[31] But attention to physical health was only one aspect of the total human mobilization effort. The Japanese also concentrated heavily on the "spiritual" aspect of mobilization. Koreans would fight harder, work harder, and generally be more cooperative, the Japanese believed, if they were able to identify themselves politically and culturally with Japan—and hence with Japanese imperialist goals. Thus was spawned what became for most Koreans the most infamous colonial policy of all: the Government-General's movement to "transform [the Korean people] into imperial subjects" (kōkoku shimminka)—better known then as now as the policy of Naisen Ittai.

Naisen Ittai does not translate easily into English. But whether one speaks of "Japanese-Korean Unity" or more literally of "Japan and Korea as One Body," the aim of the policy was clear: the total eradication of a separate Korean national identity. The policy went far beyond the realm of politics. The Japanese authorities were not only insisting, as they always had, that Koreans abandon the idea of political independence; they were now demanding, in addition, that Koreans relinquish once and for all the very idea of being Korean.

The substance of the Naisen Ittai policy was set forth in the report of the 1938 industrial commission. It was complex and comprehensive, ranging in scope from the lofty, even religious, to the mundane. The people in both Japan and Korea, first of all, were to be informed of Korea's new political status. Henceforth the peninsula was no longer to be considered a "so-called colony," as foreign countries in the West, for example, regarded their overseas territories;[32] it was to be treated as an integral part of Japan itself, and Koreans were to be given all the duties, though not necessarily all the rights, of imperial subjects

—including, of course, the duty to fight in China for the imperial cause.

As "imperial subjects," Koreans were to be inducted into the rarefied mysteries of the "national polity" (*kokutai*) and "the Japanese spirit" (*Nippon seishin*). Above all, this meant intensive indoctrination through education and practice in the principles and rites of Japanese Shintōism and the imperial cult. The government proposed "to implant a sense of reverence [for the *kokutai*] more deeply in the people" through the establishment of Shintō shrines for war heroes, and "to consider giving people as many opportunities as possible to worship the imperial portrait." The imperial oath and attendant calisthenics were to be "driven into the hearts and minds of the people," as was the "true meaning" of Japanese holidays, now to become Korean holidays as well; use of the Japanese calendar and imperial reign names was to be "strictly enforced." The martial arts were also to be encouraged as a way of furthering the Korean people's "comprehension of the Japanese spirit."[33]

The promotion of Shintōism and the imperial cult was a fundamental aspect of the colonial regime's general spiritual mobilization campaign in Korea, but it was also only a small part of a massive, far-reaching government effort to foster among the Korean people a sense of unity and common identity with Japan. One of the articles in the commission's 1938 report stressed, for example, the need to "clarify [to the Korean people] the historical relationship between Japan and Korea." What this meant was that the idea of Korea as an historically distinct and independent political power, culture, or racial entity—a view that Korean cultural nationalists had been developing and refining throughout the colonial period—was to be obliterated; instead the Government-General intended to "make clear the intermingling of diplomatic relations and culture and the mixture of bloodlines between Japan and Korea throughout Japanese and Korean history." To increase this awareness, museums and local history study societies were to be established "in areas where the connections to Japan of [the ancient Korean kingdoms of] Paekche, Silla, and Kaya were strong."[34]

The Japanese were intent on extending the concept of cultural assimilation into the most intimate aspects of Korean life. Here, of course, language was a crucial factor. Until 1938, Koreans had been able to attend schools in their own language and use Korean quite freely in public as well as at home. Now the government was insisting on "strict enforcement of the [use of the] Japanese language in daily life," including in all educational facilities, an attitude that eventually resulted in an official movement to force Koreans to adopt Japanese names. The government was also interested in "promoting the fusion of Japanese-Korean customs and habits in everyday life, including clothing, food, and housing."[35]

As in Japan itself, the Japanese used both positive and negative methods to carry out spiritual mobilization in Korea. New, full-time positions in both the central and local bureaucracy were expressly created to coordinate the various projects and activities of the movement within the government itself as well as between the government and the people, who were eventually organized at every level—province, prefectural city, county, island, township, town, village, hamlet, district, and ward—under the aegis of the Chōsen League for Concerted National Power (Kokumin Sōryoku Chōsen Remmei) and other semi-private patriotic organizations. The government also gave its formal blessing to intermarriage between Japanese and Koreans and sought ways of encouraging Japanese already in Korea to stay on.[36]

The education and training of Korean youth was a primary concern of the colonial authorities. In addition to expanding and reforming the regular educational system in accord with the goals of Naisen Ittai, the government set up "youth training centers" (*seinen kunrenjo*) all over the country under the control of the Chōsen Federation of Youth (Chōsen Rengō Seinendan). The countryside, where most of the people lived, was a special focus of attention; the Government-General's policy report of 1938 noted, for example, that spiritual guidance and control was to be extended through the youth organizations even to the farming, mountain, and fishing villages. Even Korean children were to be organized and indoctrinated through the formation of "boys clubs" (*shōnendan*) throughout the country.[37]

Negative methods were also employed. Anything that might conceivably dampen or contradict the spiritual mobilization movement was targeted for reform or reprisal. Specifically citing Buddhism, Confucianism, and Christianity, the commission's report of 1938 observed that official pressure would be exerted to make all the various religions in Korea "conform to the Japanese spirit." In a statement signaling an end once and for all to any official toleration of Korean cultural nationalism and adumbrating the forced closure of *Tonga ilbo* and other privately owned Korean-language publications two years later, the report also advocated "more thorough control of writings; speech and conduct; books; films; music; and so forth, which obstruct [the implementation of] Naisen Ittai."[38]

For most Koreans, the Naisen Ittai policy was the final and ultimate outrage of Japanese colonialism, and there were even Japanese in Korea who found the policy reprehensible; in his autobiographical novel, *Lost Names*, for example, Richard Kim has related how in the midst of the government's campaign, beginning in 1940, to coerce Koreans into adopting Japanese names, a sympathetic Japanese teacher at his school privately visited his house and apologized to his father "for inflicting on you this humiliation . . . unthinkable for one Asian people to another Asian people, especially we Asians who should have a greater respect for our ancestors."[39] In the end, of course, Koreans generally did submit to Japanese pressure in regard to the various Naisen Ittai programs, but it was no accident that the colonial authorities decided to increase the police force by some 20 percent between 1937 and 1940. Political offenses on the peninsula, invariably connected in one way or another with nationalist feeling, rose conspicuously after 1938.[40]

The Bourgeois Response

The reaction of the Korean bourgeoisie to the Naisen Ittai policy was considerably different from that of the mass of the population. During the industrial commission of 1938, which was the setting for the final formulation of the policy, Korean businessmen like Hyŏn Chunho participated in all the discussions of the committee on the "Intensification and Implementation of Naisen Ittai" and helped draft the official report quoted extensively in the previous section of this chapter. Peers member Sekiya Teizaburō, now sixty-three years old, was invited from Japan to chair the committee, perhaps because the colonial authorities thought that his personal ties with Koreans like Hyŏn and the Koch'ang Kims would help preserve Korean-Japanese amity on what was potentially a sensitive, if not explosive, nationalist issue.[41] Such concern proved unnecessary. As noted earlier, there was some anger in the bourgeois attitude toward the Japanese, and it surfaced from time to time during the 1938 industrial commission; but it was not the anger of outraged nationalism, it was more the anger of a suitor who felt his virtues were not being fully appreciated. If one thing is clear from the transcripts of the industrial commission, it is that the Korean bourgeoisie wanted the implementation of the Naisen Ittai policy as much, if not more, than the Japanese authorities themselves.

To Korea's colonial rulers the Naisen Ittai policy was primarily a means by which Koreans could be mobilized for the war in China, and their attitude toward the question of full legal and social equality for Koreans was at best ambivalent.[42] To the Korean bourgeoisie, however, for all the reasons cited earlier, the policy was a dream possibly come true, an opportunity to expand the privileges already in hand and perhaps to solve, or at least to address and alleviate, some of the existing frictions and problems. Not once did any of the Koreans on the committee voice any objections to the policy itself; on the contrary, the policy elicited universal agreement and praise. Ch'oe Rin, after asserting that the Korean people lacked a strong national character, even suggested to the committee that fostering a Korean reverence for the Japanese "national polity" through the establishment of Shintō shrines would not be a difficult problem. Hyŏn Chunho found the policy draft "virtually perfect." And Yi Sŭngu, a Korean lawyer with close ties to the business world,[43] while conceding that there were indeed nationalists and Communists among the Korean population, echoed Ch'oe's view that all Koreans would welcome the policy and added that its very implementation would destroy whatever appeal nationalism and communism had in Korea:

The Naisen Ittai matter was presented as one of the official proclamations of His Excellency the Governor-General [Minami] following his appointment, and it is something that probably all Koreans without exception will support and welcome. Up to now there have been Communists and nationalists among the Korean population. Among such nationalists, and of course Communists, there are, to be sure, people who subscribe to Marxist theory, but there are also many people, I believe, who ran after communism out of dissatisfaction with the colonial government. However, those people who tend to be drawn toward nationalism or communism are saying that if Naisen Ittai is carried out [in Korea] on the same level as in Japan, they will not run after nationalism or communism, that, indeed, they will have no reason to complain about the colonial government.[44]

The only real concern of the Koreans on the committee was that the Japanese would *not* fully carry out all the provisions of the Naisen Ittai policy draft because of the prevailing racial prejudice toward Koreans. As Yi said at the time: "What, however, about the Japanese side? . . . . If only Koreans talk about Naisen Ittai, Naisen Ittai, and the Japanese say, 'You're not a Japanese citizen,' it does no good [for Koreans] to say 'Yes, I *am* Japanese.' And when that happens—if a Korean makes a lot of effort to become Japanese and is still told by the Japanese that he [really] isn't Japanese—then he'll start feeling, 'What's the use, I'll act however I want.' "[45]

Perhaps the key provision in the policy draft for the Koreans was the article that specifically enjoined the Government-General "to make clear, with respect to the differential treatment of Japanese and Koreans in each social class, that [such treatment], both at a systemic [level] and in actual practice, should be abolished in accord with the intensification and thorough [implementation] of Naisen Ittai." Such a stipulation seemed to open the way not only for a revision of the existing bonus system (by which Japanese officials in the Government-General received as much as 60 percent more pay than their Korean counterparts),[46] but also for the eventual granting to Koreans of all the legal rights of Japanese citizenship. When a subcommittee tried to revise the draft by adding the phrase "to give serious study" to the clause quoted above—an amendment that to the Koreans seemed to weaken the force of the original and implied an indefinite shelving of the problem—Yi Sŭngu politely but vigorously opposed the change, and Sekiya and the others on the committee who had favored it finally gave in.[47]

Yi's insistence that the Japanese accept the logic of their own policy and sincerely work toward a thorough implementation of Naisen Ittai demonstrated not only the extent of bourgeois assimilation into Japanese culture by the late 1930s, but, conversely, the extent to which Yi and the other Korean businessmen on the committee had abandoned whatever nationalist aspirations they might once have had and were ready to embrace a new Japanese order that left no room for the expression of a separate Korean identity.

The Koch'ang Kims

Neither Kim Sŏngsu nor Kim Yŏnsu participated in the industrial commission of 1938 (though Yŏnsu had originally been scheduled to attend), and the transcripts of the commission that year therefore give us no hint of their attitude toward the Naisen Ittai policy. In official biographies, however, the family has made a point of distinguishing itself from "classic collaborators" like Han Sangnyong,[48] and even orthodox North Korean historians—no great admirers of the Korean bourgeoisie—have subscribed to the view that businessmen like the Kims were, at least initially, "national reformists" rather than outright comprador or "subordinate" capitalists.

To be sure, the Korean bourgeoisie was by no means a monolithic class. Within the business elite, as within any group of people, there existed a range of attitudes and behavior, and to the extent that the bourgeoisie in this period can be considered nationalistic at all, it is because of men like the Koch'ang Kims. It is important, however, to consider the form such nationalism took. Even as early as 1921, the

Kims had already begun to move away from the uncompromising demand for immediate Korean independence that had been the rallying cry of the nationalist movement of 1919 and adopted the gradualist position of "cultural nationalism," which stressed Korean educational and economic development *within* the colonial context as a prerequisite for national independence at some indeterminate date in the future. In effect, this placed the Kims in a position of yielding to the political status quo, even if in their own minds such acquiescence was only a temporary expedient. We noted earlier, for example, that Kim Sŏngsu used his newspaper, *Tonga ilbo*, to lobby the industrial commission in 1921 for a policy of economic development "centered on Koreans [rather than Japanese]." In taking this stance, however, the newspaper came very close to a public acceptance of Japanese colonial rule: "But [in advocating] a policy centered on the Korean people, [we] are not calling for the complete expulsion of the Japanese [from Korea]; we are [only advocating] the establishment of a policy whose principal goal is the development of native Korean industry."[49]

The basic assumption of the cultural nationalist movement, moreover, that is, that Koreans could somehow publish newspapers and magazines, run schools, and operate factories all on their own and with their own "nationalist" agenda within the colonial framework was laden with contradictions. The very decision to work within the limits of colonial rule was conditioned by all the various forces discussed above that inclined the bourgeoisie toward collaboration, and once the decision was made, these forces acquired even greater potency. Thus by 1938, both of the Kim brothers, and especially Yŏnsu, had come to have much in common with a "classic collaborator" like Han Sangnyong. If Han was the founder and chairman of the Chōsen Business Club, the organization that perhaps above all others epitomized the ideal of Japanese-Korean capitalist cooperation, Kim Yŏnsu was a member of the club in good standing. Both Han and the Kims relished and took full advantage of the economic opportunities that their class position in colonial society offered them and occasionally even worked together. Han, for example, was one of the original promoters of Kyŏngbang's spinning company in southern Manchuria, Kim Yŏnsu was a shareholder in Han's life insurance company, and both Han and Kim Yŏnsu joined a group of Japanese investors in setting up a new housing company in 1939.[50] Although the Kims did not, like Han and other Korean businessmen, openly indicate approval of Japanese rule in the period between 1921 and 1938, neither did they openly repudiate the colonial system like so many of the Koreans who were languishing in Japanese prisons. What remains of their private correspondence with high-ranking Japanese officials in this period reveals an extremely cordial and respectful attitude toward the colonial regime that was similar to Han's public posture and is difficult to reconcile with any serious commitment to Korean nationalism.

Even as early as the 1920s, more radical Korean nationalists who had chosen to continue fighting the Japanese by whatever means possible were attacking the Kims' position as brazen hypocrisy — bourgeois class interest masquerading as nationalism.[51] It is more likely, however, that the main factor at work here was self-deception. At least before 1938 the Kims never seem to have come to grips with the contradictions and implications of their position — they never even seem to have recognized that such contradictions existed. From the beginning they appear to have regarded what were essentially elitist and class-based activities in education and business as the very core of Korean nationalism. The famous novelist Yi Kwangsu and other Korean intellectuals in the cultural nationalist movement, for whom Kim Sŏngsu was a generous patron, also helped reinforce such self-deception by writing articles in the bourgeois press that lavished praise on Kim for his accomplishments and patriotism.[52] Even more important in this respect were the Japanese authorities themselves, whose tolerance of the cultural nationalist stance during this period allowed the Kims to straddle what would otherwise have been a much clearer line between nationalists and collaborators.

The Naisen Ittai policy, however, together with the Government-General's insistence that the Korean bourgeoisie take a leading role in its implementation, made it far more difficult to maintain this kind of double life after 1938. There was now little room for self-deception on the question of nationalism; while one might argue the potential benefits of Naisen Ittai for Koreans as individuals, or for certain Korean groups or classes, one could hardly fail to recognize the threat that Naisen Ittai posed to Korea as a separate polity and culture.[53] In that sense the policy was perhaps the final, acid test of the Kims', and the Korean bourgeoisie's, nationalist commitment.

Class Over Nation

One of the first indications that the Kims were going to accommodate themselves to the Naisen Ittai policy actually came before the industrial commission of 1938 in a Kyŏngbang board meeting held on June 25, 1938. Kim Yŏnsu presided over the meeting, which included Ch'oe

Tusŏn,[54] Kim Chaesu (younger brother of Sŏngsu and Yŏnsu), Pak Hŭngsik, Ch'oe Ch'anghak (known in colonial business circles as the Korean "gold mine king"),[55] Yi Kanghyŏn, and, finally, Hyŏn Chunho, who would of course take an active role in the Naisen Ittai discussions at the industrial commission three months later. There was no noticeable air of urgency at the meeting—most of the talk centered on the legal technicalities of establishing a Kyŏngbang branch office in Mukden—and the board voted to adjourn after only thirty minutes. But for all that, the meeting was an historic event at Kyŏngbang: for the first time since the company had been founded nineteen years earlier, the board's minutes were being officially recorded in Japanese rather than Korean. Soon thereafter Japanese became the language of all the company's official records, and eventually Kim Yŏnsu even established Japanese-language classes for his employees inside the company itself, in keeping with the 1938 industrial commission's plan "to devise appropriate measures in regard to spreading the [use] of the Japanese language."[56]

Both Sŏngsu and Yŏnsu were given positions in the General Affairs Division of the Chōsen League for Concerted National Power, the key organization in the spiritual mobilization campaign after October 1940. Yŏnsu also served as the head of the League's Social Welfare Department and joined other Korean businessmen in token labor service on Shintō shrines under construction in the countryside. In addition, he contributed 30,000 yen to the league's mobilization efforts.[57]

Either personally or through Kyŏngbang and its affiliates, Kim Yŏnsu also gave large sums of money for the "training and guidance of youth and children," which had been advocated by the industrial commission's Naisen Ittai policy committee.[58] One such donation approved by Kyŏngbang's board of directors in April 1939 for the construction of a Government-General youth training center was for 10,000 yen. Later, in July 1943, Kim joined Pak Hŭngsik and Min Kyusik in personally contributing 50,000 yen apiece for such training.[59]

Both brothers also became involved in the Government-General's efforts to recruit Korean young men into the Japanese army.

The use of Koreans to supplement the Japanese military had, of course, always been one of the major underlying purposes of the Naisen Ittai policy, and the colonial government's sudden new interest after the China Incident in upgrading the general health of the Korean people, its concern for the "training and guidance of youth and children," its emphasis on fostering the "Japanese spirit" through encouragement of the martial arts, and even its intense promotion of the use of the Japanese language were all measures designed in large part to prepare Korean youth for military service. The youth training centers, for example, which Kim Yŏnsu and Kyŏngbang were supporting with donations, were intended, according to the report of the industrial commission, "to make members feel exactly as if they were under the army conscription system in effect in Japan."[60]

The actual recruitment of Koreans took place in three stages. From February 1938 the Government-General began to accept Korean volunteers (males aged seventeen *se* and above), and one of the provisions of the Naisen Ittai policy adopted by the industrial commission later that year stressed the need "to propagate and thoroughly infuse [into the hearts and minds of the people] a [proper] spirit for the implementation of a volunteer army system."[61] A Korean conscription system was promulgated in May 1942, but it was not actually set in motion until August 1943 and initially exempted college and university students. However, apparently to mollify adverse public opinion about the draft and to provide potential draftees with models of enthusiastic Korean soldiers, the Government-General announced a "special volunteer" system in October of that same year and launched an intensive three-month propaganda campaign to recruit *hakpyŏng* or "student soldiers."[62] The Kims, along with other businessmen and educators, were asked by the Government-General to assist in the campaign.

Even before the *hakpyŏng* campaign, the Kims appear to have been lending their personal support to the war effort in several ways. The September 2, 1937, edition of *Tonga ilbo*, for example, listed Kim Sŏngsu as one of fifty-nine Koreans scheduled to go into the provinces and give lectures on the China Incident in accord with Governor-General Minami's developing Naisen Ittai policy. On October 14, 1938, Kyŏngbang's board of directors voted to donate 100,000 yen, 10 percent of the company's profits since the China Incident, to help defray the cost of "national defense";[63] according to Kim Yŏnsu in a subsequent interview with the *Maeil sinbo*, the Kyŏngbang board was concerned about "the hardships of the Japanese soldiers on the front lines." In June 1942 Kim Yŏnsu also made a contribution to the troops in China of 2,000 folding fans imprinted with the *hinomaru*.[64]

The Kims' involvement in the actual *hakpyŏng* campaign similarly took a variety of forms. In November 1943 Kim Sŏngsu, then president of Posŏng College, appears to have participated in a *hakpyŏng* symposium of government officials, educators, and students' families sponsored by the *Maeil sinbo* at Seoul's Citizens Hall (Fuminkan). There, according to the transcripts of the symposium, which were subsequently printed in the newspaper, Kim explained the reluctance among Korean students to volunteer for the Japanese army as a product of Korea's historical degeneration into "effeminacy," the result of the country's traditional pursuit of the literary arts to the neglect of the military. During this period both Sŏngsu and Yŏnsu also joined other Koreans — many of them close friends or associates like Chang Tŏksu — on lecture tours sponsored by the Government-General to exhort Korean students to join the Japanese army. Yŏnsu was even part of a Korean group that went to Japan in November 1943 to rally Korean university students in Tokyo and other Japanese cities to enlist in the imperial cause.[65]

We do not, unfortunately, have the texts of the speeches delivered by the brothers on these occasions, but we can get some idea of the general themes of such speaking tours from articles that appeared under the Kims' names in the colonial press. One such article credited to Kim Sŏngsu was published in the *Maeil sinbo* on November 6, 1943, shortly after the government's announcement of the new *hakpyŏng* system. The article was captioned "Dying for a Righteous Cause: The Responsibility of Imperial Citizens is Great" and was one of several such pieces attributed to well-known Koreans that the *Maeil sinbo* featured in a series called "Students! Join the Holy War."[66]

The article, addressed directly to the students, was designed to assuage what were clearly very serious doubts on the students' part about risking their lives in a cause for which they had little sympathy. It was a complicated mixture of flattery ("Your intellectual level is higher than the average person"), the promise of future rewards ("Exactly the same splendid treatment, indeed, rights as [people in] Japan"), and warnings ("Just imagine [what things will be like] if you fail to rally . . . and the construction of a new order in Greater East Asia is completed without our [Korean] participation"), and it was studded with typical wartime bombast about the "holy war" and "Greater East Asia." It also played on the senior-junior and student-teacher bond "I know very well that you are of course in a state of mind which neither I nor your other seniors, who are asking you with easy words to give up your lives, can even imagine"), and sought to channel the students' concerns about their family and country into a sense of obligation to take part in the war ("If you run from the line of battle in this holy war, you may well preserve your insignificant individual lives, but what will become of your brothers and sisters who were born in this land after you? Truly, you have an absolute duty to the future of Korea"). The main point of the essay, however, was clear and frequently reiterated: "Do your duty." Duty, of course, did not mean simply joining the army; it also meant "sacrifice." And "sacrifice," in turn, meant the ultimate sacrifice—a "glorious death." "I have always told you," the article said, "that in doing your duty you should not spare even [your own] life. Now, indeed, the time has come for you to put these words into action with your bodies" (see appendix 2 for the complete text).

A similar article entitled "Korean Student Soldiers Enlist in a Bright Tomorrow" appeared under Kim Yŏnsu's name in the *Keijō nippō* on January 19, 1944. Two days earlier, Korea's crop of "student soldiers" had been inducted into the Japanese army in a special ceremony at the Chōsen Shrine on Seoul's South Mountain (Namsan)—on their way to "victory and glory," as Sŏngsu himself was reputed to have said later in an interview published in the *Maeil sinbo* (January 22).[67] The *Keijō nippō* article was critical of Koreans for their "selfish thoughts and ideas" about military service (the Korean response to voluntary recruitment had continued to be disappointing) but noted that the conscription system now under way was very "heartening." It also called upon the new "student soldiers" being sent to the front to give their "full measure of service to the country":

With the great work of the conscription system underway, the correlation between "soldiers" and "Koreans" has truly deepened to a heartening degree. Until now, Koreans have been stuck in existing tradition, and [they] have been excessively narrow-minded toward the conscription system. I think this is a shortcoming of all Korean compatriots. Koreans hereafter must fling off their selfish thoughts and ideas and rally to patriotic thoughts and concepts grounded in morality. This is literally [a time of] war. What a glorious [sight] you are, Student Soldiers, who are bravely departing for the front, facing such a great trial and bearing on your shoulders the fate of the Empire. You have a duty ordained by destiny to smash the United States and England by all means, and so you must absolutely be victorious. Your victory is not only the parent that will give birth to a new Korea; it is also the only way to preserve the peace of all East Asia. I beg you to ground [yourself] in what is ethically and morally right and give [your] full measure of service to the country.[68]

There is some question as to the degree of enthusiasm with which the Kims, and especially Kim Sŏngsu, took part in the implementation of the Naisen Ittai policy, including the *hakpyŏng* campaign. In 1949,

Kim Yŏnsu, on trial by the South Korean National Assembly for anti-nationalist activities, claimed that his involvement in Naisen Ittai had been "forced" upon him by the colonial authorities, and subsequent authorized biographies and other writings by close friends and associates in the past four decades have invariably echoed the view that the Kims' participation had been minimal and coerced.[69]

For obvious reasons such statements must be regarded with a certain skepticism. There is no compelling evidence that either of the Kims ever seriously protested or attempted to dissociate himself from the Naisen Ittai movement.[70] The evidence, as we have seen, tends to suggest that the attitude of both brothers toward Naisen Ittai, at least in the end, was similar to that demonstrated by the Korean members of the Naisen Ittai committee at the industrial commission of 1938.

On the other hand, we must also beware of leaping to conclusions. The existing primary material is limited, and some of it, such as the information culled from the strictly controlled and propagandistic wartime press of the 1940s, also needs to be viewed with caution. We do not know, for example, whether the Kims actually wrote (or endorsed) the articles that appeared under their names in the press during the *hakpyŏng* campaign, or whether the newspapers simply attached their names to the articles without their permission. And even in those cases where there is no doubt as to the participation of one or both brothers in a certain Naisen Ittai event or activity, there is little indication in the available documentation of their motivation or attitude.

It is probable that we shall never fathom the full complex of ideas and emotions that were at play here. Fortunately, however, a few personal letters written by the Kims to Sekiya Teizaburō in the 1940s have been deposited for scholarly use in the National Diet Library. While these letters do not specifically refer to Naisen Ittai, taken together with all the other available documentation, and placed in the context of the Kims' various activities during the colonial period as described in this book, they do allow us to come as close as perhaps we ever shall to the respective attitudes of the two brothers toward the Naisen Ittai policy at the time.

For Kim Yŏnsu, who was essentially a businessman with close economic ties to the Government-General and strong vested interests in the imperial system, a man who, as Honorary Consul-General of Manchuria, led the imperial bows and sake toasts in Seoul at the tenth anniversary celebration of the founding of Manchukuo in 1942, the decision to participate in Naisen Ittai activities was probably made with a modicum of anxiety and, indeed, with great expectations about

Kyŏngbang's future in a postwar Asia under Japanese political control. His personal letters to Sekiya from 1939 on are filled with pledges to devote himself to the development of his business, especially in Manchuria, and to contribute to the war effort,[71] which, of course, he eventually did in numerous concrete ways. A basically positive attitude toward Naisen Ittai along the lines evinced by the Koreans who attended the Government-General's industrial commission of 1938 seems entirely consistent with everything we know of his background, personality, and professional concerns.

Kim Sŏngsu is a far more elusive and problematic figure. His public involvement in Naisen Ittai activities was certainly less than that of his brother and of many other prominent Koreans, and his strong ties to the cultural nationalist movement tend to argue against a positive attitude on his part toward Naisen Ittai; as a publisher, let alone as an advocate of cultural nationalism, he could hardly have been pleased, for example, by the Government-General's decision to close down the privately owned Korean-language press in 1940. On the other hand, we must note that he was no less immune than his brother and other members of his personal circle like Hyŏn Chunho to the forces that were pushing the Korean bourgeoisie toward collaboration,[72] and his relationship with the colonial authorities since the 1920s had, in fact, been a history of cordial accommodation.

A letter, written (and marked "Confidential") by Kim Sŏngsu in his own hand to Sekiya Teizaburō on July 8, 1945, offers a final, tantalizing glimpse into Kim's mind only weeks before Korea's liberation from Japanese rule. Kim had written to Sekiya about a month earlier (May 29) expressing concern for Sekiya and his family in the wake of unconfirmed reports of Allied bombing in Sekiya's section of Tokyo.[73] Sekiya had written back to assure Kim that he and his family were safe, and Kim had responded with the following letter:

132 Kye-dong
Seoul
July 8 [1945]

The Right Honorable Lord Sekiya Teizaburō
3 Kioi-chō
Kōjimachi-ku
Tokyo.
Confidential

Dear Lord Sekiya:
    [I] have read your gracious letter, for which [I] thank you very much. [I]

could not have been more pleased [by the news] that your home suffered no damage from the air raids by enemy planes, and [also by the news] that [you] are healthier than ever. I was alarmed, however, to hear that all the homes in your vicinity were burned down by the air raids. I can imagine how desolate [you] must feel.

As for Bureau Director Ōshima,[74] whom you kindly introduced to me, I had the honor of seeing [him] at Vice-Governor-General Endō's[75] residence, and [he] is [indeed] a most wonderful person. In fact, I would have liked to invite [him] for a little dinner, but because my wife and children have evacuated to Yŏnch'ŏn County in Kyŏnggi Province and I am alone in Seoul, I was unable to do so. So [I] am deeply sorry that I was unable to show him [my] hospitality. [I] have the honor of meeting Vice-Governor-General Endō from time to time, and [he] has been gracious enough to favor me with his kindness. He is truly a gentle and modest person, and [his] public esteem is also increasing with each day.

[I] am afraid that the sweets [I sent you] were somehow lost in the mail. I inquired at the post office hoping to send [some sweets] again, but [they] absolutely would not accept this kind of parcel. So once again things did not turn out as I had wished.

With the increasing seriousness of the war, I can well imagine how busy you must be. I beg you, please, take good care of yourself and your health.

Please by all means give my regards to Lady Sekiya.

With that, [I] remain,

Respectfully yours,
Kim Sŏngsu.[76]

While Kim's letter says nothing directly about Naisen Ittai, it is nevertheless revealing and suggestive on a number of levels. It is clear, for example, that neither the war nor the Naisen Ittai policy had adversely affected Kim's warm personal relationship with Sekiya or become a stumbling block in the way of amicable social intercourse with high-ranking colonial officials. Kim writes as one who seems to share some of the basic concerns of his Japanese acquaintances, including the progress of the war and the popular standing of the colonial government; in any case, his reference to "enemy planes" and enthusiastic impressions of Bureau Director Ōshima and Vice-Governor-General Endō, including his comment about Endō's growing "public esteem," all seem largely incompatible with a Korean nationalist perspective, especially in the summer of 1945.[77]

While it in no way diminishes the genuine affection for Sekiya that permeates the letter, there is also undoubtedly an element of self-interest here, a desire to reinforce an old personal connection that had proven useful in the past, and it is not inconceivable that Kim might have deliberately colored or exaggerated his real feelings to please Sekiya. Nevertheless, even if one chooses to stress the manipulative aspect of the letter, it is difficult to escape the conclusion that Kim had somehow made his peace with Naisen Ittai by the end of the colonial period, if not earlier, and was laying the groundwork for continued personal and professional interaction with the Japanese authorities. If, as one suspects, he was somewhat less sanguine about such a future than his brother, he was also apparently prepared to accept it. At the very least, one can say that he seems to have been keeping his options open in the event Japan won the war.

The End of Bourgeois Nationalism

The Kims' participation in the Naisen Ittai movement marked the end of bourgeois nationalism during the colonial period. As in a classic tragedy, a fatal flaw had been present from the beginning. The nationalist efforts of the Korean bourgeoisie after 1919 had always been fraught with paradox, and the final denouement was in that sense far from startling. Indeed, in retrospect it seems eminently predictable: the logic of Korean capitalist development within the colonial context pointed from the beginning to the creation of a bourgeoisie that was more Japanese than Korean in both interests and ethos.

Equally predictable, moreover, was the popular reaction to the bourgeoisie's support of the Naisen Ittai policy. The decades of colonialism, and especially the last eight years, had been full of grudging resignation and compromise for most Koreans, but it is clear from the great spontaneous outburst of nationalist feeling and activity at the time of Liberation that the terrible trial of war and Naisen Ittai, far from destroying popular nationalist sentiment, had in fact inflamed it. In the first flush of freedom in August 1945, when Koreans all over the country were ripping down Japanese war posters and flags and smashing the windows of Japanese shops and homes, one of the first objects singled out for retribution was the local Shintō shrine, the key symbol of the hated Naisen Ittai policy.[78] Soon thereafter the focus of anger shifted to those Koreans who had served or collaborated with the colonial regime and its policies.

The popular judgment on collaboration took into account the complexities of individual experience and motivation that had characterized the bourgeois response to Naisen Ittai. Kim Sŏngsu, for example, because of his important role in the cultural nationalist movement and his relatively low public profile during the war, received far less criticism than his brother, who was widely regarded as an active collaborator. But even Kim Sŏngsu, who probably more than any other single individual epitomized the strengths and weaknesses of the bourgeois nationalist position, suffered a certain fall from grace during the Naisen Ittai period.[79] As for the bourgeoisie as a whole, of whom Yŏnsu was perhaps a more representative figure, the Naisen Ittai years had greatly eroded whatever credentials for political leadership the class had possessed in 1919 and the early 1920s and made the establishment of a genuine hegemony over other classes a far from certain prospect.

Conclusion
The Colonial Legacy

Korea's first great industrialization, begun modestly towards the end of World War I, expanded rapidly and dramatically in the 1930s after the Japanese seizure of Manchuria and the outbreak of the Sino-Japanese War, only to be abruptly truncated by Japan's defeat in World War II. The incompleteness of the pre-1945 industrialization effort, together with its inescapable taint of colonialism, have led many scholars to underestimate the importance of the colonial era in shaping the South Korean political economy that we know today. Colonialism, however, for better or worse, was both the catalyst and the cradle of industrial development in Korea, and in studying it, we are brought face to face with the very origins of modern Korea itself.

The colonial transformation was profound and multifaceted, but most striking of all, perhaps, was the aspect of social change. Colonial industrialization altered not only the physical appearance of the peninsula, but the social landscape as well. Other scholars have already noted the emergence between 1919 and 1945 of a new urban intelligentsia, a small core of white-collar managers and technicians, and a modern labor force.[1] These same years also saw the first stirrings of a native capitalist class. Korean entrepreneurship under the Japanese was restricted, but it was by no means entirely blocked. And even if some businessmen like the Koch'ang Kims had not completely cut their ties to the land by 1945, they had nevertheless taken an irrevocable step into industrial civilization.

Businessmen like the Kims represented only the tip of the proverbial iceberg: they were merely the biggest and most conspicuous figures in a pre-1945 capitalist class whose full dimensions await more extensive and systematic study. We know, for example, that there were many Korean businessmen during the colonial period who never attained the status of the Kims but who later became well-known figures in South Korea. Some were originally connected with Kyŏngbang;[2] others were not. But all shared a common past: like the Kims, their first business experience had been in the world of colonial capitalism before 1945, and all of them, in one way or another, had participated in the rapid industrialization of the late colonial era. And their numbers were significant; a recent study commissioned and supervised by this author suggests that nearly 60 percent of the founders of South Korea's top fifty *chaebŏl* had some kind of colonial business experience.[3]

Few if any Koreans, of course, would have predicted such social continuity in August 1945. Although there was no question of a return to the preindustrial past, Korean capitalism faced a major crisis at the end of World War II when the empire that had given it birth and sustenance suddenly ceased to exist. The Allied victory had severed the economic lifelines of capitalist growth, and even if new financial, technological, and marketing channels could be found and developed, a basic political problem remained: Korea's bourgeoisie had won its economic success under Japanese rule at the expense of its own hegemony in Korean society, and its position in the volatile post-Liberation political context was tenuous at best. In the end, capitalism survived only in the south, and only, it would seem, with substantial economic, political, and ultimately military, assistance from the United States.[4]

The complex and fascinating story of that survival lies beyond the scope of this book. What interests us here is the colonial social legacy that the south consequently inherited. When Park Chung Hee, himself a product of colonial training,[5] decided in the 1960s to launch an economic program of rapid industrial development, he had at his disposal a core of veteran businessmen, many of whom had been tempered not only in the economic reconstruction of the 1950s, but first and foremost in the rapid industrial growth of the late 1930s and early 1940s. In 1961, when Park first seized power in a army coup d'état, Kim Yŏnsu was still, sixteen years after Liberation, one of Korea's premier business figures, chairman of the businessmen's organization that under Park would eventually become the Federation of Korean Industries (FKI). Yŏnsu, in fact, would continue to take an active part in Korea's new industrialization throughout the sixties and into the seventies; in 1971, at the age of seventy-five, he would even receive the Park government's coveted "Gold Pagoda Industrial Medal" as the nation's most successful exporter.[6]

Since Park's plans for development were predicated, moreover, on the re-establishment of close economic ties with Japan, men like Kim Yŏnsu were clearly priceless assets, especially in the first decade after 1961, when the diplomatic relationship between South Korea and

Japan was normalized and the groundwork of economic cooperation between the two countries firmly laid. Even before Park took power, in the last months of the ill-fated Chang Myŏn regime, the Korean business community, led by Kim Yŏnsu, had already begun reinstituting regular channels of communication with the Japanese private sector.[7] Later, Kim Yongwan, Yŏnsu's brother-in-law and successor, both at Kyŏngbang and in the FKI, would bring Yŏnsu's efforts to fruition during the initial stormy period of Korean-Japanese normalization. In April 1965, for example, two months before the formal Korean ratification of the normalization treaty and in the midst of widespread student demonstrations and mounting public fears and criticism of a new "economic invasion" by Japan, Kim Yongwan welcomed a forty-member delegation of Japan's business elite to Seoul for a formal joint Korean-Japanese economic symposium, the first such conference of Japanese and Korean businessmen in Korea since the colonial period. Kim continued, of course, to guide the new course of Korean-Japanese capitalist cooperation during his long second tenure as FKI chairman from 1970 to 1977.[8]

The legacy of colonial industrialization actually went beyond the creation of a native capitalist class. Colonialism bequeathed to the postwar period not only a social basis for future development but also an historically based model of successful capitalist growth, successful at least in the narrow sense of stimulating rapid industrialization. Not surprisingly, the model shared a number of elements in common with its contemporary Japanese archetype: the pivotal economic function of the state, the concentration of private economic power in the hands of a small number of large business groups or *chaebŏl* (*zaibatsu*), the emphasis on exports, and the threat or actuality of war as a stimulus for economic growth. In other ways, however, the model was less Japanese than Korean-colonial in character; Japanese colonialism, and the particular form that such colonialism took in Korea, gave rise to patterns of industrial development on the peninsula that were distinctively different from those in Japan itself.

Here two aspects of the model seem particularly worthy of note. The first was the overwhelming predominance of the state in economic affairs: the colonial government was a pervasive and dictatorial economic force, clearly master of both the economy and the bourgeoisie in a way that was inconceivable even in Japan itself. This is not to say, however, that the basic government-business relationship in colonial Korea was adversarial: indeed, the two sides tended to function more often than not as an effective unit. If the Government-General was the overall planner and coordinator of economic activity and the ultimate allocator of credit, the business community was the sometimes eager, sometimes reluctant, but generally well-rewarded, servant of state policy in the private sector. Not infrequently their roles overlapped as bureaucrats became stockholders and officers in private firms and businessmen came to participate both formally and informally in the policy-making process. In spite of the basic inequality of the relationship and occasional disagreement, the unitary bond between government and business seems to have been strong, maintained through a combination of shared Confucian values and a bedrock of material interest.

A second major element in the colonial development model was the subordination of Korean capitalism to its Japanese counterpart, an inevitable consequence not only of the more advanced state of Japanese capitalism but also of Korea's status as a Japanese colony. Such subordination took the form of a considerable dependence on individual Japanese companies and/or business groups in many of the principal aspects of capitalist enterprise, and especially in the area of technological development. Kyŏngbang, perhaps the most sophisticated example of Korean capitalism at the time, was a case in point. Throughout the colonial period the Kyŏngbang *chaebŏl* relied heavily on Japanese corporate associates like Yagi Shōten, C. Itoh, and Kureha Spinning for its procurement of raw materials and marketing, and above all for its equipment, spare parts, and technical expertise.

The model described above was bequeathed to the post-1945 world in a dual sense. It became, first of all, part of the living heritage of the Koreans who had participated in it, whether directly, like Kim Yŏnsu, or more peripherally, like Yi Pyŏngch'ŏl and Park Chung Hee, and could be resurrected, consciously or unconsciously, in modified form in any later Korean attempt at capitalist industrialization. Perhaps we shall never know exactly what model, if any, Park Chung Hee had in mind for Korean economic development in the early 1960s, though he does appear to have had a strong admiration for Meiji Japan.[9] What *is* clear, however, is that the South Korean pattern of capitalist development that did finally emerge was far more reminiscent of colonial Korea than of anything else, including Meiji Japan.[10]

There was also another way in which the colonial model was passed on to the postwar world. Korea's first industrialization under the Japanese left an indelible mark on the country. To acknowledge this is not to fall prey to any kind of historical determinism; it is, rather, a matter of historical common sense. Capitalist industrialization had been initiated in a particular way, which meant that it would be most easily and successfully continued in a similar fashion. All of the key elements, in a sense, worked together. Colonialism had, for example, produced a native capitalist class, but it was a class that was accustomed to extensive government direction and patronage and to massive support from a stronger, more advanced capitalist system. After Liberation, and especially after the Korean War, the United States was willing to some extent to assume the role of capitalist "elder brother" in Korea, but the government of Syngman Rhee seems to have lacked the kind of determined commitment to economic growth that had been one of the hallmarks of the Government-General. It was not until the 1960s and the advent of the economically oriented Park regime that all the crucial elements of the colonial model were once again in full play. With the normalization of relations with Japan in 1965, and the resulting influx of Japanese capital and technology, South Korea's pattern of industrialization seemed, despite important differences, all the more to resemble the colonial prototype.

There is a third aspect to the colonial capitalist legacy, a political dark side that is closely bound up with the social and economic aspects already discussed. Barrington Moore has argued eloquently that both dictatorship and democracy have social roots,[11] and, indeed, one need hardly be a materialist to agree with him; even Isaiah Berlin, for example, has suggested that "without the pressure of social forces, political ideas are stillborn."[12] In any capitalist society, furthermore, it seems inevitable that the bourgeoisie will play a major role in shaping that country's politics, In nineteenth-century Europe the bourgeois political impulse tended to be liberal, even revolutionary, and where the bourgeosie was strong, so too was the liberal element in the political spectrum. Even where liberalism stumbled, as in Germany, the bourgeoisie was still a critical variable. Thus David Landes has written that the German bourgeoisie "traded, in effect, its political birthright for the pottage of economic advantage and vicarious prowess."[13] Moore, paraphrasing Marx and Engels, has said much the same thing: "Marx and Engels in their discussion of the abortive 1848 revolution in Germany, wrong though they were on other major features, put their finger on this decisive ingredient: a commercial and industrial class that is too weak and dependent to take power in its own right and which therefore throws itself into the arms of the landed aristocracy and the royal bureaucracy, exchanging the right to rule for the right to make money."[14]

In Korea, too, the bourgeoisie on the eve of Liberation found itself in league with the forces of authoritarianism. The reason for this, how-ever, had little, if anything, to do with a stifling of bourgeois liberalism through an unholy coalition of landed and industrial interests. The Korean bourgeoisie had never possessed a liberal birthright. To no small extent its very social origins were bound up with an aristocratic political culture that meshed ascriptive status with bureaucratic au-thority and hierarchy. Even more important, Korean capitalism had been spawned within the matrix of Japanese colonialism. This meant that the bourgeoisie developed under the aegis of, and in close collabo-ration with, the Japanese colonial state, a form of dictatorship that had no real precedent in the Yi dynasty's five-hundred-year history[15] or, for that matter, in Japanese history either, a highly functional, *sui generis* product of Japanese colonial needs and goals. The dictator-ship of the Government-General, however, was no barrier to entrepre-neurial success. Quite the opposite: Korean capitalism experienced its first great burst of growth and prosperity under this repressive state structure, and by 1945 the Korean bourgeoisie had become thoroughly conditioned to working within an authoritarian political framework. Indeed, the political wisdom that Korean capitalists carried with them into the postwar world was that dictatorship was both economically efficient and profitable.

The specifically colonial nature of the pre-1945 industrialization ef-fort, moreover, worked to transform the Korean bourgeoisie's basic contentment with authoritarianism into a more consciously antidemo-cratic attitude by 1945. Participation in the colonial industrialization process involved Korean capitalists not only in the economic exploita-tion of their own workers but ultimately in the Japanese attempt to eradicate a separate and distinct sense of national identity in the Ko-rean people as a whole. Thus unable or unwilling to compromise with less privileged classes and lacking sufficient nationalist credentials, the Korean bourgeoisie found its political position within the native soci-ety increasingly unstable and came to rely more and more on the op-pressive powers of the Government-General. By the end of the colonial period, dictatorship had become not only a comfortable political mode for the accumulation of capital, but a political prerequisite for Korean bourgeois survival in the midst of widespread economic and nationalist discontent.

All things considered, the colonial capitalist legacy was clearly more mixed than blessed. If, on the one hand, it gave fair promise of a vibrant, reconstituted industrial economy on the Korean peninsula, it also implied that the price of such development might well be high:

obtrusive state power and a high degree of foreign dependency, two conditions that many Koreans, living in a postcolonial world charged with democratic and nationalist emotions, would eventually find uncomfortable and even come to resent. To be sure, the colonial legacy would not be the sole factor in the molding of the South Korean political economy after 1948. Nevertheless, in looking at the recent transformation of that country, especially during the crucial two decades of rapid industrialization under Park Chung Hee, it is difficult for the colonial scholar to shake off an uncanny feeling of *déjà vu*, a sense that history not only prevailed, as one might expect, but that it prevailed with a vengeance.

Protectorate and Colonial Administrations, 1905–45

Residents-General and Vice-Residents-General 1905–10

Residents-General (Tōkan) 統監

1.	Itō Hirobumi	伊藤博文	1905 (12/21)–1909 (6/14)
2.	Sone Arasuke	曽弥荒助	1909 (6/14)–1910 (5/30)
3.	Terauchi Masatake	寺内正毅	1910 (5/30)–1910 (9/30)

Vice-Residents-General (Fukutōkan) 副統監

1.	Sone Arasuke	曽弥荒助	1907 (9/21)–1909 (6/15)
2.	Yamagata Isaburō	山県伊三郎	1910 (7/4)–1910 (9/30)

Governors-General and Vice-Governors-General 1910–45

Governors-General (Sōtoku) 總督

1.	Terauchi Masatake	寺内正毅	1910 (10/1)–1916 (10/9)
2.	Hasegawa Yoshimichi	長谷川好道	1916 (10/16)–1919 (8/12)
3.	Saitō Makoto	齋藤 實	1919 (8/12)–1927 (12/10)
4.	Ugaki Kazunari/Kazushige (Acting Governor-General)	宇垣一成	1927 (4/15)–1927 (10/1)
5.	Yamanashi Hanzō	山梨半造	1927 (12/10)–1929 (8/17)
6.	Saitō Makoto	齋藤 實	1929 (8/17)–1931 (6/17)
7.	Ugaki Kazunari	宇垣一成	1931 (6/17)–1936 (8/4)
8.	Minami Jirō	南 次郎	1936 (8/5)–1942 (5/29)
9.	Koiso Kuniaki	小磯國昭	1942 (5/29)–1944 (7/27)
10.	Abe Nobuyuki	阿部信行	1944 (7/24)–1945 (9/28)

Vice-Governors-General (Seimu Sōkan) 政務總監

1.	Yamagata Isaburō	山県伊三郎	1910 (10/1)–1919 (8/12)
2.	Mizuno Rentarō	水野錬太郎	1919 (8/12)–1922 (6/12)
3.	Ariyoshi Chūichi	有吉忠一	1922 (6/15)–1924 (7/4)
4.	Shimooka Chūji	下岡忠治	1924 (7/4)–1925 (11/22)
5.	Yuasa Kurahei	湯浅倉平	1925 (12/3)–1927 (12/23)
6.	Ikegami Shirō	池上四郎	1927 (12/23)–1929 (4/4)
7.	Kodama Hideo	児玉秀雄	1929 (6/22)–1931 (6/19)
8.	Imaida Kiyonori	今井田清徳	1931 (6/19)–1936 (8/4)
9.	Ōno Rokuichirō	大野緑一郎	1936 (8/5)–1942 (5/29)
10.	Tanaka Takeo	田中武雄	1942 (5/29)–1944 (7/23)
11.	Endō Ryūsaku	遠藤柳作	1944 (7/24)–1945 (10/24)

SOURCE: Ajia Keizai Kenkyūsho: Tosho shiryōbu, *Kyū shokuminchi kankei kikan kankōbutsu sōgō mokuroku: Chōsen hen* [Union catalog of publications by the former colonial institutions: Korea] (Tokyo: Ajia Keizai Kenkyūsho, 1974), p. 203.

"Dying for a Righteous Cause

The Responsibility of Imperial Citizens Is Great"

[In the past] I have continually been saying [this] to you in the classroom or as the occasion arose, and it is hardly necessary to say [it] again here and now, but [please bear with me]. On the one hand you have been exerting yourself in intellectual endeavors, and at the same time you have worked hard at ethical cultivation. Education, [proceeding] from these two directions, will develop you into a complete human being. In a period like the present, when a new international order is being built, you too, [I am sure], clearly realize the necessity of stressing the ethical side [of education] all the more. Today, as you face the [prospect] of battle, I want to reiterate my ideas, which I have frequently expressed to you [even] in ordinary times. In a word: "Do your duty."

[In the past] I have [also] always told [you] that in doing your duty you should not spare even [your own] life. Now, indeed, the time has come for you to put these words into action with your bodies.

I know very well that you are of course in a state of mind which neither I nor other seniors, who are asking you with easy words to offer up your lives, can even imagine. Even yesterday morning, when I called you all together and looked down from the dais into your many eyes, I felt a profound emotion that is difficult to express in mere words. But I am speaking with the conscience of a long-time educator. Frankly, even as I make of you this final one-sentence request, "Die for [your] duty," I do not of course expect you to accept it without any doubts or questions. Your intellectual level is higher than the average person, such that it is natural [for you] to regard any proposition with skepticism. Furthermore, I am not demanding blind servility at a time like the present when you have to make an immediate decision on [the question of] a glorious death.

But I am confident [enough] to think that I [as an educator] know more than other kinds of people about such doubts and anxieties—so confident [in fact] that [I] do not approve of an attitude which categorically denies your doubts. I intend, rather, to join you in looking forward to the day when,

Credited to Kim Sŏngsu, in *Maeil sinbo*, November 6, 1943.

262

after working through these anxieties, you firmly grasp the shining goal on the other side. Because I know very well that only if the commitment to a glorious death has been tempered by such a process of anxiety will [it] be more unshakeable than any other resolution.

This being the case, when I tell you to "offer your lives for the sake of duty," you naturally should have a clear idea of what kind of duty I am talking about. As an educator, as someone who has been entrusted by your parents to mold you, their precious [children], into fine, whole human beings, I am absolutely unable to say anything false or contrary to my conscience. In a position of such great responsibility, I intend to speak with fearless honesty. When [I] speak of the duty that currently confronts us, you too know very well [what I mean]. This is the duty that you and all we Korean compatriots owe to the Greater East Asia holy war, through which [we] are welcoming a new dawn and endeavoring to develop a great enterprise in human history. You received your life from this land, and you have been enjoying all kinds of blessings up to now, including the gift of a decent human temperament and character. The blessings from the state, the family, and the society, together constitute these [various blessings]. Such blessings in the past are [now] calling on each of you to fulfill that duty. A far greater and graver duty, moreover, is the duty to the future.

Just imagine [what things will be like] if you fail to rally to the Greater East Asia holy war, and the construction of a new order in Greater East Asia is completed without our [Korean] participation. As beings who turned rotten even as they received [the gift of] life in Greater East Asia, we will never be able to redeem our existence in this historic period. If you run from the line of battle in this holy war, you may well preserve your insignificant individual lives, but what will become of your brothers and sisters who were born in this land after you? Truly, you have an absolute duty to the future of Korea.

I suspect your anxieties are now confronting this [very] point. But the moments are ticking away one by one regardless of such anxieties and questions on your part. The construction of a Greater East Asia is moving ahead with no time to spare for your trifling existence. If you lose the chance of a lifetime that this advance offers [you], and Korea, as a result, falls behind this [advance], we will cease being part of the construction of Greater East Asia and will be unable, moreover, to become in an honorable fashion a part of the Empire as imperial subjects. Only when you fulfill the duty mentioned above will you live on in this land and be able to enjoy, as a part of the Empire, exactly the same treatment, indeed, rights, as [people in] Japan. It is generally said about duties and rights that in Western societies duty is owed as a result of the assertion of rights, while in the East rights have traditionally appeared as a matter of course from doing [one's] duty. Ever since I have been advocating that we become imperial subjects, I have heard you frequently demanding your rights as imperial subjects from the general society. But if [we] consider [this matter] dispassionately, Japan has been discharging all kinds of duties for as long as 3,000 years in the course of bringing glory to the Empire of today. But we [Koreans], on the other hand, have had barely thirty years. Considering the difference between 3,000 years and 30 years, can [you dare to] demand equal rights? You must realize that this is a mistake—[the result] of your being dazzled by the doctrines of Westerners who only advocate rights. But I have a certain idea here [that I want to share with you]. With respect to carrying out [one's] duty, the length of time is not that important. The importance of a duty lies not in the time it takes but in the nature of the duty itself. Is it not possible that we, even in a short period of time, by carrying out a great duty can match the sacrifice rendered by the Japanese over a long period of time? Now, at this [very] moment, we have before us the greatest opportunity to perform this duty.

I declare to you that your sacrifice will absolutely not be in vain. [It] is a sacrifice for this peninsula that gave you life, and with it, this peninsula will attain the qualifications [necessary] for imperial membership; thus it may be said that the future of Korea rests solely on your course of action.

Notes

The following abbreviations are used in the Notes.

Chōsen GKKY: Nakamuro Sukeyoshi, ed. *Chōsen ginkō kaisha kumiai yōroku* [Digest of Korean banks, companies, and associations]. Keijō: Tōa Keizai Jinhōsha, 1933.

JAS: Journal of Asian Studies

JKS: Journal of Korean Studies

KO: Cho Yonggu, ed. *Kyŏngsŏng Pangjik osimnyŏn* [Fifty years of Kyŏngbang]. Seoul: Kyŏngsŏng Pangjik CH, 1969.

KSS: Ko Cheuk, ed. *Inch'on Kim Sŏngsujŏn* [The biography of Kim Sŏngsu]. Seoul: Inch'on Ki'nyŏmhoe, 1976.

KY: Pak Inhwan, ed. *Kyŏngbang yuksimnyŏn* [Sixty years of Kyŏngbang]. Seoul: CH Kyŏngbang, 1980.

KYS: Kim Sanghyŏng, ed. *Sudang Kim Yŏnsu* [Kim Yŏnsu]. Seoul: Sudang Ki'nyŏm Saŏphoe, 1971.

SY: Kim Sanghong, ed. *Samyang osimnyŏn: 1924–1974* [Fifty years of Samyang: 1924–1974]. Seoul: CH Samyangsa, 1974.

Part I. The Rise of Korean Capitalism

1. Tuho was the natural son of Min Ch'iu, who was, in turn, the natural brother of Min Ch'igu. Both father and son, however, had adoptive parents as well. Chi'u's adoptive father was Min Sŭnghyŏn, and Tuho's was Min Ch'isŏ. See the Yŏhŭng Min genealogy in the *Mansŏng taedongbo* [Grand genealogy of the 10,000 names] (Seoul, n.p., n.d.); see also James B. Palais, *Politics and Policy in Traditional Korea* (Cambridge, Mass.: Harvard University Press, 1975), pp. 302–3 nn. 5, 6.

2. Pak Tubyŏng Chŏn'gi Wiwŏnhoe, *Yŏn'gang Pak Tubyŏng* [Pak Tubyŏng] (Seoul: Haptong T'ongsinsa Ch'ulp'an'guk, 1975), pp. 25–26.

3. The Chōsen Business Club (Chōsen Jitsugyō Kurabu). See chap. 4.

4. Tuho's son was Min Yŏnghwi, an early supporter and official of the Hansŏng Bank. See Cho Kijun, *Han'guk kiŏpkasa* [A history of Korean entre-

preneurs] (Seoul: Pagyŏngsa, 1974), p. 135. Min Yŏnghwi and his sons Kyusik, Taesik, and Chungsik later founded the Tongil Bank in Seoul in 1931—the result of a merger of the Hanil and Hosŏ Banks. In 1943, when all the existing Korean banks were merged to form the Chohŭng Bank, Min Kyusik became the new bank's first chairman. See "Manmok chusi hanŭn samdae chaengp'aejŏn" [Three big competitions everyone is watching], Samch'ŏlli 4 (April 1932): 46–48; also Emura Koji, "Ŭnhaeng tuch'wi inmulp'yŏng: Tongŭn tuch'wi Min Taesikssi" [Profile of a bank president: Tongil bank president Min Taesik], Samch'ŏlli 8 (Feb. 1936): 51–55; also Pak Chongt'ae, ed., Chohŭng Ŭnhaeng p'alsibo'nyŏnsa: Ch'urok [The eighty-five-year-history of the Chohŭng Bank: Supplement] (Seoul: CH Chohŭng Ŭnhaeng, 1982), p. 36. Along with Han Sangnyong, Pak Yŏngch'ŏl, Kim Yŏnsu, and other Korean and Japanese businessmen, Min Kyusik took an active role in the formation and management of the Chōsen Trust Company (Chōsen Shintaku KK), established in 1932 (authorized capital: 10 million yen) with the financial backing of the Bank of Chōsen, the Chōsen Industrial Bank, and the Oriental Development Company. Around the same time, Min Kyusik, Kim Yŏnsu, and Pak Hŭngsik joined a core of Japanese investors in establishing the Chōsen Urban Management Company (Chōsen Toshi Keiei KK), a real estate brokerage, management, and financing firm with an authorized capital of 500,000 yen. See Cho Kijun, Han'guk kiŏpkasa, p. 138; also Nakamura Sukeyoshi, ed., Chōsen ginkō kaisha kumiai yōroku (hereafter cited as Chōsen GKKY) [Digest of Korean banks, companies, and associations] (Keijō: Tōa Keizai Jihōsha, 1933), pp. 57, 361–62. Min Kyusik was also a stockholder in the Kyŏngsŏng Spinning and Weaving Company founded by Kim Sŏngsu in 1919. See Kyŏngsŏng Pangjik CH, List of Stockholders, Nov. 30, 1944, p. 10. Pak Munhoe's most famous son was Pak Sŭngjik, who became a leading Korean textile merchant during the colonial period and was a close associate of Kim Yŏnsu. See chap. 6.

5. By "bourgeoisie" I mean, essentially, what Marx and Engels meant by the term, as indicated in Engels's note to the 1888 English edition of the Communist Manifesto: "the class of modern Capitalists, owners of the means of social production and employers of wage labor." These are the machine-factory owners, historically the core class of industrial capitalist civilization. See Robert C. Tucker, ed., The Marx-Engels Reader, 2nd ed., rev. and enl. (New York and London: W. W. Norton, 1978), p. 473. By extension, however, I also include in the category "bourgeoisie" those businessmen who regularly and directly service the core bourgeoisie in one way or another—bankers, brokers, traders, insurance-company owners, etc.

6. For a discussion of the Japanese perspective on Korean history before 1945 and its connection with Japanese colonial policy in Korea, see Cho Kijun, Han'guk chabonjuŭi sŏngnipsaron [Discourses on the formative history of Korean capitalism], rev. ed. (Seoul: Taewangsa, 1981), pp. 20–23.

7. There is an extensive literature on this subject both in North and South

Korea. Some of the major South Korean works include Wŏn Yuhan, *Han'guk hugi hwap'yesa yŏn'gu* [Studies in the monetary history of the late Yi dynasty] (Seoul: Han'guk Yŏn'guwŏn, 1975); Yu Wŏndong, *Han'guk kŭndae kyŏngjesa yŏn'gu* [Studies in the modern economic history of Korea] (Seoul: Ilch'ungsa, 1977); Kang Man'gil, *Chosŏn hugi sangŏp chabon ŭi paltal* [The development of commercial capital in the late Yi dynasty] (Seoul: Koryŏ Taehakkyo Ch'ulp'anbu, 1974); Kim Yongsŏp, *Chosŏn hugi nongŏpsa yŏn'gu* [Studies in the agrarian history of the late Yi dynasty], 2 vols. (Seoul: Ilchogak, 1974) —especially 2: 182ff. Articles by Wŏn, Yu, and Kang have been included (both in Korean and English) in Chun Shin-yong, ed., *Economic Life in Korea*, Korean Culture Series no. 8 (Seoul: International Cultural Foundation, 1978). A brief overview and critique of the South Korean literature is included in Cho Kijun, *Han'guk chabonjuŭi sŏngnipsaron*, pp. 34–41. For a good critical synopsis of the North Korean literature, see Yŏng-ho Ch'oe, "Reinterpreting Traditional History in North Korea," *Journal of Asian Studies* (hereafter JAS) 40, no. 3 (May 1981): 503–23.

8. See, for example, Edward W. Wagner, "The Ladder of Success in Yi Dynasty Korea," *Occasional Papers on Korea*, no. 1 (April 1974), pp. 1–8; Wagner, "Social Stratification in Seventeenth-Century Korea: Some Observations from a 1663 Seoul Census Register," *Occasional Papers on Korea*, no. 1 (April 1974), pp. 36–54; Susan Shin, "The Social Structure of Kŭmhwa County in the Late Seventeenth Century," *Occasional Papers on Korea*, no. 1 (April 1974), pp. 9–35, and "Economic Development and Social Mobility in Pre-Modern Korea: 1600–1860," *Peasant Studies* 7, no. 3 (Summer 1978): 187–97; Fujiya Kawashima, "Clan Structure and Political Power in Yi Dynasty Korea: A Case Study of the Munhwa Yu Clan" (Ph.D. diss., Harvard University, 1972); John N. Somerville, "Stability in Eighteenth Century Ulsan," *Korean Studies Forum*, no. 1 (Autumn–Winter 1976–77), pp. 1–18. See also James B. Palais, "Stability in Yi Dynasty Korea: Equilibrium Systems and Marginal Adjustment," *Occasional Papers on Korea*, no. 3 (June 1975), pp. 1–18, and his *Politics and Policy*, pp. 4–22.

9. Palais, *Politics and Policy*, pp. 64, 310–11 n. 16; Max Weber, *The Protestant Ethic and the Spirit of Capitalism*, trans. Talcott Parsons (1958. New York: Charles Scribner's Sons, Lyceum, 1958), p. 58.

10. Thorstein Veblen, *The Theory of Business Enterprise* (Clifton, N. J.: Augustus M. Kelley, 1973), p. 1.

11. Karl Marx, *Capital: A Critique of Political Economy*, trans. Samuel Moore and Edward Aveling (from the 3rd German edition) and ed. Frederick Engels, 3 vols. (New York: International Publishers, n.d.) 1:368. Karl Polanyi, who sees the early growth of Western capitalism in terms of the gradual triumph of the idea of a self-regulating market economy, also stresses the technological impetus for such an idea: "We do not intend to assert that the machine caused that which happened, but we insist that once elaborate machines and plants were used for production in a commercial society, the idea of a self-

regulating market was bound to take shape." Karl Polanyi, *The Great Transformation: The Political and Economic Origins of Our Time* (1944; reprint, Boston: Beacon Press, 1957), p. 40. Yŏng-ho Ch'oe in "Reinterpreting Traditional History," p. 515, notes that "practically no attention was given to the technological aspect during the debates [on Korean capitalistic development] in North Korea." The same might well be said of South Korean scholarship.

12. Recently the search for capitalist sprouts in the pre-1876 period has been generating criticism in South Korea as well. See the discussion on Korean capitalism by several well-known scholars in the monthly magazine *Sindonga*: "Han'guk ŭi chabonjuŭi wa chayujuŭi" [Capitalism and liberalism in Korea], *Sindonga* (August 1986), pp. 276–95.

13. Cho Kijun, *Han'guk chabonjuŭi sŏngnipsaron*, p. 45.

1. Merchants and Landlords: The Accumulation of Capital, 1876–1919

1. Susan B. Hanley and Kozo Yamamura, *Economic and Demographic Change in Preindustrial Japan, 1600–1868* (1977; reprint, Princeton: Princeton University Press, 1977), pp. 45, 351 n. 42.

2. See Howard Hibbett, *The Floating World in Japanese Fiction* (New York: Oxford University Press, paperback, 1959), especially pt. 1, pp. 2–96.

3. Seoul's population at the beginning of the nineteenth century was said to be 200,000. See Susan Shin, "Economic Development and Social Mobility in Pre-Modern Korea," p. 197 n. 7. On the population of Korea as a whole during the Yi dynasty, see Palais, *Politics and Policy*, pp. 64, 312, n. 20.

4. See, for example, Ihara Saikaku, *This Scheming World*, trans. Masanori Takatsuka and David C. Stubbs (Rutland, Vt.: Charles E. Tuttle Co., Inc., 1965); idem, *The Japanese Family Storehouse, or the Millionaires' Gospel Modernised*, trans. G. W. Sargent (Cambridge: Cambridge University Press, 1959). See also idem, *Worldly Mental Calculations*, trans. Ben Befu (Berkeley, Los Angeles, London: University of California Press, 1976).

5. See Johannes Hirschmeier and Tsunehiko Yui, *The Development of Japanese Business 1600–1973* (Cambridge: Harvard University Press, 1975), pp. 11–69; also John G. Roberts, *Mitsui: Three Centuries of Japanese Business* (New York, Tokyo: John Weatherhill, 1973), pp. 3–84.

6. In Chun Shin-yong, ed., *Economic Life in Korea*, p. 279.

7. See Yi Kibaek, *Han'guksa sillon* [A new history of Korea], rev. ed. (Seoul: Ilchogak, 1982), pp. 228-31, 314-15; also Han Ugŭn, *Han'guk t'ongsa* [A comprehensive history of Korea] (Seoul: Ŭryu Munhwasa, 1970), pp. 240–43, 401–9. A first-rate English translation of Yi Kibaek's work is now available: see Ki-baik Lee, *A New History of Korea*, trans. Edward W. Wagner with Edward J. Schultz (Cambridge: Harvard University Press, 1984). There is also an English translation of Han Ugŭn's book: see Woo-keun Han, *The History of Korea*, trans. Kyung-shik Lee and ed. Grafton K. Mintz (1970; reprint, Honolulu: University Press of Hawaii, 1974).

8. Cho Kijun, *Han'guk kiŏpkasa*, pp. 270–71.

9. Ibid., pp. 274–79.

10. Ernst Oppert, *A Forbidden Land: Voyages to the Corea* (New York: G. P. Putnam's Sons, 1880), p. 174.

11. Kajimura Hideki, *Chōsen ni okeru shihonshugi no keisei to tenkai* [The formation and development of capitalism in Korea] (Tokyo: Ryūkei Shosha, 1977), pp. 43, 53.

12. See Hilary Conroy, *The Japanese Seizure of Korea 1868–1910: A Study of Realism and Idealism in International Relations.* (1960. Philadelphia: University of Pennsylvania Press, 1974), pp. 442–91.

13. Peter Duus, "Economic Dimensions of Meiji Imperialism: The Case of Korea, 1895–1910," in Ramon H. Myers and Mark R. Peattie, eds., *The Japanese Colonial Empire, 1895–1945* (Princeton: Princeton University Press, 1984), pp. 131–61.

14. See Martina Deuchler, *Confucian Gentlemen and Barbarian Envoys: The Opening of Korea, 1875–1885* (Seattle: University of Washington Press, 1977), pp. 69–84 passim.

15. From a letter written by Max von Brandt, the minister of the North German Union, to Baron de Rehfus in Peking. Quoted in Albert A. Altman, "Korea's First Newspaper: The Japanese *Chōsen shinpō*," *JAS* 43, no. 4 (August 1984): 685.

16. Isabella Bird Bishop, *Korea and Her Neighbours* (New York: Fleming H. Revell Co., 1897), p. 296.

17. Cho Kijun, *Han'guk kiŏpkasa*, p. 282.

18. On the *yugŭijŏn*, see Yi Kibaek, *Han'guksa sillon*, pp. 225–26; also Cho Kijun, *Han'guk kiŏpkasa*, p. 34; also Kim Pyŏngha, "Yugŭijŏn" [The six licensed stores], in Kwŏn Oik et al., eds., *Kyŏngjehak taesajŏn* [The unabridged dictionary of economics], rev. and exp. (Seoul: Pagyŏngsa, 1980), pp. 1089–90.

19. On the *kongin*, see Yi Kibaek, *Han'guksa sillon*, pp. 265–67, 272, also Cho Kijun, *Han'guk kiŏpkasa*, pp. 225–26; also Ch'oe T'aeho, "Kongin" [The tribute men], in Kwŏn Oik et al., eds., *Kyŏngjehak taesajŏn*, p. 199. Cho Kijun, *Han'guk kiŏpkasa*, p. 226. Ibid., pp. 44–45. The abolition of special commercial privileges was part of the so-called Kabo Reform program implemented by the government at the time.

20. Paek Yunsu was originally a silk merchant in Chongno. According to Cho Kijun, the two main reasons Paek was able to survive were his good relationship with the Chinese merchant-importers from whom he purchased his cloth and that his customers were, primarily, members of the royal family, high government officials, and other wealthy Koreans. Paek and his family were active in Korean business circles (especially the textile industry) during the colonial period and throughout the 1950s, but their "T'aech'ang Group" (T'aech'ang Chaebŏl) did not survive the military coup in 1961. See Cho Kijun, *Han'guk kiŏpkasa*, pp. 184–90.

21. Japanese currency did not officially become legal tender in Korea until 1905, but as the influx of Japanese goods into Korea continued to increase in the 1890s, it became a popular medium of exchange among businessmen in the port cities. See Cho Kijun, *Han'guk chabonjuŭi sŏngnipsaron*, pp. 205, 210.

22. Quoted in Cho Kijun's *Han'guk chabonjuŭi sŏngnipsaron*, p. 212. Koreans were forced by the government to turn in their old nickel and copper cash, for which they received *at most* only 50 percent of the face value of the old coins. The most debased coins were merely confiscated and no reimbursement paid at all. See H.I.J.M.'s Residency General, *Annual Report for 1907 on Reforms and Progress in Korea* (Seoul, 1908), pp. 48–51.

23. On the *kaekchu* and *yŏgak*, see Yi Kibaek, *Han'guksa sillon*, p. 273; also Ch'oe Hojin, "Kaekchu" and "Yŏgak," in Kwŏn Oik et al., eds., *Kyŏngjehak taesajŏn*, pp. 53–54, 994. See also Pak Wŏnsŏn, *Kaekchu* [The Kaekchu] (Seoul: Yŏnse Taehakkyo Ch'ulp'anbu, 1968). It is difficult to know how to translate these terms. Edward W. Wagner, in his translation of Yi Kibaek's history, calls the *kaekchu* "inland market traders" and the *yŏgak* "coastal market traders," but this distinction is not explicit in Yi's own work, and Ch'oe Hojin regards *yŏgak* as simply another name for *kaekchu*.

24. See Yi Kibaek, *Han'guksa sillon*, pp. 350–51; also Ch'oe Hojin, "Kaekchu," *Kyŏngjehak taesajŏn*, pp. 53–54.

25. Cho Kijun, *Han'guk kiŏpkasa*, pp. 185, 196–97.

26. Ko Sŭngje, *Han'guk kŭm'yungsa yŏn'gu* [Studies in Korean financial history] (Seoul: Ilchogak, 1970), pp. 241–42.

27. Cho Kijun, *Han'guk kiŏpkasa*, pp. 140–42.

28. Ko Sŭngje, *Han'guk kŭm'yungsa yŏn'gu*, pp. 239–44.

29. See Yi Kibaek, *Han'guksa sillon*, p. 351; also Cho Kijun, *Han'guk kiŏpkasa*, pp. 35–37, 229–31.

30. See Chōsen Menshifushō Rengōkai, *Chōsen mengyōshi* [The history of the Korean cotton industry] (Keijō: Chōsen Menshifushō Rengōkai, 1929), pp. 32–34, 299–300. Other colonial sources have the company being founded in 1905 rather than 1907—see *Chōsen GKKY*, p. 250, and Cho Kijun, *Han'guk kiŏpkasa*, pp. 198–200.

31. Chōsen Sōtokufu, *Chōsen Sōtokufu tōkei nempō, 1911* [The statistical yearbook of the Government–General of Korea, 1911], 3 vols. (Keijō: Chōsen Sōtokufu, 1913) 1: 223.

32. This was Pak Yonghŭi, whose father, Pak Sŏngil of P'aju, although a big landlord by 1919, had originally been a *kaekchu*: see Cho Kijun, *Han'guk kiŏpkasa*, p. 256.

33. Leroy P. Jones and Il Sakong, *Government, Business, and Entrepreneurship in Economic Development: The Korean Case*, Studies in the Modernization of the Republic of Korea: 1945-1975 (Cambridge: Council on East Asian Studies, Harvard University, 1980), p. 228.

34. See Song Chan-shik, "Genealogical Records," *Korea Journal* 17 (May 1977): 15–24.

35. Jones and Sakong, *Government, Business, and Entrepreneurship*, p. 228.

36. Cho Kijun, *Han'guk kiŏpkasa*, pp. 397–98; Kim Yŏngmo, *Chosŏn chibaech'ŭng yŏn'gu* [Studies of the Yi dynasty ruling class] (Seoul: Ilchogak, 1982), pp. 371–91.

37. While there were probably some large landowning families who did not have a prominent history in the Chosŏn bureacracy or who were not regarded by their contemporaries as genuine aristocrats or yangban—just as there were probably some bureaucrats who managed to attain high office without the benefit of a landed background—there was nevertheless in general a close correlation in Yi Korea between social status, officeholding, and land-ownership. See Palais, *Politics and Policy*, p. 64.

38. See Cho Kijun, *Han'guk kiŏpkasa*, pp. 114–18.

39. In Dae-Sook Suh, *Documents of Korean Communism 1918–1948* (Princeton: Princeton University Press, 1970), p. 156.

40. Kim Yongsŏp, "Hanmal-ilcheha ŭi chijuje—sarye 3: Naju Yissiga ŭi chijuro ŭi sŏngjang kwa kŭ nongjang kyŏngyŏng" [The landlord system of the late Yi dynasty and Japanese colonial period—case study 3: The rise of the Naju Yi family as landlords, and the management of their agricultural estate], *Chindan hakpo* 42 (August 1976): 41.

41. On the formation of the Oriental Development Company, see Karl Moskowitz, "The Creation of the Oriental Development Company: Japanese Illusions Meet Korean Reality," *Occasional Papers on Korea*, no. 2 (March 1974), pp. 73–121.

42. Kim Yongsŏp, "Hanmal-ilcheha ŭi chijuje—sarye 1: Kanghwa Kimssiga ŭi ch'usugirul t'onghaesŏ pon chiju kyŏngyŏng" [The landlord system of the late Yi dynasty and Japanese colonial period—case study 1: The landlord management of the Kanghwa Kim family as seen through their harvest records], *Tonga munhwa*, no. 11 (December 1972), p. 36.

43. Andrew J. Grajdanzev, *Modern Korea* (New York: International Secretariat, Institute of Pacific Relations, 1944), p. 106. According to the Harvard modernization study on rural development, "most of the rented land (over 80 percent) . . . was owned by Koreans." See Sung Hwan Ban, Pal Yong Moon, Dwight Perkins, with contributions by Vincent Brandt, Albert Keidel, John E. Sloboda, *Rural Development*, Studies in the Modernization of the Republic of Korea: 1945–1975 (Cambridge: Council on East Asian Studies, Harvard University, 1982), p. 284. Such figures, of course, are only for cultivated land. If the total amount of land (forests, etc.) is considered, the Japanese figure is probably closer to 50 percent. See Grajdanzev, *Modern Korea*, p. 110.

44. Between 1913 and 1939, the number of pure proprietors on the one hand and mixed proprietors and tenants on the other hand decreased from

21.7 percent to 19 percent and from 38.9 percent to 25.3 percent, respectively, whereas the number of pure tenants rose from 39.4 percent to 55.7 percent. See Sang-Chul Suh, *Growth and Structural Changes in the Korean Economy, 1910–1940* (Cambridge: Council on East Asian Studies, Harvard University, 1978).

45. Cho Kijun, "Irin nongŏp imin kwa Tongyang Ch'ŏksik Chusik Hoesa" [Japanese agricultural immigrants and the Oriental Development Company] in Yun Pyŏngsŏk, Sin Yongha, An Pyŏngjik, eds., *Han'guk kŭndaesaron I: Ilche singminji sidae ŭi sahoe kyŏngje* [Discourses on modern Korean history I: Society and economy in the Japanese colonial period] (Seoul: Chisik Sanŏpsa, 1979), p. 64.

46. Moskowitz, "Creation of the Oriental Development Company," pp. 98–102 and passim.

47. See Sin Yongha, *Chosŏn t'oji chosa saŏp yŏn'gu* [Studies on the Korean cadastral survey] (Seoul: Chisik Sanŏpsa, 1982), pp. 103–4. For English works on this subject see Edwin Harold Gragert, "Landownership Change in Korea under Japanese Rule: 1900–1935" (Ph.D. diss., Columbia University, 1982) and Edward J. Baker, "The Role of Legal Reforms in the Japanese Annexation and Rule of Korea, 1905–1919," in David R. McCann et al., eds., *Studies on Korea in Transition* (Honolulu: Center for Korean Studies, University of Hawaii, 1979), pp. 17–42, esp. 36–38.

48. Kim Yongsŏp, "Hanmal-ilcheha ŭi chijuje — sarye 1," pp. 36, 40.

49. William W. Lockwood, *The Economic Development of Japan: Growth and Structural Change 1868–1938* (Princeton: Princeton University Press, 1954), p. 56. The price of rice in Korea also rose dramatically during this period. In 1910, the price of unpolished rice in Seoul was 9.35 yen per *sŏk*; by 1920, the price had risen to 37.36 yen. See Kim Yongsŏp, "Hanmal-ilcheha ŭi chijuje — sarye 1," p. 49.

50. Ko Cheuk, ed., *Inch'on Kim Sŏngsujŏn (hereafter cited as KSS)* [The biography of Kim Sŏngsu] (Seoul: Inch'on Ki'nyŏmhoe, 1976), p. 43.

51. In the 518 years of the Yi dynasty, a total of only 12 Ulsan Kims, including Kim Inhu, passed the top-level *munkwa* examination — and none at all between 1610 and 1834, a gap of over 200 years. See Edward W. Wagner, "*Munkwa* Project" (Computer printouts, Harvard University, 1971). KSS, p. 43.

52. Kim Sanghyŏng, ed., *Sudang Kim Yŏnsu* (hereafter cited as *KYS*) [Kim Yŏnsu] (Seoul: Sudang Ki'nyŏm Saŏphoe, 1971), p. 135.

53. Among the Kims' Korean landholdings during the colonial period were the following *nongjang*, organized and controlled by Yohyŏp's grandson, Kim Yŏnsu, through the Samyang Company, founded (by Yŏnsu) in 1924: Changsŏng Estate (S. Chŏlla; est. 1924); Chulp'o Estate (N. Chŏlla; est. 1925–26); Koch'ang Estate (N. Chŏlla; est. 1925–26); Myŏnggo Estate (N. Chŏlla; est. 1925–26); Sint'aein Estate (N. Chŏlla; est. 1925–26); Pŏpsŏng Estate (S. Chŏlla; est. 1927); Yŏnggwang Estate (S. Chŏlla; est. 1931); Sonbul

Estate (S. Chŏlla; est. 1937); Haeri Estate (N. Chŏlla; est. 1938). See Kim Sanghong, ed., *Samyang osimnyŏn: 1924–1974* (hereafter cited as *SY*) [Fifty years of Samyang: 1924-1974] (Seoul: CH Samyangsa, 1974), passim. See also *KYS*, passim.

54. *SY*, passim; *KYS*, passim. Reclaimed land was not subject to the South Korean land reforms undertaken between 1948 and 1958: see Sung Hwan Ban et al., *Rural Development*, pp. 285–87.

55. Discussion with officials of the Haeri Branch of the Samyang Salt Company (Samyang Yŏm'ŏpsa), including Kim Sangdŏk and Pak Yundo, at the company, Tongho-ri, Haeri-myŏn, N. Chŏlla, October 1982. Between Aug. 12 and Sept. 11, 1987, about 150 to 250 of Samyang's tenants occupied Samyang's main office in Seoul to force the company to listen to a number of longstanding grievances. Eventually a settlement was reached that allowed the tenants to purchase their land at a relatively favorable price set by the government. As of May 1988 most of the tenants had purchased part or all of their land, but they are still linked to Samyang because of the company's control of the water system in the area. My thanks to Fred Hiatt and Nancy Abelman for providing me with information about this incident.

56. James S. Gale, *Korean Sketches* (Chicago, New York, Toronto: Fleming H. Revell, 1898), p. 11.

57. See Patricia M. Bartz, *South Korea* (Oxford: Clarendon Press, 1972), p. 183.

58. Yasutaka Masanori, ed., *Gunzan kaikōshi* [The history of the opening of the port of Kunsan] (Gunzan: Gunzanfu, 1925), pp. 113–14.

59. *KSS*, pp. 43–44.

60. *KYS*, pp. 54–55. See also Yi Hŭisŭng's preface in Kim Hwajin, ed., *Chisan yugo chŏn* [The complete posthumous writings of Chisan] (Taejŏn: Hoesangsa, 1966). Chisan was Kim Kyŏngjung's pen name.

61. From June 1982 to October 1983.

62. See C. I. Eugene Kim and Han-Kyo Kim, *Korea and the Politics of Imperialism 1876–1910* (Berkeley and Los Angeles: University of California Press, 1967), pp. 203–4.

63. Regarding the Kims' various bureaucratic posts, see Kim Hwangjung, ed. *Ulsan Kimssi chokpo* [The Ulsan Kim genealogy], 3 vols. (Changsŏng, S. Chŏlla: Kim Hwangjung, 1977) 2:112. See also Kim Yongsŏp, "Hanmal-ilcheha ŭi chijuje — sarye 4: Kobu Kimssiga ŭi chiju kyŏngyŏng kwa chabon chŏnhwan" [The landlord system of the late Yi dynasty and Japanese colonial period — case study 4: Landlord management and capital conversion in the Kobu Kim family], *Han'guksa yŏn'gu*, no. 19 (February 1978), p. 70.

64. *KSS*, p. 58. See also Kim Yongsŏp, "Hanmal-ilcheha ŭi chijuje — sarye 4," p. 69.

65. This is an extrapolation from 1925 figures. See Yasutaka, ed., *Gunzan kaikōshi*, p. 113, and Gunzanfu, *Gunzanfushi* [The history of Kunsan] (Gunzan, 1935), p. 179.

66. *SY,* p. 98.

67. Gunzanfu, *Gunzanfushi,* pp. 191–92.

68. Kim Yongsŏp, "Hanmal-ilcheha ŭl chijuje—sarye 4," pp. 90–91, 97, 101–6.

69. Ibid., pp. 91–92. The average yearly income for Kijung's branch of the family between 1918 and 1924 was about 7,000 *sŏk*: see Kim Yongsŏp, "Hanmal-ilcheha ŭi chijuje—sarye 4," p. 109. Kyŏngjung's lands, on the other hand, were producing between 15,000 and 20,000 *sŏk* per year: see *KSS,* p. 46; *KYS,* pp. 53, 134. See also *SY,* p. 74.

70. Kim Yongsŏp, "Hanmal-ilcheha ŭi chijuje—sarye 4," pp. 92–94.

71. Ibid., pp. 92–94.

72. *KSS,* p. 43.

73. For the list of Yŏnil Chŏngs who passed the *munkwa* examination in the Yi dynasty, see Wagner, *"Munkwa* Project."

74. *KSS,* p. 43.

75. See information sign in front of Kim Sŏngsu–Kim Yŏnsu birthplace, Inch'on, Koch'ang County, N. Chŏlla Province.

76. According to Edward W. Wagner, no less than 90 percent of those Koreans in the Yi dynasty who reached the position of High State Councillor had passed the *munkwa* examination: see Wagner, "Ladder of Success," p. 1.

77. See C. Kenneth Quinones, "The Impact of the Kabo Reforms upon Political Role Allocation in Late Yi Korea, 1884–1902," *Occasional Papers on Korea,* no. 4 (September 1975), pp. 1–13.

78. Kim Hwangjung, ed., *Ulsan Kimssi chokpo* 2: 112; Carlos Kenneth Quinones, "The Prerequisites for Power in Late Yi Korea: 1864–1894" (Ph.D. diss., Harvard University, 1975), p. 51.

79. See n. 63, above.

80. See Quinones, "Impact of the Kabo Reforms," p. 7; Palais, *Politics and Policy,* p. 7.

81. *KYS,* p. 51; also *KSS,* p. 44.

82. Grajdanzev, *Modern Korea,* p. 108.

83. These are 1921 figures. See Hoon K. Lee, *Land Utilization and Rural Economy in Korea* (Chicago: University of Chicago Press, 1936), p. 145.

84. Kim Yongsŏp, "Hanmal-ilcheha ŭi chijuje—sarye 4," pp. 85–87, 109.

85. By 1924, Kijung's family had increased its 1918 holdings by about 120 *chŏngbo* and had a total of 1,978 tenants, 5 of whom were Japanese. Kim Yongsŏp, "Hanmal-ilcheha ŭi chijuje—sarye 4," pp. 85, 88.

86. *SY,* p. 66.

2. An Industrial Bourgeoisie: Transition and Emergence, 1919–45

1. Cho Kijun, *Han'guk kiŏpkasa,* pp. 52, 54.

2. Ibid., pp. 55–56. See also Yi Kibaek, *Han'guksa sillon,* pp. 346–47.

3. See Cho Kijun, *Han'guk kiŏpkasa*, pp. 56, 59, 108–80 passim, 397. Min Pyŏngsŏk (Yŏhŭng Min clan) passed the *munkwa* examination in 1879: see Wagner, "*Munkwa* Project"; see also Kita Tadai, *Chōsen jinji kōshinroku* [Who's who in Korea] (Keijō: Chōsen Shimbunsha, 1935), p. 392.

4. Kwŏn T'aeŏk, "Kyŏngsŏng Chingnyu Chusik Hoesa ŭi sŏngnip kwa kyŏngyŏng" [The founding and management of the Kyŏngsŏng Cord Company, Ltd.], *Han'guk saron*, no. 6 (December 1980); pp. 298–99. My thanks to Soon Won Park for bringing this article to my attention.

5. The president of the company (as of 1915) was Yun Ch'iso, the father of Yun Posŏn and the first cousin of Yun Ch'iho. See Kwŏn T'aeŏk, "Kyŏngsŏng Chingnyu," p. 300. See also Yun Yonggu, *Haep'yŏng Yunssi taedongbo* [The Haep'yŏng Yun genealogy], 5 vols. (Seoul: Haep'yŏng Yunssi Taedongbo Kanhaeng Wiwŏnhoe, 1983) 3: 558–59, 617. My thanks to Edward W. Wagner and the late Sungha Kim of Harvard for helping me to trace these connections in the clan genealogy. See also Pak Inhwan, ed. *Kyŏngbang yuksimnyŏn* (hereafter cited as *KY*) [Sixty years of Kyŏngbang], (Seoul: CH Kyŏngbang, 1980), p. 50.

6. Kwŏn T'aeŏk, "Kyŏngsŏng Chingnyu," p. 302, 304, 306.

7. Ibid., p. 305.

8. Ibid., p. 300.

9. See *KSS*, p. 156. Kwŏn T'aeŏk, "Kyŏngsŏng Chingnyu," suggests that the traditional market, although limited (p. 315) and in danger of becoming stagnated (pp. 315–16), was not yet in actual decline in 1917 (pp. 314–15) and that the company's problems were due less to the market than to the economic fluctuations of the First World War and to internal management difficulties. Later in the article, however, he does cite decreasing demand in the large cities (such as Seoul) as a factor in the company's eventual failure (p. 315).

10. *KSS*, pp. 41, 47, 350.

11. The *Tonga ilbo*, one of South Korea's major newspapers and the core of a large-scale publishing empire, was founded by Kim Sŏngsu in 1920. In 1932, Kim took over and developed the Posŏng Junior College (Posŏng Chŏnmun Hakkyo), which later became Koryŏ University. See *KSS*, pp. 91–107. After August 1945, Kim was a pivotal figure in the formation and financing of the conservative Korean Democratic party (KDP), which became the main opposition party in South Korea in the 1950s. See Bruce Cumings, *The Origins of the Korean War: Liberation and the Emergence of Separate Regimes* (Princeton: Princeton University Press, 1981), pp. 92–99; also *KSS*, pp. 491–522; Gregory Henderson, *The Politics of the Vortex* (Cambridge: Harvard University Press, 1968), pp. 274–78; Sungjoo Han, *The Failure of Democracy in South Korea* (Berkeley and Los Angeles: University of California Press, 1974), pp. 34–35. Kim was also vice-president of the Republic of Korea under Syngman Rhee (May 1951 to May 1952).

12. See James B. Palais, "Stability in Yi Dynasty Korea: Equilibrium Systems and Marginal Adjustments," *Occasional Papers on Korea*, no. 3 (June 1975), pp. 1–18.

13. As in China, "self-strengthening" in Korea originally meant the adoption of Western technology (especially military technology), and it was in this sense that King Kojong first initiated such a movement as early as 1879: see Deuchler, *Confucian Gentlemen*, p. 99. The Kaehwadang, on the other hand, tended from the beginning to see "self-strengthening" in broader terms (Meiji Japan rather than China was their model): a multifaceted process of modernization that embraced culture and values as well as technology. It was in this latter sense that the term *chagang* was being used on the eve of the annexation in 1910. See Yi Kibaek, *Han'guksa sillon*, pp. 327–34, 387; also Deuchler, *Confucian Gentlemen*, pp. 151–52, 199–202. An excellent English-language study of the Enlightenment movement is also now available: see Vipan Chandra, *Imperialism, Resistance, and Reform in Late Nineteenth-Century Korea: Enlightenment and the Independence Club* (Berkeley: Institute of East Asian Studies, University of California-Berkeley, 1988).

14. See, for example, any issue of the *Honam hakpo*, first published in June 1908.

15. See, for example, Yun Chuch'an, "Chesŏng kaeryang" [Some improvements in character], *Honam hakpo*, no. 3 (August 1908), p. 39.

16. See Yi Kibaek, *Han'guksa sillon*, pp. 391–94.

17. *KSS*, p. 59.

18. *KSS*, pp. 45–46. See also Kim Yongsŏp, "Hanmal-ilcheha ŭi chijuje—sarye 4," pp. 78–79.

19. See the *Honam hakpo*, no. 1 (June 1908), pp. 57–58 (the second character of Kim Kyŏngjung's name is misprinted there). See also Kim Yongsŏp, "Hanmal-ilcheha ŭi chijuje—sarye 4," pp. 79–80.

20. Or 13 *se*. See *KSS*, p. 48.

21. On Ko Chŏngju, see *KSS*, pp. 49–50. See also Wagner, "Munkwa Project"; *Honam hakpo*, no. 1 (June 1908), pp. 57–58; Kim Yongsŏp, "Hanmal-ilcheha ŭi chijuje—sarye 4," p. 79. Ko Chŏngju was the father of Ko Kwangjun, whose son, Ko Cheuk, eventually became president of *Tonga ilbo* and the editor of *KSS*: see *KSS*, pp. 49, 66.

22. *KSS*, p. 59.

23. See, for example, Namgung Yŏng's article, "A Congratulatory Address" (in English) celebrating the first issue of the magazine in *Sangŏpkye*, no. 1 (October 1908), pp. 4–5. See also "Sangyongŏ Han-Il-Yŏng taejo" [A comparison of commercial terms in Korean, Japanese, and English], *Sangŏpkye*, no. 3 (December 1908), pp. 15–16. Yun Chŏngha, the editor of the magazine, was originally from S. Chŏlla. In 1908 he was a student at the Tokyo Higher Commercial School. After graduation, he returned to Korea and became the first editor of the *Sanggong wŏlbo*, the monthly journal of the Korean Chamber of Commerce and Industry. Later he helped Kim Sŏngsu set up the

Kyŏngsŏng Spinning and Weaving Company and was one of the original stock-
holders. See *Sangŏpkye*, no. 1 (October 1908), p. 1. See also Cho Kijun,
Han'guk kiŏpkasa, pp. 158, 203–4. See also Kyŏngsŏng Pangjik CH, Record
of the General Stockholders Meetings, Minutes of the General Meeting to
Establish the Company, Oct. 5, 1919. Mun Sangu was the publisher of
Sangŏpkye. After his return to Korea he worked at the Hanil Bank in Seoul,
where he helped the wealthy S. Kyŏngsang landlord Yun Sangŭn set up the
Kup'o Bank in 1912, and eventually Yun made him the bank's manager
(chibaein). It is not clear exactly when Mun established his connection with
the Kims. It may have been through Yun, who was one of the original supporters of Kyŏngbang and served on the company's first board of directors. In
any case, by 1932 Mun was the manager *(chibaein)* of Kim Yŏnsu's Haedong
Bank in Seoul and eventually became a Kyŏngbang stockholder and auditor
(kamsayŏk). See *Sangŏpkye*, no. 1 (October 1908). Also Cho Kijun, *Han'guk
kiŏpkasa*, pp. 146, 300. See also Kyŏngsŏng Pangjik CH, Record of the Board
of Directors Meetings, Minutes of Board Meeting no. 1, Oct. 5, 1919, and
Board Meeting no. 90, Oct. 7, 1940; also List of Stockholders, Nov. 30, 1944,
p. 10.

24. This was the famous "gentlemen's sightseeing group" *(sinsa yuramdan)*.
See Deuchler, *Confucian Gentlemen*, pp. 101–2.

25. It was Ko Chŏngju's belief, for example, that one had to go to Shanghai
or Tokyo to experience the full impact of the "new learning," and his school
was designed in large part to prepare students (including his own children)
for such trips abroad: see *KSS*, pp. 49–50, 61.

26. Ibid., pp. 64, 67–68. Song Chinu (1890–1945) was originally from the
Ch'angp'yŏng area, and his father had been a close friend of Ko Chŏngju:
see *KSS*, p. 56. The exceptionally close relationship between Kim and Song
that began in Ch'angp'yŏng lasted until Song's assassination in 1945. While
Song was the older (by one year) and more outspoken and publicly visible
of the two men, he was dependent on Kim's immense financial resources for
his various activities (while in Tokyo, for example, Kim helped pay Song's
tuition at Meiji University Law School), and most of his activities seem to
have been a reflection of Kim's own personal interest. In 1962, Yu Chin'o
characterized the relationship between the two men in the *Tonga ilbo*:

As everyone knows, Kim Sŏngsu and Song Chinu were not just close friends; as unique
kindred spirits, they seemed to become one and the same person spiritually and physically. They spent their whole lives together—Kim behind the scenes as the chief of
staff, making plans and providing the capital for each undertaking, Song as the field
general leading the men into battle. As a result, on the surface Song appeared to be
the senior of the two in appearance, self-confidence, and action. But one wonders
whether Kim was not in fact the senior. Given Song's openness and Kim's delight in
humor, whenever the two of them were together in the same drinking party, they would
generally tease each other unmercifully. . . .But if Kim ever seriously made the slightest
sharp remark, Song would just close his mouth tight and blink (*KSS*, pp. 207–8).

27. Ch'ang Nanggaek, "Paengman changja ŭi paengmanwŏn'gwan: Chakko ssŭgosiptanŭn Kim Sŏngsussi" [Millionaires look at their millions: I want to keep spending, says Kim Sŏngsu], Samch'ŏlli 7 (September 1935): 47.

28. *KYS*, pp. 77–78. Yŏnsu's wife (like Sŏngsu's) came from a prominent S. Chŏlla family with good connections in the bureaucracy. Her father, Pak Pongju (Ch'ungju Pak clan), had passed the *munkwa* examination in 1894 and subsequently served as the magistrate of Kobu (Koch'ang) County and as a second minister (*ch'amp'an*) on one of the government boards. See *KYS*, p. 81; Wagner, "*Munkwa* Project."

29. *KSS*, pp. 780–81; *KYS*, pp. 329–30.

30. *KSS*, p. 781; *KYS*, p. 330.

31. See Vipin Chandra, "An Outline Study of the Ilchin-hoe (Advancement Society) of Korea," *Occasional Papers on Korea*, no. 2 (March 1974), pp. 58–68.

32. See Kim Sŏngsu, "Ōkuma Shigenobu wa Chosŏn yuhaksaeng" [Ōkuma Shigenobu and Korean students in Japan], Samch'ŏlli 6 (May 1934): 97. See also Edwin O. Reischauer and Albert Craig, *Japan: Tradition and Transformation* (Boston: Houghton Mifflin Co., 1978), p. 142.

33. See Takafusa Nakamura, *Economic Growth in Prewar Japan*, trans. Robert A. Feldman (New Haven: Yale University Press, 1983), pp. 22, 147.

34. Ibid., pp. 23–24, 35, 60–63, 66, 151.

35. See Keizo Seki, *The Cotton Industry of Japan* (Tokyo: Japan Society for the Promotion of Science, 1956), pp. 21–23. See also Sampei Takako, *Nippon mengyō hattatsushi* [The history of the development of the Japanese cotton industry] (Tokyo: Keiō Shobō, 1941), pp. 164–83.

36. See Kajimura, *Chōsen ni okeru shihonshugi*, pp. 40–43, 127–42. According to Kajimura, the influx of foreign goods began even before 1876, but the native industries were able to hold their own until the 1890s (after the Sino-Japanese War). Thereafter Japanese penetration of the Korean economy escalated as Japan became more and more of an exporter of manufactured goods (and especially textiles).

37. See *KY*, p. 33. See also *KYS*, p. 102; Cho Kijun, *Han'guk kiŏpkasa*, pp. 260–61; Yi Kanghyŏn [L. Saeng], "Kongin ŭige koham" [A message to Korean workers], *Sanggong wŏlbo*, no. 19 (May 1911), pp. 3–5.

38. See Nakamura, *Economic Growth*, pp. 153, 213. See also Kozo Yamamura, "The Japanese Economy, 1911–1930: Concentration, Conflicts, and Crises," in Bernard S. Silverman and H. D. Harootunian, eds., *Japan in Crisis: Essays on Taishō Democracy* (Princeton: Princeton University Press, 1974), pp. 301–9. See also Ushisaburo Kobayashi, *The Basic Industries and Social History of Japan 1914–1918* (New Haven: Yale University Press, 1930), pp. 11–53, 239–42, 272–74. See also Janet E. Hunter, ed., *Concise Dictionary of Japanese History* (Berkeley and Los Angeles: University of California Press, 1984), pp. 178–79.

39. Hoon K. Lee, *Land Utilization*, pp. 262–66.

40. For a chart of the rice prices per *sŏk* obtained by the Kims (Kijung's family only) between 1918 and 1924, see Kim Yongsŏp, "Hanmal-ilcheha ŭi chijuje: sarye 4," p. 110. Nishimura is quoted in Hoon K. Lee, *Land Utilization*, pp. 127–28.

41. Kim Yongsŏp, "Hanmal-ilcheha ŭi chijuje: sarye 4," pp. 90–91.

42. See Hoon K. Lee, *Land Utilization*, p. 176.

43. See Sang-Chul Suh, *Growth and Structural Changes*, p. 74. See also Hoon K. Lee, pp. 118–31. The financing terms for such land improvement projects were quite generous. Kim Yŏnsu, for example, was granted a 175,000-yen loan from the Chōsen Industrial Bank for a land reclamation project in Sonbul Township, Hamp'yŏng County, S. Chŏlla Province—and that later became part of Kim's Sonbul Estate (Sonbul Nongjang). The first half of the principal was to be paid back at 4.6 percent interest, the second half at 6.7 percent, over a period of 20 years with a four-year grace period. See letter to Kim Yŏnsu from Hamp'yŏng County Magistrate, Jan. 16, 1936, Hapcha Hoesa Samyangsa Papers, CH Samyangsa, Seoul.

44. See Hoon K. Lee, *Land Utilization*, p. 170.

45. Arno S. Pearse, *The Cotton Industry of Japan and China* (Manchester: International Cotton Federation, 1929), pp. 20–21. See also Sampei Takako, *Nippon mengyō hattatsushi*, pp. 164–73.

46. See Sang-Chul Suh, *Growth and Structural Changes*, pp. 7–10. Also Hochin Choi, "The Process of Industrial Modernization in Korea," *Journal of Social Sciences and Humanities*, no. 26 (June 1967), pp. 8–11. For a good synopsis and analysis of the Company Law, see Kobayashi Hideo, " 'Kaisha Rei' kenkyū nōto" [Research notes on the "Company Law"], *Kaikyo*, no. 3 (December 1975), pp. 21–36.

47. Kobayashi, " 'Kaisha Rei,' " p. 25.

48. Ibid., pp. 26–28.

49. See Kawai Akitake, *Chōsen kōgyō no gendankai* [The present stage of Korean industry] (Keijō: Tōyō Keizai Shimpōsha, 1943), pp. 108–10.

50. See Nakamura, *Economic Growth*, pp. 152–55. See also Kawai, *Chōsen kōgyō*, pp. 108–10.

51. See Kobayashi, " 'Kaisha Rei,' " pp. 35–36. At the time of the annexation in 1910, Japan promised the other foreign powers that the existing tariff rates would continue as they were for the next ten years. After 1920, however, Japan began to eliminate tariffs between Korea and Japan, and by 1923 all tariffs, except on liquors and textiles, had been abolished. The reason for retaining these two tariffs was not to protect such industries in Korea, but to preserve an important source of tax revenue for the Government-General. The tariff on cloth had originally been 7.5 percent, but it was revised downward in 1927 to 5 percent. See Government-General of Chosen, *Annual Report on Administration of Chosen: 1935–1936* (Keijo, 1936), pp. 53–54. See also Kawai, *Chōsen kōgyō*, pp. 102–3.

52. See, for example, Shiomi Tsunesaburō, "Chōsen ni okeru bōseki kōgyō

no genjō (II)" [The present condition of the spinning industry in Korea: II] *Dai Nippon Bōseki Rengōkai geppō*, no. 589 (November 1941), p. 63.

53. Chōsen Sōtokufu, *Sangyō Chōsa Iinkai giji sokkiroku* [The stenographic record of the proceedings of the industrial commission] (September 1921), Special Committee on Sec. 1, pp. 1–25.

54. See Cho Kijun, *Han'guk chabonjuŭi sŏngnipsaron*, pp. 476–77; F. C. Jones, *Manchuria Since 1931* (London: Royal Institute of International Affairs, 1949), p. 124.

55. On Yamamoto's role in the establishment of Chōbō, see Shiomi Tsunesaburō, "Chōsen ni okeru . . . ," p. 63. For a listing of the officers and major shareholders in the company (including Yamamoto) in 1933, see *Chōsen GKKY*, pp. 130–31. Yamamoto also served as Chōbō's president; see Chōsen Ginkō Chōsaka, *Saikin Chōsen ni okeru daikōgyō yakushin to sono shihon keitō* [The recent rapid advance and capital connections of large-scale industry in Korea], Research Report no. 16 (March 1935), unpaginated chart at the end of the report. On Yamamoto as continental empire builder, see Roberts, *Mitsui*, passim.

56. Chōsen Sōtokufu, *Sangyō Chōsa Iinkai giji sokkiroku*, Special Committee on Sec. 1, pp. 3–4, 6–7; Kondō Ken'ichi, ed., *Chōsen Sōtokufu shiryō senshū: Saitō Sōtoku no bunka tōchi* [Selected documents of the Government-General of Korea: The enlightened rule of Governor-General Saitō], Yūhō Series (Tokyo: Yūhō Kyōkai, 1970), p. 70.

57. Kobayashi, " 'Kaisha Rei,' " pp. 28–29.

58. Frank Prentiss Baldwin, Jr., "The March First Movement: Korean Challenge and Japanese Response" (Ph.D. diss., Columbia University, 1969), chaps. 5, 7.

59. Ibid., chap. 8. Also Wonmo Dong, "Japanese Colonial Policy and Practice in Korea, 1905–1945: A Study in Assimilation" (Ph.D. diss., Georgetown University, 1965), pp. 245–55, 293–313. Yi Kibaek, *Han'guksa sillon*, pp. 407–8.

60. Baldwin points out that Hara Kei, prime minister at the time, regarded any talk of Korean independence as ridiculous and unthinkable: see Baldwin, "March First Movement," p. 183.

61. Ibid., pp. 207–13.

62. Ibid., pp. 96, 99, 119–22 and chap. 4 n. 4. Also *Chōsen san'ichi dokuritsu sōjō jiken: Gaikyō, shisō oyobi undō* [The Korean March First independence riots: The general situation, ideology, and activities], reprint of the original report of the Chōsen Kempeitai Shireibu (Tokyo: Gannandō Shoten, 1969), pp. 107–8.

63. Between January and March 1919, Kim Sŏngsu and his two main associates at Chungang School, Song Chinu (principal of the school at the time) and Hyŏn Sangyun (a Chungang instructor) met regularly to exchange ideas about the independence movement with Ch'oe Rin, the principal of the Posŏng School (then owned and run by the Ch'ŏndogyo) and the person whom Bald-

win calls "the driving force behind the March First Movement." According to Hyŏn, Kim also contributed "thousands of yen" to another important figure in the movement, the Presbyterian minister Yi Sŭnghun. As usual, Kim kept a low public profile and, apparently at the urging of friends, deliberately absented himself from Seoul on March 1 (he was in Chulp'o) to avoid being directly implicated in the movement and thereby risk the possible closing of Chungang School. Song and Hyŏn were subsequently arrested by the Japanese police. See *KSS*, pp. 128–35. Also Baldwin, "March First Movement," pp. 54, 247 n. 22, 249–50 n. 33.

64. This movement was originally launched in P'yŏngyang in July 1920 by Cho Mansik and other Christian nationalists, and later spread all over the country. In January 1923, Song Chinu and others reorganized the movement on a national basis by incorporating over twenty groups into the Association to Promote Korean Goods (Chosŏn Mulsan Changnyŏhoe). Kim Sŏngsu's newspaper, the *Tonga ilbo*, actively supported the movement. Nationalistic sentiment notwithstanding, Song's reorganization and active promotion of the movement on a national scale coincided nicely with the first appearance of Kyŏngbang's cotton cloth in the Korean market in April 1923. See *KSS*, pp. 244–47; Cho Kijun, *Han'guk chabonjŭui sŏngnipsaron*, pp. 527–53; Kim Yongsŏp, "Hanmal-ilcheha ŭi chijuje—sarye 4," pp. 124–31.

65. Quoted in Kang Tongjin, *Nihon no Chōsen shihai seisakushi* [Studies in the history of Japan's policy of control in Korea] (Tokyo: Tōkyō Daigaku Shuppankai, 1979), p. 203. The original document is included among the Saitō Makoto papers (no. 742) in the National Diet Library: see Kang, pp. 225 n. 123, 457. There is also a Korean version of Kang's book: see Kang Tongjin, *Ilcheŭi Han'guk ch'imnyak chŏngch'aeksa* [The history of the Japanese imperial policy of aggression in Korea], Onŭrŭi Sasang Sinsŏ Series no. 14 (Seoul: Han'gilsa, 1980). The same document is also quoted in Kim Chunch'ŏl, *Ilcheha ŭi Han'guk minjok chabon kwa minjok sahak e kwanhan yŏn'gu* [Studies of Korean national capital and national private education under Japanese imperialist rule] (Seoul: Sangjosa, 1984), p. 206. Kim identifies the document as a proposal from Vice-Minister of War Yamanashi to Governor-General Saitō: see p. 207 n.7.

66. As mentioned earlier, the main impetus for the abolition of the Company Law was economic and came from within Japan itself, but the March First movement also made the law's abolition desirable from a political point of view. See Kobayashi, " 'Kaisha Rei,' " pp. 34–35.

67. See Chōsen Sōtokufu, *Sangyō Chōsa Iinkai giji sokkiroku*, General Session, Day 2, pp. 173–74. See also *Tonga ilbo*, Sept. 6, 1921, p. 2. The Koreans attending the conference were: Hyŏn Kibong, Chŏng Chaehak, Cho Pyŏngnyŏl, Han Sangnyong, Pak Yŏnggun, Song Pyŏngjun, Yi Wanyong, Ch'oe Hŭisun, and Cho Chint'ae.

68. Chōsen Sōtokufu, *Sangyō Chōsa Iinkai giji sokkiroku*, General Session, Day 2, p. 144; General Session, Day 1, pp. 41, 75; General Session, Day

2, p. 160; Special Committee on Sec. 1, Day 3, pp. 9,10; General Session, Day 1, p. 75; General Session, Day 2, p. 160; General Session, Day 1, pp. 8, 40–41; Special Committee on Sec. 1, Day 3, pp. 2, 105, 129.

69. See Baldwin, "March First Movement," pp. 186–91.

70. *Tonga ilbo*, Sept. 13, 1919.

71. Cumings, *Origins of the Korean War*, pp. 66–67.

72. Cumings, in fact, makes this same point; ibid., p. 7.

73. See Jones and Sakong, *Government, Business, and Entrepreneurship*, pp. 23–24. Edward S. Mason et al., *The Economic and Social Modernization of the Republic of Korea*, Studies in the Modernization of the Republic of Korea: 1945–1975 (Cambridge: Council on East Asian Studies, Harvard University, 1980), p. 76 (table).

74. Grajdanzev, *Modern Korea*, p. 177.

75. Suh, *Growth and Structural Changes*, p. 103.

76. Ibid., p. 85.

77. See the *Chōsen jitsugyō kurabu* 17 (May 1939): 90.

78. Ibid., pp. 91–98.

79. Ibid.

80. See, for example, Suh, *Growth and Structural Changes*, p. 110.

81. See Paul W. Kuznets, *Economic Growth and Structure in the Republic of Korea* (New Haven: Yale University Press, 1977), p. 21. According to a 1941 study by the Seoul Chamber of Commerce and Industry, over 90 percent of the city's factories were unincorporated establishments, and about 60 percent of those were Korean-owned. See Daniel Sungil Juhn, "Entrepreneurship in an Underdeveloped Economy: The Case of Korea, 1890–1940" (D.B.A. diss., George Washington University, 1965), pp. 138–39. See Kyŏngsŏng Pangjik CH, Business Report for the Thirty-Sixth Fiscal Period, May 31, 1945.

82. See Jones and Sakong, *Government, Business, and Entrepreneurship*, p. 25.

83. See Kim Chunggil, ed., *Hwasin osimnyŏnsa: 1926–1976* [A fifty-year history of Hwasin: 1926–1976] (Seoul: Hwasin Sanŏp CH, 1977), pp. 97-98. Also Myŏng Chuhyŏn, ed., *OB isimnyŏnsa* [A twenty-year history of the OB Company] (Seoul: Tongyang Maekchu CH, 1972), pp. 61–62.

84. See Jones and Sakong, *Government, Business, and Entrepreneurship*, p. 25.

85. See, for example, Daniel Juhn's study of Korean entrepreneurship in Seoul and P'yŏngyang in Juhn, "Entrepreneurship," pp. 129–63. For a good study of the development of the Korean-owned knitwear industry in P'yŏngyang, see Kajimura Hideki, *Chōsen ni okeru shihonshugi*, pp. 143–212. See also Cho Kijun, *Han'guk kiŏpkasa*, passim.

86. See Jones and Sakong, *Government, Business, and Entrepreneurship*, p. 28. Also Juhn "Entrepreneurship," p. 122. See, for example, *Chōsen GKKY*, passim. See also Gary R. Saxonhouse, "Working Koreans in Korea and Japan in the Inter-War Period" (Unpublished paper, Dept. of Economics, University

of Michigan, Ann Arbor, Michigan). My thanks to Prof. Saxonhouse for send-ing me a copy.

87. See Yi Pyŏngch'ŏl, "Chaegye hoego" [Memoirs of the business world], in *Chaegye hoego wŏllo kiŏpinp'yŏn I* [Memoirs of the business world: Senior businessmen, vol. 1] (Seoul: Han'guk Ilbosa Ch'ulp'an'guk, 1984), pp. 280–88, 294–97.

88. See Ku Chagyŏng, ed., *Yŏn'am Ku Inhoe* [Ku Inhoe] (Yŏn'am Ki'nyŏm Saŏphoe, 1979), pp. 72–75, 116–18. Unlike Yi and Ku, Chŏng came from poor peasant stock in Kangwŏn Province. See Pak Tongsun, *Chaebŏl ŭi ppuri* [The roots of the business groups] (Seoul: CH T'aech'ang Unhwasa, 1980), pp. 350, 355–56; see also Jones and Sakong, *Government, Business, and Entrepreneurship*, pp. 354, 356.

89. Yi Pyŏngch'ŏl, "Chaegye hoego," p. 288; Ku Chagyŏng, ed., *Yŏn'am Ku Inhoe*, p. 105; Pak Tongsun, *Chaebŏl ŭi ppuri*, p. 355.

90. What is important to grasp here is that Kyŏngbang was an exceptional Korean company during the colonial period only in its scale and scope of operation. Even smaller Korean companies, such as those founded by Yi and Ku, often tended to exhibit patterns of growth quite similar, though on a smaller scale, to Kyŏngbang's, enjoying, for example, access to funding from the Chōsen Industrial Bank and other Japanese financial organizations. See Yi Pyŏngch'ŏl, "Chaegye hoego," p. 289; Ku Chagyŏng, ed., *Yŏn'am Ku Inhoe*, p. 118. See also Kajimura Hideki, *Chōsen ni okeru shihonshugi*, p. 169. While Chŏng Chuyŏng appears to have relied on personal rather than bank loans to finance his business during the colonial period, like the Kims he profited from the war boom after 1937. See Pak Tongsun, *Chaebŏl ŭi ppuri*, p. 356.

91. This was Chungang School. See *KSS*, pp. 91–119.

92. See Kwŏn T'aeŏk, "Kyŏngsŏng Chingnyu," pp. 310–17.

93. *KSS*, pp. 155–56.

94. *KSS*, pp. 156–59; *KYS*, pp. 103–4. The Company Law was not officially repealed until April 1920. See Kobayashi Hideo, " 'Kaisha Rei,' " p. 35. Kim Sŏngsu and his associates applied to the Government-General Bureau of Indus-try (Shokusan Kyoku) for permission to establish Kyŏngbang in mid-August, 1919. Permission was granted on Oct. 5, 1919. See *KY*, pp. 33, 51.

95. Kyŏngsŏng Pangjik CH, Record of the General Stockholders Meetings, Minutes of the General Meeting to Establish the Company, Oct. 5, 1919.

96. Ibid. It is recorded in the minutes of the meeting, for example, that a certain Kohari Jūkichi seconded a motion by Kim Sŏngsu to amend a phrase in the company's articles of incorporation.

97. Yŏnsu graduated from Kyoto Imperial University in April 1921 and returned immediately to Korea. A year later he was appointed managing direc-tor of Kyŏngbang (a position he shared with Yi Kanghyŏn). See *KYS*, pp. 96, 107; Kyŏngsŏng Pangjik CH, Record of the Board of Directors Meetings, Board Meeting no. 16, April 26, 1922; see also *KYS*, pp. 247–48.

98. Sŏngsu continued to control a considerable number of shares in the company both personally and through various members of his family, as well as through various corporate entities such as the Chungang Institute. See Kyŏngsŏng Pangjik CH, List of Stockholders, Nov. 30, 1944. In 1929 Sŏngsu became an official adviser (komun) to the company, a post he resigned in 1939. See Kyŏngsŏng Pangjik CH, Record of the Board of Directors Meetings, Minutes of Board Meeting no. 44, Mar. 20, 1929; Minutes of Board Meeting no. 83, Sept. 14, 1939.

99. See "Manmok chusi hanŭn samdae chaengp'aejŏn," p. 46.

Part II. The Patterns of Growth

1. For a good general introduction to the term, see the entry for "national bourgeoisie" in Tom Bottomore, ed., A Dictionary of Marxist Thought (Cambridge: Harvard University Press, 1983), pp. 345–46; see also the "national bourgeoisie" listing in C. D. Kernig, ed., Marxism, Communism and Western Society: A Comparative Encyclopedia (New York: Herder and Herder, 1973) 6: 5–8. See also Kajimura Hideki, Chōsen ni okeru shihonshugi, pp. 217–24; also Ko Pyŏngu, "Minjok chabon," in Kwŏn Oik et al., eds., Kyŏngjehak taesajŏn, p. 624. One of the best expositions of the difference between "national" and "comprador" capital was given by Mao Tse-tung in 1939 in a work called The Chinese Revolution and the Chinese Communist Party: see Selected Works of Mao Tse-tung (Peking: Foreign Language Press, 1975) 2: 320–21. A similar exposition can be found in a work by Kim Ilsŏng entitled Chosŏn kongsanjuŭijadŭl ŭi immu [The mission of Korean Communists] that was allegedly written in 1937: see Kim Ilsŏng chŏjakchip [The works of Kim Ilsŏng] (P'yŏngyang: Chosŏn Nodongdang Ch'ulp'ansa, 1979) 1:159ff. On the doubtful authenticity of such pre-1945 writings by Kim Ilsŏng, see Dae-Sook Suh, Korean Communism 1945– 1980: A Reference Guide to the Political System (Honolulu: University Press of Hawaii, 1981), pp. 9–10.

2. See, for example, the 1966 debate between Hŏ Changman and Kim Hŭiil in the Yŏksa kwahak: Hŏ Changman, "1920 nyŏndae minjok kaeryangjuŭi ŭi kyegŭp kich'o haemyŏng essŏ chegi toenŭn myŏkkaji munje" [Various problems in elucidating the class basis of the national reformism of the 1920s], Yŏksa kwahak 3 (1966): 37–43; Kim Hŭiil, "Minjok kaeryangjuŭi ŭi kyegŭpchŏk kich'o nŭn yesok purŭjyoaji ida" [The class basis of national reformism was the comprador bourgeoisie], Yŏksa kwahak 4 (1966): 38–46. See also Kajimura Hideki, Chōsen ni okeru shihonshugi, pp. 225–31. North Korean scholars tend to use the term yesok ("subordinate" or "servile") rather than the usual maep'an to describe the comprador bourgeoisie, but the two terms seem to be interchangeable. In North Korean dictionaries, for example, maep'an chabon is used to define yesok chabon and vice versa. For a good general overview of recent scholarly trends in South Korea on the question of "national capital" formation during the colonial period, see Yi Sŭngnyŏl,

"Ilche sigi minjok chabonga nonjaeng" [The debate on national capitalists in the period of Japanese imperialism], *Yŏksa pip'yŏng* (Summer 1990), pp. 56–67. See also Yi Han'gu, *Ilcheha Han'guk kiŏp sŏllip undongsa* [The history of efforts to establish Korean companies under Japanese imperialism] (Seoul: Tosŏ Ch'ulp'an: Ch'ŏngsa, 1989), especially pp. 180–229.

3. Cho Kijun, "Han'guk minjok kiŏp kŏnsŏl ŭi sasangjŏk paegyŏng: Inch'on Kim Sŏngsu ŭi minjok kiŏp hwaltong" [The intellectual background behind the establishment of Korean nationalist businesses: The nationalist business activities of Kim Sŏngsu] in Kwŏn Ogi, ed., *Inch'on Kim Sŏngsu ŭi aejok sasang kwa kŭ silch'ŏn* [The patriotism of Kim Sŏngsu in thought and deed] (Seoul: Tonga Ilbosa, 1982), p. 145.

4. Cho Kijun, "Han'guk minjok kiŏp kŏnsŏl," p. 146.

5. See, for example, Kajimura, *Chōsen no okeru shihonshugi*, pp. 213–42.

3. Class and State: The Financial Nexus

1. See James B. Palais, *Politics and Policy*, pp. 6–16; Palais, "Political Leadership in the Yi Dynasty" in Dae-Sook Suh and Chae-Jin Lee, eds., *Political Leadership in Korea* (Seattle: University of Washington Press, 1976), pp. 3–35; Palais, "Stability in Yi Dynasty Korea," pp. 1–17. See also Edward Willett Wagner, *The Literati Purges: Political Conflict in Early Yi Korea* (Cambridge: East Asian Research Center, Harvard University, 1974), pp. 1–22, 51–69, 121–23.

2. See Alexander Gerschenkron, *Economic Backwardness in Historical Perspective* (Cambridge: Harvard University Press, 1962), pp. 5–30.

3. See Edward I-te Chen, "The Attempt to Integrate the Empire: Legal Perspectives," in Ramon H. Myers and Mark R. Peattie, eds., *The Japanese Colonial Empire, 1895–1945*, p. 259.

4. Chen, "Attempt to Integrate the Empire," pp. 262–66. For a new theoretical and historical study of the modern Korean state, see Jung-eun Woo, "State Power, Finance, and Industrialization of Korea" (Ph.D. diss., Columbia University, 1988).

5. The exception was Admiral Saitō Makoto (1919–27 and 1929–31).

6. For biographical sketches of Ugaki, Minami, and Koiso, as well as of other Korean *sōtoku*, see Shimonaka Yasaburō, ed., *Dai jimmei jiten* [Great biographical dictionary], 10 vols. (Tokyo: Heibonsha, 1953–55); also Itō Dōjin, ed., *Gendai jimbutsu jiten* [Modern biographical dictionary] (Tokyo: Asahi Shimbunsha, 1977). See also Ugaki Kazunari, *Ugaki nikki* [The Ugaki diary] (Tokyo: Asahi Shimbunsha, 1954); Mitarai Tatsuo, *Minami Jirō* [Minami Jirō] (Tokyo: Minami Jirō Denki Kankōkai, 1957).

7. See Richard Storry, *The Double Patriots: A Study of Japanese Nationalism* (Boston: Houghton Mifflin Company, 1957), pp. 37–38.

8. T. A. Bisson, *Japan's War Economy* (New York: International Secretariat, Institute of Pacific Relations, 1945), pp. 3, 100–2.

9. See Jones, *Manchuria Since 1931*, pp. 35–39.

10. See Chalmers Johnson, *MITI and the Japanese Miracle: The Growth of Industrial Policy, 1925–1975* (Stanford: Stanford University Press, 1982), pp. 124–25.

11. Jones, *Manchuria Since 1931*, pp. 147–49. See also Roberts, *Mitsui*, pp. 320, 323. New work is now in progress that challenges the conventional view of the Kwantung Army as radically anticapitalist. See Y. Tak Matsusaka, "The Kwantung Army and the Reorganization of the South Manchuria Rai way Company" (Paper presented at the 42nd Annual Meeting of the Association for Asian Studies, Chicago, April 7, 1990).

12. As opposed to the more radically anticapitalist "Imperial Way Faction" (Kōdōha). See Storry, *Double Patriots*, p. 138 n.1. Such army factions, however, were neither comprehensive nor always clear-cut: see James B. Crowley, "Japanese Army Factionalism in the Early 1930's," *JAS* 21, no. 3 (May 1962): 309–26.

13. See Kobayashi Hideo, *Daitōa Kyōeiken no keisei to hōkai* [The rise and fall of the greater East Asia co-prosperity sphere] (Tokyo: Ochanomizu Shobō, 1975), pp. 79–89. On Noguchi in Korea, see also Barbara Ann Molony, "Technology and Investment in the Prewar Japanese Chemical Industry" (Ph.D. diss., Harvard University, 1982), chap. 8. I am grateful to Stephen Erickson for bringing this dissertation to my attention.

14. Kobayashi Hideo, *Daitōa Kyōeiken*, p. 211; Grajdanzev, *Modern Korea*, pp. 213–15.

15. *Kokutai No Hongi: Cardinal Principles of the National Entity of Japan*, trans. John Owen Gauntlett; ed. Robert King Hall (Cambridge: Harvard University Press, 1949), pp. 169–70.

16. See Minami's speech to the delegates of the 1936 industrial commission in Chōsen Sōtokufu, *Chōsen Sangyō Keizai Chōsakai shimon tōshinsho* [The final report of the commission on the industry and economy of Chōsen] (October 1936), p. 102.

17. Quoted in Masao Maruyama, *Thought and Behavior in Japanese Politics*, ed. Ivan Morris (London: Oxford University Press, 1963), pp. 105–6.

18. See *Kokutai No Hongi*, p. 95; see also Bruce Cumings, "Corporatism in North Korea," *Journal of Korean Studies* 4 (1982–83): 282–83.

19. Chōsen Sōtokufu, *Chōsen Sangyō Keizai Chōsakai kaigiroku* [The proceedings of the commission on the industry and economy of Chōsen] (October 1936), Committee no. 2, p. 378.

20. See Cho Kijun, *Han'guk kiŏpkasa*, pp. 37–40.

21. Ibid., pp. 44–47.

22. Kwŏn T'aeŏk, "Kyŏngsŏng Chingnyu," pp. 298–99.

23. According to Kim Yongwan, the Kims had been ranked as the third richest family in Korea based on a study of Korean property undertaken by the Chōsen Industrial Bank sometime around or before the time of Kyŏngbang's founding. The wealthiest Korean at the time was Min Yŏnghwi,

followed by Paek In'gi of North Chŏlla (with about 60,000 sŏk worth of land). Kim Yongwan, taped interview, Seoul, April 13, 1984.

24. See Grajdanzev, *Modern Korea*, p. 114.

25. *KY*, pp. 52–53, 59, 66–67, 542–48.

26. See, for example, Kyŏngsŏng Pangjik CH, Record of the Board of Directors Meetings, Minutes of Board Meeting no. 27, Nov. 7, 1924; Minutes of Board Meeting no. 41, Jan. 11, 1929; Minutes of Board Meeting no. 52, Sept. 15, 1932.

27. See *KY*, pp. 53–54: *KSS*, pp. 162–63.

28. On Sŏngsu's income for 1919, see Kim Yongsŏp, "Hanmal ilcheha ŭi chijuje—sarye 4," pp. 109–10. On his investment in Kyŏngbang, see *KSS*, pp. 163–64. Sŏngsu's investment amounted to only 2,500 yen (12.5 yen X 200 shares).

29. The 1919 income from land rents for Kijung's branch of the family amounted to about 7,200 sŏk or about 130,000 yen according to the average rice price for that year (18.12 yen per sŏk). Kyŏngjung's holdings were about 2.5 times larger, and on that basis we may estimate his 1919 income from rents to have been about 18,000 sŏk or about 326,000 yen, thus making the total rents of the two branches of the family (who lived together as a single household) about 456,000 yen. See Kim Yongsŏp, "Hanmal ilcheha ŭi chijuje—sarye 4," pp. 109–10, 113; *KSS*, pp. 164–66; *KY*, p. 59.

30. The 8 percent figure is based on a survey by the Chōsen Industrial Bank. See Suh, *Growth and Structural Changes*, p. 85. The 19 percent figure comes from a survey by the Chōsen Industrial Bank in 1937. See *Chōsen jitsugyō kurabu* 17 (May 1939): 90.

31. *KY*, pp. 251, 522–24.

32. *KY*, pp. 545–48.

33. Or 3,000 of 20,000 total shares. Kyŏngjung owned 2,000 shares, Kijung owned 800 shares, and Sŏngsu owned 200 shares. See *KSS*, pp. 162–64. Another source gives 650 shares for Kijung's portion: see *KY*, p. 59.

34. Most of this stock was controlled in one way or another by Kim Yŏnsu. See Kyŏngsŏng Pangjik CH, List of Stockholders, Nov. 30, 1944.

35. Daniel S. Juhn, "Nationalism and Korean Businessmen," in C. I. Eugene Kim and Doretha E. Mortimore, eds., *Korea's Response to Japan: The Colonial Period, 1910-1945*, Korean Studies Series 5 (Kalamazoo: Center for Korean Studies, Western Michigan University, 1977), p. 49.

36. See Jung Young Lee, *Sokdam: Capsules of Korean Wisdom*, 2d ed. (Seoul: Seoul Computer Press, 1983), pp. 35, 102.

37. Kyŏngsŏng Pangjik CH, Record of the General Stockholders Meetings, Minutes of the 37th Regular Meeting, Dec. 29, 1945. There is also an extant list of company stockholders from Nov. 30, 1944, but since by that time so many Koreans had taken Japanese names, the nationality of the stockholders is sometimes difficult to distinguish. The figure of 5.6 percent, however, may represent only a portion of the total Japanese shares in the company at the

end of the colonial period. It is not clear, for example, whether the 57 "Japanese stockholders" *[Ilbon'in chuju]* mentioned in the minutes included Japanese corporate entities that continued to operate as Korean institutions under American supervision after Liberation, e.g., the Chōsen Industrial Bank. As of Nov. 30, 1944, four Japanese-controlled banks alone held 21,285 shares or about 8.2 percent of the company's stock, which strongly suggests that such corporate bodies were not included among the 57 "Japanese stockholders," whose total holdings were listed in the minutes at only 14,660 shares. The actual percentage of Japanese shares in the company by the end of the colonial period may thus have been close to 14 percent. See Kyŏngsŏng Pangjik CH, List of Stockholders, Nov. 30, 1944.

38. See *KY*, pp. 60–62; *KSS*, pp. 168–72; *KYS*, pp. 112–16. Yi submitted his resignation, but the board refused to accept it. See Kyŏngsŏng Pangjik CH, Record of the Board of Directors Meetings, Board Meeting no. 8, June 21, 1920.

39. See *KY*, p. 68.

40. Kajimura Hideki, *Chōsen ni okeru shihonshugi*, pp. 40–52; Chōsen Menshifushō Rengōkai, *Chōsen mengyōshi*, pp. 38, 53.

41. Chōsen Menshifushō Rengōkai, *Chōsen mengyōshi*, pp. 35–53.

42. Ibid., pp. 89–92. See also *KY*, pp. 65, 299; *KYS*, pp. 118–19.

43. See *KY*, p. 63. See also Chōsen Menshifushō Rengōkai, *Chōsen mengyōshi*, pp. 89–92.

44. See Chōsen Sōtokufu, *Sangyō Chōsa Iinkai giji sokkiroku*, General Session, Day 1, pp. 77–78. See also Kawai Akitake, *Chōsen kōgyō no gendankai*, p. 108.

45. Chōsen Sōtokufu, *Sangyō Chōsa Iinkai giji sokkiroku*, General Session, Day 5, pp. 246–47.

46. See the remarks by Diet Member Matsumura Tsunejirō in Chōsen Sōtokufu, *Sangyō Chōsa Iinkai giji sokkiroku*, General Session, Day 2, pp. 161–63. Also see the remarks of Nishimura Yasukichi (Director, Bureau of Industry) in Chōsen Sōtokufu, *Sangyō Chōsa Iinkai giji sokkiroku*, General Session, Day 1, pp. 76–77.

47. *Tonga ilbo*, June 11, 1922, p. 2.

48. See the story in *Tonga ilbo*, Sept. 13, 1921, p. 3.

49. See, for example, the editorial criticizing the final report of the 1921 industrial commission as a policy centered on Japanese rather than Korean interests: *Tonga ilbo*, Sept. 23, 1921. See also Kim Yongsŏp, "Hanmal ilcheha ŭi chijuje — sarye 4," pp. 124–31.

50. According to *KY*, p. 71, the first subsidy was received in 1925 to help cover losses in 1924, but this is not correct. See Kyŏngsŏng Pangjik CH, Record of the Board of Directors Meetings, Minutes of Board Meeting no. 24, Mar. 27, 1924. See also *KY*, p. 523. The total amount of subsidies was 254,788.36 yen; Kyŏngbang's paid-up capital was 1 million yen at the time. See *KY*, pp. 70–71, 248, 503, 523.

51. Ibid., p. 523.

52. Ibid., p. 248.

53. Kyŏngsŏng Pangjik CH, Record of the Board of Directors Meetings, Minutes of Board Meeting no. 26, Sept. 19, 1924.

54. Ibid., Minutes of Board Meeting no. 9, July 2, 1920. See also *KY*, pp. 60–62; *KSS*, pp. 168–71; *KYS*, pp. 114–16.

55. *KY,* pp. 230, 532, 544.

56. "Keijō Bōseki [*sic*] Kaisha no naiyō o kiku: Keijō Bōseki [*sic*] Kabushiki Kaisha Shihainin Ri Jōushi" [Getting the facts on the Kyŏngsŏng Spinning and Weaving Company: Company Manager Mr. Yi Sangu], *Chōsen jitsugyō kurabu* 10 (December 1932): 17.

57. Kyŏngsŏng Pangjik CH, Record of the Board of Directors Meetings, Minutes of Board Meeting no. 41, Jan. 11, 1929; Record of the Board of Directors Meetings, Minutes of Board Meeting no. 52, Sept. 15, 1932. According to *KY*, p. 90, the loan was from the Bank of Chōsen, but this is incorrect.

58. Kyŏngsŏng Pangjik CH, Balance Sheet, May 31, 1945. See also *KY*, p. 503; Record of the Board of Directors Meetings, Minutes of Board Meeting no. 57, Mar. 16, 1935; Record of the Board of Directors Meetings, Minutes of Board Meeting no. 62, Feb. 6, 1936; Loan Ledger (unnumbered), Chōsen Industrial Bank Section (First entry: June 5, 1944), pp. 1–2; See also *KY*, p. 97.

59. See Kyŏngsŏng Pangjik CH, Itemized Expense Ledger (Yongin ledger no. 120), Interest Sec., Dec. 2, 1939–May 15, 1940; Itemized Expense Ledger (Yongin ledger no. 30), Interest Sec., June 6, 1940–Nov. 30, 1940; Itemized Expense Ledger (Yongin ledger no. 150), Dec. 2, 1940–May 31, 1941.

60. See, for example, *Report of the Mission on Japanese Combines, Part II: Analytical and Technical Data*, Department of State Publication 2628, Far Eastern Series 14 (Washington, D.C.: Department of State, 1946), pp. 36–67.

61. On the Chōsen Industrial Bank, see Honda Hideo, ed., *Chōsen Shokusan Ginkō nijūnenshi* [A twenty-year record of the Chōsen Industrial Bank] (Keijō: Chōsen Shokusan Ginkō, 1938). See also Cho Kijun, *Han'guk chabonjuŭi sŏngnipsaron*, pp. 477–85. See also Karl Moskowitz, "Current Assets: The Employees of Japanese Banks in Colonial Korea" (Ph.D. diss., Harvard University, 1979), pp. 32–39.

62. See Ogura Masatarō, ed., *Chōsen sangyō nempō, 1943* [Chōsen industrial yearbook, 1943] (Keijō: Tōyō Keizei Shimpōsha, 1943), pp. 70, 146–47. See also Cho Kijun, *Han'guk chabonjuŭi sŏngnipsaron*, pp. 444–47, 480–82.

63. Honda Hideo, ed., *Chōsen Shokusan Ginkō nijūnenshi*, p. 46.

64. As was the bank's board of directors. See ibid., p. 37.

65. See Kita Tadai, *Chōsen jinji kōshinroku*, pp. 378–79. On the position of *kanrikan*, see Honda Hideo, ed., *Chōsen Shokusan Ginkō nijūnenshi*, p. 37.

66. See *Chōsen GKKY*, p. 2.

67. On Korean banks during the late Chosŏn and colonial periods, see Ko Sŭngje, *Han'guk kŭm'yungsa yŏn'gu*, passim. See also Cho Kijun, *Han'guk*

kiŏpkasa, pp. 108–80, and *Han'guk chabonjuŭi sŏngnipsaron*, pp. 474–85; Pak Chongt'ae, ed., *Chohŭng Ŭnhaeng p'alsibo'nyŏnsa*, pp. 5–38. See also Tongŭn Ki'nyŏm Saŏphoe, *Tongŭn Kim Yongwan* [Kim Yongwan] (Seoul: Tongŭn Ki'nyŏm Saŏphoe, 1979), p. 86, and *Chōsen GKKY*, pp. 1–15.

68. Cho Kijun, *Han'guk chabonjuŭi sŏngnipsaron*, p. 475.

69. Ibid., pp. 474–75.

70. *Chōsen GKKY*, pp. 2, 8. Cho Kijun, *Han'guk chabonjuŭi sŏngnipsaron*, p. 474.

71. See, for example, Kyŏngsŏng Pangjik CH, Record of the Board of Directors Meetings, Minutes of Board Meeting no. 58, Mar. 16, 1935; Minutes of Board Meeting no. 62, Feb. 6, 1936; Minutes of Board Meeting no. 98, Dec. 10, 1941. See also Kyŏngsŏng Pangjik CH, Itemized Expense Ledger (unnumbered), Feb. 17, 1934–Feb. 16, 1935, or any subsequent such expense ledger.

72. See above, nn. 57–59. See also Kyŏngsŏng Pangjik CH, Loan Ledger (unnumbered), Chōsen Industrial Bank Section (First entry: June 5, 1944), pp. 1–8; Chōsen Industrial Bank Section (First entry: Dec. 11, 1944), pp. 19–26; Chōsen Industrial Bank Section (First entry: June 1, 1945), pp. 42–48. On the Chōsen Industrial Bank's involvement in financing for Kyŏngbang's Manchurian subsidiary, see also *KYS*, p. 171.

73. Honda Hideo, ed., *Chōsen Shokusan Ginkō nijūnenshi*, p. 144b.

74. See *KYS*, pp. 145–47; "Manmok chusi hanŭn samdae chaengp'aejŏn," pp. 48–49; *Chōsen GKKY*, pp. 12–13.

75. "Manmok chusi hanŭn samdae chaengp'aejŏn," p. 48; *Chōsen GKKY*, p. 13.

76. See Roberts, *Mitsui*, passim.

77. "Manmok chusi hanŭn samdae chaengp'aejŏn," p. 46.

78. *Chōsen GKKY*, pp. 3, 13.

79. Kim Yongwan (1904–) of the Kwangsan Kim clan married one of Kim Sŏngsu's (and Yŏnsu's) sisters (Kim Chŏmhyo) in 1915. After being educated in Japan, he was brought into the Samyang-Kyŏngbang business network, where he served in various managerial positions during the colonial period, becoming a managing director of Kyŏngbang in 1944. After Liberation he went on to become president and later chairman of the company, as well as the founding father and honorary chairman of the Federation of Korean Industries and a member of the South Korean Presidential Advisory Council on State Affairs.

80. Kim Yongwan, taped interview, Seoul, Apr. 13, 1984.

81. Kyŏngsŏng Pangjik CH, Itemized Expense Ledger (unnumbered), Interest Sec., Feb. 17–Sept. 29, 1934, and Itemized Expense Ledger (unnumbered), Interest Sec., Nov. 11, 1935–May 21, 1936.

82. *KY*, p. 147.

83. Kyŏngsŏng Pangjik CH, Record of the Board of Directors Meetings, Minutes of Board Meeting no. 26, Sept. 19, 1924.

84. Ibid.

85. Honda Hideo, ed., *Chōsen Shokusan Ginkō nijūnenshi*, chart, p. 78a.

86. See Grajdanzev, *Modern Korea*, p. 207. Honda Hideo, ed., *Chōsen Shokusan Ginkō nijūnenshi*, chart, p. 78a.

87. Honda Hideo, ed., *Chōsen Shokusan Ginkō nijūnenshi*, chart, p. 78a.

88. Kyŏngsŏng Pangjik CH, Itemized Expense Ledger (Yongin ledger no. 335), Interest Sec., May 25, 1938–Nov. 30, 1938; Itemized Expense Ledger (Yongin ledger no. 275), Interest Sec., Dec. 5, 1938–May 31, 1939; Itemized Expense Ledger (Yongin ledger no. 120), Interest Sec., Dec. 2, 1939–May 15, 1940; Itemized Expense Ledger (Yongin ledger no. 30), Interest Sec., June 6, 1940–Nov. 30, 1940.

89. Ibid., Loan Ledger (unnumbered), Chōsen Industrial Bank Sec. (First entry: June 5, 1944), pp. 1–2.

90. See *KY*, p. 545.

91. See above, n. 89. Interest rates for long-term loans at the Chōsen Industrial Bank in June, 1937, were averaging around 6.7 percent: see Chōsen Sōtokufu, *Chōsen Sōtokufu tōkei nempō, 1937*, p. 148. Another documented long-term loan from the Chōsen Industrial Bank was taken out by Kyŏngbang's affiliate, the Chungang Commercial and Industrial Company, on July 30, 1941. The principal was 148,000 yen, to be paid back over ten years at 6.0 percent yearly interest after an eight-month grace period. See Kyŏngsŏng Pangjik CH, Loan Ledger (unnumbered), Chōsen Industrial Bank Sec. (First entry: June 5, 1944), p. 3 (notation at top of page) and p. 4 (attached memo). This was also well below the average yearly interest rate of 6.6 percent being charged by the bank in July, 1941: see Chōsen Sōtokufu, *Chōsen Sōtokufu tōkei nempō, 1941*, p. 132.

92. Kyŏngsŏng Pangjik CH, Itemized Expense Ledger (Yongin ledger no. 150), Interest Sec., Dec. 2, 1940–May 31, 1941; Itemized Expense Ledger (unnumbered), Interest Sec., Dec. 1, 1941–May 30, 1942.

93. Chōsen Sōtokufu, *Chōsen Sōtokufu tōkei nempō, 1941*, p. 132.

94. Usually 1.5 sen per hundred yen per day. See above, nn. 89, 91.

95. See Chōsen Sōtokufu, *Sangyō Chōsa Iinkai giji sokkiroku*, Special Committee on Sec. One, Day 3, p. 29.

96. See Naitō Yasohachi, ed., *Semman sangyō taikan* [Korea-Manchuria industrial encyclopedia] (Tokyo: Jigyō to Keizai Sha, 1940), Korea sec., Biographies, pp. 112–13.

97. Ibid., p. 112.

98. Kim Yongwan, taped interview, Seoul, Apr. 13, 1984.

99. Ibid. See also Aruga's own remarks on this subject at the industrial commission of 1938—Chōsen Sōtokufu, *Chōsen Sōtokufu Jikyoku Taisaku Chōsakai kaigiroku* [The proceedings of the Chōsen Government-General commission on policy for the current situation] (September 1938), committee no. 1, Day 1, pp. 105–7.

The Chinese characters for "Aruga" can also be read as "Ariga" in Japanese, and one finds the latter in some English-language works in reference to the Chōsen Industrial Bank president. Nevertheless, in both the *Seoul Press*, the English-language newspaper published in Korea during the colonial period, and also in Japanese biographical dictionaries where the names are also rendered in *kana*, one invariably finds "Aruga" rather than "Ariga." See *Seoul Press*, passim; Shimonaka Kunihiko, ed. *Nihon jimmei daijiten: gendai* [Great biographical dictionary of Japan: Modern Period], p. 34.

100. Kim Chunggil, ed., *Hwasin osimnyŏnsa, 1926–1976*, pp. 121–24. Kim Yongwan, taped interview, Seoul, Apr. 13, 1984.

101. This was a commonly used term. See Naitō Yasohachi, ed., *Semman sangyō taikan*, Korea Sec., Biographies, p. 112.

102. *Report of the Mission on Japanese Combines, Part I: Analytical and Technical Data*, p. 22.

103. Pearse, *Cotton Industry of Japan and China*, p. 141.

104. On Pak Yŏnghyo, see Han'guk Inmyŏng Taesajŏn P'yŏnch'ansil, *Han'guk inmyŏng taesajŏn* [Great Korean biographical dictionary] (Seoul: Sin'gu Munhwasa, 1967), p. 286. See also Yi Kibaek, *Han'guksa sillon*, pp. 327–31, 290–95. See also Conroy, *Japanese Seizure of Korea*, passim; Harold F. Cook, "Pak Yong-hyo: Background and Early Years," *Journal of Social Sciences and Humanities*, no. 31 (December 1969), pp. 11–24.

105. See Kita Tadai, *Chōsen jinji kōshinroku*, pp. 413–14.

106. *KY*, pp. 51–52. Kim Yongwan also stressed that Kim Sŏngsu, because of his youth, needed someone older to deal with the colonial authorities: Kim Yongwan, taped interview, Seoul, Mar. 30, 1984.

107. Cho Kijun, *Han'guk chabonjuŭi sŏngnipsaron*, p. 480.

108. See Honda Hideo, ed., *Chōsen Shokusan Ginkō nijūnenshi*, pp. 45, 264, 266. Pak's photograph also appears at the beginning of the book along with the photographs of other bank officials.

109. See Naitō Yasohachi, ed., *Semman sangyō taikan*, Korea Sec., Biographies, pp. 112–13.

110. *Chōsen GKKY*, pp. 4, 57.

111. Ogura Masatarō, ed., *Chōsen sangyō nempō, 1943*, p. 147.

112. See Honda Hideo, ed., *Chōsen Shokusan Ginkō nijūnenshi*, appendix, pp. 65, 109.

113. Samyang Tongjehoe, Securities Ledger (Yongin ledger no. 289), pp. 13–15. The Samyang Tongjehoe (Samyang Foundation) was established by the Kyŏngbang board of directors in April 1939. It replaced an earlier, similar foundation called the Friends of Kyŏngbang (Kyŏngbang Sauhoe). Such foundations were funded by sizable company donations (the initial donation voted by the board was 200,000 yen) and by automatic deductions from white-collar salaries. See Kyŏngsŏng Pangjik CH, Record of the Board of Directors Meetings, Minutes of Board Meeting no. 81, Apr. 18, 1939; Minutes of Board Meeting no. 95, May 10, 1941. See also Kyŏngsŏng Pangjik CH, Salary and Allowance Sheet (P'yŏngyang Ginning Factory), May 1945.

114. Kyŏngsŏng Pangjik CH, List of Stockholders, Nov. 30, 1944.

115. Auditors, like directors, were ordinarily elected by vote of the share-holders, but in this case the shareholders simply voted to have Kim Yŏnsu designate an auditor. See Kyŏngsŏng Pangjik CH, Record of the General Stockholders Meetings, Minutes of the 26th Regular Meeting, Dec. 26, 1939. On Nakatomi's background and affiliation with the Chōsen Industrial Bank, see Naitō Yasohachi, ed., *Semman sangyō taikan*, Korea Sec., Biographies, p. 22. In 1944, Nakatomi personally owned 700 shares of Kyŏngbang stock: see Kyŏngsŏng Pangjik CH, List of Stockholders, Nov. 30, 1944. p. 9.

116. On Shiraishi, see Kita Tadai, *Chōsen jinji kōshinroku*, pp. 232–33. On Tanegashima, see Naitō Yasohachi, ed., *Semman sangyō taikan*, Korea Sec., Biographies, pp. 173–74. On Terada and Hayashi, see Honda Hideo, ed., *Chōsen Shokusan Ginkō nijūnenshi*, pp. 280–81 and Kita Tadai, *Chōsen jinji kōshinroku*, p. 379. In 1944, Shiraishi and Hayashi each held 300 Kyŏngbang shares, Tanegashima had 100, and Terada had 50; Kyŏngsŏng Pangjik CH, List of Stockholders, Nov. 30, 1944, pp. 7–10.

117. Kondō Tokuzō (500 Kyŏngbang shares), for example, was Commercial Finance Section chief of the bank in 1938. On Kondō, see Kita Tadai, *Chōsen jinji kōshinroku*, p. 188; Honda Hideo, ed., *Chōsen Shokusan Ginkō nijūnenshi*, appendix, p. 114; Naitō Yasohachi, ed., *Semman sangyō taikan*, pp. 74–75; Kyŏngsŏng Pangjik CH, List of Stockholders, Nov. 30, 1944, p. 6. Matsui Sanjirō (570 Kyŏngbang shares) was Industrial Finance Section chief of the bank during this same period. On Matsui, see Kita Tadai, *Chōsen jinji kōshinroku*, p. 436; Honda Hideo, ed., *Chōsen Shokusan Ginkō nijūnenshi*, pp. 263, 266, and appendix, p. 113; Kyŏngsŏng Pangjik CH, List of Stockholders, Nov. 30, 1944, p. 11.

118. On Watanabe (76 Kyŏngbang shares), see Naitō Yasohachi, ed., *semman sangyō taikan*, p. 94; Honda Hideo, *Chōsen Shokusan Ginkō nijūnenshi*, appendix, p. 112; Kyŏngsŏng Pangjik CH, List of Stockholders, Nov. 30, 1944, p. 13.

119. On Noda (300 Kyŏngbang shares), see Naitō Yasohachi, ed., *Semman sangyō taikan*, Korea Sec., Biographies, p. 31; Honda Hideo, ed., *Chōsen Shokusan Ginkō nijūnenshi*, p. 265 and appendix, pp. 108, 111; Kyŏngsŏng Pangjik CH, List of Stockholders, Nov. 30, 1944, p. 9.

120. On Hayashi Shigeki (100 Kyŏngbang shares), see Naitō Yasohachi, ed., *Semman sangyō taikan*, Korea Sec., Biographies, p. 80 and Korea Sec., Companies, p. 40; Honda Hideo, ed., *Chōsen Shokusan Ginkō nijūnenshi*, p. 265 and appendix, p. 108; Pak Chongt'ae, ed., *Chohŭng Ŭnhaeng p'alsibo'nyŏnsa*, p. 18; Ogura Masatarō, ed., *Chōsen sangyō nempō, 1943*, p. 140. See also Kyŏngsŏng Pangjik CH, List of Stockholders, Nov. 30, 1944, p. 10.

121. On Imori, see Kita Tadai, *Chōsen jinji kōshinroku*, pp. 27–28; see also Ogura Masatarō, ed., *Chōsen sangyō nempō, 1943*, p. 147; Kyŏngsŏng Pangjik CH, List of Stockholders, Nov. 30, 1944, p. 1.

122. On Hayashi, see Kita Tadai, *Chōsen jinji kōshinroku*, pp. 378–79; Honda Hideo, ed., *Chōsen Shokusan Ginkō nijūnenshi*, p. 263; Kyŏngsŏng Pangjik CH, List of Stockholders, Nov. 30, 1944, p. 10.

123. Samyang Tongjehoe, Securities Ledger (Yongin ledger no. 289), pp. 1, 8, 19; see also Ogura Masatarō, ed., *Chōsen sangyō nempō*, 1943, pp. 70, 86, 140. Although the company's primary business was operating the railroad, it was also involved in the lumber and automotive industries and in the development of extensive property holdings in central Kyŏnggi and Kangwŏn Provinces—the area through which the railroad ran. See Naitō Yasohachi, ed., *Semman sangyō taikan*, Korea Sec., Companies, p. 40.

124. Kyŏngsŏng Pangjik CH, Securities Ledger (Yongin ledger no. 293), p. 37. Pak Hŭngsik was the president of this company and several Koreans, including Kim Yŏnsu, were on the board of directors (others were Pak Ch'un'gŭm and Pang Ŭisŏk): see *Maeil sinbo*, Oct. 2, 1944. See also Kim Chunggil, ed., *Hwasin osimnyŏnsa, 1926–1976*, p. 203.

125. There were at least two Industrial Bank employees (Honda Hideo and Yamaguchi Shigemasa) on the company's board of directors (Honda was a managing director), and Aruga Mitsutoyo was also a consultant to the company. See *Maeil sinbo*, Oct. 2, 1944. On Honda and Yamaguchi, see Kita Tadai, *Chōsen jinji kōshinroku*, pp. 425, 487. See also Honda Hideo, ed., *Chōsen Shokusan Ginkō nijūnenshi*, p. 280.

4. Class and State: Partners in Management

1. A list of the participants in the 1921 conference may be found in *Tonga ilbo*, Sept. 6, 1921; see also Chōsen Sōtokufu, *Sangyō Chōsa Iinkai giji sokkiroku*, General Session, Day 2, pp. 173–74. For a list of the participants in the 1936 conference, see idem, *Chōsen Sangyō Keizai Chōsakai shimon tōshinsho*, pp. 79–87. For the 1938 conference, see idem, *Chōsen Sōtokufu Jikyoku Taisaku Chōsakai shimon tōshinsho* [The final report of the Chōsen Government-General commission on policy for the current situation] (September 1938), pp. 183–90.

2. See, for example, Pak's speech as chairman of the group's organizing committee, quoted in *Tonga ilbo*, July 29, 1921, p. 2.

3. Chōsen Sōtokufu, *Chōsen Sangyō Keizai Chōsakai kaigiroku*, Committee no. 2, pp. 386–89.

4. Chōsen Sōtokufu, *Chōsen Sōtokufu Jikyoku Taisaku Chōsakai shimon tōshinsho*, p. 188. Although invited, Kim was unable to attend the 1938 conference; see idem, *Chōsen Sōtokufu Jikyoku Taisaku Chōsakai kaigiroku*, p. 6.

5. See Chōsen Sōtokufu, *Chōsen Sangyō Keizai Chōsakai shimon tōshinsho*, pp. 27–33.

6. Quoted in Maruyama, *Thought and Behavior*, pp. 105–6.

7. See, for example, the rules of order for the 1936 commission in Chōsen Sōtokufu, *Chōsen Sangyō Keizai Chōsakai shimon tōshinsho*, pp. 77–78.

8. *The Japan Weekly Chronicle — Commercial Supplement*, Jan. 30, 1936, p. 43.

9. Chōsen Sōtokufu, *Chōsen Sangyō Keizai Chōsakai shimon tōshinsho*, pp. 27–28.

10. See, for example, Miyabayashi Taiji, "Chōsen orimono gyōkai no tembō" [A look at the Chōsen textile world], *Chōsen jitsugyō* (formerly *Chōsen jitsugyō kurabu*) 18 (March 1940): 102–6.

11. See Zenkoku Keizai Chōsa Kikan Rengōkai Chōsen Shibu, *Chōsen keizai nempō, 1940* [Chōsen economic yearbook: 1940] (Tokyo: Kaizōsha, 1940), pp. 3–50, esp. 34ff.

12. Ibid., pp. 3–50. See also Kyŏngsŏng Pangjik CH, Business Report for the 35th Fiscal Period, Nov. 30, 1944, p. 5.

13. Chōsen Sōtokufu, *Chōsen Sangyō Keizai Chōsakai shimon tōshinsho*, pp. 31–32.

14. See *KY*, pp. 121–22. See also Kyŏngsŏng Pangjik CH, Business Report for the 35th Fiscal Period, Nov. 30, 1944, pp. 2–4; Kyŏngsŏng Panjik CH, Contract of Merger (with Tonggwang Chesa CH), July 4, 1944.

15. The information in this section on the Government-General's control of the Korean textile industry is taken from a variety of sources, including Hashiguchi Shūkō, ed., *Chōsen sen'i yōran* [The Chōsen textile handbook] (Keijō: Chōsen Orimono Kyōkai, 1943), pp. 3–51, esp. 1–4, 11–14; Kyŏngsŏng Pangjik CH, Business Reports, 1942–1945; *KY*, pp. 113–15.

16. Zenkoku Keizai Chōsa Kikan Rengōkai Chōsen Shibu, ed., *Chōsen nempō, 1940*, pp. 44–45.

17. On the Chōsen Spinners Association (Chōsen Bōseki Kōgyō Kumiai), see Hashiguchi Shūkō, ed., *Chōsen sen'i yōran*, pp. 13–14, 269.

18. Discussion with officials of the Haeri Branch of the Samyang Salt Company (Samyang Yŏm'ŏpsa), including Kim Sangdŏk and Pak Yundo, at the company, Haeri, North Chŏlla, October 1982.

19. See *KYS*, pp. 189–96. According to the biography, one of the things Matsuzawa was asking in return was for Kim to take Pak Yŏngch'ŏl's place as Honorary Consul-General of Manchukuo in Seoul (Pak had recently died). Kim agreed to accept the post.

20. Quoted in Anthony Sampson, *The Sovereign State: The Secret History of ITT* (Sevenoaks, Kent: Hodder and Stoughton, 1974), p. 177.

21. See Naitō Yasohachi, ed., *Semman sangyō taikan*, Korea Sec., Industries, pp. 134–35. For a recent article on Japanese-Korean business interaction in the Seoul branch of the Chamber, see Dennis McNamara, "The Keishō and the Korean Business Elite," *JAS* 48, no. 2 (May 1989): 310–23.

22. See "Honkai no enkaku to jigyō" [The history and activities of this club], *Chōsen jitsugyō* (formerly *Chōsen jitsugyō kurabu*) 18 (March 1940): 3.

23. "Kaiin meibo" [The list of club members], *Chōsen jitsugyō kurabu* 14 (June 1936): 85–117.

24. Han Sangnyong was unquestionably one of the most interesting and important Korean businessmen in the period between 1876 and 1945. Han (born 1880) was the maternal nephew and protégé of Korean Prime Minister Yi Wanyong (who signed the treaty of annexation in 1910), and his exalted background, ability to speak Japanese (he spent three years attending school in Japan), and general charm and sociability allowed him to develop close personal relationships with high-ranking Japanese officials and businessmen (including Shibusawa Eiichi), who provided him with invaluable support for his various business undertakings. Han began his business career in the Hansŏng Bank, of which he later became president (1923), but his business interests were wide-ranging, and he eventually became personally involved in one way or another with many different companies, including the Kims' cotton textile subsidiary in Manchuria. In 1941, the governor of North Ch'ungch'ŏng Province, Yu Man'gyŏm, wrote: "It may well be said that Han's personal history is in fact the history of the Korean business world in miniature." In spite of his obvious historical significance as a prominent early Korean entrepreneur, however, Han—as Karl Moskowitz has pointed out—has been generally ignored in conventional Korean historiography because of his unabashedly pro-Japanese stance throughout the colonial period (Han appears to have been a strong supporter, for example, of Japanese-Korean assimilation throughout his career: see chap. 8). See Cho Kijun, Han'guk kiŏpkasa, pp. 128–39; Han Ikkyo, ed., Kan Sōryūkun o kataru [Speaking of Han Sangnyong] (Keijō: Kan Sōryū Kanreki Kinenkai, 1941), p. 501, quotation by Yu Man'gyŏm. See also Karl Moskowitz, "Korean Development and Korean Studies—A Review Article," JAS 42 (November 1982): 85.

25. Han Sangnyong, "Jitsugyō Kurabu no enkaku" [The history of the Chōsen Business Club] Chōsen jitsugyō kurabu 7 (September 1929): 2.

26. "Kaimu" [Club Business], Chōsen jitsugyō kurabu 14 (November 1936): 187.

27. See "Shinnyū kaiin (2)" [New club members:2] Chōsen jitsugyō kurabu 14 (February 1936): 65.

28. Kim Yongwan, taped interview, Seoul, Apr. 13, 1984.

29. Han Sangnyong, "Jitsugyō Kurabu no enkaku," p. 2.

30. Ibid., pp. 2–3. See also "Chōsen Jitsugyō Kurabu seiritsu no keika to genjō" [The establishment and present circumstances of the Chōsen Business Club], Chōsen jitsugyō kurabu 15 (June 1937): 164; see also "Semman keizai sangyō zadankai (I)" [Symposium on Korean-Manchurian economy and industry: I], Chōsen jitsugyō kurabu 15 (May 1937): 32.

31. "Chōsen o hagukumishi nyūjō meishi: Kangei daigosankai" [A grand welcoming luncheon for the visiting dignitaries who have nurtured Chōsen], Chōsen jitsugyō kurabu 13 (October 1935): 33.

32. Chōsen Sōtokufu, Sangyō Chōsa Iinkai giji sokkiroku, Special Committee on Sec. 1, p. 1.

33. Chōsen Sōtokufu, *Chōsen Sangyō Keizei Chōsakai shimon tōshinsho*, p. 1.

34. "Semman keizai sangyō zadankai (II)" [Symposium on Korean-Manchurian economy and industry: II], *Chōsen jitsugyō kurabu* 15 (June 1937): 90, comments by Aikawa.

35. Kobayashi Hideo, *Daitōa Kyōeiken no keisei to hōkai*, p. 88.

36. Ibid., p. 79.

37. Chōsen Sōtokufu, *Chōsen Sangyō Keizai Chōsakai shimon tōshinsho*, pp. 29–30.

38. Chōsen Sōtokufu, *Chōsen Sangyō Keizai Chōsakai kaigiroku*, Committee no. 2, p. 380.

39. See Chōsen Sōtokufu, *Chōsen Sōtokufu Jikyoku Taisaku Chōsakai shimon tōshinsho*, pp. 135–45.

40. See, for example, Kyŏngsŏng Pangjik CH, Record of the Board of Directors Meetings, Minutes of Board Meeting no. 77, Oct. 14, 1938; Minutes of Board Meeting no. 85, Oct. 28, 1939; Minutes of Board Meeting no. 98, Dec. 10, 1941; Minutes of Board Meeting no. 100, Feb. 5, 1942.

41. Kyŏngsŏng Pangjik CH, Securities Ledger (Yongin ledger no. 203); Securities Ledger (unnumbered; first entry is for one-yen Special National Defense Bonds, Sept. 9, 1943); Samyang Tongjehoe, Securities Ledger (Yongin ledger no. 289), pp. 22, 39.

42. See Ogura Masatarō, ed., *Chōsen sangyō nempō*, pp. 124–25; see also Shiomi Tsunesaburō, "Chōsen ni okeru bōseki kōgyō no genjō (II)," pp. 66ff; Zenkoku Keizai Chōsa Kikan Rengōkai Chōsen Shibu, ed., *Chōsen keizai nempō, 1940*, pp. 253–54, 258–59.

43. Ogura Masatarō, ed., *Chōsen sangyō nempō*, pp. 124–25; Chōsen Sōtokufu, *Chōsen Sōtokufu Jikyoku Taisaku Chōsakai shimon tōshinsho*, p. 144.

44. Ogura Masatarō, ed., *Chōsen sangyō nempō*, pp. 124–25 (Suwŏn is incorrectly cited here as the location of the factory); Shashi Henshū Iinkai, ed., *Kureha Bōseki sanjūnen* [Thirty years of Kureha spinning] (Ōsaka: Kureha Bōseki KK, 1960), pp. 92–93, 235. See also Keizo Seki, *Cotton Industry of Japan*, pp. 198–200.

45. See Kim Sangjun (eldest son of Kim Yŏnsu), Stock Certificates (102 shares), Kanegafuchi Industries (Kanegafuchi Kōgyō KK), all purchased on Feb. 1, 1944; also Kim Sangjun, Stock Certificates (500 shares), Kawasaki Heavy Industries (Kawasaki Jūkōgyō KK), all purchased Oct. 18, 1943. These certificates are included among the Hapcha Hoesa Samyangsa Documents, CH Samyangsa, Seoul. Kanegafuchi Industries, established in 1944, represented a merger of Kanegafuchi Spinning and its associate, Kanegafuchi Jitsugyō (set up by the spinning company in 1938 to engage in the heavy chemical industry and other nontextile fields). Kawasaki Heavy Industries was engaged in a variety of areas, including shipbuilding, rolling stock, marine

transportation, steel, and aircraft. On Kanegafuchi and Kawasaki, see Hiroshi Matsumura, ed., *Diamond's Japan Business Directory, 1975* (Tokyo: Diamond Lead Co., Ltd., Spring 1975), pp. 174, 848.

46. See Samyang Tongjehoe, Securities Ledger (Yongin ledger no. 289), pp. 7, 44; Ogura Masatarō, ed., *Chōsen sangyō nempō*, p. 114. On the crucial importance of liquid fuel to Japan's war effort, see Bisson, *Japan's War Economy*, pp. 164–65.

47. See Samyang Tongjehoe, Securities Ledger (Yongin ledger no. 289), p. 12; Ogura Masatarō, ed., *Chōsen sangyō nempō*, p. 103; Naitō Yasohachi, ed., *Semman sangyō taikan*, Korea Sec., Companies, p. 44; Taniura Takao, "Haebanghu Han'guk sangŏp chabon ŭi hyŏngsŏng kwa palchŏn" [The formation and development of Korean commercial capital after Liberation], trans. An Pyŏngjik, in Chin Tŏkkyu et al., *1950 nyŏndae ŭi insik* [Understanding the 1950s], Onŭrŭi Sasang Sinsŏ no. 22 (Seoul: Han'gilsa, 1981), pp. 304–6.

48. See Bisson, *Japan's War Economy*, pp. 118–22.

49. See R. J. Francillon, *Japanese Aircraft of the Pacific War* (London: Putnam and Co., 1970, 1979), pp. 10–18.

50. Ibid., p. 36.

51. Edwin W. Pauley, *Report on Japanese Assets in Soviet-Occupied Korea to the President of the United States* (June 1946), pp. 28–29. Pauley's report on the Shōwa Aircraft Company (prepared by A. B. Einig) specifically identifies the aircraft being produced in P'yŏngyang as "the 86 Type army medium training plane," but the "type numbers" of Japanese army aircraft during this period began with number 87, i.e., there was no "Type 86." See Francillon, *Japanese Aircraft of the Pacific War*, pp. 48, 540. What Einig apparently meant was the Kokusai Ki-86 Army Type 4 Primary Trainer, production of which began in 1944, and which replaced the Ki-17 as the Japanese army's standard primary trainer. See Francillon, pp. 504–5, 538. According to a 1947 report on the Japanese aircraft industry by the United States Strategic Bombing Survey, such trainers, being "cheap to build and. . . expendable," were "obviously intended for the final kamikaze effort against invasion." The report also noted that "trainers produced after 1 April 1945 were scheduled, for the most part, to be used as kamikaze or special attack suicide planes." See *The United States Strategic Bombing Survey*, 10 vols. (New York: Garland Publishing, 1976) 7: 68.

52. On the Chōsen Aircraft Company, see *Maeil sinbo*, Oct. 2, 1944; Oct. 7, 1944. See also Kim Chunggil, ed., *Hwasin osimnyŏnsa, 1926–1976*, pp. 203–6. According to the Hwasin company history (p. 206), the war ended before the new company was able to produce even one plane.

53. Ibid. See also Kyŏngsŏng Pangjik CH, Securities Ledger (Yongin ledger no. 293), p. 37.

54. See, for example, Han Sangnyong, "Nentō shokan" [Thoughts on the New Year], *Chōsen jitsugyō kurabu* 18 (January 1940): 11; Kim Yehyŏn, "Shina jihengo ni shosubeki Hantōjin no yōi" [Korean strategies in the after-

math of the China Incident], *Chōsen jitsugyō kurabu* 16 (March 1938): 64. See also Yoshida Shigeru's memo to Konoe (1942) in J. W. Dower, *Empire and Aftermath: Yoshida Shigeru and the Japanese Experience, 1878–1954* (Cambridge: Council on East Asian Studies, Harvard University, 1979), p. 230.

55. See *KY*, pp. 123–25, 252, 532–33. See also Kyŏngsŏng Pangjik CH, Business Report for the 34th Fiscal Period, May 31, 1944; Business Report for the 35th Fiscal Period, Nov. 30, 1944; Business Report for the 36th Fiscal Period, May 31, 1945.

56. Kyŏngsŏng Pangjik CH, Business Report for the 34th Fiscal Period, May 31, 1944, p. 3. Idem, Record of the Board of Directors Meetings, Minutes of Board Meeting no. 114, Oct. 5, 1944.

57. Kyŏngsŏng Pangjik CH, Business Report for the 30th Fiscal Period, May 31, 1942, p. 6.

58. See *KY*, pp. 522–25.

59. See, for example, Kyŏngsŏng Pangjik CH, Business Report for the 30th Fiscal Period, May 31, 1942, p. 6; Business Report for the 36th Fiscal Period, May 31, 1945.

60. Kim Yongwan, taped interview, Seoul, Mar. 30, 1984.

61. Kyŏngsŏng Pangjik CH, Business Report for the 35th Fiscal Period, Nov. 30, 1944, p. 5; see also Business Report for the 34th Fiscal Period, May 31, 1944, p. 3, as well as Business Report for the 35th Fiscal Period, Nov. 30, 1944, p. 7.

62. See *KY*, p. 251.

63. Ibid., pp. 522–25. See also Kyŏngsŏng Pangjik CH, Business Reports (30th, 34th, 35th, and 36th Fiscal Periods), Profit and Loss Statements, May 31, 1942; May 31, 1944; Nov. 30, 1944; May 31, 1945.

64. See *Tonga ilbo*, April 11, 1939, p. 8. Like so many of the Government-General's measures during this period, this particular restriction represented an extension of Japanese wartime controls to Korea. The 6 percent figure was later raised to 8 percent; dividends above that figure had to be approved by the government. See Jerome B. Cohen, *Japan's Economy in War and Reconstruction* (Minneapolis: University of Minnesota Press, 1949), p. 18. See also *The Japan Weekly Chronicle—Commercial Supplement*, Dec. 22, 1938, p. 188; *KY*, p. 251.

65. Kyŏngsŏng Pangjik CH, Business Report for the 36th Fiscal Period, Balance Sheet, May 31, 1945.

66. See *The Japan Weekly Chronicle—Commercial Supplement*, Dec. 22, 1938, p. 188.

67. *KY*, pp. 522–25.

68. See Kyŏngsŏng Pangjik CH, Business Report for the 36th Fiscal Period, Balance Sheet, May 31, 1945; *Chōsen GKKY*, p. 134.

69. Kyŏngsŏng Pangjik CH, Business Report for the 36th Fiscal Period, May 31, 1945, pp. 1–3.

70. *KY*, pp. 524–25.

5. Between Metropole and Hinterland: The Acquisition of Raw Materials and Technology

1. The terms *dependence* and *dependency* have come to be almost exclusively associated in recent years with the work of so-called dependency theorists like Paul Baran, Andre Gunder Frank, and, above all, Immanuel Wallerstein. Korea's—and the Korean bourgeoisie's—dependency on Japan and Japanese capitalism, however, was quite different from the dependency relationship discussed by Wallerstein and others. For Wallerstein, the key determinant of dependency is a country's particular economic position within a capitalist world economy of competing nation-states. According to this view, political factors are largely irrelevant in establishing dependency, and, indeed, are more or less a consequence of economics. Wallerstein says quite explicitly that "to understand the internal class contradictions and political struggles of a particular state, we must first situate it in the world-economy. We can then understand the ways in which various political and cultural thrusts may be efforts to alter or preserve a position within the world-economy which is to the advantage or disadvantage of particular groups located within a particular state." In colonial Korea, however, the situation was reversed. The political factor, i.e., Korea's status as a Japanese colony, was the primary determinant of Korea's—and the Korean bourgeoisie's—economic position vis-à-vis Japan and Japanese capitalism. The above quotation is from the essay, "The Present State of the Debate on World Equality," in Immanuel Wallerstein, *The Capitalist World-Economy* (Cambridge: Cambridge University Press, 1979), pp. 53–54. Also included in this same volume is another essay, "The Rise and Future Demise of the World Capitalist System: Concepts for Comparative Analysis," pp. 1–36, which offers a concise, overall view of Wallerstein's general theory.

2. Chōsen Sōtokufu, *Sangyō Chōsa Iinkai giji sokkiroku*, General Session, Day 1, p. 75.

3. Ibid., pp. 75–76.

4. See Keizo Seki, *Cotton Industry of Japan*, pp. 18–19, 21.

5. *KY*, p. 54.

6. See, for example, Kim Yŏnsu's remarks at the industrial commission of 1936 in Chōsen Sōtokufu, *Chōsen Sangyō Keizai Chōsakai kaigiroku*, Committee no. 2, p. 387.

7. "Keijō Bōseki [sic] Kaisha no naiyō o kiku," p. 17.

8. *KY*, pp. 92, 249.

9. Ibid.

10. See Keizo Seki, Cotton Industry of Japan, pp. 111–21.

11. On Tōyō Menka, see *Chōsen GKKY*, p. 403; Kozo Yamamura, "General Trading Companies in Japan: Their Origins and Growth," in Hugh Patrick, ed., *Japanese Industrialization and Its Social Consequences* (Berkeley and Los

Angeles: University of California Press, paperback, 1976), pp. 169–71, 174–76, 180–82; Pearse, *Cotton Industry of Japan and China*, pp. 39–40.

12. Pearse, *Cotton Industry of Japan and China*, pp. 39–41.

13. Until 1927, Kyŏngbang's business office (as opposed to its factory, which was in Yŏngdŭngp'o) and Tōyō Menka's Seoul branch office were both located at Ŭlchiro Il-ga, one of the centers of the city's cloth trade. In 1927 Kyŏngbang moved its business office to what is now Namdaemunno Il-ga, present location of Kyungbang Corner, Ltd. (CH Kyŏngbang K'onŏ), a Kyŏngbang domestic sales subsidiary. See *Chōsen GKKY*, p. 403; *KY*, pp. 67, 404–6. Eventually Tōyō Menka also had an office in Yŏngdŭngp'o: see Hashiguchi Shūkō, ed., *Chōsen sen'i yōran*, p. 118.

14. This was especially true in the provinces, where Kyŏngbang did much of its business. See Chōsen Menshifushō Rengōkai, *Chōsen mengyōshi*, pp. 233–35.

15. Kim Yongwan, taped interview, Seoul, Apr. 13, 1984. Kyŏngbang's relationship with Yagi Shōten had a long history that went back to Yi Kanghyŏn's first trip to Japan on Kyŏngbang's behalf shortly after the company was founded. See *KY*, p. 60.

16. See Pearse, *Cotton Industry of Japan and China*, pp. 46–47.

17. "Keijō Bōseki [sic] Kaisha no naiyō o kiku," p. 17.

18. See Hashiguchi Shūkō, ed., *Chōsen sen'i yōran*, p. 113; Kyŏngsŏng Pangjik CH, List of Stockholders, Nov. 30, 1944, p. 1.

19. Kim Yongwan, taped interview, Seoul, Mar. 30, 1984. Another company that figured prominently in Kyŏngbang's procurement of raw materials was the C. Itoh Trading Company (Itō Chū Shōji KK) — not surprisingly, considering Kyŏngbang's extremely close relationship with the C. Itoh Group. Many of the original vouchers for such transactions are still extant. See, for example, Kyŏngsŏng Pangjik CH, Vouchers (Yongin voucher pack dated Oct. 21, 1938–Oct. 25, 1938).

20. Shiomi Tsunesaburō, "Chōsen ni okeru bōseki kōgyō no genjō: I" [The present condition of the spinning industry in Korea: I], *Dai Nippon Bōseki Rengōkai geppō*, no. 587 (September 1941), p. 11.

21. See Pak Cheŭl, "Han'guk myŏnbang chigŏp ŭi sajŏk yŏn'gu: 1876–1945 nyŏnŭl chungsim ŭro" [A historical study of the cotton spinning and weaving industry in Korea with emphasis on the period 1876–1945] (Ph.D. diss., Kyŏnghŭi Taehakkyo, 1980), pp. 17–67; Kajimura Hideki, *Chōsen ni okeru shihonshugi*, pp. 11–142, esp. 52–91. For a brief historical sketch of the traditional Korean cotton industry in English, see Sung Jae Koh, *Stages of Industrial Development in Asia: A Comparative History of the Cotton Industry in Japan, India, China, and Korea* (Philadelphia: University of Pennsylvania Press, 1966), pp. 260–84.

22. See Keizo Seki, *Cotton Industry of Japan*, p. 104.

23. Ibid. American upland cotton is "the standard American cotton and

the one by which all other cottons are compared for properties and characteristics." See George E. Linton, *The Modern Textile Dictionary* (New York: Duell, Sloan, and Pearse, 1954), p. 705.

24. Sung Jae Koh, *Stages of Industrial Growth*, pp. 307–10.

25. Shiomi Tsunesaburō, "Chōsen ni okeru bōseki kōgyō no genjō: I," pp. 11–15, 102.

26. Ibid.

27. See, for example, "Semman keizai sangyō zadankai (II)," comments by Kamata, p. 113.

28. Chōsen Sōtokufu, *Chōsen Sangyō Keizai Chōsakai kaigiroku*, Committee no. 2, pp. 381–82.

29. Ibid., pp. 386–89. See also Linton, *Modern Textile Dictionary*. The Japanese Cotton Spinners Association also noted that production of thick, coarse yarns (with counts under 22 or 19) was a "unique characteristic" of the spinning industry in Korea. See Shiomi Tsunesaburō, "Chōsen ni okeru bōseki kōgyō no genjō: II," p. 68.

30. See Keizo Seki, *Cotton Industry of Japan*, p. 36.

31. Pearse, *Cotton Industry of Japan and China*, pp. 123–25.

32. *The Japan Weekly Chronicle — Commercial Supplement*, Dec. 24, 1936, p. 270.

33. See Yi Chaegon, "Eitōhō no san daikōjō o miru" [A look at three large-scale factories in Yŏngdŭngp'o], *Chōsen jitsugyō kurabu* 14 (June 1936): 74. The blend was about 60–40 (Indian-American). See Chōsen Sōtokufu, *Chōsen Sotōkufu Jikyoku Taisaku Chōsakai shimon tōshinsho*, p. 46.

34. Chōsen Sōtokufu, *Chōsen Sangyō Keizai Chōsakai kaigiroku*, Committee no. 2, p. 313.

35. Shiomi Tsunesaburō, "Chōsen ni okeru bōseki kōgyō no genjō: II," p. 73.

36. See Jones, *Manchuria Since 1931*, pp. 176–78.

37. See Keizo Seki, *Cotton Industry of Japan*, pp. 104–5.

38. Japanese interest in China as an alternative source of cotton actually antedated the Sino-Japanese War; it had, in fact, been growing since the seizure of Jehol in 1933 had given Japan easy access to the North China Plain. See, for example, Tien-Tsung Sih, "Japan and Cotton Industry in North China," *Council of International Affairs (Nanking) Information Bulletin* 3, no. 6 (March 1937): 123–37. See also Mitsubishi Economic Research Bureau, *Japanese Trade and Industry: Present and Future* (Tokyo: Mitsubishi Economic Research Bureau, 1936), pp. 236–37.

39. Mitsubishi Economic Research Bureau, *Japanese Trade and Industry*, p. 236. See also Keizo Seki, *Cotton Industry of Japan*.

40. Chōsen Sōtokufu, *Chōsen Sōtokufu Jikyoku Taisaku Chōsakai shimon tōshinsho*, p. 46.

41. See Kyŏngsŏng Pangjik CH, Business Report for the 35th Fiscal Period, Nov. 30, 1944, p. 5. See also Keizo Seki, *Cotton Industry of Japan*, p. 372.

42. See Gary Saxonhouse, "A Tale of Technical Diffusion in the Meiji Period," *Journal of Economic History* 34 (March 1974): 151–52, 162.

43. Ibid., pp. 152, 162.

44. Japanese hank-cop reelers were developed in 1888; the Meiji constitution was promulgated in 1889. Ibid., p. 154.

45. See Keizo Seki, *Cotton Industry of Japan*, p. 23.

46. Ibid., pp. 23–24.

47. At 60 looms per worker, however, the cloth tended to suffer. The average was about 24 looms per worker. Pearse, *Cotton Industry of Japan and China*, pp. 79–80. Charles K. Moser, *The Cotton Textile Industry of Far Eastern Countries* (Boston: Pepperell Manufacturing Co., 1930), p. 32.

48. Pearse, *Cotton Industry of Japan and China*, p. 80.

49. Ibid., pp. 80, 87.

50. Ibid., p. 78.

51. Moser, *Cotton Textile Industry of Far Eastern Countries*, p. 31.

52. Lockwood, *Economic Development of Japan*, pp. 332–33.

53. See Han's comments at the industrial commission of 1921. Chōsen Sōtokufu, *Sangyō Chōsa Iinkai giji sokkiroku*, General Session, Day 2, p. 158.

54. See Chōsen Sōtokufu, *Chōsen Sangyō Keizai Chōsakai shimon tōshinsho*, pp. 29–30; Chōsen Sōtokufu, *Chōsen Sōtokufu Jikyoku Taisaku Chōsakai shimon tōshinsho*, p. 141.

55. See Grajdanzev, *Modern Korea*, p. 157. See also Juhn, "Entrepreneurship in an Underdeveloped Economy," pp. 174–75; also Kobayashi Hideo, *Daitōa Kyōeiken no keisei to hōkai*, pp. 210–11.

56. George M. McCune, *Korea Today* (Cambridge: Harvard University Press, 1950), p. 140.

57. *KY*, p. 273.

58. See for example, Kyŏngsŏng Pangjik CH, Property Ledger (Yongin ledger no. 453), pp. 86–100. In 1938 Toyoda also proposed that Kyŏngbang join it in setting up a textile factory in China's Honan Province (in Changte; also called Anyang), but Kyŏngbang declined.

59. *KY*, pp. 273–74.

60. And many other companies as well. See, for example, Kyŏngsŏng Pangjik CH, Property Ledger (Yongin Ledger no. 453) passim; Kyŏngsŏng Pangjik CH, Machinery and Tools Purchase Ledger (Yongin ledger no. 417). There are also hundreds, perhaps thousands, of extant bills and receipts attesting to such purchases in Kyŏngbang's vault at Yongin—a sampling (photocopied) of which is in the possession of the author.

61. *KY*, p. 274.

62. Kyŏngsŏng Pangjik CH, Property Ledger (Yongin ledger no. 453), p. 100.

63. Ibid., pp. 160, 165.

64. Kyŏngsŏng Pangjik CH, Record of the Board of Directors Meetings, Board Meeting no. 103, May 27, 1942. Kyŏngbang had actually been station-

ing representatives in Osaka since the spring of 1935 (when the company decided to become a spinning as well as a weaving operation). In 1942, however, the decision was taken to expand the Osaka operation and open a formal representative office (*ch'ulchangso*). See Cho Yonggu, ed., *Kyŏngsŏng Pangjik osimnyŏn* (hereafter cited as *KO*) [Fifty years of Kyŏngbang] (Seoul: Kyŏngsŏng Pangjik CH, 1969), pp. 159–60. It is clear from company documents that one of the main reasons behind the decision to expand and upgrade the Osaka office was to facilitate the purchase and shipping of machinery for Kyŏngbang's new subsidiary in Manchuria. See, for example, Kyŏngsŏng Pangjik CH, Osaka Representative Office: Statements of Expenses For One-Day Business Trips Within and Outside the City, May 30, 1942, and June 3, 1942. Even the location of Kyŏngbang's Osaka offices reflected the company's close relationship with special Japanese friends like C. Itoh and Yagi Shōten. Before 1942, Kyŏngbang's representatives in Osaka operated out of the Kureha Spinning Company's offices in the C. Itoh Trading Company Building (C. Itoh owned Kureha). See *KO*, picture, p. 160; also Shashi Henshū Iinkai, *Kureha Bōseki sanjūnen*, picture of C. Itoh Trading Company Building, p. 48. After 1942, Kyŏngbang moved to an office at Minami Kyūtarō Nichōme, where Yagi Shōten's head office was also located. See Hashiguchi Shūkō, ed., *Chōsen sen'i yōran*, pp. 88, 113.

65. See Kyŏngsŏng Pangjik CH, Transfer Slip (regarding payment for 1,000 cheese bobbins from Yamamoto Jūjirō Honten, Kuwana), July 1, 1942; Inspection Voucher for Goods Received (1,000 cheese bobbins from Tōa Yoriito KK, Osaka), July 11, 1942.

66. Kyŏngsŏng Pangjik CH, Invoice (from branch office of Takashimaya), June 8, 1942.

67. Lockwood, *Economic Development of Japan*, pp. 510–12.

68. Chōsen Ginkō Chōsaka, *Kōgyō kin'yū no genjō to sono taisaku* [The present state of industrial financing and an appropriate policy], Research Report no. 25 (July 1936), p. 19.

69. Chōsen Sōtokufu, *Chōsen Sangyō Keizai Chōsakai kaigiroku*, Committee no. 4, pp. 613–14.

70. Ibid., p. 613. Keijō Higher Industrial School was founded by the Korean government in 1905, and in 1916 the Japanese raised its status to that of a technical college. To be eligible for entrance, a student had to have graduated from higher common school (middle school), which during the colonial period was a five-year course (after six years of common or elementary school). In his remarks at the industrial commission in 1936, Noguchi said that Keijō Industrial only offered courses in mining and mechanical engineering, but this was inaccurate and an exaggeration. In fact, the school offered courses in spinning and weaving, applied chemistry, ceramics, civil engineering, architecture, and mining. In contrast to Tokyo Industrial College (Tokyo Higher Industrial School until 1929), however, Keijō Industrial offered no courses in more sophisticated areas such as dyeing and electrochemistry—or even in

mechanical or electrical engineering. See Government-General of Chosen, ed., *Annual Report on Administration of Chosen: 1922–1923* (Keijō, 1924), p. 88; Mombushō Jitsugyō Gakumukyoku, *Jitsugyō gakkō ichiran* [A survey of vocational schools] (Tokyo: Mombushō Jitsugyō Gakumukyoku, 1936), p. 133; Sakudō Yoshio and Etō Takendo, eds., *Tōkyō Kōgyō Daigaku kyūjūnenshi* [A ninety-year history of the Tokyo Industrial College] (Tokyo: Zaikai Hyōron Shinsha, 1975), p. 431. See also Juhn, "Entrepreneurship in an Undeveloped Economy," pp. 93–94. The Japanese followed a similar industrial educational policy in Taiwan. There, as in Korea, the assumption was that one "could always obtain technicians from the home country." See E. Patricia Tsurumi, *Japanese Colonial Education in Taiwan, 1895–1945* (Cambridge: Harvard University Press, 1977), p. 53.

71. Chōsen Sōtokufu, *Chōsen Sangyō Keizai Chōsakai kaigiroku*, Committee no. 4, p. 611.

72. See Chōsen Sōtokufu, *Chōsen Sangyō Keizai Chōsakai shimon tōshinsho*, pp. 57–60.

73. By 1945 about 19 percent of the technicians in the manufacturing and construction industries in Korea were Korean. In high-technology industries, however, such as metals and chemicals, this figure was only 11 percent. See Mason et al., *Economic and Social Modernization of the Republic of Korea*, pp. 76–77.

74. *KYS*, p. 154; "Keijō Bōseki [sic] Kaisha no naiyō o kiku," p. 16.

75. *KYS*, p. 105.

76. Kim Yongwan, taped interview, Seoul, Mar. 30, 1984.

77. *KYS*, p. 154.

78. Kyŏngsŏng Pangjik CH, Record of the Board of Directors Meetings, Minutes of Board Meeting no. 2, Oct. 6, 1919.

79. Tongǔn Ki'nyŏm Saǒphoe, *Tongǔn Kim Yongwan*, p. 92.

80. Kyŏngsŏng Pangjik CH, Record of the Board of Directors Meetings, Minutes of Board Meeting no. 88, Apr. 27, 1940.

81. Kim Yongwan, taped interview, Seoul, Mar. 30, 1984.

82. Yamamura, "General Trading Companies in Japan," pp. 171–72, 177–78. Yamamura's information is taken from the C. Itoh centennial history, *Itō Chū Shōji hyakunen*, published in 1964.

83. Kim Yongwan, taped interview, Seoul, Apr. 13, 1984. Kyŏngbang's current chairman, Kim Kakchung, told me that his father (and former Kyŏngbang chairman) Kim Yongwan was a close friend of the current president of C. Itoh. Kim Kakchung, interview, Seoul, Mar. 29, 1984. Later, during a tour of the Yŏngdŭngp'o factory, I noticed that Kyŏngbang's machinery from Toyoda had been purchased through the C. Itoh Company.

84. Kim Yongwan, taped interview, Seoul, Mar. 30, 1984. See also Ogura Masatarō, ed., *Chōsen sangyō nempō, 1943*, pp. 124–25.

85. Kim Yongwan, taped interview, Seoul, Apr. 13, 1984. See also above, n. 70.

86. Hashiguchi Shūkō, ed., *Chōsen sen'i yōran*, p. 390. Kim Yongwan, taped interview, Seoul, Mar. 30, 1984.

87. See, for example, Kyŏngsŏng Pangjik CH, receipt from Kureha Bōseki KK (for monthly payment of allowance, food, and bonus expenses incurred by four Kyŏngbang trainees at Kureha's factory in Kureha), June 11, 1942; receipt from Kureha Bōseki KK (for monthly payment of allowance, food, and bonus expenses incurred by three Kyŏngbang trainees at Kureha's factory in Daimon), June 15, 1942; receipt from Kureha Bōseki KK (for allowance, food, and bonus expenses incurred by four Kyŏngbang trainees at Kureha's factory in Nyūzen), June (n.d.), 1942. See also Kyŏngsŏng Pangjik CH, Osaka Representative Office: Income and Expenditure Report nos. KB123, KB126, June 1942. Kyŏngbang's higher-level technicians also appear to have been in the habit of making short field trips to Japanese textile factories. See, for example, Kyŏngsŏng Pangjik CH, Travel Expense Statement (submitted by the head of Kyŏngbang's spinning department for inspection tour of factories in the Osaka, Hokuriku, and Shikoku areas between June 11 and June 29, 1941), July 1, 1941.

88. Kim Yongwan, taped interview, Seoul, Mar. 30, 1984.

6. Between Metropole and Hinterland: The Quest for Markets

1. Kyŏngbang was participating in these fairs, which generally went on for one to two months, as early as 1924; other such fairs in which Kyŏngbang participated were held in 1929, 1935, and 1940. See *KY*, p. 328.

2. *KYS*, pp. 98–100.

3. *KY*, p. 90.

4. Ibid., pp. 299–300.

5. Ibid., pp. 65–66.

6. *Sanŏpkye*, no. 2 (January 1924), advertisement opposite first page of table of contents.

7. See "Keijō Bōseki [sic] Kaisha no naiyō o kiku," p. 16.

8. See Cho Kijun, *Han'guk kiŏpkasa*, pp. 184–85, 196–200; also Pak Tubyŏng Chŏn'gi Wiwŏnhoe, *Yŏn'gang Pak Tubyŏng*, pp. 25–32; also Myŏng Chuhyŏn, ed., *OB isimnyŏnsa*, pp. 64–67.

9. Cho Kijun, *Han'guk kiŏpkasa*, p. 199; Pak Tubyŏng Chŏn'gi Wiwŏnhoe, *Yŏn'gang Pak Tubyŏng*, p. 32.

10. Chōsen Menshifushō Rengōkai, *Chōsen mengyōshi*, pp. 32–34, 299–301. See also Myŏng Chuhyŏn, ed., *OB isimnyŏnsa*, pp. 67–68.

11. Cho Kijun, *Han'guk kiŏpkasa*, pp. 198–99.

12. Pak Tubyŏng Chŏn'gi Wiwŏnhoe, *Yŏn'gang Pak Tubyŏng*, p. 76. See also Chōsen Menshifushō Rengōkai, *Chōsen mengyōshi*, p. 33.

13. Chōsen Menshifushō Rengōkai, *Chōsen mengyōshi*, pp. 24, 299–300.

14. On C. Itoh's investment in Kongik, see Cho Kijun, *Han'guk kiŏpkasa*,

p. 199; information on Kyŏngbang's introduction to the C. Itoh company from Kim Yongwan, taped interview, Seoul, Apr. 13, 1984.

15. Kim Yongwan, taped interview, Seoul, Mar. 30, 1984. The textile industry was not the only area in which the Paks and the Kims worked together during the colonial period. When the Shōwa Kirin Beer Company, Ltd., was established by Mitsubishi in Yŏngdŭngp'o in 1933, both Pak Sŭngjik and Kim Yŏnsu participated as shareholders and directors in the new company. After Liberation, management and eventual control of Shōwa Kirin fell to Pak's eldest son, Tubyŏng, who used the company (now OB Beer) as a base for creating the Tusan business group. See Myŏng Chuhyŏn, ed., *OB isimnyŏnsa*, pp. 60–64. See also Chōsen Ginkō Chōsaka, *Saikin Chōsen ni okeru daikōgyō yakushin to sono shihon keitō*, unpaginated chart at the end of the report.

16. Pak's social background is somewhat murky. His recently published memoirs and the Hwasin company history portray his father as a well known and respected figure in Yonggang Country (South P'yŏngan Province), but neither Pak nor his writers make any attempt to claim yangban status for the family and do not, in fact, even tell us which Pak clan the family belonged to—an aspect of family history that most Koreans with any aristocratic pretensions, however shaky, would hardly fail to mention. According to Pak, the family, which had been living in Yonggang for ten generations, had by the sixth or seventh generation become "wealthy farmers" (*t'oho*) with an income of 2,000 *sŏk*. By the time Pak was born, however, the family appears to have lost much of its former wealth (though this is never clearly spelled out in the sources), and Pak seems to have been forced to rely on his wits rather than on an inheritance to support his mother (his older brother had died in 1910 and his father in 1916). See Pak Hŭngsik, "Chaegye hoego" [Memoirs of the business world] in *Chaegye hoego wŏllo kiŏbinp'yŏn II* [Memoirs of the business world: Senior businessmen, vol. 2] (Seoul: Han'guk Ilbosa Ch'ulp'anguk, 1984): 166–67; Kim Chunggil, ed., *Hwasin osimnyŏnsa: 1926–1976*, p. 69.

17. Pak Hŭngsik, "Chaegye hoego," pp. 167–68; Kim Chunggil, ed., *Hwasin osimnyŏnsa: 1926–1976*, pp. 74–75.

18. Pak Hŭngsik, "Chaegye hoego," pp. 168–78; Kim Chunggil, ed., *Hwasin osimnyŏnsa: 1926–1976*, pp. 75–101.

19. Kim Chunggil, ed., *Hwasin osimnyŏnsa: 1926–1976*, pp. 97–98.

20. At his trial for anti-nationalist activities in 1949 Pak acknowledged that he had been a shareholder (about 1,000 shares) and an auditor in the company. See Kim Yŏngjin, ed., *Panminja taegongp'angi* [Record of the public trial of the traitors] (Seoul: Hanp'ung Ch'ulp'ansa, 1949), p. 56.

21. Regarding Pak's relationship with Aruga, see Pak Hŭngsik, "Chaegye hoego," p. 188; also Kim Chunggil, ed., *Hwasin osimnyŏnsa: 1926–1976*, p. 122, and on Pak and Ugaki, idem, pp. 97–98.

22. See Kim Yŏngjin, ed., *Panminja*, pp. 61–62.

23. Kim Chunggil, ed., *Hwasin osimnyŏnsa: 1926–1976*, pp. 102–31.

24. Kyŏngsŏng Pangjik CH, Sales Premiums Ledger, Dec. 1, 1938–Nov. 31, 1939 (Yongin ledger no. 11), p. 1.

25. Kim Chunggil, ed., *Hwasin osimnyŏnsa, 1926–1976*, pp. 180–81.

26. See Hashiguchi Shūkō, ed., *Chōsen sen'i yōran*, pp. 122–23.

27. See Kim Chunggil, *Hwasin osimnyŏnsa: 1926–1976*, p. 143; also Hashiguchi Shūkō, ed., *Chōsen sen'i yōran*, pp. 115–16. According to the Hwasin company history, this company was forced to dissolve in 1940; according to the *Chōsen sen'i yōran*, however, it was still in operation as of February 1943.

28. See Kim Chunggil, *Hwasin osimnyŏnsa: 1926–1976*, p. 143. At the end of 1944 Pak personally held 1,340 Kyŏngbang shares but also controlled 16,766 additional shares in the company through CH Hwasin and Hwasin Trading. Kyŏngbang had a total of 260,000 shares at the end of 1944. See Kyŏngsŏng Pangjik, CH, List of Stockholders, Nov. 30, 1944.

29. See Ko Wŏnbyŏn, ed., *Panminja choesanggi* [Record of the crimes of the traitors] (Seoul: Paeg'yŏp Munhwasa, 1949), p. 16.

30. See Kyŏngsŏng Pangjik CH, Sales Premiums Ledger, Dec. 1, 1938–Nov. 31, 1939 (Yongin ledger no. 11), passim.

31. Ibid.

32. Ibid. See Kyŏngsŏng Pangjik CH, Daily Sales Ledger, May 6, 1943–Oct. 23, 1943 (Yongin ledger no. 462), pp. 1–217 passim.

33. See Kyŏngsŏng Pangjik CH, Table of Rebate Rates, in the company's Sales Premiums Ledger, Dec. 1, 1938–Nov. 31, 1939 (Yongin ledger no. 11).

34. Kawai Akitake, *Chōsen kōgyō no gendankai*, pp. 109–10.

35. Ernest Hemingway, *The Snows of Kilimanjaro and Other Stories* (New York: Charles Scribner's Sons, 1927), p. 3.

36. Martin's report is in Edwin W. Pauley, *Report on Japanese Assets in Manchuria to the President of the United States* (July 1946), Appendix 12, Plant Inspection Report 1-K-8.

37. *The Manchoukuo Year Book (1942)* (Hsinking: Manchoukuo Year Book Co., 1942), p. 117.

38. On the Yongjŏng Trading Company, see *Chomei shōkō annai* [Guide to major commerce and industry] (Osaka: KK Shōgyō Kōshinjo, 1942), Chōsen-Manchū Section, p. 98. See also Kyŏngsŏng Pangjik CH, List of Stockholders, Nov. 30, 1944, p. 12. Kyŏngbang's 1944 list of stockholders names a certain Toyoda Tomihisa as president of Yongjŏng, but the *Chomei shōkō annai* names Kang as president, as does a Kyŏngbang dividend statement to the Yongjŏng Trading Company dated July 7, 1942. Conclusion: by 1944 either Kang had adopted a Japanese name or had been succeeded by someone else as president of Yongjŏng.

39. Jones, *Manchuria Since 1931*, p. 73.

40. Ibid., pp. 72–73 and 178–79.

41. *SY*, pp. 131–50, 169–71.

42. Ibid., pp. 138, 141.

43. Ibid., pp. 142, 144, 146, 170.

44. Ibid., pp. 162–167.

45. Peter Duus, "Economic Dimensions of Meiji Imperialism," p. 159.

46. On Kada, see Kita Tadai, *Chōsen jinji kōshinroku*, p. 103.

47. Chōsen Sōtokufu, *Sangyō Chōsa Iinkai giji sokkiroku*, Special Committee on Sec. 1, Day 3, p. 10.

48. Ibid., p. 7.

49. Grajdanzev, *Modern Korea*, p. 201. See also Cho Kijun, *Han'guk chabonjuŭi sŏngnipsaron*, pp. 475–77; Jones, pp. 124–28; Grajdanzev, *Modern Korea*, p. 201. See also Cho Kijun, *Han'guk chabonjuŭi sŏngnipsaron*, p. 476.

50. See Han Sangnyong, *Namboku Shina oyobi Manshū shisatsu hōkokusho* [Report of the mission to north and south China and Manchuria] (Keijō: KK Kanjō Ginkō, 1917), p. 179.

51. Chōsen Sōtokufu, *Sangyō Chōsa Iinkai giji sokkiroku*, Special Committee on Sec. 1, Day 3, p. 1.

52. See Han Sangnyong, "Namboku Manshū o shisatsu shite" [Mission to north and south Manchuria], *Chōsen jitsugyō kurabu* 10 (April 1932): 3.

53. "Zaikai hempen" [Business notes], *Chōsen jitsugyō kurabu* 10 (June 1932): 40.

54. See Kudō Sanjirō, "Chōsen tai Manshū bōeki no jūnen" [Ten years of Chōsen-Manchurian trade], *Chōsen jitsugyō* 20 (September 1942): 2. On the Government-General's role in the organization, see Chōsen Sōtokufu, *Chōsen Sangyō Keizai Chōsakai shimon tōshinsho*, p. 37.

55. See, for example, "Zaikai hempen," p. 37. See also the list of participants and the transcript of the May 27, 1932, Symposium on Chōsen-Manchurian Trade (Semman Bōeki Zadankai) in *Chōsen jitsugyō kurabu* 10 (June 1932): 31–66 and *Chōsen jitsugyō kurabu* 10 (July 1932): 41–65. See also Furuta Renzaburō (Manager of the Bank of Chōsen, Dairen Branch), "Manshūkoku ni tsuite" [On Manchukuo], *Chōsen jitsugyō kurabu* 10 (October 1932): 14–15; Yamanari Kyōroku (Vice-Governor of the Central Bank of Manchukuo), "Manshūkoku no kin'yū jijō (I)" [Financing in Manchukuo, Part I], *Chōsen jitsugyō kurabu* 11 (March 1933): 31–33 (continued in the April and May issues); Dōmoto Sadakazu (director of the Bureau of Industry, Chōsen Government-General), "Manshūkoku sangyō no taisei to Semman bōeki ni tsuite" [Manchurian industry and Chōsen-Manchurian trade], *Chōsen jitsugyō kurabu* 13 (April 1935): 2–7.

56. Chōsen Sōtokufu, *Chōsen Sangyō Keizai Chōsakai shimon tōshinsho*, p. 27.

57. Ibid., pp. 35–37.

58. Cho Kijun, *Han'guk kiŏpkasa*, p. 199.

59. "Semman bōeki zadankai" [Symposium on Chōsen-Manchurian

Trade], *Chōsen jitsugyō kurabu* 10 (June 1932): 31–36, and *Chōsen jitsugyō kurabu* 10 (July 1932): 41–65.

60. "Zaikai hempen," *Chōsen jitsugyō kurabu* 10 (June 1932): 37.

61. See Han's speech, "Jikyoku to Manshū" [Manchukuo and the current situation], on the first anniversary of the Manchurian Incident, published in the *Chōsen jitsugyō kurabu* 10 (October 1932): 25–31. Han continued to deliver similar commemorative speeches on the incident thereafter: see, for example, his 1936 speech in Han Ikkyo, ed., *Kan Sōryū o kataru*, pp. 760–71.

62. "Semman keizai sangyō zadankai (I)," p. 46. See also *KY*, p. 106.

63. See Jones, *Manchuria Since 1931*, pp. 70–71.

64. Han Sangnyong, "Namboku Manshū o shisatsu," pp. 6, 13. See also Han Sangnyong, "Jikyoku to Manshū," p. 31.

65. F. C. Jones, pp. 72–75.

66. On the Yinkow Spinning and Weaving Company, see Sakai Kazuo, "Manshū keikōgyō no hatten katei ni kansuru oboegaki" [A note on the process of development of light industry in Manchukuo], *Dai Nippon Bōseki Rengōkai geppō*, no. 583 (May 1941): 6. We do not know the exact amount of Kim Yŏnsu's investment in the Yingkow mill. Extant records, however, show that he controlled at least 132 shares by the end of the colonial period. See Samyang Tongjehoe, Securities Ledger (Yongin ledger no. 289), pp. 18, 37.

67. See *Chōsen jitsugyō kurabu* 12 (March 1934): 51 (box at bottom of page).

68. See Han Sangnyong, "Manshū Jihen sanjūnen o mukaete" [Celebrating the third anniversary of the Manchurian Incident], *Chōsen jitsugyō kurabu* 12 (October 1934): 11. Kim Yŏnsu was a good example of one of these businessmen.

69. Kudō Sanjirō, "Chōsen tai Manshū bōeki no jūnen," p. 4.

70. Shiomi Tsunesaburō, "Chōsen ni okeru bōseki kōgyō no genjō (II)," pp. 70–73. See also Keizo Seki, *Cotton Industry of Japan*, p. 196; Jerome B. Cohen, *Japan's Economy in War and Reconstruction*, p. 15.

71. Chōsen Menshifushō Rengōkai, *Chōsen mengyōshi*, pp. 89–92.

72. See *KY*, pp. 64–66, 310; *KYS*, pp. 118–19; Kyŏngsŏng Pangjik CH, Record of the Board of Directors Meetings, Minutes of Board Meeting no. 27, Nov. 7, 1924. See also *KY*, p. 65.

73. *KY*, p. 54

74. The tour was sponsored by the P'yŏngyang municipal government and lasted about a month. See *KYS*, pp. 98–100 (including map of area visited). On Yŏnsu's appointment to Kyŏngbang, see *KYS*, p. 107.

75. *KYS*, pp. 129–30. Also Kim Yongwan, taped interview, Seoul, Mar. 30, 1984.

76. On the popularity of this type of sheeting in Manchuria, see Richard A. Krause, *Cotton and Cotton Goods in China, 1918–1936* (New York: Gar-

land Publishing, 1980), K-1 (appendix K). This is the type of sheeting that Kyŏngbang was producing: see Kim Yŏnsu's own remarks at the 1936 Government-General industrial commission in Chōsen Sōtokufu, *Chōsen Sangyō Keizai Chōsakai kaigiroku*, Committee no. 2, p. 387. See also *KYS*, p. 130; *KY*, p. 74.

77. *KYS*, p. 130.

78. *KY*, p. 7.

79. "Keijō Bōseki [sic] Kaisha no naiyō o kiku," p. 16; *KY*, p. 544.

80. *KY*, pp. 90, 325, 545; *KYS*, p. 132; *SY*, pp. 134–35.

81. *KY*, pp. 90, 301, 522.

82. Ibid., pp. 102, 545.

83. Sakai Kazuo, "Manshū keikōgyō no hatten katei ni kansuru oboegaki," p. 6.

84. See Miyabashi's outspoken criticism (in 1932) of the existing Manchurian tariff in "Semman bōeki zadankai (II)," pp. 48–49. At the time he was chairman of the Keijō Wholesalers Federation. He also served as director–general of the Chōsen Cotton Yarn and Cloth Merchants Association: see chap. 4. On the revision of the tariff in 1933, see Jones, *Manchuria Since 1931*, pp. 191–92.

85. Sakai Kazuo, "Manshū keikōgyō no hatten katei ni kansuru oboegaki," p. 6.

86. Before the establishment of Manchukuo, the tariff on cotton piece goods imported into Manchuria from Japan (and Korea) was running as high as 36 percent (see Miyabayashi's remarks in "Semman bōeki zadankai [II]," p. 48). In 1933, the ad valorem tariff on cotton piece goods ranged between 12.0 and 12.5 percent, depending on the item. In 1934 it was raised to between 17.5 and 25 percent. By 1938, all cotton piece goods (with the exception of terry pile cloth and corduroy) were being assessed a 25 percent duty. See South Manchuria Railway Company, *Fifth Report on Progress in Manchuria to 1936* (Dairen: South Manchuria Railway Company, 1936), p. 39; South Manchuria Railway Company, *Sixth Report on Progress in Manchuria to 1939* (Dairen: South Manchuria Railway Company, 1939), p. 217. See also Jones, *Manchuria Since 1931*, p. 193.

87. Shiomi Tsunesaburō, "Chōsen ni okeru bōseki kōgyō no genjō (II)," pp. 71–72.

88. *KY*, p. 522. By 1937 colonial businessmen were even beginning to look back rather fondly on earlier Manchurian tariff arrangements with the Chinese. See the remarks of Kudō Sanjirō (director of the Chōsen Trade Association) in "Semman keizai sangyō zadankai (II)," pp. 107–8. See also Chōsen Sōtokufu, *Chōsen Sangyō Keizai Chōsakai shimon tōshinsho*, pp. 36–37; Chōsen Sōtokufu, *Chōsen Sōtokufu Jikyoku Taisaku Chōsakai shimon tōshinsho*, p. 80.

89. Shiomi Tsunesaburō, "Chōsen ni okeru bōseki kōgyō no genjō (I)," p. 8; (II), pp. 63–64.

90. Chōsen Sōtokufu, *Chōsen Sangyō Keizai Chōsakai kaigiroku*, Committee no. 2, pp. 388–89.

91. In 1944 customs duties were completely abolished between Japan and Manchukuo. See Jones. *Manchuria Since 1931*, p. 204. "Difficulties in the supply of capital goods from Japan combined with the exigencies of war to modify the concept of Manchuria as a fully-equipped industrial base" (p. 205).

92. Shiomi Tsunesaburō, "Chōsen ni okeru bōseki kōgyō no genjō (II)," pp. 71–72.

93. The purpose of the restriction was to encourage export outside the Yen Bloc and thereby acquire foreign exchange to purchase war-related raw materials. Shiomi Tsunesaburō, "Chōsen ni okeru bōseki kōgyō no genjō (II)," pp. 71–72.

94. *KY*, pp. 104–5.

95. Kim Kakchung (current Kyŏngbang chairman; son of Kim Yongwan and nephew of Sŏngsu and Yŏnsu), interview, Yŏngdŭngp'o office, Mar. 29, 1984. Mr. Kim said his uncle (Yŏnsu) had believed the Japanese were "strong enough to hold Manchuria." *KY*, pp. 546–47.

96. Letter from Kim Yŏnsu to Sekiya Teizaburō, Sept. 25, 1939. Sekiya Teizaburō Bunsho 1081, Kenseishiryō Shitsu, Kokuritsu Kokkai Toshōkan (Sekiya Teizaburō Papers, Constitutional Documents Room, National Diet Library, Tokyo, Japan). Sekiya (1875–1950) was a graduate of the law college of Tokyo Imperial University in 1899. That same year he passed the Civil Service Examination and entered the Home Ministry, subsequently serving in a number of official posts in Taiwan, Korea, and Kwantung. In Korea he was director of the Bureau of Education from 1910 to 1917 as well as chief secretary (Shokikanchō) of the Central Council (Chūsūin), a Korean advisory organ to the governor-general. After returning to Japan, he served in the Imperial Household Ministry, becoming a vice-minister in 1921. In 1933 he left the Imperial Household Ministry and was appointed by the emperor to the House of Peers. When Kim Yŏnsu wrote to him in 1939, Sekiya was also an auditor of the Bank of Japan. See Shimonaka Yasaburō, ed., *Dai jimmei jiten* 3–4: 523; Tsunesaburo Kamesaka, ed., *Who's Who in Japan: Fourteenth Annual Edition (1931–1932)* (Tokyo: Who's Who in Japan Publishing Office, 1932) and *Who's Who in Japan with Manchoukuo and China: Nineteenth Annual Edition* (Tokyo: Who's Who in Japan Publishing House, 1938).

97. *KY*, pp. 107–8; Kim Yongwan, taped interview, Seoul, Mar. 30, 1984.

98. *KY*, p. 106. The total authorized textile (including dye) capital was about 88 million yen in 1938: see South Manchuria Railway Company, *Sixth Report on Progress in Manchuria to 1939*, p. 77. In the sources, the capital of Manchurian companies, including the SMSC, was normally stated in yuan, the Manchurian currency, rather than in yen, but the two currencies were equivalent in value (i.e., 1 yuan equaled 1 yen), and I have converted yuan to yen for the sake of clarity and consistency.

99. *KY*, pp. 106–7. See also Edwin M. Martin's report on the factory in

Pauley, *Report on Japanese Assets in Manchuria to the President of the United States*, Appendix 12, Plant Inspection Report 1-K-8. In 1940 Kanebō's mill in Mukden had about 30,818 spindles and 888 looms. See Osanaga Yoshimasu, ed., *Manshū keizai zusetsu* [The Manchurian economy in graphs] (Dairen: Dairen Shōkō Kaigisho, 1940), p. 96; Sakai Kazuo, "Manshū keikōgyō no hatten katei ni kansuru oboegaki," p. 6. *KY*, pp. 235–36. Kim Kakchung also said that the factory in Manchuria had "over 3,000 workers." Kim Kakchung, interview, Yŏngdŭngp'o, Mar. 29, 1984.

100. *KY*, p. 106.

101. Ibid., pp. 106–7. The original board of directors included Kim Yŏnsu (president), Ch'oe Tusŏn, Pak Hŭngsik, Ko Wŏnhun, and Min Kyusik. Hyŏn Chunho and Kim Sayŏn served as auditors.

102. Chōsen Sōtokufu, *Chōsen Sangyō Keizai Chōsakai kaigiroku*, General Session (final), Oct. 24, 1936, pp. 665–67.

103. See *KY*, pp. 108–9; Kim Yŏngsŏn, "Kwiguk yŏlch'a" [The train home], *Sabo Kyŏngbang* [The Kyŏngbang bulletin] (November 1970): 7. Kim was responsible for bringing the girls back to Korea after Liberation. His fascinating account of the trip through Russian lines was serialized in Kyŏngbang's official monthly bulletin between November 1970 and June 1971. Kim Kakchung, interview, Yŏngdŭngp'o, Mar. 29, 1984.

104. See South Manchuria Railway Company, *Sixth Report on Progress in Manchuria to 1939*, map (folded) following table of contents.

105. See Minami Manshū Tetsudō KK, *Minami Manshū Tetsudō ryōkō annai* [The South Manchuria Railway travel guide] (Dairen: Minami Manshū Tetsudō KK, 1919), pp. 72–74. See also *The Manchoukuo Year Book (1942)*, pp. 731–34, and Jones, *Manchuria Since 1931*, pp. 206, 210–11.

106. South Manchuria Railway Company, *Sixth Report on Progress in Manchuria to 1939*, pp. 77–79; Jones, *Manchuria Since 1931*, pp. 210–11.

107. See Kim Sanghyŏp (second son of Yŏnsu and later prime minister of. the Republic of Korea from June 1982 to October 1983), Stock Certificates (1,420 shares), Mukden Bank of Commerce and Industry (KK Hōten Shōkō Ginkō), purchased at various times between July 1940 and April 1943, Hapcha Hoesa Samyangsa Documents, CH Samyangsa, Seoul. On the Mukden Bank of Commerce and Industry, see Zaiseibu Rizaiji, ed., *Manshūkoku ginkō sōran* [Compendium of Manchurian banks] (Hsinking: Bureau of Finance, 1935), p. 116.

108. See Kim Sangjun (eldest son of Yŏnsu), Stock Certificates (300 shares), Manchurian Real Estate and Development Company (Manshū Tochi Tatemono KK), all purchased on Aug. 13, 1941, Hapcha Hoesa Samyangsa Documents, CH Samyangsa, Seoul.

109. Naitō Yasohachi, ed., *Semman sangyō taikan*, Manchurian Sec., Companies, p. 94.

110. Kim Sangjun (eldest son of Yŏnsu), Stock Certificates (284 shares), Manchurian Paper Company (Manshū Seishi KK), purchased on Apr. 28,

1943, and Feb. 1, 1944, Hapcha Hoesa Samyangsa Documents, CH Samyangsa, Seoul. On the Manchurian Paper Company, see Kanahara Kaoru, ed., *Manshū ginkō kaisha nenkan, 1942* [The Manchurian bank and company yearbook, 1942], no. 8 (Dairen: Dairen Shōkō Kaigisho, 1943), p. 366. Kim Sangjun (eldest son of Yŏnsu), Stock Certificates (700 shares), Manchurian-Mongolian Woolen Company (Mammō Keiori KK), purchased in 1941 and 1942, Hapcha Hoesa Samyangsa Documents, CH Samyangsa, Seoul. On the company, see Naitō Yasohachi, ed., *Semman sangyō taikan*, Manchurian Sec., Companies, p. 39. See also Pauley, *Report on Japanese Assets in Manchuria to the President of the United States*, p. 221.

111. Osanaga Yoshimasu, ed., *Manshū keizai zusetsu*, p. 96.

112. See Hashiguchi Shūkō, ed., *Chōsen sen'i yōran*, p. 269. The Chōsen Spinners Association (Chōsen Bōseki Kōgyō Kumiai), established in 1940, was apparently the successor to the Federation of Chōsen Spinners (Chōsen Bōseki Dōgyōkai Rengōkai), of which Kim Yŏnsu had also served as chairman: see chap. 4. Such organizations were promoted by the Government-General in the late 1930s as part of the semi-war and wartime economic mobilization. According to Kim Yongwan, however, a cooperative organization of Korean and Japanese spinners had already been in existence as early as the 1920s—long before the Government-General instituted any kind of formal controls. Kim Yongwan, taped interview, Seoul, Apr. 13, 1984. A record (possibly only partial) of Kyŏngbang's shares in Kanebō, Tōyōbō, and Dai Nippon can be found in Kyŏngsŏng Pangjik CH, Securities Ledger (Yongin ledger no. 293), passim. On the Chōbō shares, see Samyang Tongjehoe, Securities Ledger (Yongin ledger no. 289), pp. 16–17.

113. Kim Sangjun (eldest son of Yŏnsu), Stock Certificates (1,200 shares), Dairen Machine Works (Dairen Kikai Seisakujo), all purchased on Oct. 1, 1944, Hapcha Hoesa Samyangsa Documents, CH Samyangsa, Seoul. The Dairen Machine works (with a branch office in Mukden) was a huge company (the authorized capital in 1944 was 60 million yuan according to stock certificates) engaged primarily in the production of rolling stock and items related to railroad construction both in Manchuria and north China. See Naitō Yasohachi, ed., *Semman sangyō taikan*, Manchurian Sec., Companies, pp. 35–36.

114. Kim Sangjun (eldest son of Yŏnsu), Stock Certificates (400 shares), South Manchurian Gas Company (Minami Manshū Gasu KK), all purchased on June 1, 1943, Hapcha Hoesa Samyangsa Documents, CH Samyangsa, Seoul. The company was originally established in 1925 by the South Manchuria Railway as a wholly owned subsidiary but was opened to the public in 1935. It had an authorized capital of 20 million yuan in 1944 (see stock certificates) and was Manchuria's first and only gas company. See Naitō Yasohachi, ed., *Semman sangyō taikan*, Manchurian Sec., Companies, pp. 58–59.

115. Kim Sanghong (third son of Yŏnsu), Stock Certificates (300 shares),

Manchurian Bearing Company (Manshū Bearingu Seizō KK), all purchased on July 16, 1942, Hapcha Hoesa Samyangsa Documents, CH Samyangsa, Seoul. The company had an authorized capital of 8 million yuan in 1942 (see stock certificates) and was manufacturing and selling ball bearings, roller bearings, and related items. See Sakamoto Zensaburō, ed., *Manshū ginkō kaisha nenkan, 1938* [The Manchurian bank and company yearbook, 1938], no. 4 (Dairen: Dairen Shōkō Kaigisho, 1938), p. 433. See also Jones, *Manchuria Since 1931*, pp. 160, 163–64.

116. *SY*, 168–69; *KYS*, p. 168.

117. Han Sangnyong, *Namboku Shina oyobi Manshū shisatsu hōkokusho*, p. 1.

118. Chōsen Sōtokufu, *Chōsen Sangyō Keizai Chōsakai kaigiroku*, Committee no. 2, p. 377.

119. Chōsen Sōtokufu, *Chōsen Sōtokufu Jikyoku Taisaku Chōsakai shimon tōshinsho*, pp. 77, 82–83.

120. Ibid., p. 83.

121. Kim Yehyŏn, "Shina jihengo ni shosubeki Hantōjin no jōi," pp. 64–65. Kim was a consultant to the Chōsen Fire and Marine Insurance Company KK (Chōsen Kasai Kaijō Hoken KK), principally owned by the Chōsen Industrial Bank and the Bank of Chōsen. See "Kaiin meibo," p. 107; also *Chōsen GKKY*, pp. 16–17.

122. Han Sangnyong, "Hokushi o mite" [Looking at north China], *Chōsen jitsugyo* 18 (July 1940): 67–68.

123. *KY*, pp. 100, 105–6. It was not until September, 1939, that Kyŏngbang received permission to build a factory from the Manchurian authorities (see p. 178). After the Japanese advance into China, the company may have held off making a final decision to build in Manchuria until the possibilities of building a factory in China proper had first been thoroughly explored.

124. *KY*, p. 105.

125. Ibid.

126. Ibid., pp. 105–6.

127. Chŏn Sŭngbŏm, "Daitōa sensō to Chōsen keizai no shinro" [The greater East Asia war and the course of the Korean economy], *Chōsen jitsugyō* 20 (March 1942): 14.

128. Hashiguchi Shūkō, ed., *Chōsen sen'i yōran*, p. 122.

129. Ibid., p. 88. Changte, located about midway on the Peking-Hankow railway line, had a population of about 2,500 in the 1940s and was the most important industrial city in Honan Province. Noted for its cotton production, it had offices of all of Japan's major cotton traders: Tōyō Menka, Nippon Menka, Gōshō, and others. Korea also seems to have been prominent in Changte's business life. In addition to the Kyŏngbang office, there was a branch of the Bank of Chōsen and even a "Chōsen Inn" (Chōsen Ryōkan). See Tsukamoto Yoshitaka, ed., *Chūgoku kōshō meikan* [Directory of trade and industry in China] (Tokyo: Nippon Shōgyō Tsūshinsha, 1942), pp. 477–500.

130. As noted earlier, Kyŏngbang had at one point considered establishing such a factory in Changte as a joint venture with Toyoda, but there is no evidence of such an investment in Kyŏngbang's records. Sources on the factory itself also make no mention of any Kyŏngbang involvement either in equity or management. What we do know of the factory is that it was originally founded and operated by Chinese, who apparently fled in the wake of the Japanese invasion. It then came under the control and supervision of the Japanese Honan army, who, in turn, entrusted its management to Kanebō. See Kojima Seiichi, *Hokushi keizai dokuhon* [The North China economic reader] (Tokyo: Sensō Shobō, 1939), pp. 171–72.

Part III. Class and Society

1. See the editorials in *Tonga ilbo*, May 10–11, 1921. See also Michael Edson Robinson, *Cultural Nationalism in Colonial Korea, 1920–1925* (Seattle: University of Washington Press, 1988), pp. 69–77.

2. See Antonio Gramsci, *Selections from the Prison Notebooks*, ed. and trans. by Quintin Hoare and Geoffrey Nowell Smith (New York: International Publishers, paperback, 1971). See also Ronald Aminzade, *Class, Politics, and Early Industrial Capitalism: A Study of Mid-Nineteenth-Century Toulouse, France* (Albany: State University of New York Press, 1981). For an excellent interpretation of Gramsci's work, see Walter L. Adamson, *Hegemony and Revolution: A Study of Antonio Gramsci's Political and Cultural Theory* (Berkeley and Los Angeles: University of California Press, paperback, 1980).

3. There is, of course, an enormous literature on this subject reaching back into the nineteenth century itself, but one of the best studies is by Barrington Moore, Jr.: *Social Origins of Dictatorship and Democracy: Lord and Peasant in the Making of the Modern World* (Boston: Beacon Press, 1966), especially chap. 1. For a detailed case study of the role of the British cotton spinners in the struggle for political reform, see Rhodes Boyson, *The Ashworth Cotton Enterprise: The Rise and Fall of the Family Firm, 1818–1880* (Oxford: Clarendon Press, 1970).

7. "Without Any Trouble": Capitalist Views and Treatment of the Working Class

1. Grajdanzev, *Modern Korea*, p. 179.

2. See, for example, Takahashi Kamekichi, *Gendai Chōsen keizairon* [A discourse on the contemporary Korean economy] (Tokyo: Sensō Shobō, 1935), pp. 402–3. See also Shiomi Tsunesaburō, "Chōsen ni okeru bōseki kōgyō no genjō (II)," p. 63; also Grajdanzev, *Modern Korea* (citing Takahashi), p. 151.

3. Minami Manshū Tetsudō KK, Keizai Chōsakai Daiichibu, *Chōsenjin rōdōsha ippan jijō* [General conditions of Korean workers] (Minami Manshū

Tetsudō KK, 1933), p. 79. See also Grajdanzev, *Modern Korea* (who cites this source), p. 178.

4. The original Factory Law was passed in 1911; it was then revised in 1923 (effective for the most part in 1926, although grace periods of three or more years were stipulated for certain articles). One of the most important provisions (effective July 1, 1929) was the abolition of night work for juveniles (under 14) and females. A health insurance law was also passed in 1922 (effective in 1927). See Andrew Gordon, *The Evolution of Labor Relations in Japan: Heavy Industry, 1853–1955*, Subseries on the History of Japanese Business and Industry, Harvard East Asian Monographs 117 (Cambridge: Council on East Asian Studies, Harvard University, 1985), pp. 67–68, 210–11. See also Iwao F. Ayusawa, *A History of Labor in Modern Japan* (Honolulu: East-West Center Press, 1966), pp. 106–11; Pearse, *Cotton Industry of Japan and China*, pp. 102–12. See also Takafusa Nakamura, *Economic Growth in Prewar Japan*, p. 228; Grajdanzev, *Modern Korea*, pp. 154, 179.

5. Pearse, *Cotton Industry of Japan and China*, p. 93.

6. Shiomi Tsunesaburō, "Chōsen ni okeru bōseki kōgyō no genjō (II)," p. 63.

7. See Takahashi Kamekichi, *Gendai Chōsen keizairon*, p. 67. Kim Yongwan also said that Kyŏngbang's wages were slightly lower than those of the Japanese textile companies in Korea. Kim Yongwan, taped interview, Seoul, Mar. 30, 1984.

8. In Korean: *saeng-chiok kat'ŭn kongwŏndŭl ŭi saenghwal*, from an article in the *Chŏn'guk nodongja sinmun* [National worker's news], Nov. 1, 1945. The article was describing working life at Kyŏngbang during the colonial period.

9. Compare, for example, working conditions at Kyŏngbang described in this chapter with the general labor conditions described in Minami Manshū Tetsudō KK, Keizai Chōsakai Daiichibu, *Chōsenjin rōdōsha ippan jijō*, pp. 72–80. See *KY*, p. 230.

10. *KY*, pp. 229–30. See also Kim Yŏngsŏn, "Kwiguk yŏlch'a," *Sabo Kyŏngbang* (November 1970), p. 7; Kim Yongwan, taped interview, March 30, 1984, Seoul; *KYS*, p. 131.

11. *KY*, pp. 108, 230.

12. Pearse, *Cotton Industry of Japan and China*, pp. 102–3.

13. Kim Yongwan, taped interview, Seoul, Apr. 13, 1984. *Tonga ilbo*, May 31, 1931 (interview with Yi Kanghyŏn). Kim Yongwan said the working time was eleven hours with an hour's break for meals, but it is clear from newspaper interviews with Kyŏngbang's management and striking workers that forty minutes of rest was the rule at least as late as 1931. One of the demands of the Kyŏngbang workers who struck in 1931, for example, was for an extension of the rest time from forty minutes to one hour. See *Tonga ilbo*, May 30, 1931.

14. See "Keijō Bōseki [*sic*] Kaisha no naiyō o kiku," p. 17. One of the

demands made by Kyŏngbang's striking workers in 1931 was for the adoption of a special six-hour workday for juveniles.

15. On Japan, see Pearse, *Cotton Industry of Japan and China*, p. 103. The usual (not legal) arrangement in Korea was also two days of rest per month, although a survey of factories with ten or more workers in 1931 showed that 35 percent of them had no rest days at all (Granjdanzev, *Modern Korea*, p. 184). Kyŏngbang's wage records from 1945 clearly show that workers were strongly encouraged, if not expected, to work thirty days per month. Only those workers who put in the full thirty days received the maximum "perfect attendance" bonus. Those who worked twenty-nine days received a slightly lower bonus. Workers who put in no more than twenty-eight days received no bonus at all. See Kyŏngsŏng Pangjik CH, Wage Sheet (Ŭllyul Cotton Ginning Factory), May 31, 1945. Newspaper accounts of Kyŏngbang's strikes in 1928 and 1931 also suggest that workers may well have been putting in thirty-day months during peacetime (i.e., maximum 21 yen monthly pay divided by maximum 70 sen daily wage = thirty days). See *Tonga ilbo*, June 4, 1928; also May 31, 1931 (interview with worker Song Kwangmun).

16. For a description of the effect of such an environment on the workers' physical well-being, see Yasue Aoki Kidd, *Women Workers in the Japanese Cotton Mills, 1880–1920* (Ithaca, N.Y.: China-Japan Program, Cornell University, 1978), pp. 32–45. See also Joseph G. Montalvo, ed., *Cotton Dust: Controlling an Occupational Health Hazard* (American Chemical Society, 1982), passim.

17. Yi Chaegon, "Eitōho no san daikōjō o miru," p. 75.

18. Kim Kakchung (son of Kim Yongwan; nephew of Sŏngsu and Yŏnsu), interview, Yŏngdŭngp'o, Mar. 29, 1984.

19. In explaining the negative attitude of Manchurian-Chinese toward Manchurian-Koreans, Han Sangnyong wrote in 1932 that the Chinese "mistakenly" regarded the Koreans as "trailblazers in the Japanese invasion of Manchuria." See Han Sangnyong, "Namboku Manshū o shisatsu shite," p. 6. See also chap. 6, above.

20. *KY*, p. 230

21. See *Tonga ilbo*, May 30, 1931; May 31, 1931. See also Kidd, *Women Workers*, p. 29.

22. *Tonga ilbo*, May 30, 1931; May 31, 1931.

23. See *KY*, pp. 238–39.

24. See *KY*, p. 87.

25. Kim Yongwan, interview, Seoul, Mar. 30, 1984. See also *KY*, pp. 238–39.

26. See Kim Chunggil, ed., *Hwasin osimnyŏnsa: 1926–1976*, pp. 171–76. See photographs of the colonial Chōsen Hotel (interior and exterior) in Chōsen Sōtokufu, Tetsudōkyoku, *Hantō no kin'ei* [The peninsula in pictures] (Keijō: Chōsen Sōtokufu, Tetsudōkyoku, 1937), p. 30.

27. A term commonly used by Japanese police and reporters during this

period to refer to groups regarded as subversive by the authorities, especially Socialists and Communists, but also anti-imperialists, anarchists, and nationalists. See, for example, Chōsen Sōtokufu, Keimukyoku Hoanka, *Kōtō keisatsuhō* [The higher police report], no. 2 (Keijō: Chōsen Sōtokufu, Keimukyoku, n.d.; reprint ed., Tokyo: Gannandō, 1962), table of contents.

28. Saxonhouse, "A Tale of Technical Diffusion in the Meiji Period," p. 161.

29. *KY*, p. 230. See also Yi Chaegon, "Eitōho no san daikōjō o miru," p. 75. *Tonga ilbo*, May 30, 1931.

30. Moser, *Cotton Textile Industry of Far Eastern Countries*, pp. 17–25; *Tonga ilbo*, June 4, 1928.

31. The highest monthly wage is based on thirty workdays per month. See Yi Chaegon, "Eitōho no san daikōjō o miru," pp. 74–75. This was still true as late as 1936.

32. See Minami Manshū Tetsudō KK, Keizai Chōsakai Daiichibu, *Chōsenjin rōdōsha ippan jijō*, pp. 78–79. The Chōsen Spinning and Weaving Company in Pusan, for example, was paying a minimum wage of 30 sen to its workers in 1930. See *Tonga ilbo*, Jan. 11, 1930. *Tonga ilbo* (interview with striking Kyŏngbang worker Song Kwangmun), May 31, 1931. Minami Manshū Tetsudō KK, Keizai Chōsakai Daiichibu, *Chōsenjin rōdōsha ippan jijō*, p. 78. Kim Yongwan, taped interview, Seoul, Mar. 30, 1984.

33. The figure of 15 yen is only a crude approximation, based on the average of the highest (70 sen) and lowest (30 sen) daily wages paid at Kyŏngbang around 1930 and assuming thirty workdays per month. As an average, it is probably too high, since most of Kyŏngbang's workers were paid far less than the maximum wage. Food cost is based on five sen per three meals per day times thirty days. See Minami Manshū Tetsudō KK, Keizai Chōsakai Daiichibu, *Chōsenjin rōdōsha ippan jijō*, p. 71.

34. The figure of 5.25 yen per month is one-half the total amount for such items in the report of the Japanese Cotton Spinners Association (to take into account, in a very rough way, Korea's lower standard of living). See Pearse, *Cotton Industry of Japan and China*, pp. 98–99.

35. Based on a Government-General estimate from 1931. See Minami Manshū Tetsudō KK, Keizai Chōsakai Daiichibu, *Chōsenjin rōdōsha ippan jijō*, p. 71.

36. *Tonga ilbo*, May 30, 1931.

37. Minami Manshū Tetsudō KK, Keizai Chōsakai Daiichibu, *Chōsenjin rōdōsha ippan jijō*, p. 71.

38. Most large-scale factories in Korea (as in Japan) gave both their white-collar personnel (*shokuin*) and factory workers (*jūgyōin*) various kinds of emoluments in addition to the regular monthly salaries or wages. These included, for example, regular and special bonuses (*shōyo*) as well as small allowances (*teate*) for continuous service, perfect attendance, quality work,

or for extra duty. See Minami Manshū Tetsudō KK, Keizai Chōsakai Daiichibu, *Chōsenjin rōdōsha ippan jijō*, p. 80.

What about Kyŏngbang? Article 35 of the company's original articles of incorporation (adopted on Oct. 5, 1919) stipulated that up to 15 percent of the company's profits per fiscal period should be distributed jointly as bonuses to the company officers, white-collar staff, and workers before the distribution of any corporate dividends. All such distributions were subsequently voted on by the company's board of directors and duly recorded in the board minutes. Kyŏngbang's board minutes show clearly that prior to 1938 all corporate profits were either distributed as dividends or placed in the company's legal reserve: there is no record of any profits being used as bonuses for anyone. The reason seems obvious. Before the late 1930s Kyŏngbang's profits were relatively small, and the company was interested in attracting as much equity capital as possible. From 1938 on, however, profits were soaring (see chap. 4), and the company's vital role in the wartime industrial structure opened the way to cheap bank loans, thereby reducing its dependence on equity financing. From this period on, the board also regularly began to distribute part of the profits as bonuses. Such bonuses went first of all to the members of the board itself and secondly to the white-collar staff; there is, however, no record of any profits being converted to bonuses for workers. On the contrary, Kyŏngbang's articles of incorporation were amended at the end of 1939 to make only company officers eligible for bonuses from corporate profits. In 1941, when the articles were amended once more, the white-collar staff was again made eligible for such bonuses. It is possible that bonuses were paid out to workers from sources other than corporate profits (working capital, corporate reserves), but there is no record of this either in the official company histories or the minutes of Kyŏngbang's board of directors meetings. The only bonus for workers recorded in the board minutes was part of a general special bonus — voted to all officers, white-collar staff, and workers — on the company's twentieth anniversary in 1939. There is also evidence from extant company wage sheets in 1945 that at least by the end of the colonial period Kyŏngbang was following the Japanese example of giving workers small allowances for such things as extra duty, perfect attendance, positions of responsibility, and outstanding work. In general, however, bonuses and allowances seem to have played a relatively minor role in supplementing workers' incomes at Kyŏngbang. See Kyŏngsŏng Pangjik CH, Record of the Board of Directors Meetings, Oct. 5, 1919-June 28, 1945, passim. See also Kyŏngsŏng Pangjik CH, Semimonthly Wage Sheets (P'yŏngyang Cotton Ginning Factory), Apr. 15–May 15, 1945.

39. It is not clear whether Kyŏngbang's girls paid a portion of their income directly to the company each month for their dormitory space or whether their contribution to the cost of the dormitory was figured into the calculation of their monthly wage. Moser, *Cotton Textile Industry of Far Eastern Coun-*

tries, pp. 18–19; Pearse, *Cotton Industry of Japan and China*, p. 98. As in Japan, Kyŏngbang's girls paid 15 sen per day for three meals. See Minami Manshū Tetsudō KK, Keizai Chōsakai Daiichibu, *Chōsenjin rōdōsha ippan jijō*, p. 71. Assuming the cost of such meals to have been approximately 1/2 what it was in Japan, or 22.5 sen (1/2 of 45 sen), Kyŏngbang's girls were paying 2/3 of the total cost.

40. See Yi Chaegon, "Eitōho no san daikōjō o miru," p. 75; Pearse, *Cotton Industry of Japan and China*, p. 92. *KY*, p. 260.

41. Yi Chaegon, "Eitōho no san daikōjō o miru," p. 75. *Chŏn'guk nodongja sinmun*, Nov. 1, 1945.

42. See the article on Chōbō's striking workers (especially the eighth demand in the workers' list of demands), *Tonga ilbo*, Jan. 13, 1930.

43. *KO*, pp. 191, 194.

44. See the *Chŏn'guk nodongja sinmun*, Nov. 1, 1945.

45. On Kyŏngbang's educational programs, see *KY*, pp. 238–41.

46. *Chŏn'guk nodongja sinmun*, Nov. 1, 1945.

47. Pearse, *Cotton Industry of Japan and China*, p. 93.

48. Kozo Yamamura, "Then Came the Great Depression: Japan's Interwar Years," in Herman Van der Wee, ed., *The Great Depression Revisited: Essays on the Economics of the Thirties* (The Hague: Nijhoff, 1972), pp. 197–98. See Kenneth B. Pyle, *The Making of Modern Japan*, Civilization and Society: Studies in Social, Economic, and Cultural History (Lexington, Mass.: D.C. Heath, paperback, 1978), p. 114. Pearse's report was published in July 1929; Kanebō's strike broke out in early April the following year. On the strike, see the front page of *Japan Times & Mail*, April 11, 1930.

49. Kim Yunhwan, *Han'guk nodong undongsa (I): Ilchehap'yŏn* [History of the Korean labor movement, vol. 1: Under Japanese imperialism], Ch'ŏngsa Sinsŏ 13 (Seoul: Tosŏ Ch'ulp'an Ch'ŏngsa, paperback, 1982), pp. 41–43, 297.

50. Iwao F. Ayusawa, *History of Labor in Modern Japan*, p. 106.

51. Quoted in Kenneth B. Pyle, "Advantages of Followership: German Economics and Japanese Bureaucrats, 1890–1925," *Journal of Japanese Studies* 1 (Autumn 1974): 143.

52. Chōsen Sōtokufu, *Chōsen Sōtokufu Jikyoku Taisaku Chōsakai shimon tōshinsho*, pp. 121–22. On the Sampō Movement, see Gordon, *Evolution of Labor Relations in Japan*, pp. 299–326. Chōsen Sōtokufu, *Chōsen Sōtokufu Jikyoku Taisaku Chōsakai shimon tōshinsho*, p. 119. Kim Yunhwan, *Han'guk nodong undongsa (I): Ilchehap'yŏn*, pp. 322–23.

53. See Okiayu Toshihiro, *Chōsen hōritsu hanrei ketsugi sōran* [A survey of Chōsen laws, precedents, and decisions] (Keijō: Osaka Yagō Shoten, 1927), passim. See also Kim Yunhwan, *Han'guk nodong undongsa (I): Ilchehap'yŏn*, pp. 140–41.

54. See Okudaira Yasuhiro, *Chian Iji Hō shōshi* [A concise history of the peace preservation law] (Tokyo: Chikuma Shobō, 1977), p. 60.

55. Grajdanzev, *Modern Korea*, p. 182. See Okiayu Toshihiro, *Chōsen hōritsu hanrei ketsugi sōran*, pp. 85–87.

56. See Kim Yunhwan, *Han'guk nodong undongsa (I): Ilchehap'yŏn*, p. 111. See also Chong-Sik Lee, *The Korean Workers' Party: A Short History*, Histories of Ruling Communist Parties (Stanford: Hoover Institution Press, paperback, 1978), pp. 15–19, 23–24; Cumings, *Origins of the Korean War*, pp. 77–78. See also Robinson, *Cultural Nationalism in Colonial Korea;* Kim Yunhwan, *Han'guk nodong undongsa (I): Ilchehap'yŏn*, pp. 112–15, 121–22; Chong-Sik Lee, *Korean Workers' Party*, pp. 18–19, 23–24.

57. Kim Yunhwan, *Han'guk nodong undongsa (I): Ilchehap'yŏn*, pp. 123, 125. See also Chong-Sik Lee, *The Korean Workers' Party*, p. 24; Dae-Sook Suh, *The Korean Communist Movement, 1918–1948* (Princeton: Princeton University Press, 1967), p. 63.

58. See *Tonga ilbo*, May 9, 1926; May 13, 1926. See also Chōsen Sōtokufu, Keimukyoku, *Kōtō Keisatsu kankei nempyō*, p. 199. The Sihŭng Nou Sangjohoe was established in Yŏngdŭngp'o on Dec. 25, 1925. See Kim Yunhwan, *Han'guk nodong undongsa (I): Ilchehap'yŏn*, p. 179.

59. *Tonga ilbo*, May 9, 1926.

60. Ibid., May 13, 1926.

61. Kim Yongwan, taped interview, Seoul, Apr. 13, 1984.

62. *Tonga ilbo*, May 9, 1926.

63. The police arrested the leaders of the Sangjohoe merely on suspicion of subversive activities. As Police Inspector Rifu said at the time: "We're just asking questions to ascertain the facts. It's difficult to say whether we'll turn up any violations of the Public Order and Police Law or whether we'll soon be letting them go." See *Tonga ilbo*, May 9, 1926.

64. Chōsen Sōtokufu Keimukyoku, *Kōtō Keisatsu kankei nempyō*, p. 199; *Tonga ilbo*, May 9, 1926.

65. *Tonga ilbo*, May 9, 1926.

66. Ibid.

67. Ibid.

68. See *KY*, pp. 268, 269; *KYS*, pp. 234, 235. *Tonga ilbo*, May 9, 1926.

69. Robinson, *Cultural Nationalism in Colonial Korea*, pp. 74–75.

70. See Kajimura Hideki, *Chōsen ni okeru shihonshugi*, pp. 175–77.

71. *Tonga ilbo*, Apr. 14, 1925.

72. Ibid., May 9, 1926. By the time this article appeared (the first on the strike), the Sangjohoe's leaders were already undergoing interrogation at the Yŏngdŭngp'o police station.

73. Ibid.

74. Ibid.

75. Ibid., May 13, 1926. The strike began on the morning of May 7 and ended on the morning of the 10th: see *Tonga ilbo*, May 9, 1926; May 13, 1926.

76. *Tonga ilbo*, May 30, 1931.

77. United States Department of Commerce, Bureau of Foreign and Domestic Commerce, Office of the Commercial Attaché, American Embassy, Tokyo, "Japan Monthly Trade & Economic Letter—July 1929."

78. In July 1928, for example, Kyŏngbang's board of directors voted to separate the company's production and sales activities and turn sales over to an affiliate, the Chungang Commercial and Industrial Company, "to keep the original production cost low and economize on sales expenditures." Kyŏngsŏng Pangjik CH, Record of the Board of Directors Meetings, Minutes of Board Meeting no. 44, July 20, 1928.

79. Or about 31 percent of the total processing cost of a bale of yarn (factory production + operating expenses + depreciation + interest). In either case, labor was the single most important factor in determining the final cost of the product. See Keizo Seki, *Cotton Industry of Japan*, p. 92.

80. See *Keijō nippō*, June 2, 1928. According to the *Tonga ilbo*, the wage cut was only about 14 percent. *Tonga ilbo*, June 4, 1928.

81. *Keijō nippō*, June 5, 1928.

82. Ibid., June 8, 1928; *Seibu mainichi shimbun*, June 8, 1928.

83. *Tonga ilbo*, June 4, 1928. Kyŏngsŏng Pangjik CH, Record of the Board of Directors Meetings, Minutes of Board Meeting no. 36, Mar. 1, 1928.

84. Kyŏngsŏng Pangjik CH, Record of the Board of Directors Meetings, Minutes of Board Meeting no. 42, Mar. 1, 1929; Minutes of Board Meeting no. 46, Mar. 1, 1930; Minutes of Board Meeting no. 49, Mar. 1, 1931.

85. *The Japan Chronicle—Weekly Commercial Supplement*, Sept. 3, 1930, p. 106.

86. Kyŏngsŏng Pangjik CH, Record of the Board of Directors Meetings, Minutes of Board Meeting no. 47, May 29, 1930.

87. Ibid. See Kyŏngsŏng Pangjik CH, Record of the Board of Directors Meetings, Minutes of Board Meeting no. 52, Sept. 15, 1932; see also *KY*, p. 544.

88. *KY*, p. 544.

89. Kyŏngsŏng Pangjik CH, Record of the Board of Directors Meetings, Minutes of Board Meeting no. 52, Sept. 15, 1932.

90. See Kyŏngsŏng Pangjik CH, Record of the Board of Directors Meetings, Minutes of Board Meeting no. 49, Mar. 1, 1931. See also Kyŏngsŏng Pangjik CH, Record of the General Stockholders Meetings, Minutes of the 13th Regular Meeting, Mar. 16, 1931.

91. *Taikyū nippō*, May 30, 1931.

92. See *Tonga ilbo*, May 30, 1931; May 31, 1931.

93. Ibid., May 31, 1931.

94. Ibid., May 30, 1931.

95. Ibid., May 31, 1931.

96. Ibid.

97. Ibid.

98. Ibid.

99. *Keijō nippō*, May 31, 1931; *Tonga ilbo*, May 31, 1931.

100. See, for example, the 1933 "Platform of the Chŏlla Namdo League" in Dae-Sook Suh, ed., *Documents of Korean Communism*, pp. 174–75.

101. *Tonga ilbo*, May 31, 1931; *Keijō nippō*, May 31, 1931.

102. Quoted in Dae-Sook Suh, ed., *Documents of Korean Communism*, p. 293.

103. On the Wŏnsan strike, see Kim Yunhwan, *Han'guk nodong undongsa (I): Ilchehap'yŏn*, pp. 162–76.

104. *Chōsen shimbun*, June 1, 1931.

105. *Maeil sinbo*, June 1, 1931; *Chōsen shimbun*, June 1, 1931.

106. *Maeil sinbo*, June 1, 1931; *Chōsen shimbun*, June 1, 1931.

107. *Keijō nippō*, June 1, 1931.

108. Ibid., June 2, 1931; *Maeil sinbo*, June 1, 1931.

109. *Tonga ilbo*, June 1, 1931; *Keijō nippō*, June 2, 1931.

110. *Keijō nippō*, June 1, 1931; June 2, 1931.

111. Ibid., May 31, 1931. See also *Keijō nippō*, June 1, 1931.

112. *Tonga ilbo*, June 2, 1931; *Keijō nippō*, June 4, 1931.

113. *Keijō nippo*, June 4, 1931.

114. Ibid., June 5, 1931.

115. *Tonga ilbo*, June 6, 1931; *Chōsen shimbun*, June 5, 1931; *Keijō nippō*, June 5, 1931.

116. Kim Yunhwan also makes this point. The peak year for strikes was 1934; thereafter the number of strikes per year gradually decreased. See Kim Yunhwan, *Han'guk nodong undongsa (I): Ilchehap'yŏn*, p. 297. At the Government-General's industrial commission of 1936, moreover, the banker Pak Yŏngch'ŏl noted that Korean discontent with Japanese rule was considerably mitigated during the five years following the Japanese invasion of Manchuria. See Chōsen Sōtokufu, *Chōsen Sangyō Keizai Chōsakai kaigiroku*, General Session (final), p. 666.

117. "Keijō Bōseki [*sic*] Kaisha no naiyō o kiku," p. 17; Yi Chaegon, "Eitōho no san daikōjō o miru," p. 74. See, for example, Kyŏngsŏng Pangjik CH, Semimonthly Wage Sheet (P'yŏngyang Cotton Ginning Factory), Apr. 15, 1945.

118. Grajdanzev, *Modern Korea*, pp. 179–80; Yi Chaegon, "Eitōho no san daikōjō o miru," pp. 74–75.

119. See Kyŏngsŏng Pangjik CH, Record of the Board of Directors Meetings, Minutes of Board Meeting no. 78, Dec. 10, 1938; Minutes of Board Meeting no. 77, October 14, 1938; see n. 37, above.

120. See Kim Yunhwan, *Han'guk nodong undongsa (I): Ilchehap'yŏn*, p. 297.

121. See Cohen, *Japan's Economy in War and Reconstruction*, pp. 11, 277; *Wartime Legislation in Japan: A Selection of Important Laws Enacted or Revised in 1941* (Tokyo: Nippon Shogyo Tsushin Sha, n.d.), p. 34.

122. Kim Yongwan, taped interview, Seoul, Apr. 13, 1984.
123. *Chŏn'guk nodongja sinmun*, Nov. 1, 1945.

8. Class Over Nation: Naisen Ittai and the Korean Bourgeoisie

1. See part 3. See also Marc Bloc, *Feudal Society,* trans. by L. A. Manyon (Chicago: University of Chicago Press, Phoenix Books, 1964) 2, *Social Classes and Political Organization:* 352–55. See also Albert O. Hirschmann, *The Passions and the Interests: Political Arguments for Capitalism Before its Triumph* (Princeton: Princeton University Press, 1977); Hirschmann, *Rival Views of Market Society and Other Recent Essays* (New York: Viking, Elisabeth Sifton Books, 1986), chaps. 2, 5. See also Robert L. Heilbroner, *The Nature and Logic of Capitalism* (New York: W. W. Norton, paperback, 1985).

2. Ch'ang Nanggaek, "Paengman changja ŭi paengmanwŏn'gwan," p. 45. In responding to King Hui of Liang, Mencius said: "Why must your Majesty use that word 'profit?' What I am provided with are counsels to benevolence and righteousness, and these are my only topics." See James Legge, *The Works of Mencius* (New York: Dover Publications, 1970), p. 126.

3. For a fascinating account of one Korean's transition from disillusionment to radical nationalism after 1919, see Nym Wales [Helen Foster Snow] and Kim San, *Song of Arian: A Korean Communist in the Chinese Revolution* (San Francisco: Ramparts Press, 1941), pp. 57–98. See also Chong-Sik Lee's excellent chapter on collaboration and resistance during the late colonial period (based on colonial police reports) in Chong-Sik Lee, *Politics of Korean Nationalism*, pp. 257–73, esp. 266–70.

4. Two new works provide an excellent introduction to Korean nationalism and *sadae*: see Robinson, *Cultural Nationalism*, pp. 14–19; and Vipan Chandra, *Imperialism, Resistance, and Reform in Late Nineteenth-Century Korea: Enlightenment and the Independence Club* (Berkeley: Institute of East Asian Studies, University of California, Berkeley, 1988), chap. 1. For a fascinating account of how Sinocentrism impeded a Korean understanding of Western science and cosmology, see Donald L. Baker, "Jesuit Science through Korean Eyes," JKS 4 (1982–83): 207–39, esp. 220–21.

5. Quoted in Gari Keith Ledyard, "The Korean Language Reform of 1446" (Ph.D. diss., University of California, Berkeley, 1966), pp. 104–5.

6. See Chandra, *Imperialism, Resistance, and Reform*; Chandra, "An Outline Study of the Ilchin-hoe [Advancement Society] of Korea."

7. Hyŏn Chunho was the son of Hyŏn Kibong, a wealthy S. Chŏlla (Yŏngam) landlord-entrepreneur who had already made a name (and money) for himself in the world of finance by the early 1920s. (Kibong was one of the Korean businessmen invited to the Government-General's industrial commission in 1921.) Chunho, who inherited his father's property, including control of the Honam Bank (founded 1920), was born in 1889 (two years before

Kim Sŏngsu and seven years before Kim Yŏnsu) and majored in law at Meiji University in Tokyo. Like the Kims, he was profoundly impressed by Japan's version of capitalism and sought to re-create it in Korea on his return home. He first met Sŏngsu (and Song Chinu) at the Ch'angp'yŏng School in S. Chŏlla founded by Sŏngsu's father-in-law (see chap. 2), and the two boys later renewed their acquaintance as students in Tokyo. The personal relationship eventually blossomed into a profitable business relationship as well. Sŏngsu helped the Hyŏns establish the Honam Bank, and Chunho took an active role in the promotion and development of Kyŏngbang, both as a shareholder and as a member of the board of directors. In 1944, Chunho held 1,016 shares of Kyŏngbang stock in his own name and 3,630 shares in the name of the Hakp'a Estate, his consolidated agricultural estate in S. Chŏlla. In 1950 he was executed in his home province by the North Korean army. See Cho Kijun, *Han'guk kiŏpkasa*, pp. 151–68; Kwŏn Ogi, ed., *Inch'on Kim Sŏngsu*, p. 419; *Tonga ilbo*, Sept. 6, 1921. See also Kyŏngsŏng Pangjik CH, List of Stockholders, Nov. 30, 1944. There is also an authorized biography of Hyŏn Chunho: see Son Chŏngyŏn, *Musong Hyŏn Chunho* (Kwangju: Chŏnnam Maeil Ch'ulp'an'guk, 1977).

8. Chōsen Sōtokufu, *Chōsen Sōtokufu Jikyoku Taisaku Chōsakai kaigiroku*, Committee no. 1, pp. 104–5. Hyŏn's language is almost a pidgin Japanese that indiscriminately mixes high and low forms and is full of grammatical errors. The terms "patron" [*oyabun*] and "follower" [*kobun*], for example, are commonly used in the gangster underworld, and the term "big brother" [*aniki*] sounds crude and impolite when used outside the family. Hyŏn, of course, had no intention whatsoever of being impolite; he was simply speaking bad Japanese. A good contemporary comparison might be with the kind of English one hears today in the It'aewŏn section of Seoul, which caters primarily to the United States Eighth Army headquartered just down the street.

9. There were periods in East Asian history, as during the Ch'ing dynasty, for example, when the yangban saw themselves as the inheritors and preservers of a universal culture from which the Chinese themselves (under Manchu rule) had strayed. See, for example, Gari Ledyard's article, "Korean Travelers in China over Four Hundred Years, 1488–1887," *Occasional Papers on Korea*, no. 2 (March 1974), pp. 1–42.

10. Albert Memmi, *The Colonizer and the Colonized* (Boston: Beacon Press, paperback, 1967), pp. 69–76.

11. The translation is by Gary Saxonhouse, "Working Koreans in Korea and Japan in the Inter-War Period." The original is in Takahashi Kamekichi, *Gendai Chōsen keizairon*, pp. 402–3.

12. In Otis Cary, ed., *From a Ruined Empire: Letters—Japan, China, Korea, 1945–46* (Tokyo: Kodansha International, 1984), p. 195.

13. Chōsen Sōtokufu, *Chōsen Sangyō Keizai Chōsakai kaigiroku*, General

Session (final), pp. 666–67. Like the Koch'ang Kims, Pak Yŏngch'ŏl was originally from the North Chŏlla area; his father, Pak Kisun, a rice broker turned landlord, had, like Kim Yohyŏp and his family, become rich on the Korea-Japan rice trade after 1876 and transferred some of his assets into modern enterprise (banking). In 1900, at twenty-one, Pak Yŏngch'ŏl had gone to Tokyo to complete his education; he had graduated from the Japanese Military Academy in 1903 and later served with the Japanese Imperial Guard Cavalry in Korea and Manchuria during the Russo-Japanese War. After the annexation he turned his ambition first to the colonial bureaucracy, in which he eventually came to hold a number of high posts, including the governorship of Kangwŏn and North Hamgyŏng Provinces, and then to the banking business he had inherited from his father. In 1936, he was president of the Chōsen Commercial Bank, Honorary Consul-General of Manchuria, and the holder of numerous directorships and auditorships in colonial business firms. On Pak, see chap. 1; also Kita Tadai, *Chōsen jinji kōshinroku*, p. 414; Pak Yŏngch'ŏl, *Gojūnen no kaiko* [Fifty years of memories] (Keijō: Pak Yŏngch'ŏl, 1929), passim. See also *KYS*, p. 194. On Son Kijŏng's Olympic victory, see the *New York Times*, Aug. 10, 1936.

14. See Chōsen Sōtokufu, *Chōsen Sōtokufu Jikyoku Taisaku Chōsakai kaigiroku*, Committee no. 1, pp. 75, 104–5. See also Wonmo Dong, "Japanese Colonial Policy and Practice in Korea," p. 254.

15. Memmi, *Colonizer and the Colonized*, p. 120.

16. Chōsen Sōtokufu, *Chōsen Sangyō Keizai Chōsakai kaigiroku*, General Session (final), p. 667.

17. Warren Tsuneishi, a Japanese-American interpreter and translator attached to the 24th Corps of the United States Army in Korea in September 1945, made the following observation at the time: "That the Japanese have succeeded to some extent in the Japanization of Korea . . . is clear. This is most evident in the matter of language. I have met very few Koreans, at least in Seoul, who do not have a good command of Japanese." In Otis Cary, ed., *From a Ruined Empire*, pp. 33–34.

18. On the *Maeil sinbo*, see Chong Chin-sok, "A Study of the *Maeil Sinbo* (Daily News): Public Information Policy of the Japanese Imperialists and Korean Journalism under Japanese Imperialism," *Journal of Social Sciences and Humanities*, no. 52 (December 1980), pp. 59–114.

19. Chōsen Sōtokufu, *Chōsen Sōtokufu Jikyoku Taisaku Chōsakai kaigiroku*, Committee no. 1, p. 72.

20. On Ch'oe Rin's role in the March First movement, see Baldwin, *The March First Movement*, passim. Like Kim Sŏngsu, Ch'oe had gradually moderated his nationalist stance after 1919 and played a leading role in the Home Rule Movement of the late 1920s, which advocated Korean political autonomy within the Japanese Empire. See Scalapino and Lee, *Communism in Korea* 1, *The Movement*: 98–100.

21. See Alexander Gerschenkron, *Economic Backwardness in Historical Perspective* (Cambridge: Harvard University Press, 1962); Ronald P. Dore, "The Late Development Effect," in Hans Dieter-Evans, ed., *Modernization in South-East Asia* (London: Oxford University Press, 1973).

22. Chōsen Sōtokufu, *Sangyō Chōsa Iinkai giji sokkiroku*, General Session, Day 2, p. 159.

23. See, for example, *Tonga ilbo*, Sept. 11, 1921 (announcement by Temporary Chairman Pak Yŏnghyo of general meeting of the Congress of Korean Industry), and Sept. 16, 1921 (proposals of the Congress of Korean Industry). See also the editorials in *Tonga ilbo*, on Sept. 10, Sept. 11, Sept. 12, and Sept. 20, 1921.

24. See Chōsen Sōtokufu, *Sangyō Chōsa Iinkai giji sokkiroku*, General Session, Day 2, p. 159; General Session, Day 5, pp. 244–45.

25. See Chōsen Sōtokufu, *Chōsen Sōtokufu Jikyoku Taisaku Chōsakai kaigiroku*, Committee no. 1, p. 103.

26. Letter from Kim Sŏngsu to Saitō Makoto, Dec. 30, 1927. Saitō Makoto Bunsho 4–121, Kenseishiryō Shitsu, Kokuritsu Kokkai Toshōkan [Saitō Makoto Papers, Constitutional Documents Room, National Diet Library], Tokyo.

27. Chōsen Sōtokufu, *Chōsen Sangyō Keizai Chōsakai kaigiroku*, General Session (final), p. 666.

28. Ko Wŏnbyŏn, *Panminja choesanggi*, p. 85. In September 1945 a Korean manager of the Bando (Hantō) Hotel had said exactly the same thing to one of the American army interpreters: "I did not think it [liberation] possible even in my dreams." See Otis Cary, ed., *From A Ruined Empire*, p. 32.

29. See Robinson, *Cultural Nationalism*, esp. chaps. 2 and 3. See also chap. 2, above.

30. Chōsen Sōtokufu, *Chōsen Sōtokufu Jikyoku Taisaku Chōsakai shimon tōshinsho*, p. 85. See also Henderson, *Korea: The Politics of the Vortex*, pp. 103–12.

31. Chōsen Sōtokufu, *Chōsen Sōtokufu Jikyoku Taisaku Chōsakai shimon tōshinsho*, pp. 85–96.

32. Ibid., p. 2.

33. Ibid., pp. 2–3, 5, 6.

34. Ibid., p. 3.

35. Ibid., pp. 4, 5.

36. Ibid., pp. 4, 6. See also Kokumin Sōryoku Chōsen Remmei, ed. "Kokumin Sōryoku tokuhon" [The concerted national power reader], *Chōsen jitsugyō* 19 (October 1941): 41–45 and *Chōsen jitsugyō* 19 (December 1941): 39–44.

37. *Chōsen jitsugyō* 19 (December, 1941): 4–5.

38. Ibid., pp. 5–6. On the forced closure of *Tonga ilbo* in 1940, see Chong Chin-sok, "A Study of the *Maeil Sinbo* (Daily News): Public Information Pol-

icy of the Japanese Imperialists and Korean Journalism under Japanese Imperialism," pp. 80–81.

39. Richard E. Kim, *Lost Names: Scenes from a Korean Boyhood* (New York: Praeger, 1970), p. 109.

40. See Wonmo Dong, "Japanese Colonial Policy and Practice in Korea," pp. 348–49. See also Chong-sik Lee, *The Politics of Korean Nationalism* (Berkeley and Los Angeles: University of California Press, 1963), pp. 266–70.

41. Note Hyŏn's complimentary remarks about Sekiya as a man familiar with Korean conditions and his positive attitude about Sekiya's chairmanship of the Naisen Ittai committee: Chōsen Sōtokufu, *Chōsen Sōtokufu Jikyoku Taisaku Chōsakai Kaigiroku*, Committee no. 1, p. 102. Sekiya was a strong supporter of Naisen Ittai, and like Aruga Mitsutoyo, who also made a point of cultivating relationships with the Korean elite, he was probably one of those Japanese who genuinely supported full assimilation of Koreans on equal terms with Japanese. There is an article by him on the Naisen Ittai policy in *Maeil sinbo:* see "Hwangmin ŭi t'aedo rŭl t'angma" [Assiduous application of the moral principles of imperial subjects], *Maeil sinbo*, Sept. 26, 1944.

42. The rhetoric of Naisen Ittai, of course, especially during the Pacific War, explicitly promised Koreans equal treatment and rights in the new East Asian order that would follow a Japanese victory, and the exigencies of the war did create new opportunities for Koreans in managerial, technical, and other areas that might not otherwise have arisen. See Saxonhouse, "Working Koreans in Korea and Japan in the Inter-War Period," pp. 45–61. There were also highly placed figures like Aruga Mitsutoyo, for example, who were powerful advocates of genuine Japanese-Korean equality (note, for example, Aruga's comments on discrimination against Koreans at the industrial commission of 1938: Chōsen Sōtokufu, *Chōsen Sōtokufu Jikyoku Taisaku Chōsakai kaigiroku*, Committee no. 1, pp. 105–7), and in the last months of the war Koreans (as well as Taiwanese) did become legally eligible for membership in the Japanese Diet. The government in Tokyo announced in March 1945 that the lower house would be open to Koreans beginning with the next general election and a month later seven Koreans, including Han Sangnyong, received imperial nominations to the House of Peers. See *Maeil sinbo*, Mar. 19, Mar. 27, April 2, and April 4, 1945. See also Henderson, *Politics of the Vortex*, p. 105 (Henderson says six Koreans were appointed, but the correct number is seven). On the other hand, such measures came very late in the war and may well have reflected more of a desperate hope to galvanize the empire for the final battle than a true commitment to Japanese–Korean equality. All things considered, it is probably safe to say that to the end the Japanese attitude toward such equality remained ambivalent at best.

43. Chōsen Sōtokufu, *Chōsen Sōtokufu Jikyoku Taisaku Chōsakai kaigiroku*, Committee no. 1, pp. 72, 102. On Yi Sŭngu, see Ko Wŏnbyŏn,

Panminja choesanggi, pp. 82–86. Yi was an auditor in the Tongil Bank (see chap. 3, above) and had also been an auditor in a Korean-run finance and brokerage firm in Seoul called Kyŏngsŏng Siksan CH and president of another such Korean-run firm called Namch'angsa. Both finance firms had gone out of business in the mid-1930s. See *Chōsen GKKY*, pp. 8, 21, 41. Yi was also a member of the Chūsūin, the Government-General's Korean advisory council. See Chōsen Sōtokufu, *Chōsen Sōtokufu Jikyoku Taisaku Chōsakai shimon tōshinsho*, p. 185. On the Chūsūin (Central Council), see Grajdanzev, *Formosa Today*, pp. 243–45.

44. Chōsen Sōtokufu, *Chōsen Sōtokufu Jikyoku Taisaku Chōsakai kaigiroku*, Committee no. 1, p. 76.

45. Ibid., p. 77.

46. Chōsen Sōtokufu, *Chōsen Sōtokufu Jikyoku Taisaku Chōsakai shimon tōshinsho*, p. 3; Wonmo Dong, "Japanese Colonial Policy and Practice in Korea," p. 254.

47. See Chōsen Sōtokufu, *Chōsen Sōtokufu Jikyoku Taisaku Chōsakai kaigiroku*, Committee no. 1, pp. 173–77. See also Chōsen Sōtokufu, *Chōsen Sōtokufu Jikyoku Taisaku Chōsakai shimon tōshinsho*, p. 3.

48. See Chōsen Sōtokufu, *Chōsen Sōtokufu Jikyoku Taisaku Chōsakai kaigiroku*, p. 6; *KSS*, p. 410.

49. *Tonga ilbo*, Sept. 20, 1921 (editorial).

50. And was subsequently appointed a consultant (*sōdanyaku*) to the company. See Han Ikkyo, ed., *Kan Sōryūkun o kataru*, pp. 430, 440; *Chōsen GKKY*, p. 16.

51. See L. Saeng, "Ssŏttŏn t'arŭl pŏsŏnanŭn mulsan changnyŏ" [Goods promotion unmasked], *Kaebyŏk*, no. 40 (October 1923), pp. 53–59, esp. 56–57. See also Robinson, *Cultural Nationalism*, chap. 4.

52. In the September 1930 edition of the magazine *Tonggwang*, for example, Yi Kwangsu wrote a piece on Kim that was so effusive that it even provoked a satirical response in *Samch'ŏlli* several months later. See Yu Kwangyŏl, "Yi Kwangsu ŭi 'Kim Sŏngsuron' ŭl pakham" [A critique of Yi Kwangsu's "Essay on Kim Sŏngsu"], *Samch'ŏlli* 3 (October 1931): 44. Yi was indebted to Kim for, among other things, his university education at Waseda. See Kwŏn Ogi, ed., *Inch'on Kim Sŏngsu*, pp. 187–89.

53. Facing public outrage and prosecution from the South Korean National Assembly for his active wartime collaboration, the novelist Yi Kwangsu published an essay in 1948 stating that he had believed at the time that collaboration would eventually work to the advantage of the Korean people by giving them the right to speak out in the future, and by improving their material benefits, educational and occupational opportunities, and legal status relative to Japanese. Despite its obviously defensive and self-serving intent, this statement has a certain ring of truth about it. It is similar in tone and substance to many of the comments by Koreans who attended the Government-General's industrial commission in 1938, and the question of Japanese-Korean equality

was of course one of the few issues on which most Koreans, regardless of class, could agree. Yi is far less convincing in his essay, however, when he goes on to say that he regarded such potential improvements in Korean life as bringing Korea itself a step closer to independence. It is hard to believe that a man of Yi's intelligence and sophistication did not realize what Naisen Ittai implied for the fate of Korean political and cultural independence. It seems much more likely that, like Yi Sŭngu and others on the Naisen Ittai committee in 1938, Yi had come to regard Korean independence as more or less improbable, if not impossible, and had decided to embrace Naisen Ittai as a way for Koreans as individuals to achieve full equality within a postwar Japanese empire. See Yi Kwangsu, *Na ŭi kobaek* [My confession], in Sŏ Chaesu, ed., *Yi Kwangsu chŏnjip* 13 (Seoul: Samjungdang, 1962–1964): 267–75.

54. Ch'oe Tusŏn (1894–1974) was the younger brother of Ch'oe Namsŏn (1890–1957), the author of the March 1, 1919, Declaration of Independence. Tusŏn was a close associate of the Kims. Like his older brother (and Kim Sŏngsu), he was educated at Waseda University (graduated 1917), where he majored in philosophy. He also spent some time in Germany at the University of Jena and the University of Berlin. During the colonial period, in addition to his role as Kyŏngbang stockholder (460 shares in 1944) and officer, he assisted Kim Sŏngsu in his various educational projects, serving as principal of Kim's Chungang School and managing director of Posŏng College. After Liberation he served as president of Kim Sŏngsu's newspaper, the *Tonga ilbo* (appointed 1947), prime minister of the Republic of Korea (1963–1964, in the first cabinet of Pak Chŏnghŭi), and chairman of Kyŏngbang (appointed 1964). See Kwŏn Ogi, ed., *Inch'on Kim Sŏngsu; KSS*, p. 793; Tongŭn ki'nyŏm Saŏphoe, *Tongŭn Kim Yongwan*, p. 314. See also Kyŏngsŏng Pangjik CH, List of Stockholders, Nov. 30, 1944.

55. Ch'oe Ch'anghak was born in 1891 (same year as Kim Sŏngsu) in N. P'yŏngan Province. Unlike the Kims, however, he does not seem to have come from a landlord and educated background, but rather got his start in business as part of a group of itinerant peddlers. See Kita Tadai, *Chōsen jinji kōshinroku*, p. 203. In 1944, Ch'oe held 1,815 Kyŏngbang shares: see Kyŏngsŏng Pangjik CH, List of Stockholders, Nov. 30, 1944.

56. Kyŏngsŏng Pangjik CH, Record of the Board of Directors Meetings, Minutes of Board Meeting no. 74, June 25, 1938, and List of Annual Payments to Japanese Language Class Instructors, n.d. (in Yongin voucher pack dated Oct. 21, 1938–Oct. 25, 1938). Also see Chōsen Sōtokufu, *Chōsen Sōtokufu Jikyoku Taisaku Chōsakai shimon tōshinsho*, p. 4.

57. See *Maeil sinbo*, Nov. 15, 1942, Jan. 7, 1941, and Jan. 19, 1941. For an interview with Kim Yŏnsu as the League's social welfare director, see ibid., Feb. 28, 1943.

58. Chōsen Sōtokufu, *Chōsen Sōtokufu Jikyoku Taisaku Chōsakai shimon tōshinsho*, pp. 4–5. See also Chong-Sik Lee, *Politics of Korean Nationalism,*

pp. 265–66, 322n. 32. By the end of World War II about 187,000 Koreans were in the Japanese army and over 22,000 in the Japanese navy. See Chong-Sik Lee, *Japan and Korea: The Political Dimension* (Stanford, Calif.: Hoover Institution Press, 1985), p. 25.

59. Kyŏngsŏng Pangjik CH, Record of the Board of Directors, Minutes of Board Meeting no. 81, Apr. 18, 1939; *Maeil sinbo*, July 22, 1943.

60. Chōsen Sōtokufu, *Chōsen Sōtokufu Jikyoku Taisaku Chōsakai shimon tōshinsho*, pp. 4–5.

61. See Chōsen Sōtokufu, *Shisei sanjūnen* [Thirty years of administration] (Keijō, 1940), pp. 803–5; Chōsen Sōtokufu, *Chōsen Sōtokufu Jikyoku Taisaku Chōsakai shimon tōshinsho*, p. 6.

62. A full conscription system (no exemptions) was put into effect in February 1944. See *KSS*, pp. 431, 790–91.

63. It is not clear from the newspaper, however, if Kim actually did participate in this lecture tour. Kyŏngsŏng Pangjik CH, Record of the Board of Directors Meetings, Minutes of Board Meeting no. 77, Oct. 14, 1938. See also *Maeil sinbo*, Oct. 16, 1938.

64. *Maeil sinbo*, Oct. 16, 1938, and June 21, 1942. A record of such donations and other information on Korean collaboration during the Naisen Ittai period are available in Kil Chinhyŏn, *Yŏksa e tasi munnŭnda* [A second look at history] (Seoul: Samminsa, 1984), pp. 300–301, 312. This is a recent compilation from existing journalistic sources of the record of the 1949 South Korean National Assembly trials of pro-Japanese collaborators and includes as a supplement a reprint of *Ch'inilp'a kunsang* [The pro-Japanese groups] originally published in 1948, probably the most detailed listing of the various Korean individuals and organizations who supported Naisen Ittai and the Japanese war effort between 1937 and 1945. In checking the references, I discovered a number of mistakes, especially with respect to dates, and scholars are advised always to check the reference against the original sources cited, such as the *Maeil sinbo*.

65. The transcripts of the symposium are in *Maeil sinbo*, Nov. 9, 1943. Several months earlier, when the conscription system was officially put into effect, a long article attributed to Sŏngsu and focusing on the problem of Korean "effeminacy" had also appeared in the newspaper: see *Maeil sinbo*, Aug. 5, 1943. *KSS*, pp. 430–31; see also the interview with Kim Yŏnsu regarding his *hakpyŏng* trip to Japan in *Maeil sinbo*, Nov. 9, 1943.

66. The other contributors were Ch'oe Namsŏn (Nov. 5, 1943), Yang Chusam (Nov. 9, 1943), Hyŏn Sangyun (Nov. 11, 1943). I am grateful to Joseph Nowakowski and Milan Hejtmanek for obtaining copies of these articles for me. The articles all read like speeches addressed to a student audience and may in fact have been publicly delivered. See Cumings, *Origins of the Korean War*, pp. 148–49.

67. *Maeil sinbo*, Jan. 22, 1944.

68. *Keijō nippō*, Jan. 19, 1944. See also the interview with Kim Yŏnsu in the Korean-language *Maeil sinbo* on the occasion of the implementation of the conscription system: *Maeil sinbo*, Aug. 1, 1943.

69. On Kim Yŏnsu at the antinationalist trials, see Ko Wŏnbyŏn, *Panminja choesanggi*, pp. 66–68. On the antinationalist trials in general, see Ch'oe Chunghŭi, "Panmin t'ŭgwi e kwanhan punsŏkchŏk yŏn'gu" [An analytical study of the anti-nationalist committee] (M.A. thesis, Ehwa University, 1976). Yŏnsu's official biography acknowledges his participation in the *hakpyŏng* campaign in Japan, but says that he was "forced" to participate and that after delivering one short and innocuous speech at Meiji University, he checked into a hospital and did not complete the lecture tour. See *KYS*, pp. 215–19. The biography makes no reference to any of Yŏnsu's articles or interviews in the Korean- or Japanese-language press or to any of his financial contributions to the war effort. Sŏngsu's official biography also acknowledges that he was "forced" to join a *hakpyŏng* lecture tour to Ch'unch'ŏn in 1943, but says that when called upon to speak, he simply deferred to the next speaker, his friend and associate, Chang Tŏksu (by prearranged agreement with Chang) (*KSS*, pp. 430–31). The biography further acknowledges one *hakpyŏng* newspaper article by Sŏngsu (*Maeil sinbo*, Jan. 22, 1944) but says that it was completely fabricated by a reporter after a nominal interview and after Sŏngsu had refused to contribute an article himself (*KSS*, pp. 432–34). The biography makes no mention of the article reputedly by Sŏngsu that is quoted extensively in this chapter. Nor does it mention Sŏngsu's apparent participation in the *hakpyŏng* symposium at Citizens Hall.

70. The Kims' continued free use of their Korean names throughout the Naisen Ittai period raises more questions than it answers. Many of the Korean businessmen engaged in the war effort whose well established names were also, in a sense, important business trademarks were exempted from the Government-General's injunction to Koreans to adopt Japanese names, and a prosecutor examining Pak Hŭngsik at the South Korean antinationalist trials in 1949 also noted that the Japanese authorities allowed some "trustworthy" Koreans to retain their names to preserve the illusion that the name change movement was voluntary (Pak had also continued to use his Korean name). See Ko Wŏnbyŏn, *Panminja choesanggi*, p. 20; Kim Yŏngjin, ed., *Panminja taegongp'angi*, p. 62.

In a recent article in *Tonga ilbo*, Yi Ch'ŏlsŭng has written that Kim Sŏngsu instructed him at the time to organize an underground anti-*hakpyŏng* movement, which failed because of Japanese suppression. This statement must be regarded with extreme skepticism. Apart from Yi's sudden assertion, nearly fifty years after the fact, there is no evidence that Kim Sŏngsu, or Yi himself for that matter, was ever involved in such a movement; even the authorized biographies, which border on hagiography, fail to mention such a fact. Yi's impartiality on this point must also be called into question, first because his

334 NOTES

article was clearly written to counter a growing revisionist critique of Kim by South Korean students (especially students at Koryŏ University, which is still under the control of the Kim family), and second, because of his position as an advisor to the Association of Friends of Koryŏ University. Yi further diminishes his credibility by attempting to brand the students' criticism of Kim as a product of "leftist," i.e., Communist, agitation. See Yi Ch'ŏlsŭng, "Inch'on ŭl paro alcha" [Let's understand Inch'on correctly], Tonga ilbo, July 15, 1989. I thank Kyu Hyun Kim for bringing this article to my attention.

71. Kim Yŏnsu was appointed Honorary Consul-General of Manchukuo in June 1939; see KYS, p. 335. In that capacity he hosted an annual celebration on March 1 at his consulate for staff, Manchukuo residents in Korea, and other interested parties to commemorate the founding of the Manchukuo state. In addition to food and toasts, the ceremonies included ritual bows for both the Japanese and Manchukuo emperors. For a description of these events, see Maeil sinbo, March 2, 1942, or March 2, 1943. See letters from Kim Yŏnsu to Sekiya Teizaburō, Sept. 25, 1939; Jan. 12, 1943; and July 21, 1943; Sekiya Teizaburō Bunsho 1081, 875–2, and 875–1, Kenseishiryō Shitsu, Kokuritsu Kokkai Toshōkan [Sekiya Teizaburō Papers, Constitutional Documents Room, National Diet Library], Tokyo.

72. Other key figures in the cultural nationalist movement became active collaborators, including Ch'oe Namsŏn and Yi Kwangsu. See Ch'oe's own statement on his collaboration in Ko Wŏnbyŏn, Panminja choesanggi, pp. 52–61. On Yi Kwangsu, see above, n. 53.

73. Letter from Kim Sŏngsu to Sekiya Teizaburō, May 29, 1945. Sekiya Teizaburō Bunsho 876–2, Kenseishiryō Shitsu, Kokuritsu Kokkai Toshōkan [Sekiya Teizaburō Papers, Constitutional Documents Room, National Diet Library], Tokyo.

74. To date I have not been able precisely to identify Bureau Director Ōshima. He does not appear to have been a bureau director in the Government-General when Kim Sŏngsu wrote to Sekiya in 1945. He may have been a former Government-General bureau director on visit to Korea, or he may have been a visiting bureau director (present or former), whose bureaucratic affiliation was with a different part of the empire, such as Manchukuo, Taiwan, or even Japan itself.

75. Endō was vice-governor-general from July 24, 1944, to Oct. 24, 1945. In addition to being the second highest-ranking official in the colony, the vice-governor-general, whose official title was the Secretary-General of Political Affairs (Seimu Sōkan), was the head of the Chūsūin, the Korean advisory council to the Government-General. Kim Sŏngsu was listed as a member of the Chūsūin at the time of its dissolution by the American Military Government in November 1945. See Cumings, Origins of the Korean War, pp. 148, 498 n.64.

76. Letter from Kim Sŏngsu to Sekiya Teizaburō, July 8, 1945, Sekiya

Teizaburō Bunsho 876–1, Kenseishiryō Shitsu, Kokuritsu Kokkai Toshōkan [Sekiya Teizaburō Papers, Constitutional Documents Room, National Diet Library], Tokyo.

77. They are, on the other hand, consistent in tone and substance with some of the articles and interviews credited to Kim Sŏngsu in the *Maeil sinbo* during this period. See, for example, the newspaper's reputed interview with Kim on the occasion of Governor-General's Koiso's appointment as Japanese prime minister. *Maeil sinbo*, July 24, 1944.

78. For a powerful account of such liberation activities in one Korean town, see Richard Kim, *Lost Names*, pp. 164–70.

79. Although the most severe attacks on Yŏnsu as a "national traitor" came from the political left and from his own workers at Kyŏngbang, the general public's outrage at his wartime activities was such that he was eventually brought to trial in 1949 by the South Korean National Assembly for "antinationalist acts." Kim's public display of contrition at the trial and, even more important, political subversion of the Assembly's prosecuting committee by the Syngman Rhee regime, eventually gained him an acquittal. See *Chŏn'guk nodongja sinmun*, Nov. 1, 1945; Dec. 1, 1945. See also *KY*, p. 138; *KYS*, pp. 234–35; Kil Chinhyŏn, *Yŏksa e tasi munnŭnda*, pp. 12–22, 109–10; Ch'oe Chunghŭi, "Panmin t'ŭgwi e kwanhan punsŏkchŏk yŏn'gu."

Sŏngsu's nationalist reputation was still good enough in September 1945 for his name to be included in the cabinet list (as minister of education) of the ill-fated Korean People's Republic (KPR), a leftist-oriented coalition government established after the Japanese surrender and before the arrival of American troops. He did not, however, entirely escape charges of being a collaborator. See Cumings, *Origins of the Korean War*, pp. 148–49. On the establishment of the KPR and the American reaction to it, see ibid., pp. 68–100, 135–78. Since 1945, family, friends, and associates have assiduously cultivated Sŏngsu's image as a nationalist, an effort that has been greatly bolstered by the immense resources and influence of the family's publishing empire and educational foundations. Recently, however, students and scholars have been engaged in a critical reassessment of Sŏngsu's colonial past, and the question of his collaboration remains today a highly controversial issue.

Conclusion: The Colonial Legacy

1. See Robinson, *Cultural Nationalism in Colonial Korea;* Karl Moskowitz, "Current Assets: The Employees of Japanese Banks in Colonial Korea"; and Soon Won Park, "The Emergence of a Factory Labor Force in Colonial Korea: A Case Study of the Onoda Cement Company" (Ph.D. diss., Harvard University, 1985).

2. For example, in 1938 Kim Yongwan (who had married Sŏngsu's younger sister, Kim Chŏmhyo, in 1917 at the age of 13) moved from the executive

directorship of the Chungang Commercial and Industrial Company (a Kyŏngbang affiliate; originally Kyŏngsŏng Chingnyu) to a managing director-ship in Kyŏngbang proper. He personally held 1,366 shares in the company at the end of 1944. See Tongŭn Ki'nyŏm Saŏphoe, ed., *Tongŭn Kim Yongwan*, pp. 308, 310; Kyŏngsŏng Pangjik CH, List of Stockholders, Nov. 30, 1944. Yi Toyŏng was born in 1910. Although his father was a poor tenant farmer, his grandfather had been a wealthy landlord (who had bequeathed everything to his eldest son, Toyŏng's brother) and the family belonged to a clan (the Yŏn'an Yi) with impeccable yangban credentials (see Wagner, "*Munkwa* Proj-ect."). Perhaps for that reason, his family was able to see him married to the daughter of a very wealthy Yŏhŭng Min landlord, who helped send Toyŏng to the best colonial schools, including Keijō Imperial University, where he studied law. Eventually Yi became a white-collar employee of Kyŏngbang and a small stockholder (70 shares) in the company as well: see Kyŏngsŏng Pangjik CH, List of Stockholders, Nov. 30, 1944 (listed under his Japanese surname "Masaki"). After Liberation, Yi acquired a valuable talc mine, the profits from which allowed him gradually to create his own business group (Ilsin Sanŏp) in South Korea and also to establish Hongik University. Kyunghoon Lee (elder son of Toyŏng), interview, Seattle, Dec. 22, 1985. Along with Kim Yŏnsu, Kim Yongwan, Yi Pyŏngch'ŏl, and other colonial businessmen, Yi played a prominent role in the early 1960s in helping to reopen and promote Korean-Japanese economic ties through the Federation of Korean Industries (FKI); Yi was, in fact, a vice-chairman (Kim Yongwan was chairman) of the FKI in 1964–65 (the normalization treaty was ratified in Korea in August 1965). See No Inhwan, ed., *Chŏn'gyŏng isimnyŏnsa* [A twenty-year history of the FKI] (Seoul: Chŏn'guk Kyŏngjein Yŏnhaphoe, 1983), p. 617.

Kim Yongju was born in 1905 in S. Kyŏngsang Province and graduated from Pusan Commercial School in 1923. After graduation he worked at the Chōsen Industrial Bank for three years both in the bank's head office and in its branch in P'ohang. In 1926, he resigned from the bank and went into the marine trading and transport business in P'ohang with a number of other Korean (and Japanese) businessmen—eventually becoming president of the P'ohang Transport Company (P'ohang Unsu CH) in 1933. He was also a substantial Kyŏngbang stockholder (2,878 shares) during the colonial period. His postcolonial career has been even more impressive, combining both busi-ness (chairman of the Chŏnbang Group: based on the Chŏnbang Spinning Company—formerly Kanebō's factory in Kwangju—and ranked as Korea's thirty-ninth largest business group in 1975) and politics (Democratic party [Minjudang] assemblyman in 1960). He has been an active and high-ranking member of a number of important business organizations, including the FKI (vice-chairman), the Association of Korean Managers (chairman), and the Ko-rean Spinners and Weavers Association (chairman). He has also been very active in promoting Korean-Japanese economic relations. In 1950–51 he served as the South Korean government's official representative in Japan and was a key member during the Park years of the ongoing Committee on Korean-Japanese Cooperation. See Kim Yongju, "Chaegye hoego" [Memoirs of the business world], in *Chaegye hoego wŏllo kiŏbinp'yŏn II* [Memoirs of the business world: Senior businessmen, vol. 2] (Seoul: Han'guk Ilbosa Ch'ulp'an'guk, 1984), pp. 21–161; Sekai Seikei Chōsakai, ed., *Kankoku-Kita Chōsen jimmei jiten (1975)* [Biographical dictionary of North and South Korea: 1975] (Tokyo: Sekai Seikei Chōsakai, 1975), p. 133; Honda Hideo, ed., *Chōsen jinji kōshinroku*, p. 154; *Chōsen GKKY*, pp. 97–98; Pae Tŏkchin, ed., *Panghyŏp samsimnyŏnsa* [A thirty-year history of the Spinners Association] (Seoul: Taehan Pangjik Hyŏphoe, 1977), pp. 647–50. See also Kyŏngsŏng Pangjik CH, List of Stockholders (Kim is listed under his Japanese surname "Kaneda"), Nov. 30, 1944.

3. This study was undertaken at my request by Kyu Hyun Kim, a graduate student in History and East Asian Languages at Harvard, using the Korean-language resources of the Harvard-Yenching Library, including biographical dictionaries, official corporate histories and biographies and autobiographies, and a variety of other published materials on South Korea's *chaebŏl*. The list of top fifty *chaebŏl* came from Han'guk Ilbo Sa Kyŏngjebu, *Han'guk ŭi 50 tae chaebŏl* [Korea's fifty major financial groups] (Seoul: Kyŏngyŏng Nŭngnyul Yŏn'guso, 1985). Kim found that twenty-nine of the fifty founders (58%) had had some kind of colonial business experience either as entrepreneurs or as employees (often in Japanese companies). Seven other founders had had some other kind of colonial experience (in the colonial bureaucracy, for example) that might arguably have contributed to the development of managerial skills. While Kim's conclusions are necessarily tentative pending further study, corroboration, and refinement, they strongly suggest, as does this book, that the Koch'ang Kims represented only the top stratum of a growing new social class and that there is a great need for more empirical research on the colonial era as a formative period of Korean capitalism.

4. The most comprehensive work on this subject is Bruce Cumings' two-volume study of the origins of the Korean War (second volume recently published by Princeton University Press). For a good overview of American economic aid to South Korea, see also David C. Cole, "Foreign Assistance and Korean Development," in David C. Cole, Youngil Lim, and Paul W. Kuznets, *The Korean Economy—Issues of Development* (Berkeley: Institute of East Asian Studies, 1980), pp. 1–29.

5. Park graduated at the top of his class from the Manchukuo Military Academy in 1942. After completing two more years of study at the Japanese Imperial Military Academy in Tokyo, he received a commission as a second lieutenant and was assigned to the Kwantung army. By the end of the war he had been promoted to first lieutenant. See Chŏn Mokku, *Chŏn'gi Pak Chŏnghŭi* [The biography of Park Chung Hee] (Seoul: Kyoyuk P'yŏngnon Sa,

1964), pp. 83–91. The best English-language works on Park's background are Henderson, *Politics of the Vortex*, esp. pp. 106–10, and Kim, *Politics of Military Revolution in Korea*, esp. pp. 89–92.

6. See Kim Yŏnsu, "Chaegye hoego" [Memoirs of the business world] in *Chaegye hoego wŏllo kiŏbinp'yŏn I* [Memoirs of the business world: Senior businessmen, vol. 1] (Seoul: Han'guk Ilbosa Ch'ulp'an'guk, 1984), p. 276. On the "Gold Pagoda Industrial Medal," see Jones and Sakong, *Government, Business, and Entrepreneurship*, p. 98. Yŏnsu died in 1979.

7. See Tongŭn Ki'nyŏm Saŏphoe, ed., *Tongŭn Kim Yongwan*, p. 196. See also No Inhwan, ed., *Chŏn'gyŏng isimnyŏsa*, p. 342.

8. See Tongŭn Ki'nyŏm Saŏphoe, ed., *Tongŭn Kim Yongwan*, pp. 195–200. Kim Yongwan was the FKI's chairman from 1964 to 1966 and again from 1970 to 1977: see No Inhwan, ed., *Chŏn'gyŏng isimnyŏnsa*, pp. 617–68. See also Kwan Bong Kim, *The Korea-Japan Treaty Crisis and the Instability of the Korean Political System* (New York: Praeger Publishers, 1971).

9. See Park Chung Hee, *The Country, the Revolution and I* (Seoul: Hollym Corporation, 1970; 1st ed., 1962), pp. 117–20, 140.

10. Two of South Korea's most important new export areas—electronics and automobiles—provide a case in point. Nearly 100 percent of the key parts for Korea's VCRs, facsimile machines, and computer terminals are being supplied by Japanese companies. As for automobiles: 15 percent of the Hyundai Motor Company, which has been exporting its Hyundai Excel to the United States, is owned by the Mitsubishi group, and the car itself is equipped with a Mitsubishi engine and other key Mitsubishi components (axles, for example). See *Business Week*, Dec. 23, 1985, p. 50; also *Business Korea* (April 1986), p. 99.

11. See Moore, *Social Origins of Dictatorship and Democracy*.

12. Isaiah Berlin, *Four Essays on Liberty* (Oxford: Oxford University Press, paperback, 1979), p. 120.

13. Landes, "Japan and Europe," p. 177.

14. Moore, *Social Origins of Dictatorship and Democracy*, p. 437.

15. As noted above, Korea's traditional politics were certainly far from democratic in the current Western sense of the word. Still, they were not despotic: in terms of guarding its prerogatives against monarchical encroachment, the Korean aristocracy was among the most zealous and successful the world has ever seen, in England or elsewhere. Edward W. Wagner, for example, has suggested that the relationship between the Yi ruling house and the yangban "at its finest point of balance represented a kind of constitutional monarchy." To see the authoritarianism of South Korea simply or even primarily as an extension of the Chosŏn political tradition thus seems grossly inaccurate: the power wielded by a contemporary South Korean president is something of which few, if any, Yi dynasty kings dared dream and which none attained, Wagner, *Literati Purges*, p. 2. See also chap. 3.

Guide To Romanization

The following is a list of Korean, Japanese, and Chinese names and terms that appear in the main text. In romanizing Korean and Japanese, I have been guided, respectively, by the McCune-Reischauer and Hepburn systems, except in the case of familiar names such as Seoul or Tokyo, where I have adopted the standard English spellings without any diacritical markings. The Chinese names listed below, with the exception of Manchukuo, follow the orthography of pre-1945 English-language newspapers and maps.

Akashi 明石

an 안

aniki 兄貴

Antung 安東

Anyang (city in Korea) 安養

Anyang (city in China) 安陽

Aruga Mitsutoyo 有賀光豊

assen kikan 斡旋機關

Bandai 萬代

betto tsumitatekin 別途積立金

budan seiji 武斷政治

bunka seiji 文化政治

Ch'abung 茶棚

chaebŏl/zaibatsu 財閥

chagang 自強

ch'ambong 參奉

ch'amp'an 參判

Chang Myŏn 張勉

Chang Tŏksu 張德秀

Chang Usŏk 張禹錫

Ch'angp'yŏng 昌平

changgi/shōgi 將棋

Changsha 長沙

Changsŏng 長城

Changte 彰德

chibaein 支配人

Chientao 間島

Chikchoguk 織造局

chingnyu 織紐

Chinju 晋州

Ch'inmok tanch'e 親睦團體

Chinnamp'o 鎮南浦

chinsa 進士

Chiphyŏnjŏn 集賢殿

Cho Kijun 趙璣濬

Chōbō 朝紡

Ch'oe Ch'anghak 崔昌學
Ch'oe Malli 崔萬理
Ch'oe Rin 崔麟
Ch'oe Tusŏn 崔斗善
chokumei 勅命
Chŏlla 全羅
Chŏn Sŭngbŏm 全承範
Chŏng Chuyŏng 鄭周永
chŏngbo 町步
Ch'ŏngjin 清津
Chongno Sa-ga 鐘路四街
Ch'ŏnil 天一
Chŏnju 全州
Chŏnp'yŏng 全評
chōsakai 調査會
Chōsen Bōeki Kyōkai
　朝鮮貿易協會
Chōsen Bōseki Kōgyō Kumiai
　朝鮮紡績工業組合
Chōsen Bōshoku KK
　朝鮮紡織株式會社
Chōsen Hikōki Kōgyō KK
　朝鮮飛行機工業株式會社
Chōsen Jitsugyō Kurabu
　朝鮮實業倶楽部
Chōsen Kin'yu Kumiai Rengōkai
　朝鮮金融組合聯合會
Chōsen Menka Dōgyō Kumiai
　朝鮮棉花同業組合
Chōsen Menshifushō Rengōkai
　朝鮮綿絲布商聯合會
Chōsen Rengō Seinendan
　朝鮮聯合青年團

Chōsen Sen'i Sangyōkai
　朝鮮纖維産業會
Chōsen Shōgyō Ginkō
　朝鮮商業銀行
Chōsen Shokusan Ginkō
　朝鮮殖産銀行
Chōsen shimbun 朝鮮新聞
Chosŏn (dynasty) 朝鮮
Chosŏn Nodong Chohap Chŏn'guk
　P'yŏngŭihoe
　朝鮮勞動組合全國評議會
Chosŏn Nodong Kongjehoe
　朝鮮勞動共済會
Chosŏn Nonong Ch'ongdongmaeng
　朝鮮勞農總同盟
Chosŏnin Sanŏp Taehoe
　朝鮮人産業大會
Chosŏn Ŭnhaeng 朝鮮銀行
ch'ulchangso 出張所
Chulp'o 茁浦
Chun Doo Hwan (Chŏn Tuhwan)
　全斗煥
Ch'unch'ŏn 春川
Chungang Hakkyo 中央學校
Chungch'uwŏn/Chūsūin 中樞院
chusik hoesa (CH)/kabushiki
　kaisha (KK) 株式會社

Dai Nippon 大日本
Dai Nippon Bōseki Rengōkai
　大日本紡績聯合會
Dairen 大連
dōtai 胴體

Edo 江戸
Endō 遠藤

Fujii 藤井
fukokuji 府告示
Fuminkan 府民館
furei 府令
Fushun 撫順

gun no shitei kōjō 軍の指定工場
Gōshō KK 江商株式會社

Haedong 海東
Haeju 海州
Haeri 海里
hakhoe 學會
hakpyŏng 學兵
Hamgyŏng 咸鏡
hammyŏng hoesa 合名會社
Han (river in Korea) 漢
Han Sangnyong 韓相龍
han'gŭl 한글
Hanil 韓一
Hansŏng 漢城
Hansŏng sunbo 漢城旬報
Hanyang 漢陽
hap 合
hapcha hoesa 合資會社
Harbin 合爾賓
Hayashi Shigeki 林茂樹
Hayashi Shigezō 林繁藏
Hayashi Yutaka 林豊
heitambu 兵站部

hinomaru 日の丸
hojo 補助
Honam 湖南
Honam hakpo 湖南學報
Honan 河南
Hsinking 新京
Hwanghae 黃海
Hwangsŏng sinmun 皇城新聞
Hwasin 和信
Hwasin Sangsa CH
   和信商事株式會社
Hwasun 和順
Hyŏn Chunho 玄俊鎬
Hyundai (Hyŏndae) 現代

iinkai 委員會
Ikuta 生田
Ilbon'in chuju 日本人株主
Ilchinhoe 一進會
ilgŭpche 日給制
Imori Meiji 伊森明治
Inch'on 仁村
Inch'ŏn 仁川
Iri 裡里
Itagaki Taisuke 板垣退助
Itō Hirobumi 伊藤博文

jifu 慈父

Kabo 甲午
Kada Naoji 賀田直治
Kaehwadang 開化黨
kaekchu 客主

Kaesŏng 開城

kamikaze 神風

kamsayŏk 監査役

kamyŏk 監役

Kanai Noburu 金井延

Kanebō 鐘紡

Kanegafuchi 鐘淵

Kang Chaehu 姜載厚

Kang Man'gil 姜萬吉

Kanghwa 江華

kangje chŏgŭm 強制貯金

Kangwŏn 江原

kanrikan 管理官

Kapsin 甲申

Katō 加藤

Kawasaki 川崎

Kaya 伽倻

keigo 警護

Keijō nippō 京城日報

keizai keisatsu 經濟警察

Kim Chaesu 金在洙

Kim Chonghan 金宗漢

Kim Chŏngho 金正浩

Kim Il Sung (Kim Ilsŏng) 金日成

Kim Inhu 金麟厚

Kim Kijung 金祺中

Kim Kyŏngjung 金暻中

Kim Sanghyŏp 金相浹

Kim Sayŏn 金思演

Kim Sŏngsu 金性洙

Kim T'aebong 金泰峯

Kim Yŏbaek 金汝伯

Kim Yohyŏp 金堯莢

Kim Yongju 金龍周

Kim Yŏngmo 金泳謨

Kim Yongwan 金容完

Kim Yŏnsu 金秊洙

Kirita 桐田

Kita Ikki 北一輝

Ko Chŏngju 高鼎柱

Kobayashi Hideo 小林英夫

Kobu 古阜

kobun 子分

kobushi 拳

Koch'ang 高敞

Koiso Kuniaki 小磯國昭

Kojong 高宗

kōkoku shinmhinka 皇國臣民化

Kokumin Sōryoku Chōsen Remmei
國民總力朝鮮聯盟

kokutai 國體

Kokutai no hongi 國體の本義

komun 顧問

kondankai 懇談會

Kongik/Kōeki 共益

kongin 貢人

Kōnoike 鴻池

konshinkai 懇親會

kōtō keisatsu 高等警察

Koryŏ 高麗

Ku Inhoe 具仁會

Kudae 九臺

Kŭmho 錦湖

kumiai 組合

kun 君

kŭndaehwa 近代化

Kunsan 群山

kunsu 郡守

Kuomintang 國民黨

Kup'o 龜浦

kurabu 倶楽部

Kureha 呉羽

Kuwana 桑名

kwalliin 管理人

Kwangju 廣州

Kwantung 關東

kyōdō no fukuri 共同の福利

kyōei 共榮

Kyoha 蛟河

Kyŏnggi 京畿

Kyŏngsang 慶尚

Kyŏngsŏng/Keijō 京城

Kyŏngsŏng Chingnyu CH
　京城織丑株式會社

Kyŏngsŏng Pangjik CH
　京城紡織株式會社

kyōson 共存

Kyoto (Kyōtō) 京都

Kyujanggak 奎章閣

Kyūshū 九州

Liao 遼

Maeha 梅河

Maeil sinbo 毎日新報

maenga 萌芽

Manchukuo 滿洲國

mansŏkkun 萬石君

Manp'ojin 滿浦鎮

Mantetsu 滿鐵

Marumiya 丸宮

Masan 馬山

Mataichi 又一

Matsui 松井

Matsuzawa Tatsuo 松澤龍雄

Meiji 明治

Mempu Tōsei Iinkai
　綿布統制委員會

Min Ch'igu 閔致久

Min Kyusik 閔奎植

Min Pyŏngsŏk 閔丙奭

Min Sŭngho 閔升鎬

Min Taesik 閔大植

Min Tuho 閔斗鎬

Min Yŏnghwi 閔泳徽

Minami Jirō 南次郎

minjok chabon 民族資本

Minobe Shunkichi 美濃部俊吉

Mishima Tarō 三島太郎

Mitsubishi 三菱

Mitsui 三井

Mitsui Bussan 三井物産

Miyabayashi Taiji 宮林泰司

Mizuno Rentarō 水野錬太郎

Mokp'o 木浦

Mukden 奉天

Mun Sangu 文尚宇

munkwa 文科

Murakami Shōten 村上商店

Muromachi 室町

musubi 結び

Myŏngwŏlgwan 明月館

myŏnhoe 面會

Naichi 内地

Naichi dōhō 内地同胞

Naisen Ittai 内鮮一體

Najin 羅津

Nakamura Takafusa 中村隆英

Nakatomi Keita 中富計太

Namman Pangjŏk CH
　南滿紡績株式會社

Namsan 南山

Nichiman Ittai 日滿一體

Nippon Chisso 日本窒素

Nippon Menka KK
　日本棉花株式會社

Nippon seishin 日本精神

Nishihara 西原

Nishimura 西村

Nissen Yūwa 日鮮融和

Noda Shingo 野田新吾

Nogami 野上

Noguchi Jun 野口遵

nongjang 農場

Noryangjin 鷺梁津

Nosawa 能澤

Ōji 王子

ōja 王者

Ōkubo Toshimichi 大久保利通

Ōkuma Shigenobu 大隈重信

Ōkura Kihachirō 大倉喜八郎

ondol 온돌

Ōnishi Shōten KK
　大西商店株式會社

Osaka (Ōsaka) 大阪

Ōshima 大島

otōto 弟

oyabun 親分

Ozaki 尾崎

Paek In'gi 白寅基

Paek Yunju 白潤洙

Paekche 百濟

Pak Hŭngsik 朴興植

Pak Kisun 朴基順

Pak Munhoe 朴文會

Pak Sŭngjik 朴承稷

Pak Yŏngch'ŏl 朴榮喆

Pak Yŏnghyo 朴泳孝

Pansŏk 盤石

Park Chung Hee (Pak Chŏnghŭi)
　朴正熙

Peking 北京

Penhsihu 本溪湖

Pisŏwŏn 秘書院

pojŭngin 保證人

pŏlgŭm chedo 罰金制度

pongsa 奉事

Pujŏn 赴戰

Pulloch'o 不老草

Pusan 釜山

p'yŏng 坪

P'yŏngyang 平壤

Rhee Syngman (Yi Sŭngman)
李承晩
rengōkai 聯合會

sāberushugi サーベル主義
sadae 事大
Saeki Tasuke 佐伯多助
Saigō Takamori 西郷隆盛
saihensei 再編成
Saitō Makoto 齋藤實
sake 酒
Samch'ŏk 三拓
Samch'ŏlli 三千里
Samnam 三南
Sampin 三品
Sampō 産報
Samsung (Samsŏng) 三星
Samyang 三養
Sanggong wŏlbo 商工月報
sangjohoe 相助會
Sangŏpkye 商業界
Sangyō Hōkoku Undō
産業報國運動
sarang 사랑
se 歳
seikanron 征韓論
seinen kunrenjo 青年訓練所
seirei 政令
seisen 聖戰
Sejong 世宗
sekai keizaisen 世界經濟戰
Sekiya Teizaburō 關屋貞三郎

sembu kōsaku 宣撫工作
sen 錢
Seoul 서울
Shanghai 上海
Shantung 山東
Shibusawa Eiichi 澁澤榮一
Shintō 神道
Shioda 鹽田
Shiraishi Jinkichi 白石甚吉
shōgyō 商業
Shōkō Kaigisho 商工會議所
Shokugin Ōkoku 殖銀王國
Shokuginkei 殖銀系
shōnendan 少年團
Siangtan 湘潭
Sihŭng 始興
Sihŭng Nou Sangjohoe
始興勞友相助會
Silla 新羅
Sim Sangik 沈相翊
Sin Ch'ŏlhun 申哲勳
Sin T'aehwa 申泰和
Sinŭiju 新義州
Sŏdaemun 西大門
sŏdang 書堂
sŏk 石
Son Kijŏng 孫基禎
Song Chinu 宋鎭禹
Song Kwangmun 宋光文
Song Pyŏngjun 宋秉畯
Sŏn'gonggam 繕工監
sōtoku 總督

Ssangnimdong 雙林洞

Suchiatun 蘇家屯

Sugihara 杉原

Taedong 大同

Taegu 大邱

T'aegŭksŏng 太極星

Taehan Hŭnghakhoe 大韓興學會

Taejŏn 大田

taenim 대님

taiatari 體當たり

Taisei 大星

Taishō 大正

Takada 高田

Takahashi Kamekichi 高橋龜吉

Takase 高瀬

Takashimaya 高島屋

Tamyang 潭陽

tan 反

Tanegashima Shigeru 種子島蕃

teate 手當て

Terada Kazuichi 寺田數一

Tiehsi 鐵西

Tientsin 天津

Tōjō Hideki 東条英機

Tōkyō asahi shimbun
　東京朝日新聞

tōdori 頭取

togŭpche 都給制

t'oho 土豪

tojobu 賭租簿

tokubetsu teiri kashitsuke
　特別低利貸し付け

Tokugawa 徳川

Tokyo (Tōkyō) 東京

Tonga ilbo 東亞日報

Tonggwang 東光

Tonggwang 東光

Tongil 東一

tosa 都事

Tōseiha 統制派

Tōyō Menka KK 東洋棉花株式會社

Tōyōbō 東洋紡

Toyoda 豊田

Tsuda Shingo 津田信吾

Tsingtao 青島

t'ŭgyak p'anmaejŏm 特約販賣店

Tuman (Tumen) 豆滿

Tungchow 通州

Tusan 斗山

ude 腕

Ugaki Kazunari 宇垣一成

ŭibyŏng 義兵

Ŭigŭmbu 義禁府

Ŭijŏngbu 議政府

Ŭiju 義州

Ulsan 蔚山

umi no oya 生みの親

Unggi 雄基

Waseda 早稲田

Watanabe Toyohiko 渡邊豊日子

Wŏnju 原州

Wŏnsan 元山

Yagi Shōten　八木商店
Yamamoto Jōtarō　山本条太郎
Yamato　大和
yangban　兩班
Yangp'yŏngdong　楊坪洞
yen　圓
Yi (dynasty)　李
Yi Hwang (T'oegye)　李滉 (退溪)
Yi Kanghyŏn　李康賢
Yi Kwangsu　李光洙
Yi Pyŏngch'ŏl　李秉喆
Yi Sangu　李常雨
Yi Sŭngu　李升雨
Yi Toyŏng　李道榮
Yingkow　營口

yŏgak　旅閣
Yŏnch'ŏn　漣川
Yŏngdŭngp'o　永登浦
Yonggang　龍岡
Yongjŏng　龍井
Yŏngsin　永信
Yŏnil Chŏng　延日鄭
Yu Kilchun　俞吉濬
yugŭijŏn　六矣廛
Yun Ch'iho　尹致昊
Yun Chŏngha　尹定夏
Yun Chubok　尹柱福
Yun Posŏn　尹潽善
Yun Tŏgyŏng　尹德榮

Bibliography

Unpublished Sources

Chaedan Pŏbin Samyang Tongjehoe. Papers, 1939–1945. Chusik Hoesa Kyŏngbang, Yongin.

Hapcha Hoesa Samyangsa. Papers, 1924–1945. Chusik Hoesa Samyangsa. Seoul.

Kyŏngsŏng Pangjik Chusik Hoesa, Papers, 1919–1945. Chusik Hoesa Kyŏngbang. Seoul and Yongin. Company business and fiscal reports, lists of stockholders, and the records of the board and stockholders meetings are kept at the company's head office in Seoul (Yŏngdŭngp'o). All other papers (ledgers, vouchers, etc.) are stored in the company's vault at its factory in Yongin.

Saitō Makoto Bunsho. Kenseishiryō Shitsu, Kokuritsu Kokkai Toshōkan [Saitō Makoto Papers, Constitutional Documents Room, National Diet Library]. Tokyo.

Sekiya Teizaburō Bunsho. Kenseishiryō Shitsu, Kokuritsu Kokkai Toshōkan [Sekiya Teizaburō Papers, Constitutional Documents Room, National Diet Library]. Tokyo.

Official and Company Sources

Chōsen Ginkō Chōsaka. Kōgyō kin'yū no genjō to sono taisaku [The present state of industrial financing and an appropriate policy]. Research Report no. 25 (July 1936). Keijō, 1936.

———. Saikin Chōsen ni okeru daikōgyō yakushin to sono shihon keitō [The recent rapid advance and capital connections of large-scale industry in Korea]. Research Report no. 16 (March 1935). Keijō, 1935.

Chōsen Kempeitai Shireibu. Chōsen san'ichi dokuritsu sōjō jiken: Gaikyō, shisō oyobi undō [The Korean March First independence riots: The general situation, ideology, and activities]. Reprint of original. Tokyo: Gannandō Shoten, 1969.

Chōsen Sōtokufu. Chōsen. Keijō: 1911–1942.

———. Chōsen Sangyō Keizai Chōsakai kaigiroku [The proceedings of the commission on the industry and economy of Chōsen]. Keijō, October 1936.

———. *Chōsen Sangyō Keizai Chōsakai shimon tōshinsho* [The final report of the commission on the industry and economy of Chōsen]. Keijō, October 1936.

———. *Chōsen Sōtokufu Jikyoku Taisaku Chōsakai kaigiroku* [Proceedings of the Chōsen Government-General commission on policy for the current situation]. Keijō, September 1938.

———. Chōsen Sōtokufu Jikyoku Taisaku Chōsakai shimon tōshinsho [The final report of the Chōsen Government-General commission on policy for the current situation]. Keijō, September 1938.

———. *Chōsen Sōtokufu tōkei nempō, 1911* [The statistical yearbook of the Government-General of Korea, 1911]. 3 vols. Keijō: Chōsen Sōtokufu, 1913.

———. *Chōsen Sōtokufu tōkei nempō, 1937* [Statistical yearbook of the Government-General of Korea, 1937]. Keijō, 1939.

———. *Chōsen Sōtokufu tōkei nempō, 1941* [Statistical yearbook of the Government-General of Korea, 1941]. Keijō, 1943.

———. *Sangyō Chōsa Iinkai giji sokkiroku* [The stenographic record of the proceedings of the industrial commission]. Keijō, September 1921.

———. *Shisei sanjūnen* [Thirty years of administration]. Keijō, 1940.

Chōsen Sōtokufu, Keimukyoku. *Kōtō Keisatsu kankei nempyō* [Chronological table of the higher police]. Reprint of 1930 edition. Tokyo: Gannandō, 1962.

Chōsen Sōtokufu, Keimukyoku Hoanka. *Kōtō keisatsuhō* [The higher police report]. No. 2. Reprint. Tokyo: Gannandō, 1962.

Chōsen Sōtokufu, Tetsudōkyoku. *Hantō no kin'ei* [The peninsula in pictures]. Keijō: Chōsen Sōtokufu, Tetsudōkyoku, 1937.

Cho Yonggu, ed. *Kyŏngsŏng Pangjik osimnyŏn* (cited in notes as *KO*) [Fifty years of Kyŏngbang]. Seoul: Kyŏngsŏng Pangjik CH, 1969.

Government-General of Chosen. *Annual Report on Administration of Chosen: 1922–1923.* Keijō, 1924.

Government-General of Chosen. *Annual Report on Administration of Chosen: 1935–1936.* Keijo, 1936.

Gunzanfu. *Gunzanfushi* [The history of Gunzan]. Gunzan, 1935.

Han Sangnyong. *Namboku Shina oyobi Manshū shisatsu hōkokusho* [Report of the mission to north and south China and Manchuria]. Keijō: KK Kanjō Ginkō, 1917.

H.I.J.M.'s Residency General. *Annual Report for 1907 on Reforms and Progress in Korea.* Seoul, 1908.

Honda Hideo, ed. *Chōsen Shokusan Ginkō nijūnenshi* [A twenty-year record of the Chōsen Industrial Bank]. Keijō: Chōsen Shokusan Ginkō, 1938.

Kim Chunggil, ed. *Hwasin osimnyŏnsa: 1926–1976* [A fifty-year history of Hwasin: 1926–1976]. Seoul: Hwasin Sanŏp CH, 1977.

Kim Sanghong, ed. *Samyang osimnyŏn: 1924–1974* (cited in notes as *SY*) [Fifty years of Samyang: 1924–1974]. Seoul: CH Samyangsa, 1974.

Kondo Ken'ichi, ed. *Chōsen Sōtokufu shiryō senshū: Saitō Sōtoku no bunka tōchi* [Selected documents of the Government-General of Korea: The enlightened rule of Governor-General Saitō]. Yūhō Series. Tokyo: Yūhō Kyōkai, 1970.

Minami Manshū Tetsudō KK. *Minami Manshū Tetsudō ryōkō annai* [The South Manchuria Railway travel guide]. Dairen: Minami Manshū Tetsudō KK, 1919.

Minami Manshū Tetsudō KK, Keizai Chōsakai Daiichibu. *Chōsenjin rōdōsha ippan jijō* [General conditions of Korean workers]. Minami Manshū Tetsudō KK, 1933.

Mombushō Jitsugyō Gakumukyoku. *Jitsugyō gakkō ichiran* [A survey of vocational schools]. Tokyo: Mombushō Jitsugyō Gakumukyoku, 1936.

Myŏng Chuhyŏn, ed. *OB isimnyŏnsa* [A twenty-year history of the OB Company]. Seoul: Tongyang Maekchu CH, 1972.

Pak Inhwan, ed. *Kyŏngbang yuksimnyŏn* (cited in notes as *KY*) [Sixty years of Kyŏngbang]. Seoul: CH Kyŏngbang, 1980.

Pauley, Edwin W. *Report on Japanese Assets in Manchuria to the President of the United States.* June 1946.

———. *Report on Japanese Assets in Soviet-Occupied Korea to the President of the United States.* June 1946.

Shashi Henshū Iinkai, ed. *Kureha Bōseki sanjūnen* [Thirty years of Kureha spinning]. Osaka: Kureha Bōseki KK, 1960.

South Manchuria Railway Company. *Fifth Report on Progress in Manchuria to 1936.* Dairen: South Manchuria Railway Company, 1936.

———. *Sixth Report on Progress in Manchuria to 1939.* Dairen: South Manchuria Railway Company, 1939.

United States Department of Commerce, Bureau of Foreign and Domestic Commerce. Office of Commercial Attaché, American Embassy, Tokyo. "Japan Monthly Trade and Economic Letters — July 1929."

United States Department of State. *Report of the Mission on Japanese Combines, Part II: Analytical and Technical Data.* Department of State Publication 2628, Far Eastern Series no. 14. Washington, D.C.: Department of State, 1946.

The United States Strategic Bombing Survey. 10 vols. New York and London: Garland Publishing, 1976.

Yasutaka Masanori, ed. *Gunzan kaikōshi* [The history of the opening of the port of Kunsan]. Gunzan: Gunzanfu, 1925.

Zaiseibu Rizaiji, ed. *Manshūkoku ginkō sōran* [Compendium of Manchurian banks]. Hsinking: Department of Finance, 1935.

Books and Articles in Japanese

Ajia Keizai Kenkyūsho: Tosho shiryōbu. *Kyū shokuminchi kankei kikan kankōbutsu sōgō mokuroku: Chōsen hen* [Union Catalog of Publications by the Former Colonial Institutions: Korea]. Tokyo: Ajia Keizai Kenkyūsho, 1974.

Chomei shōko annai [Guide to major commerce and industry]. Osaka: KK Shōgyō Kōshinjo, 1942.

Chŏn Sŭngbŏm. "Daitōa sensō to Chōsen keizai no shinro" [The great East Asian War and the course of the Korean economy]. *Chōsen jitsugyō* 20 (March 1942): 8–14.

"Chōsen Jitsugyō Kurabu seiritsu no keika to ganjō" [The establishment and present circumstances of the Chōsen Business Club]. *Chōsen jitsugyō kurabu* 15 (June 1937): 164.

Chōsen Menshifushō Rengōkai. *Chōsen mengyōshi* [The history of the Korean cotton industry]. Keijō: Chōsen Menshifushō Rengōkai, 1929.

"Chōsen o hagukumishi nyūjō meishi: Kangei daigosankai" [A grand welcoming luncheon for the visiting dignitaries who have nurtured Chōsen]. *Chōsen jitsugyō kurabu* 13 (October 1935): 30–39.

Dōmoto Sadakazu. "Manshūkoku sangyō no taisei to Semman bōeki ni tsuite" [Manchurian industry and Chōsen-Manchurian trade]. *Chōsen jitsugyō kurabu* 13 (April 1935): 2–7.

Furuta Renzaburō. "Manshūkoku ni tsuite" [On Manchukuo]. *Chōsen jitsugyō kurabu* 10 (October 1932): 14–15.

Han Ikkyo, ed. *Kan Sōryūkun o kataru* [Speaking of Han Sangnyong]. Keijō: Kan Sōryū Kanreki Kinenkai, 1941.

Han Sangnyong, "Hokushi o mite" [Looking at north China]. *Chōsen jitsugyō* 18 (July 1940): 56–68.

———. "Jikyoku to Manshū" [Manchukuo and the current situation] *Chōsen jitsugyō kurabu* 10 (October 1932): 25–31.

———. "Jitsugyō Kurabu no enkaku" [The history of the Chōsen Business Club]. *Chōsen jitsugyō kurabu* 7 (September 1929): 2–4.

———. "Manshū Jihen sanjūnen o mukaete" [Celebrating the third anniversary of the Manchurian Incident]. *Chōsen jitsugyō kurabu* 12 (October 1934): 2–11.

———. "Namboku Manshū o shisatsu shite" [Mission to north and south Manchuria]. *Chōsen jitsugyō kurabu* 10 (April 1932): 3–16.

———. "Nentō shokan" [Thoughts on the New Year]. *Chōsen jitsugyō kurabu* 18 (January 1940): 11–12.

Hashiguchi Shūkō, ed. *Chōsen sen'i yōran* [The Chōsen textile handbook]. Keijō: Chōsen Orimono Kyōkai, 1943.

"Honkai no enkaku to jigyō" [The history and activities of this club]. *Chōsen jitsugyo* 18 (March 1940): 2–11.

Itō Dōjin, ed. *Gendai jimbutsu jiten* [Modern biographical dictionary]. Tokyo: Asahi Shimbunsha, 1977.

"Kaiin meibo" [List of club members]. *Chōsen jitsugyō kurabu* 14 (June 1936): 85–117.

"Kaimu" [Club Business]. *Chōsen jitsugyō kurabu* 14 (November 1936): 186–187.

Kajimura Hideki. *Chōsen ni okeru shihonshugi no keisei to tenkai* [The formation and development of capitalism in Korea]. Tokyo: Ryūkei Shosha, 1977.

Kanahara Kaoru, ed. *Manshū ginkō kaisha nenkan, 1942* [The Manchurian bank and company yearbook, 1942], no. 8. Dairen: Dairen Shōkō Kaigisho, 1943.

Kang Tongjin. *Nihon no Chōsen shihai seisakushi* [Studies in the history of Japan's policy of control in Korea]. Tokyo: Tōkyō Daigaku Shuppankai, 1979.

Kawai Akitake. *Chōsen kōgyō no gendankai* [The present stage of Korean industry]. Keijō: Tōyō Keizai Shimpōsha, 1943.

"Keijō Bōseki [*sic*] Kaisha no naiyō o kiku: Keijō Bōseki [*sic*] Kabushiki Kaisha Shihainin Ri Jōusi" [Getting the facts on the Kyŏngsŏng Spinning and Weaving Company: Company manager Mr. Yi Sangu]. *Chōsen jitsugyō kurabu* 10 (December 1932): 16–17.

Kim Yehyŏn. "Shina jihengo ni shosubeki Hantōjin no yōi" [Korean strategies in the aftermath of the China Incident]. *Chōsen jitsugyō kurabu* 16 (March 1938): 64–65.

Kita Tadai. *Chōsen jinji kōshinroku* [Who's who in Korea]. Keijō: Chōsen Shimbunsha, 1935.

Kobayashi Hideo. *Daitōa kyōeiken no keisei to hōkai* [The rise and fall of the greater East Asia co-prosperity sphere]. Tokyo: Ochanomizu Shobō, 1975.

———. " 'Kaisha Rei' kenkyū nōto" [Research notes on the 'Company Law']. *Kaikyō*, no. 3 (December 1975): 21–36.

Kojima Seiichi. *Hokushi keizai dokuhon* [The north China economic reader]. Tokyo: Sensō Shobō, 1939.

Kokumin Sōryoku Chōsen Remmei, ed. "Kokumin Sōryoku tokuhon" [The concerted national power reader]. *Chōsen jitsugyō* 19 (October 1941): 41–45 and *Chōsen jitsugyō* 19 (December 1941): 39–44.

Kudō Sanjirō. "Chōsen tai Manshū bōeki no jūnen" [Ten years of Chōsen-Manchurian trade]. *Chōsen jitsugyō* 20 (September 1942): 2–5.

Matsui Kōya, ed. *Nihon shokuminchi shi 1: Chōsen* [History of the Japanese Colonies 1: Korea]. Bessatsu Ichiokunin no Shōwa Shi Series. Tokyo: Mainichi Shimbun Sha, 1978.

Mitarai Tatsuo. *Minami Jirō* [Minami Jirō]. Tokyo: Minami Jirō Denki Kankōkai, 1957.

Miyabayashi Taiji, "Chōsen orimono gyōkai no tembō" [A look at the Chōsen textile world]. *Chōsen jitsugyō* 18 (March 1940): 102–6.

Naitō Yasohachi, ed. *Semman sangyō taikan* [Korea-Manchuria industrial encyclopedia]. Tokyo: Jigyō to Keizai Sha, 1940.

Nakamura Sukeyoshi, ed. *Chōsen ginkō kaisha kumiai yōroku* (cited in notes as *Chōsen GKKY*) [Digest of Korean banks, companies and associations]. Keijō: Tōa Keizai Jihōsha, 1933.

Ogura Masatarō, ed. *Chōsen sangyō nempō, 1943* [Chōsen industrial yearbook, 1943]. Keijō: Tōyō Keizai Shimpōsha, 1943.

Okiayu Toshihiro. *Chōsen hōritsu hanrei ketsugi sōran* [A survey of Chōsen laws, precedents, and decisions]. Keijō: Osaka Yagō Shoten, 1927.

Okudaira Yasuhiro. *Chian Iji Hō shōshi* [A concise history of the Peace Preservation Law]. Tokyo: Chikuma Shobō, 1977.

Osanaga Yoshimasu, ed. *Manshū keizai zusetsu* [The Manchurian economy in graphs]. Dairen: Dairen Shōkō Kaigisho, 1940.

Pak Yŏngch'ŏl. *Gojūnen no kaiko* [Fifty years of memories]. Keijō: Pak Yŏngch'ŏl, 1929.

Sakai Kazuo. "Manshū keikōgyō no hatten katei ni kansuru oboegaki" [A note on the process of development of light industry in Manchukuo]. *Dai Nippon Bōseki Rengōkai geppō*, no. 583 (May 1941): pp. 2–6.

Sakamoto Zenzaburō, ed. *Manshū ginkō kaisha nenkan, 1938* [The Manchurian bank and company yearbook, 1938], no. 4. Dairen: Dairen Shōkō Kaigisho, 1938.

Sakudō Yoshio and Etō Takendo, eds. *Tōkyō Kōgyō Daigaku kyūjūnenshi* [A ninety-year history of the Tokyo Industrial College]. Tokyo: KK Zaikai Hyōron Shinsha, 1975.

Sampei Takako. *Nippon mengyō hattatsushi* [The history of the development of the Japanese cotton industry]. Tokyo: Keiō Shobō, 1941.

Sekai Seikei Chōsakai, ed. *Kankoku-Kita Chōsen jimmei jiten (1975)* [Biographical dictionary of North and South Korea: 1975]. Tokyo: Sekai Seikei Chōsakai, 1975.

"Semman bōeki zadankai (I-II)" [Symposium on Chōsen-Manchurian trade]. *Chōsen jitsugyō kurabu* 10 (June 1932): 31–36; *Chōsen jitsugyō kurabu* 10 (July 1932): 41–65.

"Semman keizai sangyō zadankai (I)" [Symposium on Korean-Manchurian economy and industry: I]. *Chōsen jitsugyō kurabu* 15 (May 1937): 32–57.

"Semman keizai sangyō zadankai (II)" [Symposium on Korean-Manchurian economy and industry: II]. *Chōsen jitsugyō kurabu* 15 (June 1937): 89–117.

Shimonaka Kunihiko, ed. *Nihon jimmei daijiten: gendai* [Great biographical dictionary of Japan: Modern period]. Tokyo: KK Heibonsha, 1979.

Shimonaka Yasaburō, ed. *Dai jimmei jiten* [Great biographical dictionary]. 10 vols. Tokyo: Heibonsha, 1953–55.

"Shinnyū kaiin (2)" [New club members: 2]. *Chōsen jitsugyō kurabu* 14 (February 1936): 64ff.

Shiomi Tsunesaburō. "Chōsen ni okeru bōseki kōgyō no genjō (I)" [The present condition of the spinning industry in Korea: I]. *Dai Nippon Bōseki Rengōkai geppō*, no. 587 (September 1941), pp. 7–15, 102.

―――. "Chōsen ni okeru bōseki kōgyō no genjō (II)" [The present condition of the spinning industry in Korea: II]. *Dai Nippon Bōseki Rengōkai geppō*, no. 589 (November 1941), pp. 63–73.

Takahashi Kamekichi. *Gendai Chōsen Keizairon* [A discourse on the contemporary Korean economy]. Tokyo: Sensō Shobō, 1935.

Tsukamoto Yoshitaka, ed. *Chūgoku kōshō meikan* [Directory of trade and industry in China]. Tokyo: Nippon Shōgyō Tsūshinsha, 1942.

Ugaki Kazunari. *Ugaki nikki* [The Ugaki diary]. Tokyo: Asahi Shimbunsha, 1954.

Yamanari Kyōroku. "Manshūkoku no kin'yū jijō (I-II-III)" [Financing in Manchukuo, Parts I-II-III]. *Chōsen jitsugyō kurabu* 11 (March 1933): 31–33; 11 (April 1933): 32–37; 11 (May 1933): 24–33.

Yi Chaegon. "Eitōhō no san daikōjō o miru" [A look at three large-scale factories in Yŏngdŭngp'o]. *Chōsen jitsugyō kurabu* 14 (June 1936): 74–76.

"Zaikai hempen" [Business notes]. *Chōsen jitsugyō kurabu* 10 (June 1932): 37ff.

Zenkoku Keizai Chōsa Kikan Rengōkai Chōsen Shibu. *Chōsen keizai nempō 1940* [Chōsen economic yearbook: 1940]. Tokyo: Kaizōsha, 1940.

Books and Articles in Korean

Chaegye hoego [Memoirs of the business world]. 10 vols. Seoul: Han'guk Ilbosa Ch'ulp'an'guk, 1984.

Ch'ang Nanggaek. "Paengman changja ŭi paengmanwŏn'gwan: Chakko ssŭgosiptanŭn Kim Sŏngsussi" [Millionaires look at their millions: I want to keep spending, says Kim Sŏngsu]. *Samch'ŏlli* 7 (September 1935): 44–48.

Chin Tŏkkyu et al. *1950 nyŏndae ŭi insik* [Understanding the 1950s]. Onŭrŭi Sasang Sinsŏ, no. 22. Seoul: Han'gilsa, 1981.

Cho Kijun. *Han'guk chabonjuŭi sŏngnipsaron* [Discourses on the formative history of Korean capitalism]. 1973. Rev. ed. Seoul: Taewangsa, 1981.

―――. *Han'guk kiŏpkasa* [A history of Korean entrepreneurs]. Seoul: Pagyŏngsa, 1974.

―――. "Han'guk minjok kiŏp kŏnsŏl ŭi sasangjŏk pae'gyŏng: Inch'on Kim Sŏngsu ŭi minjok kiŏp hwaltong" [The intellectual background behind the establishment of Korean nationalist businesses: The nationalist business activities of Kim Sŏngsu]. In Kwŏn Ogi, ed. *Inch'on Kim Sŏngsu ŭi aejok sasang kwa kŭ silch'ŏn*, pp. 85–155.

―――. "Irin nongŏp imin kwa Tongyang Ch'ŏksik Chusik Hoesa" [Japanese agricultural immigrants and the Oriental Development Company]. In Yun Pyŏngsŏk, Sin Yongha, and An Pyŏngjik, eds. *Han'guk kŭndaesaron I: Ilche singminji sidae ŭi sahoe kyŏngje*, pp. 53–71.

Ch'oe Chunghŭi. "Panmin t'ŭgwi e kwanhan punsŏkchŏk yŏn'gu" [An analytical study of the Anti-Nationalist Committee]. M.A. thesis, Ewha University, 1976.

Ch'oe Hojin. "Kaekchu." In Kwŏn Oik et al., eds. *Kyŏngjehak taesajŏn*, pp. 53–54.

———. "Yŏgak." In Kwŏn Oik et al., eds. *Kyŏngjehak taesajŏn*, pp. 994–95.

Ch'oe T'aeho. "Kongin" [The tribute men]. In Kwŏn Oik et al., eds. *Kyŏngjehak taesajŏn*, p. 199.

Chŏn, Mokku. Chŏn'gi Pak Chŏnghŭi [Biography of Park Chung Hee]. Seoul: Kyoyuk P'yŏngnon Sa, 1966.

Emura Koji, "Ŭnhaeng tuch'wi inmulp'yŏng: Tongŭn tuch'wi Min Taesikssi [Profile of a bank president: Tongil Bank President Min Taesik]. *Samch'ŏlli* 8 (February 1936): 51–55.

Han'guk Ilbo Sa Kyŏngjebu. *Han'guk ŭi 50 tae chaebŏl* [Korea's fifty major financial groups]. Seoul: Kyŏngyŏng Nŭngnyul Yŏn'guso, 1985.

Han'guk Inmyŏng Taesajŏn P'yŏnch'ansil. *Han'guk inmyŏng taesajŏn* [Great Korean biographical dictionary]. Seoul: Sin'gu Munhwasa, 1967.

"Han'guk ŭi chabonjuŭi wa chayujuŭi" [Capitalism and liberalism in Korea]. *Sindonga* (August 1986): 276–95.

Han U'gŭn. *Han'guk t'ongsa* [A comprehensive history of Korea]. Seoul: Ŭryu Munhwasa, 1970.

Hŏ Changman. "1920 nyŏndae minjok kaeryangjuŭi ŭi kyegŭp kich'o haemyŏng essŏ chegi toenŭn myŏkkagi munje" [Various problems in elucidating the class basis of the national reformism of the 1920s]. *Yŏksa kwahak* 3 (1966): 37–43.

Hŏ Yu. *Kim Sŏngsu* [Kim Sŏngsu]. Seoul: Tongsŏmunsa, 1984.

Kang Man'gil. *Chosŏn hugi sangŏp chabon ŭi paltal* [The development of commercial capital in the late Yi dynasty]. Seoul: Koryŏ Taehakkyo Ch'ulp'anbu, 1974.

Kang Tongjin. *Ilcheŭi Han'guk chimnyak chŏngch'aeksa* [The history of the Japanese imperial policy of aggression in Korea]. Onŭrŭi Sasang Sinsŏ Series, no. 14. Seoul: Han'gilsa, 1980.

Kil Chinhyŏn. *Yŏksa e tasi munnŭnda* [A second look at history]. Seoul: Samminsa, 1984.

Kim Chunch'ŏl. *Ilcheha ŭi Han'guk minjok chabon kwa minjok sahak e kwanhan yŏn'gu* [Studies of Korean national capital and national private education under Japanese imperialist rule]. Seoul: Sangjosa, 1984.

Kim Hŭiil. "Minjok kaeryangjuŭi ŭi kyegŭpchŏk kich'o nŭn yesok purŭjyoaji ida" [The class basis of national reformism was the comprador bourgeoisie]. *Yŏksa kwahak* 4 (1966): 38–46.

Kim Hwajin, ed. *Chisan yugo chŏn* [The complete posthumous writings of Chisan]. Taejŏn: Hoesangsa, 1966.

Kim Hwangjung, ed. *Ulsan Kimssi chokpo* [The Ulsan Kim genealogy]. 3 vols. Changsŏng, S. Chŏlla: Kim Hwangjung, 1977.

Kim Ilsŏng chŏjakchip [The works of Kim Ilsŏng]. 30 vols. P'yŏngyang: Chosŏn Nodongdang Ch'ulp'ansa, 1979.

Kim Pyŏngha. "Yugŭijŏn" [The six licensed stores]. In Kwŏn Oik et al., eds. *Kyŏngjehak taesajŏn*, pp. 1089–90.

Kim Sanghyŏng, ed. *Sudang Kim Yŏnsu* (cited in notes as *KYS*) [Kim Yŏnsu]. Seoul: Sudang Ki'nyŏm Saŏphoe, 1971.

Kim Sŏnghan, ed. *Sajin ŭro po nŭn Han'guk paengnyŏn (1876–1978)* [100 Years of Korea in Pictures]. Seoul: CH Tonga Ilbosa, 1978.

Kim Sŏngsu. *Ilcheha Han'guk kyŏngje saron* [Discourses on the economic history of Korea under Japanese imperialism]. Seoul: Kyŏngjinsa, 1985.

————. "Ōkuma Shigenobu wa Chosŏn yuhaksaeng" [Ōkuma Shigenobu and Korean students in Japan]. *Samch'ŏlli* 6 (May 1934): 96–99.

Kim Yŏngjin, ed. *Panminja taegongp'angi* [Record of the public trial of the traitors]. Seoul: Hanp'ung Ch'ulp'sansa, 1949.

Kim Yongju. "Chaegye hoego" [Memoirs of the business world]. In *Chaegye hoego* 2: 19–161.

Kim Yŏngmo. *Chosŏn chibaech'ŭng yŏn'gu* [Studies of the Yi dynasty ruling class]. Seoul: Ilchogak, 1982.

Kim Yŏngsŏn. "Kwiguk yŏlch'a" [The train home]. *Sabo Kyŏngbang* [The Kyŏngbang bulletin] (November 1970–June 1971).

Kim Yongsŏp. *Chosŏn hugi nongŏpsa yŏn'gu* [Studies in the agrarian history of the late Yi dynasty]. 2 vols. Seoul: Ilchogak, 1974.

————. "Hanmal-ilcheha ŭi chijuje—sarye 1: Kanghwa Kimssiga ŭi ch'usugirŭl t'onghaesŏ pon chiju kyŏngyŏng" [The landlord system of the late Yi dynasty and Japanese colonial period—case study 1: The landlord management of the Kanghwa Kim family as seen through their harvest records]. *Tonga munhwa*, no. 11 (December 1972), pp. 3–86.

————. "Hanmal-ilcheha ŭi chijuje—sarye 3: Naju Yissiga ŭi chijuro ŭi sŏngjang kwa kŭ nongjang kyŏngyŏng" [The landlord system of the late Yi dynasty and Japanese colonial period—case study 3: The rise of the Naju Yi family as landlords, and the management of their agricultural estate]. *Chindan hakpo* 42 (August 1976): 29-60.

————. "Hanmal-ilcheha ŭi chijuje—sarye 4: Kobu Kimssiga ŭi chiju kyŏngyŏng kwa chabon chŏnhwan" [The landlord system of the late Yi dynasty and Japanese colonial period—case study 4: Landlord management and capital conversion in the Kobu Kim family]. *Han'guksa yŏn'gu*, no. 19 (February 1978), pp. 65–135.

Kim Yŏnsu. "Chaegye hoego" [Memoirs of the business world]. In *Chaegye hoego* 1: 19–276.

Kim Yunhwan. *Han'guk nodong undongsa (I): Ilchehap'yŏn* [History of the Korean labor movement, vol. 1: Under Japanese imperialism]. Ch'ŏngsa Sinsŏ 13. Seoul: Tosŏ Ch'ulp'an Ch'ŏngsa, paperback, 1982.

Ko Cheuk, ed. *Inch'on Kim Sŏngsujŏn* (cited in notes as *KSS*) [The biography of Kim Sŏngsu]. Seoul: Inch'ŏn Ki'nyŏmhoe, 1976.

Ko Pyŏngu. "Minjok chabon." In Kwŏn Oik et al., eds. *Kyŏngjehak taesajŏn*, p. 624.

Ko Sŭngje. *Han'guk kŭm'yungsa yŏn'gu* [Studies in Korean financial history]. Seoul: Ilchogak, 1970.

Ko Wŏnbyŏn, ed. *Panminja choesanggi* [Record of the crimes of the traitors]. Seoul: Paegyŏp Munhwasa, 1949.

Ku Chagyŏng, ed. *Yŏn'am Ku Inhoe* [Ku Inhoe]. Yŏn'am Ki'nyŏm Saŏphoe, 1979.

Kwŏn Ogi, ed. *Inch'on Kim Sŏngsu—Inch'on Kim Sŏngsu ŭi sasang kwa ilhwa* [Kim Sŏngsu—ideas and anecdotes]. Seoul: Tonga Ilbosa, 1985.

———. *Inch'on Kim Sŏngsu ŭi aejok sasang kwa kŭ silch'ŏn* [The patriotism of Kim Sŏngsu in thought and deed]. Seoul: Tonga Ilbosa, 1982.

Kwŏn Oik et al., eds. *Kyŏngjehak taesajŏn* [The unabridged dictionary of economics]. 1964. Rev. and exp. Seoul: Pagyŏngsa, 1980.

Kwŏn T'aeŏk. "Kyŏngsŏng Chingnyu Chusik Hoesa ŭi sŏngnip kwa kyŏngyŏng" [The founding and management of the Kyŏngsŏng Cord Company, Ltd.]. *Han'guk saron*, no. 6 (December 1980), pp. 297–320.

Kwŏn Yŏngmin, ed. *Haebang 40-nyŏn ŭi munhak: 1945–1985* [Literature in the forty years since Liberation: 1945–1985]. 4 vols. Seoul: Min'ŭmsa, 1985.

L. Saeng. "Ssŏttŏn t'arŭl pŏsŏnanŭn mulsan changnyŏ" [Goods promotion unmasked]. *Kaebyŏk*, no. 40 (October 1923): 53–59.

"Manju ŭi Chosŏn kojŏk" [Ancient remains of Korea in Manchuria]. *Chōsen jitsugyō kurabu* 12 (March 1934): 51.

"Manmok chusi hanŭn samdae chaengp'aejŏn" [Three big competitions everyone is watching]. *Samch'ŏlli* 4 (April 1932): 46–53.

Mansŏng taedongbo [Grand genealogy of the 10,000 names]. Seoul, n.d.

No Inhwan, ed. *Chŏn'gyŏng isimnyŏnsa* [A twenty-year history of the FKI]. Seoul: Chŏn'guk Kyŏngjein Yŏnhaphoe, 1983.

Pae Tŏkchin, ed. *Panghyŏp samsimnyŏnsa* [A thirty-year history of the Spinners Association]. Seoul: Taehan Pangjik Hyŏphoe, 1977.

Pak Cheŭl. "Han'guk myŏnbang chigŏp ŭi sajŏk yŏn'gu: 1876–1945 nyŏnŭl chungsim ŭro" [A historical study of the cotton spinning and weaving industry in Korea with emphasis on the period 1876–1945]. Ph.D. diss., Kyŏnghŭi Taehakkyo, 1980.

Pak Chongt'ae, ed. *Chohŭng Ŭnhaeng p'alsibo'nyŏnsa: Ch'urok* [Eighty-five-year history of the Chohŭng bank: Supplement]. Seoul: CH Chohŭng Ŭnhaeng, 1982.

Pak Hŭngsik. "Chaegye hoego" [Memoirs of the business world]. In *Chaegye hoego* 2: 163–271.

Pak Tongsun. *Chaebŏl ŭi ppuri* [The roots of the business groups]. Seoul: CH T'aech'ang Unhwasa, 1980.

Pak Tubyŏng Chŏn'gi Wiwŏnhoe. *Yŏn'gang Pak Tubyŏng* [Pak Tubyŏng]. Seoul: Haptong T'ongsinsa Ch'ulp'an'guk, 1975.

Pak Ŭnsik. *Pak Ŭnsik chŏnsŏ* [The Complete writings of Pak Ŭnsik]. 3 vols. Seoul: Tan'guk Taehakkyo Ch'ulp'anbu, 1975.

Pak Wŏnsŏn. *Kaekchu* [The Kaekchu]. Seoul: Yŏnse Taehakkyo Ch'ulp'anbu, 1968.

"Sangyongŏ Han-Il-Yŏng taejo" [A comparison of commercial terms in Korean, Japanese, and English]. *Sangŏpkye*, no. 3 (December 1908), pp. 15–16.

Sin Yongha. *Chosŏn t'oji chosa saŏp yŏn'gu* [Studies on the Korean cadastral survey]. Seoul: Chisik Sanŏpsa, 1982.

Sŏ Chaesu, ed. *Yi Kwangsu chŏnjip* [Complete works of Yi Kwangsu]. 20 vols. Seoul: Samjungdang, 1962, 1964.

Son Chŏngyŏn. *Musong Hyŏn Chunho* [Hyŏn Chunho]. Kwangju: Chŏnnam Maeil Ch'ulp'an'guk, 1977.

Taniura Takao, "Haebanghu Han'guk sangŏp chabon ŭi hyŏngsŏng kwa palchŏn" [The formation and development of Korean commercial capital after Liberation]. Translated by An Pyŏngjik. In Chin Tŏkkyu et al. *1950 nyŏndae ŭi insik*, pp. 297–331.

Tongŭn Ki'nyŏm Saŏphoe. *Tongŭn Kim Yongwan* [Kim Yongwan]. Seoul: Tongŭn Ki'nyŏm Saŏphoe, 1979.

Wŏn Yuhan. *Han'guk hugi hwap'yesa yŏn'gu* [Studies in the monetary history of the late Yi dynasty]. Seoul: Han'guk Yŏn'guwŏn, 1975.

Yi Ch'ŏlsŭng, "Inch'on ŭl paro alcha" [Let's understand Inch'on correctly]. *Tonga ilbo*, July 15, 1989.

Yi Han'gu. *Ilcheha Han'guk kiŏp sŏllip undongsa* [The history of efforts to establish Korean companies under Japanese imperialism]. Seoul: Ch'ŏngsa, 1989.

Yi Kanghyŏn [L. Saeng]. "Kongin ŭige koham" [A message to Korean workers]. *Sanggong wŏlbo*, no. 19 (May 1911), pp. 3–5.

Yi Kibaek. *Han'guksa sillon* [A new history of Korea]. 1967. Rev. ed. Seoul: Ilchogak, 1982.

Yi Pyŏngch'ŏl. "Chaegye hoego" [Memoirs of the business world]. In *Chaegye hoego* 1: 277–377.

Yi Sŭngnyŏl, "Ilche sigi minjok chabonga nonjaeng" [The debate on national capitalists in the period of Japanese imperialism] *Yŏksa pip'yŏng* (Summer 1990), pp. 56–67.

Yu Kilchun. *Yu Kilchun chŏnsŏ* [The complete writings of Yu Kilchun]. 3 vols. Seoul: Ilchogak, 1971.

Yu Kwangyŏl. "Yi Kwangsu ŭi 'Kim Sŏngsuron' ŭl pakham" [A critique of Yi Kwangsu's "Essay on Kim Sŏngsu"]. *Samch'ŏlli* 3 (October 1931): 43–45.

Yu Wŏndong. *Han'guk kŭndae kyŏngjesa yŏn'gu* [Studies in the modern economic history of Korea]. Seoul: Ilch'ungsa, 1977.

Yun Chuch'an. "Chesŏng kaeryang" [Some improvements in character]. *Honam hakpo*, no. 3 (August 1908), pp. 39–45.

Yun Pyŏngsŏk, Sin Yongha, and An Pyŏngjik, eds. *Han'guk kŭndaesaron I: Ilche singminji sidae ŭi sahoe kyŏngje* [Discourses on modern Korean history I: Society and economy in the Japanese colonial period]. Seoul: Chisik Sanŏpsa, 1979.

Yun Yonggu. *Haep'yŏng Yunssi taedongbo* [The Haep'yŏng Yun genealogy]. 5 vols. Seoul: Haep'yŏng Yunssi Taedongbo Kanhaeng Wiwŏnhoe, 1983.

Books and Articles in English

Adamson, Walter L. *Hegemony and Revolution: A Study of Antonio Gramsci's Political and Cultural Theory.* Berkeley and Los Angeles: University of California Press, paperback, 1980.

Altman, Albert A. "Korea's First Newspaper: The Japanese *Chōsen shinpō.*" *Journal of Asian Studies* 43, no. 4 (August 1984): 685–96.

Aminzade, Ronald. *Class, Politics, and Early Industrial Capitalism: A Study of Mid-nineteenth-century Toulouse, France.* Albany: State University of New York Press, 1981.

Amsden, Alice H. *Asia's Next Giant: South Korea and Late Industrialization.* New York: Oxford University Press, 1989.

Anderson, Perry. "The Antinomies of Antonio Gramsci." *New Left Review* 100 (November 1976-January 1977): 5–78.

Asia Watch Committee. *Human Rights in Korea.* New York and Washington, D.C.: Asia Watch Committee, 1986.

Ayusawa, Iwao F. *A History of Labor in Modern Japan.* Honolulu: East-West Center Press, 1966.

Baker, Donald L. "Jesuit Science through Korean Eyes." *Journal of Korean Studies* 4 (1982–83): 207–39.

Baker, Edward J. "The Role of Legal Reforms in the Japanese Annexation and Rule of Korea, 1905–1919." *Harvard Law School Studies in East Asian Law, Korea*, no. 1.

Baldwin, Frank Prentiss, Jr. "The March First Movement: Korean Challenge and Japanese Response." Ph.D. diss., Columbia University, 1969.

Ban, Sung Hwan, Pal Yong Moon and Dwight Perkins, with contributions by Vincent Brandt, Albert Kleidel, and John E. Sloboda. *Rural Development.* Studies in the Modernization of the Republic of Korea: 1945–1975. Cambridge: Council on East Asian Studies, Harvard University, 1982.

Bartz, Patricia M. *South Korea.* Oxford: Clarendon Press, 1972.

Berlin, Isaiah. *Four Essays on Liberty.* 1969. Oxford: Oxford University Press, paperback, 1979.

Bird, Isabella. *Korea and Her Neighbors.* London: KPI, 1985. *See* Bishop, Isabella Bird.

Bishop, Isabella Bird, *Korea and Her Neighbors.* New York, Chicago, Toronto: Fleming H. Revell Co., 1897.

Bisson, T.A. *Japan's War Economy*. New York: International Secretariat, Institute of Pacific Relations, 1945.

Bloc, Marc. *Feudal Society*. 2 vols. Translated by L.A. Manyon. Chicago: University of Chicago Press, Phoenix Books, 1964.

Bottomore, Tom, ed. *A Dictionary of Marxist Thought*. Cambridge: Harvard University Press, paperback, 1983.

Boyson, Rhodes. *The Ashworth Cotton Enterprise: The Rise and Fall of a Family Firm, 1818-1880*. Oxford: Clarendon Press, 1970.

Brandt, Vincent S.R. *A Korean Village: Between Farm and Sea*. Cambridge: Harvard University Press, 1971.

Cary, Otis, ed. *From a Ruined Empire: Letters—Japan, China, Korea, 1945–1946*. 1975. Tokyo: Kodansha International Ltd., paperback, 1984.

Chandra, Vipan. "An Outline Study of the Ilchin-hoe (Advancement Society) of Korea." *Occasional Papers on Korea*, no. 2 (March 1974), pp. 43–72.

———. *Imperialism, Resistance, and Reform in Late Nineteenth-Century Korea: Enlightenment and the Independence Club*. Berkeley: Institute of East Asian Studies, University of California, Berkeley, 1988.

Chen, Edward I-te. "The Attempt to Integrate the Empire: Legal Perspectives." In Ramon H. Myers and Mark R. Peattie, eds. *The Japanese Colonial Empire*, pp. 240–74.

Ch'oe, Yong-ho. "Reinterpreting Traditional History in North Korea." *Journal of Asian Studies* 40, no. 3 (May 1981): 503–23.

Choi, Hochin. "The Process of Industrial Modernization in Korea." *Journal of Social Sciences and Humanities*, no. 26 (June 1967), pp. 1–33.

Chong, Chin-sok. "A Study of the *Maeil Sinbo* (Daily News): Public Information Policy of the Japanese Imperialists and Korean Journalism under Japanese Imperialism." *Journal of Social Sciences and Humanities*, no. 52 (December 1980), pp. 59–114.

Chun, Shin-yong, ed. *Economic Life in Korea*. Korean Cultural Series, no. 8. Seoul: International Cultural Foundation, 1978.

Cohen, Jerome B. *Japan's Economy in War and Reconstruction*. Minneapolis: University of Minnesota Press, 1949.

Cole, David C., and Princeton N. Lyman. *Korean Development: The Interplay of Politics and Economics*. Cambridge: Harvard University Press, 1971.

Collier, Peter and David Horowitz. *The Rockefellers: An American Dynasty*. 1976. New York: New American Library, Signet paperback, 1977.

Conroy, Hilary. *The Japanese Seizure of Korea 1868–1910: A Study of Realism and Idealism in International Relations*. 1960. Philadelphia: University of Pennsylvania Press, paperback, 1974.

Cook, Harold F. "Pak Yong-hyo: Background and Early Years." *Journal of Social Sciences and Humanities*, no. 31 (December 1969), pp. 11–24.

Crowley, James B. "Japanese Army Factionalism in the Early 1930's." *Journal of Asian Studies* 21, no. 3 (May 1962): 309–26.

362 BIBLIOGRAPHY

Cumings, Bruce. *The Origins of the Korean War: Liberation and the Emergence of Separate Regimes.* Princeton: Princeton University Press, paperback, 1981.

———. "Corporatism in North Korea." *Journal of Korean Studies* 4 (1982–83): 269–94.

———. "The Origins and Development of the Northeast Asian Political Economy." *International Organization* (Winter 1984), pp. 1–40.

Deuchler, Martina. *Confucian Gentlemen and Barbarian Envoys: The Opening of Korea, 1875-1885.* Seattle: University of Washington Press, 1977.

Diefendorf, Jeffry M. *Businessmen and Politics in the Rhineland, 1798–1834.* Princeton: Princeton University Press, 1980.

Dong, Wonmo. "Japanese Colonial Policy and Practice in Korea, 1905–1945: A Study in Assimilation." Ph.D. diss., Georgetown University, 1965.

Dore, Ronald P. "The Late Development Effect." In Hans Dieter-Evans, *Modernization in South-East Asia,* pp. 65-80. London: Oxford University Press, 1973.

Dower, J.W. *Empire and Aftermath: Yoshida Shigeru and the Japanese Experience, 1878–1954.* Cambridge: Council on East Asian Studies, Harvard University, 1979.

Duus, Peter. "Economic Dimensions of Meiji Imperialism: The Case of Korea, 1895–1910." In Ramon H. Myers and Mark R. Peattie, eds., *The Japanese Colonial Empire, 1895–1945,* pp. 128-71.

Eckert, Carter J. "The Colonial Origins of Korean Capitalism: The Koch'ang Kims and the Kyŏngsŏng Spinning and Weaving Company, 1876–1945." Ph.D. diss., University of Washington, 1986.

Francillon, R. J. *Japanese Aircraft of the Pacific War.* 1970. London: Putnam and Co., 1979.

Gale, James S. *Korean Sketches.* Chicago, New York, Toronto: Fleming H. Revell, 1898.

Gerschenkron, Alexander. *Economic Backwardness in Historical Perspective.* Cambridge: Harvard University Press, 1962.

Gold, Thomas Baron. "Dependent Development in Taiwan," Ph.D. diss., Harvard University, 1981.

Gordon, Andrew. *The Evolution of Labor Relations in Japan: Heavy Industry, 1853–1955.* Subseries on the History of Japanese Business and Industry. Harvard East Asian Monographs, no. 117. Cambridge: Council on East Asian Studies, Harvard University, 1985.

Gragert, Edwin Harold. "Landownership Change in Korea under Japanese Colonial Rule, 1900–1935." Ph.D. diss., Columbia University, 1982.

Grajdanzev, Andrew J. *Formosa Today.* New York: Institute of Pacific Relations, 1942.

———. *Modern Korea.* New York: International Secretariat, Institute of Pacific Relations, 1944.

Gramsci, Antonio. *Selections from the Prison Notebooks.* Edited and translated by Quintin Hoare and Geoffrey Nowell Smith. New York: International Publishers, paperback, 1971.

Haboush, JaHyun Kim. *A Heritage of Kings: One Man's Monarchy in the Confucian World.* New York: Columbia University Press, 1988.

Han, Sungjoo. *The Failure of Democracy in South Korea.* Berkeley and Los Angeles: University of California Press, 1974.

Han, Woo-keun. *The History of Korea.* 1970. Translated by Kyung-shik Lee and edited by Grafton K. Mintz. Honolulu: University Press of Hawaii, paperback, 1974.

Hanley, Susan B., and Kozo Yamamura. *Economic and Demographic Change in Preindustrial Japan, 1600–1868.* Princeton: Princeton University Press, paperback, 1977.

Heilbroner, Robert L. *The Nature and Logic of Capitalism.* New York: W.W. Norton, 1985.

Hemingway, Ernest. *The Snows of Kilimanjaro and Other Stories.* New York: Charles Scribner's Sons, 1927.

Henderson, Gregory. *Korea: The Politics of the Vortex.* Cambridge: Harvard University Press, 1968.

Hibbett, Howard. *The Floating World in Japanese Fiction.* New York: Oxford University Press, paperback, 1959.

Hirschman, Albert O. *The Passions and the Interests: Political Arguments for Capitalism Before its Triumph.* Princeton: Princeton University Press, 1977.

————. *Rival Views of Market Society and Other Recent Essays.* New York: Viking, Elisabeth Sifton Books, 1986.

Hirschmeier, Johannes, and Tsunehiko Yui. *The Development of Japanese Business 1600–1973.* Cambridge: Harvard University Press, 1975.

Hunter, Janet E. *Concise Dictionary of Japanese History.* Berkeley and Los Angeles: University of California Press, paperback, 1984.

Huntington, Samuel P. *Political Order in Changing Societies.* New Haven: Yale University Press, paperback, 1968.

Ihara Saikaku. *The Japanese Family Storehouse, or The Millionaires' Gospel Modernised.* Translated by G.W. Sargent. Cambridge: Cambridge University Press, 1959.

————. *This Scheming World.* Translated by Masanori Takatsuka and David C. Stubbs. Rutland, Vt.: Charles E. Tuttle, 1965.

————. *Worldly Mental Calculations.* Translated by Ben Befu. Berkeley and Los Angeles: University of California Press, 1976.

Johnson, Chalmers. *MITI and the Japanese Miracle: The Growth of Industrial Policy, 1925–1975.* Stanford, Calif.: Stanford University Press, 1982.

Jones, F.C. *Manchuria Since 1931.* London: Royal Institute of International Affairs, 1949.

Jones, Leroy P., and Il Sakong. *Government, Business, and Entrepreneurship in Economic Development: The Korean Case.* Studies in the Modernization of the Republic of Korea: 1945–1975. Cambridge: Council on East Asian Studies, Harvard University, 1980.

Juhn, Daniel S. "Nationalism and Korean Businessmen." In Kim, C.I. Eugene and Doretha E. Mortimore, eds., Korea's Response to Japan: The Colonial Period, 1910–1945, pp. 42–52.

———. "Entrepreneurship in an Underdeveloped Economy: The Case of Korea, 1890–1940." D.B.A. diss., George Washington University, 1965.

Kamesaka, Tsunesaburo, ed. Who's Who in Japan: Fourteenth Annual Edition (1931–1932). Tokyo: Who's Who in Japan Publishing Office, 1932.

———. Who's Who in Japan with Manchoukuo and China: Nineteenth Annual Edition. Tokyo: Who's Who in Japan Publishing House, 1938.

Kawashima, Fujiya. "Clan Structure and Political Power in Yi Dynasty Korea: A Case Study of the Munhwa Yu Clan." Ph.D. diss., Harvard University, 1972.

Kernig. C.D., ed. Marxism, Communism, and Western Society: A Comparative Encyclopedia. 8 vols. New York: Herder and Herder, 1973.

Keynes, John Maynard. The End of Laissez-Faire. London: Hogarth Press, 1926.

Kidd, Yasue Aoki. Women Workers in the Japanese Cotton Mills, 1880–1920. Ithaca, N.Y.: China-Japan Program, Cornell University, 1978.

Kim, C.I. Eugene and Kim Han-Kyo. Korea and the Politics of Imperialism 1876–1910. Berkeley and Los Angeles: University of California Press, 1967.

———, and Doretha E. Mortimore, eds. Korea's Response to Japan: The Colonial Period, 1910–1945. Korean Studies Series, no. 5. Kalamazoo, Mich.: Center for Korean Studies, Western Michigan University, 1977.

Kim, Key-Hiuk. The Last Phase of the East Asian World Order: Korea, Japan, and the Chinese Empire, 1860–1882. Berkeley and Los Angeles: University of California Press, 1980.

Kim, Kwan Bong. The Korea-Japan Treaty Crisis and the Instability of the Korean Political System. New York: Praeger Publishers, 1971.

Kim, Richard E. Lost Names: Scenes from a Korean Boyhood. New York: Praeger Publishers, 1970.

Kim, Se-Jin. The Politics of Military Revolution in Korea. Chapel Hill: University of North Carolina Press, 1972.

Kim, Young-Ho. "Yu Kil-chun's Idea of Enlightenment." Journal of Social Sciences and Humanities, no. 33 (December 1970), pp. 37–60.

Kobayashi, Ushisaburo. The Basic Industries and Social History of Japan 1914–1918. New Haven: Yale University Press, 1930.

Koh, Sung Jae. Stages of Industrial Development in Asia: A Comparative History of the Cotton Industry in Japan, India, China, and Korea. Philadelphia: University of Pennsylvania Press, 1966.

Kokutai no Hongi: Cardinal Principles of the National Entity of Japan. Translated by John Owen Gauntlett and edited by Robert King Hall. Cambridge: Harvard University Press, 1949.

Krause, Richard A. *Cotton and Cotton Goods in China, 1918–1936*. New York: Garland Publishing, 1980.

Kuznets, Paul W. *Economic Growth and Structure in the Republic of Korea*. New Haven: Yale University Press, 1977.

Landes, David. "Japan and Europe: Contrasts in Industrialization." In William Lockwood, ed., *The State and Economic Enterprise in Japan*, pp. 93–182.

Ledyard, Gari Keith. "The Korean Language Reform of 1446." Ph.D. diss., University of California, Berkeley, 1966.

———. "Korean Travelers in China over Four Hundred Years, 1488–1887." *Occasional Papers on Korea*, no. 2 (March 1974), pp. 1–42.

Lee, Chong-Sik. *Japan and Korea: The Political Dimension*. Stanford, Calif.: Hoover Institution Press, 1985.

———. *The Korean Workers' Party: A Short History*. Histories of Ruling Communist Parties. Stanford, Calif.: Hoover Institution Press, paperback, 1978.

———. *The Politics of Korean Nationalism*. Berkeley and Los Angeles: University of California Press, 1963.

Lee, Hoon K. *Land Utilization and Rural Economy in Korea*. Chicago: University of Chicago Press, 1936.

Lee, Jung Young. *Sokdam: Capsules of Korean Wisdom*. 2d ed. Seoul: Seoul Computer Press, 1983.

Lee, Ki-baik. *A New History of Korea*. Translated by Edward W. Wagner with Edward J. Schultz. Cambridge: Harvard University Press, 1984.

Legge, James. *The Works of Mencius*. New York: Dover Publications, 1970.

Lew, Young Ick. "The Kabo Reform Movement: Korean and Japanese Reform Efforts in Korea, 1894." Ph.D. diss., Harvard University, 1972.

Linton, George E. *The Modern Textile Dictionary*. New York: Duell, Sloan, and Pearse, 1954.

Lockwood, William W. *The Economic Development of Japan: Growth and Structural Change, 1868–1938*. Princeton: Princeton University Press, paperback, 1954.

———, ed. *The State and Economic Enterprise in Japan*. Studies in the Modernization of Japan. 1965. Princeton: Princeton University Press, paperback, 1969.

Manchester, William. *The Arms of Krupp, 1587–1968*. 1968. Toronto: Bantam, paperback, 1970.

The Manchoukuo Year Book (1942). Hsinking: Manchoukuo Year Book Co., 1942.

Maruyama, Masao. *Thought and Behavior in Japanese Politics*. Edited by Ivan Morris. London: Oxford University Press, 1963.

Marx, Karl. *Capital: A Critique of Political Economy*. Translated by Samuel Moore and Edward Aveling from the 3d German edition and edited by Frederick Engels. 3 vols. New York: International Publishers, paperback, n.d.

Mason, Edward S. et al. *The Economic and Social Modernization of the Republic of Korea.* Studies in the Modernization of the Republic of Korea: 1945–1975. Cambridge: Council on East Asian Studies, Harvard University, 1980.

Matsumura, Hiroshi, ed. *Diamond's Japan Business Directory, 1975.* Tokyo: Diamond Lead Co., Spring 1975.

Matsusaka, Y. Tak. "The Kwantung Army and the Reorganization of the South Manchuria Railway Company." Paper presented at the 42nd Annual Meeting of the Association for Asian Studies, Chicago, April 7, 1990.

McCune, George M. *Korea Today.* Cambridge: Harvard University Press, 1950.

McNamara, Dennis. "The Keisho and the Korean Business Elite." *Journal of Asian Studies* 48, no. 2 (May 1989): 310–23.

Memmi, Albert. *The Colonizer and the Colonized.* Boston: Beacon Press, 1967.

Mitsubishi Economic Research Bureau. *Japanese Trade and Industry: Present and Future.* Tokyo: Mitsubishi Economic Research Bureau, 1936.

Molony, Barbara Ann. "Technology and Investment in the Prewar Japanese Chemical Industry." Ph.D. diss., Harvard University, 1982.

Montalvo, Joseph G., ed. *Cotton Dust: Controlling an Occupational Health Hazard.* American Chemical Society, 1982.

Moore, Barrington, Jr. *Social Origins of Dictatorship and Democracy: Lord and Peasant in the Making of the Modern World.* 1966. Boston: Beacon Press, paperback, 1967.

Moser, Charles K. *The Cotton Textile Industry of Far Eastern Countries.* Boston: Pepperell Manufacturing Co., 1930.

Moskowitz, Karl. "The Creation of the Oriental Development Company: Japanese Illusions Meet Korean Reality." *Occasional Papers on Korea,* no. 2 (March 1974), pp. 73–121.

———. "Current Assets: The Employees of Japanese Banks in Colonial Korea." Ph.D. diss., Harvard University, 1979.

———. "Korean Development and Korean Studies—A Review Article." *Journal of Asian Studies* 42 (November 1982): 63–90.

Myers, Ramon H. and Mark R. Peattie, eds. *The Japanese Colonial Empire, 1895–1945.* Princeton: Princeton University Press, 1984.

Nakamura, Takafusa. *Economic Growth in Prewar Japan.* Translated by Robert A. Feldman. New Haven: Yale University Press, 1983.

Namgung, Yŏng. "A Congratulatory Address." *Sangŏpkye,* no. 1 (October 1908), pp. 4–5.

Oppert, Ernst. *A Forbidden Land: Voyages to the Corea.* New York: G. P. Putnam's Sons, 1880.

Ortega y Gasset, José. "History as a System." In Hans Meyerhoff, ed., *The Philosophy of History in Our Time,* pp. 57–64. Garden City, N.Y.: Doubleday Anchor Books, 1959.

Palais, James B. *Politics and Policy in Traditional Korea*. Cambridge: Harvard University Press, 1975.

———. "Stability in Yi Dynasty Korea: Equilibrium Systems and Marginal Adjustment." *Occasional Papers on Korea*, no. 3 (June 1975), pp. 1–18.

Park, Chung Hee. *The Country, the Revolution and I*. 1962. Seoul: Hollym Corporation, 1970.

Park, Soon Won. "The Emergence of a Factory Labor Force in Colonial Korea: A Case Study of the Onoda Cement Company." Ph.D. diss., Harvard University, 1985.

Patrick, Hugh, ed. *Japanese Industrialization and Its Social Consequences*. Berkeley and Los Angeles: University of California Press, paperback, 1976.

Pearse, Arno S. *The Cotton Industry of Japan and China*. Manchester, England: International Cotton Federation, 1929.

Peattie, Mark R. "Japanese Attitudes Toward Colonialism." In Ramon H. Myers and Mark R. Peattie, *The Japanese Colonial Empire*, pp. 80–127.

Polanyi, Karl. *The Great Transformation: The Political and Economic Origins of Our Time*. 1944. Boston: Beacon Press, paperback, 1957.

Pyle, Kenneth B. "Advantages of Followership: German Economics and Japanese Bureaucrats, 1890–1925." *Journal of Japanese Studies* 1 (Autumn 1974): 127–64.

———. *The Making of Modern Japan*. Civilization and Society: Studies in Social, Economic, and Cultural History. Lexington, Mass.: D.C. Heath, paperback, 1978.

Quinones, Carlos Kenneth. "The Prerequisites for Power in Late Yi Korea: 1864–1894." Ph.D. diss., Harvard University, 1975.

———. "The Impact of the Kabo Reforms upon Political Role Allocation in Late Yi Korea, 1884–1902." *Occasional Papers on Korea*, no. 4 (September 1975), pp. 1–13.

Reischauer, Edwin O., and Albert Craig. *Japan: Tradition and Transformation*. Boston: Houghton Mifflin Co., 1978.

Roberts, John G. *Mitsui: Three Centuries of Japanese Business*. New York, Tokyo: John Weatherhill, 1973.

Robinson, Michael Edson. *Cultural Nationalism in Colonial Korea, 1920–1925*. Seattle: University of Washington Press, 1988.

Sampson, Anthony. *The Sovereign State: The Secret History of ITT*. 1973. Sevenoaks, Kent: Hodder and Stoughton, Coronet paperback, 1974.

Saxonhouse, Gary. "A Tale of Technical Diffusion in the Meiji Period." *Journal of Economic History* 34 (March 1974): 149–65.

———. "Working Koreans in Korea and Japan in the Inter-War Period." Unpublished paper. Department of Economics, University of Michigan, Ann Arbor.

Scalapino, Robert A. and Chong-Sik Lee. *Communism in Korea*. 2 vols. Berkeley: University of California Press, 1968.

Schmitter, Philippe C. and Gerhard Lehmbruch, eds. *Trends Toward Corpo-*

ratist Intermediation. Contemporary Political Sociology, vol. 1. Beverly Hills: Sage Publications, 1979.

Seki, Keizo. *The Cotton Industry of Japan.* Tokyo: Japan Society for the Promotion of Science, 1956.

Selected Works of Mao Tse-tung. 5 vols. Peking: Foreign Language Press, 1975.

Shin, Susan. "Economic Development and Social Mobility in Pre-Modern Korea: 1600–1860." *Peasant Studies* 7, no. 3 (Summer 1978): 187–97.

———. "The Social Structure of Kŭmhwa County in the Late Seventeenth Century." *Occasional Papers on Korea,* no. 1 (April 1974), pp. 9–35.

Shin, Yong-ha. "Pak Ŭnsik's Idea of National Salvation by Industry." *Journal of Social Sciences and Humanities,* no. 50 (December 1979), pp. 17–53.

Sih, Tien-Tsung. "Japan and Cotton Industry in North China." *Council of International Affairs Information Bulletin* 3, no. 6 (March 1936): 123–37.

Silverman, Bernard, and H.D. Harootunian, eds. *Japan in Crisis: Essays on Taishō Democracy.* Princeton: Princeton University Press, 1974.

Smith, Adam. *An Inquiry into the Nature and Cause of the Wealth of Nations.* Edited by Edwin Cannan. New York: Random House, Modern Library, 1937.

Somerville, John N. "Stability in Eighteenth Century Ulsan." *Korean Studies Forum,* no. 1 (Autumn-Winter 1976–77), pp. 1–18.

Song, Chan-shik. "Genealogical Records." *Korea Journal* 17 (May 1977): 15–24.

Storry, Richard. *The Double Patriots: A Study of Japanese Nationalism.* Boston: Houghton Mifflin Co., 1957.

Suh, Dae-Sook. *Documents of Korean Communism: 1918–1948.* Princeton: Princeton University Press, 1970.

———. *Korean Communism 1945–1980: A Reference Guide to the Political System.* Honolulu: University Press of Hawaii, 1981.

———. *The Korean Communist Movement, 1918–1948.* Princeton: Princeton University Press, 1967.

———, and Chae-Jin Lee, eds. *Political Leadership in Korea.* Seattle: University of Washington Press, 1976.

Suh, Sang-Chul. *Growth and Structural Changes in the Korean Economy, 1910–1940.* Cambridge: Council on East Asian Studies, Harvard University, 1978.

Tsurumi, E. Patricia. *Japanese Colonial Education in Taiwan, 1895–1945.* Cambridge: Harvard University Press, 1977.

Tucker, Robert C. *The Marx-Engels Reader.* 2d ed. Rev. and enl. New York: W. W. Norton, 1978.

Van der Wee, Herman, ed. *The Great Depression Revisited: Essays on the Economics of the Thirties.* The Hague: Nijhoff, 1972.

Veblen, Thorstein. *The Theory of Business Enterprise*. Clifton, N.J.: Augustus M. Kelley, 1973.

Wagner, Edward W. "The Ladder of Success in Yi Dynasty Korea." *Occasional Papers on Korea*, no. 1 (April 1974), pp. 1–8.

———. "*Munkwa* Project." Computer printouts, Harvard University, 1971.

———. "Social Stratification in Seventeenth-Century Korea: Some Observations from a 1663 Seoul Census Register." *Occasional Papers on Korea*, no. 1 (April 1974), pp. 35-54.

———. *The Literati Purges: Political Conflict in Early Yi Korea*. Cambridge: East Asian Research Center, Harvard University, 1974.

Wales, Nym and Kim San. *Song of Arian: A Korean Communist in the Chinese Revolution*. San Francisco: Ramparts Press, 1941.

Wallerstein, Immanuel. *The Capitalist World-Economy*. Cambridge: Cambridge University Press, paperback, 1979.

Warren, Bill. "Imperialism and Capitalist Industrialization." *New Left Review* 81 (September-October 1973): 1–92.

Wartime Legislation in Japan: A Selection of Important Laws Enacted or Revised in 1941. Tokyo: Nippon Shogyo Tsushin Sha, n.d.

Weber, Max. *The Protestant Ethic and the Spirit of Capitalism*. 1947. Translated by Talcott Parsons. New York: Charles Scribner's Sons, Lyceum paperback, 1958.

Woo, Jung-eun. "State Power, Finance, and Industrialization of Korea." Ph.D. diss., Columbia University, 1988.

Yamamura, Kozo. "General Trading Companies in Japan: Their Origins and Growth." In Hugh Patrick, ed., *Japanese Industrialization and Its Social Consequences*, pp. 161–99.

———. "The Japanese Economy, 1911–1930: Concentration, Conflicts, and Crises." In Bernard Silverman and H.D. Harootunian, eds., *Japan in Crisis: Essays on Taishō Democracy*, pp. 299–328.

———. "Then Came the Great Depression: Japan's Interwar Years." In Herman Van der Wee, ed., *The Great Depression Revisited: Essays on the Economics of the Thirties*, pp. 182–211.

Newspapers

Chōsen shimbun [The Chōsen News].
Chŏn'guk nodongja sinmun [National Worker's News].
Japan Times and Mail.
Japan Weekly Chronicle—Commercial Supplement.
Keijō nippō [The Keijō Daily].
Maeil sinbo [The Daily News].
New York Times.

Seoul Press
Seibu mainichi shimbun [The Western Daily News].
Taikyū nippō [The Taegu Daily].
Tonga ilbo [The East Asia Daily].

Interviews

Kim Kakchung. Chairman, CH Kyŏngbang. CH Kyŏngbang Head Office, Yŏngdŭngp'o (Seoul). Interview. March 29, 1984.

Kim Sangdŏk; Pak Yundo. Samyang Salt Company (Samyang Yŏm'ŏpsa), Haeri-myŏn, Tongho-ri, N. Chŏlla. Interview, October, 1982.

Kim Yongwan. Formerly Chairman, CH Kyŏngbang and the Federation of Korean Industries. Tusan Building, Seoul. Interviews (taped), March 30, 1984; April 13, 1984.

Lee, Kyunghoon. Elder son of Yi Toyŏng. Seattle. Interview, December 22, 1985.

Index

Accommodation: of Kyŏngbang's marketing structure to colonial policies, 172; of Korean bourgeoisie with colonial authorities, 232–33; of Kim Sŏngsu with colonial authorities, 249
Advancement Society (Ilchinhoe), 35, 228
Aircraft: production of, 120–21, 298n51. *See also* Chōsen Aircraft Company
Akashi, 131
All Japan Cotton Spinners Association, 134, 191
An (family quarters), 24
Aniki (big brothers), 228, 326n8
Annexation, 5, 31, 88, 134, 167; as confirmation of Japan's role in Korean economy, 11; supporters of, 35, 47, 228; Portsmouth Treaty as precursor of, 43; and importance of land, 75; and Pak Yŏnghyo, 97; and Manchuria, 169; labor disputes before, 202; Korean-Japanese business connections before, 231; and tariffs, 279n51; and Pak Yŏngch'ŏl, 296n24
Antinationalist trials, 215, 248, 333n69
Antung, 169
Anyang (China), 186
Anyang (Korea), 121
Aristocracy, British: and development of liberal democracy, 189
Aristocracy, Korean: and link to land, 8; participation of, in March First movement, 47; political power of, 69–70, 338n15; and *sadae* legacy, 226–27. *See also* Yangban
Army Air Arsenal, 122
Army, Japanese: anticapitalist attitude of, 71–72, 286n11
Aruga Mitsutoyo, 88, 94, 98, 159; attitude toward Koreans, 94–96; founding father of Korean business world, 95; loans to Kyŏngbang and Pak Hŭngsik,

96; president, Han River Hydroelectric Company, 102; as Ariga, 291–92n99; and Chōsen Aircraft Company, 294n125; support of full assimilation, 329nn41, 42
Asia: as market for Japan, 45
Assen kikan (trade agencies), 168
Assimilation: degrees of, among Korean businessmen, 230–31. *See also* Bourgeoisie, Korean; Naisen Ittai
Association to Promote Korean Goods, 83, 281n64

Bandai Trading Company KK, 146
Bank of Agriculture and Industry, 87
Bank of Chōsen, 44, 87–91, 167, 169
Bank of Korea, 15
Banks, 88–89
Beard, Dita, 111
Berlin, Isaiah, 257
Betto tsumitatekin (special reserves), 125
Bishop, Isabella Bird, xi, 11
Bisson, T. A., 71, 120
Bituminous coal: import of, 138
Bonds. *See* War bonds
Bourgeoisie, Korean: birth of, 1; under colonialism, 6; growth of, 7, 56; emergence of industrial, 49–51; subordination of, to Japanese counterparts, 128; and tie with colonial state, 188, 233; failure to concede to working class, 189–90; and reliance on nationalism for moral leadership, 190; and authoritarianism, 190, 258; commitment to nationalism of, 225–26; and assimilation into Japanese society, 230; collaboration of, with colonial regime, 231, 284n2; end of nationalism of, 251–52
Budan seiji (military rule), 46
Bunka (cultural or enlightened), 46
Bureau of Industry, 127–28
Bureau of Railways, 109

371

Chōsen Business Club: for government-business socializing, 111; as elitist organization, 113; on Chōsen-Manchurian trade, 169; and Japanese-Korean capitalist cooperation, 242. *See also* Han Sangnyong; Kim Yongwan; Kim Yŏnsu
Chōsen Commercial Bank, 13, 229
Chōsen Cotton Yarn and Cloth Merchants Association, 116, 136, 157
Chōsen Dyers Association, 109
Chōsen Electric Cable Corporation, 109
Chōsen Electrolytic Steel Mill, 119–20
Chōsen Federation of Financial Cooperatives (Chōsen Kin'yu Kumiai Rengōkai), 87
Chōsen Forestry Development Company, 100
Chōsen Heavy Industries, Ltd., 119–20
Chōsen Hikōki Kōgyō KK. *See* Chōsen Aircraft Company
Chōsen Industrial Bank: and Kyŏngbang, 85–87, 89–91, 92, 93, 94, 99–102, 123, 125, 214; statistics compiled by (1937), 52–53; profits of, 53; as government's key financial organ, 87–91; interest rates of, 92–93; commitment of, to cooperative development, 94; and Aruga Mitsutoyo, 94–96; and Pak Yŏnghyo, 98–99; and relationships with other banks and companies, 99, 101–2; and Pak Hŭngsik, 160; and Manchurian expansion, 178; research department of, 185
Chōsen Industrial Promotion Foundation, 99–100
Chōsen Jitsugyō Kurabu. *See* Chōsen Business Club
Chōsen jitsugyō kurabu, 111, 130, 150, 158, 183
Chōsen Kin'yu Kumiai. *See* Chōsen Federation of Financial Cooperatives
Chōsen Kureha Spinning Company, 118
Chōsen League for Concerted National Power, 238, 244
Chōsen Menshifushō Rengōkai. *See* Chōsen Cotton Yarn and Cloth Merchants Association
Chōsen Oil Company, 119, 160
Chōsen Rengō Seinendan (Chōsen Federation of Youth), 238
Chōsen Savings Bank, 99

Chōsen Sen'i Sangyōkai (Chōsen Textile Industry Association), 108
Chōsen shimbun, 220
Chōsen Shōgyō Ginkō. *See* Chōsen Commercial Bank
Chōsen Shokusan Ginkō. *See* Chōsen Industrial Bank
Chōsen Shrine, 247
Chōsen Spinners Association, 108–10, 180, 314n112
Chōsen Spinning and Weaving Company, 42, 44, 57, 130; and Government-General subsidies to, 81, 83–84, 165, 192, 200; and Tōyō Menka, 161; protection of, by government, 82, 165; Kim Yŏnsu's investment in, 171; and takeover of Yingkow Spinning and Weaving Company, 171, 180; in Manchuria, 175–76; Kyŏngbang shares in, 180; and workers' demands, 200
Chōsen Textile Industry Association, 108
Chōsen Towel Association, 109
Chōsen Trade Association, 168
Chōsen Trust Company, 99
Chosŏn dynasty: economic growth in, 4; commercialization and trade in, 8–9, 11, 12; aristocracy and land in, 8, 271n37; *kaekchu* in, 12; bourgeoisie in, 15; and Kim family, 21; wealth in, 24; abdication of emperor, 31; monarchical limits of, 69, 70, 338n15; and textile trade, 152; and Pak Hŭngsik, 158; and *sadae*, 226–27; financial disarray of, 231
Chosŏn Mulsan Changnyŏhoe. *See* Association to Promote Korean Goods
Chosŏn Nodong Kongjehoe (Korean Workers Mutual Aid Society), 205
Chosŏn Nonong Ch'ongdongmaeng (Korean Worker-Peasant League), 206–7
Chosŏn Ŭnhaeng. *See* Bank of Chosŏn
Chosŏnin Sanŏp Taehoe. *See* Congress of Korean Industry
Chulp'o, port of, 20, 21, 22, 30, 32, 40, 75
Chulp'o Elementary School (formerly Yŏngsin School), 40
Chun Doo Hwan, 21
Chungang Commercial and Industrial Company, 86, 160–61
Chungang Hakkyo, 37, 280–81n63
Chungch'uwŏn (Council of Ministers Without Portfolio), 25

386 INDEX